INTERNATIONAL YEARBOOK
OF POLITICAL BEHAVIOR RESEARCH

General Editor: HEINZ EULAU, STANFORD UNIVERSITY

CONTRIBUTORS

Vilhelm Aubert, UNIVERSITY OF OSLO

Herbert Jacob, UNIVERSITY OF WISCONSIN

Fred Kort, UNIVERSITY OF CONNECTICUT

Matthew Muraskin, LL.B, MEMBER OF NEW YORK BAR

Stuart S. Nagel, UNIVERSITY OF ILLINOIS

Daniel Rosen, NEW YORK UNIVERSITY

Marvin Schick, YESHIVA UNIVERSITY

Glendon Schubert, MICHIGAN STATE UNIVERSITY

Harold J. Spaeth, UNIVERSITY OF DETROIT

Joseph Tanenhaus, NEW YORK UNIVERSITY

Ulf Torgersen, INSTITUTE FOR SOCIAL RESEARCH, OSLO

S. Sidney Ulmer, MICHIGAN STATE UNIVERSITY

Kenneth Vines, TULANE UNIVERSITY

Judicial

Decision-Making

EDITED BY GLENDON SCHUBERT
MICHIGAN STATE UNIVERSITY

THE FREE PRESS OF GLENCOE
Collier-Macmillan Limited, London

115584

For information, address:

The Free Press of Glencoe
A DIVISION OF THE MACMILLAN COMPANY,
THE CROWELL-COLLIER PUBLISHING COMPANY
60 Fifth Avenue, New York 11

DESIGNED BY SIDNEY SOLOMON

Library of Congress Catalog Card Number: 63-8422

Collier-Macmillan Canada, Ltd., Toronto, Ontario

To

C. HERMAN PRITCHETT

who blazed a trail

Preface

THE AUTHORS of the investigations reported in this fourth volume of the *International Yearbook of Political Behavior Research* have stepped into an arena of politics, where, I daresay, even angels fear to tread. That the courts are instrumentalities of the political as well as of the legal order has long been recognized, but enough ritual and mystery surround the sacerdotal ways of the legal priesthood that even disinterested inquiry into the attitudes and behavioral patterns of the judiciary may seem sacrilegious. Yet, I find it gratifying that the form such inquiry now takes is no longer the rather blustering muckraking that in the past, especially in times of political crisis, has been the characteristic response to the discovery that, after all, judges are only human. Instead of the sometimes self-righteous, sometimes indignant, and sometimes cynical disquisitions on the virtues of the law and the corruption of judges who deviate from the paths of justice, we have here scholarly efforts to analyze and explain judicial decision-making by means of studies in depth of legal attitudes and behavior and by means of some of the most advanced behavioral research techniques, which place these studies at the very frontiers of contemporary political science.

The rapid growth of behavioral studies of the judiciary, traced in Professor Schubert's introduction, can be further attested to by the fact that as late as 1957, when the first volumes of the *Yearbook* were planned, no provision was made for a collection of original research on judicial behavior such as this—despite the avowed purpose to facilitate the publication of venturesome efforts at the frontiers of political science and the other behavioral sciences. Why the growth of behavioral research on judicial decision-making occurred so rapidly at the particular point in time it did I cannot say, but even more puzzling has been the uneven development of behavioral research in different fields of political science. Why is it, for instance, that fifteen years after its publication Herbert A. Simon's *Administrative Behavior* has not been followed up by the kind of behavioral research in the field of public administration that it suggested, while in the field of public law, as the essays and bibliography in this volume demonstrate, behavioral research is flowering? Of course, there are some very excellent behavioral studies of bureaucracy, authority, and organizational decision-making, but they are the work of sociologists and social psychologists rather than of students of public administration.

I should like to offer a hypothesis here that, if not disproved, may involve an important lesson. It seems to me that scientists interested in public law, unlike those interested in public administration, never considered it their major business to tell the practitioners what to do or what not to do. In public law, unlike public administration, research and writing have always been predominantly and genuinely academic. If the practitioners of the law learned from the academicians, it was probably because of the critical acumen and analytical persuasiveness of legal research and writing. By way of contrast, the study of public administration, from its very beginnings, was program-minded, first concerning reforms of governmental structure, later concerning proper administrative procedures, and still later concerning public policies. Some theoretical aspirations notwithstanding, public administration was and still is, generally speaking, an "applied field." Thus preoccupied with so-called "practical" matters, the intellectual milieu of academic public administration has been less receptive to disinterested inquiry than the field of public law. In the program-oriented atmosphere of public administration there is little room for analytical theory or pure research. As a result, when the "behavioral revolution" struck political science, the responses in different fields were quite different—favorable in some, neutral in others, and hostile in still others. In public law, after a slow start, behavioral research was welcomed; long accustomed to rigorous logical analysis and high respect for "facts," students of public law recognized the potentialities of behavioral theories and methods. In public administration the absence of a similar tradition has evidently held up progress in behavioral research.

The lesson, it seems to me, is this: preoccupation with policy and program, with political engineering and know-how rather than knowledge, stifles theoretical development and scientific research. The process is circular: because of emphasis on practical programs, there is neglect of theory; because of neglect of theory, there is no incentive to test theoretical propositions through empirical research; because there is no research, there is no interest in methodology; instead of methodology, there is much practical lore and an appeal to common sense. How this circle can be broken in the study of public administration is, however, on the agenda of the future.

As in the previous volumes of the *Yearbook*, scholars are invited to communicate with the general editor about contributions or future volumes.

HEINZ EULAU
General Editor

Stanford, California
December, 1962

Contents

From Public Law
to Judicial Behavior

GLENDON SCHUBERT

HOW POLITICAL SCIENCE emerged in the United States in the closing decades of the nineteenth century as an academic discipline whose roots lay deep in constitutional law, constitutional history, and political philosophy is an oft-told tale.[1] Although other emphases developed as the profession grew—as evidenced by the differentiation of such fields of study as governmental structure and organization, political parties (and later, interest groups), public administration, comparative government, and international relations—the study of public law (traditionally defined as a broad synthesis of history, law, and philosophy) remained the core content of the discipline, as this was viewed by most members of the profession. During the ensuing decades, the endless variety of cases decided by courts, together with the vast number of statutes and constitutional documents enacted or revised, helped enrich the mass of raw materials available for analysis. But the decades from 1880 to 1950 saw little change in the methods of analysis employed by the political scientists, lawyers and law professors, and historians who studied public law on the basis of these data. And what is more, with a single exception, there were no theoretical developments of any importance. The exception, and it is an important one, was the insistence of a handful of pre-eminent constitutional scholars upon the political significance of the policy-making role of the United States Supreme Court.[2]

This heritage exerted a powerful influence on the study of public law. Even today almost all texts and casebooks designed for political science courses in constitutional law, administrative law, or in the judicial process—and therefore, presumably, the courses in which these books are used—define the substantive content of public law as opinions of the United States Supreme Court, the method as lawyer-like analysis of legal documents (and primarily, case reports), and the theory as a comparison of the extent to which empirical policy norms, as stated in judicial opinions, deviate from the ethical content of ideal norms excogitated from the earlier writings of eminent constitution-makers, judges, and political philosophers, or depart from the subjective value preferences of the commentators.

1

The first really major break with the past came with the publication in 1948 of C. Herman Pritchett's book *The Roosevelt Court: A Study in Judicial Politics and Values, 1937-1947*.[3] The book was seminal for two reasons. First, Pritchett conceptualized the Supreme Court as a small decision-making group, whose voting and opinion behavior could best be explained in terms of imputed differences in the attitudes of individual justices toward the recurrent issues of public policy that characterize cases that reach the Court for decision. Second, Pritchett based his analysis upon quantitative measurement of a large sample of data. As he explicitly stated, his interest was "in the social and psychological origins of judicial attitudes and the influence of individual predilections. . . ."[4] It was altogether fitting that the cornerstone for the building of a science of judicial behavior should have been laid by a former student of Charles E. Merriam—indeed, by one who followed in the footsteps of "the Chief" as Chairman of the Department of Political Science at the University of Chicago. The influence of Merriam and his students upon the establishment and the development of the behavioral approach in other fields of political science than that of public law is too well known to warrant retelling here.[5] Clearly, then, Pritchett's work can best be understood as a facet of a much broader movement that was, at the very time that he wrote, on the threshold of making its first real impact as a major trend within the profession.[6]

There was, of course, a lag of the better part of a decade before a new generation of younger political scientists began to show an interest in exploring some of the research paths that were suggested by Pritchett's book. Unquestionably, many of these younger men, themselves the products of a quite different style of graduate education than that of their elders in the field of public law, also were profoundly influenced by the published behavioral research that began to appear, during the early 1950's, in other fields of political inquiry. By about 1955, some other scholars also were beginning to build upon the foundations laid in public law by Pritchett and in other fields of political study by other researchers. Nonetheless, the first reader in political behavior, which appeared in 1956, omitted the judiciary as a relevant area of research in political behavior, and with justification in view of the dearth of relevant publication (excepting, of course, Pritchett's book).[7] An examination of the bibliography to the present volume shows that over 90 per cent of the items listed are less than five years old—a result, let it be noted, not of the selective perception of the compiler, but rather of the almost complete absence of writings on judicial behavior until very recently.

The most pronounced and obvious trend in this recent research in judicial behavior has been the shift in interdisciplinary ties that has characterized most of this work. Instead of citing law professors, historians, and philosophers, contemporary writers on judicial behavior refer to the work of sociologists, social psychologists, cultural anthropologists, statisticians, and econometricians. Predominantly, the theories and methods with which these writers work have been adapted from basic research performed by social psychologists. Sociological theories of small groups and of social stratification, and psychological theories of perception and cognition, increasingly have guided the formulation of hypotheses for investigation; and indices of group cohesion, the cumulative scale, and nonparametric statistics have provided the tools for investigation. To a lesser extent, economic theories of rational choice have provided models for pilot research. However, it is only very recently that tests of statistical significance have come into something approaching common use and acceptance as an ordinary tool of analysis; and similarly, the limitations of undimensional space as the basis for measurement and prediction of what are almost invariably complex multivariate relationships are only beginning to be recognized. These latter two contemporary accretions, both of which are conspicuously represented in the work reported in the present volume, are promising developments, since their general adoption by students of judicial behavior should go a long way toward meeting the quite legitimate complaints of traditional public law scholars about "overgeneralization" and "oversimplification" of complex reality by naive quantification. The judicial behavioralists have not been unaware of the complexity of the relationships that they sought to measure and predict. The analogy between arithmetic and calculus would be more appropriate: they had to learn to add before they could learn to integrate.

I

What have been some of the major approaches explored by these recent reports of research on judicial decision-making? Although we are still too close to the events to warrant overweening confidence in any contemporary appraisal, four approaches in particular appear to have attracted the most interest and to have been most influential.

One approach is based upon the assumption that the choices of judges, like those of other human beings, may be significantly affected by judicial attitudes toward the issues of public policy and by other psychological stimuli presented by cases which judges are asked to decide. The most important basis for research theory and method utilized thus far has been provided by the Guttman cumulative scale, as developed in *The American Soldier*. The possibility of applying Guttman scaling to the study of judicial attitudes was first suggested to the political science profession in a paper by Joseph Tanenhaus.[8] The most extensive work in empirical application of Guttman scaling to sets of judicial votes has come from Schubert and Ulmer.[9] The research done thus far in cumulative scaling indicates that there is a high degree of consistency in the attitudes of Supreme Court justices toward the recurrent issues of public policy that characterize their work load. This consistency of response in individual judicial voting in such an area of public policy as civil liberties claims appears to provide a much better general explanation of how and why the Court makes its policy choices than does the alternative traditional theory of *stare decisis,* that consistency in the manipulation of precedential legal rules and principles is a function of legal craftsmanship.

Most of the chapters in the present volume are concerned, explicitly or implicitly, with the study of judicial attitudes. Aubert analyzes differences in the opinion-writing and voting behavior of Norwegian courts-martial and he concludes that such differences cannot adequately be explained except in terms of attitudinal differences among the judges. Nagel reports on a questionnaire survey of a large sample of American judges, the results of which he is able to compare with the responses of British Tories to the same scale (which was developed by the English psychologist Hans J. Eysenck and is reported in his *The Psychology of Politics*[10]). Schubert examines the interrelationship between the attitudes of Supreme Court justices toward the political values perceived by the justices as being relevant to the decision of cases before them and toward their presumed obligation to conform to precedent choices of the same institutional group in regard to similar questions of political valuation. Spaeth examines the consistency in the manifest voting responses of a set of Supreme Court justices to the stimuli provided by a large sample of cases concerned with governmental regulation of business. He also shows that judicial attitudes toward business regulation dominated, for his sample, several other attitudinal dimensions that might plausibly be deemed relevant to judicial choice. Thus all four of these chapters focus upon the content of the responses of judges as the basis for inferences about judicial attitudes, and all necessarily discuss the stimuli to which these responses are assumed to pertain.

The two chapters by Tanenhaus and Kort also are concerned with the investigation of judicial attitudes, but with the difference that these writers focus upon the stimulus side of the stimulus-response relationship. Tanenhaus examines a large and systematic sample of jurisdictional decisions of the Supreme Court, in an attempt to isolate, through the use of correlational measurement, the most significant cues that, singly and in combination, function to assist the justices in "identifying" the relatively small subset of these cases whose merits they will want to decide upon. By a shift in the language of discourse, one can restate Tanenhaus' objective as constituting a differentiation, from among the many different stimuli presented by cases docketed with the Court, of those which are most likely to induce a favorable response from the requisite minority of Supreme Court justices, in regard to certiorari cases—the subset comprising by far the most popular category of the Court's jurisdictional decision-making. Kort classifies the manifest content of majority opinions of the Supreme Court in order to specify the categories (and the relative importance) of "facts" which are assumed to be interrelated in complex patterns of association within the minds of the perceiving justices. Thus, these "fact" syndromes function as stimuli to which the justices respond with such a high degree of individual consistency that a highly consistent pattern of collective judgment for the group (that is, for "the Court") also obtains.

Another approach to judicial decision-making, and one of historic importance, is small group analysis, which does not, however, seem to have loomed large in the work of the past half-dozen years. The identification of cluster blocs among the justices was, of course, a principal technique that characterized Pritchett's earlier work, as in *The Roosevelt Court*. However, in Pritchett's book on the Vinson Court,[11] bloc analysis assumed a very subdued role, and it has not been used at all in his more recent work. There is also one article by a sociologist, who attempted, although with substantial differences in research design, to apply Pritchett's basic technique to a non-random sample of data drawn from the decisions of the Taft, Hughes, Stone, and Vinson Courts. This study generated some novel findings and suggested several interesting hypotheses about small group behavior in the Court.[12] In another study, Schubert has suggested some refinements in technique in a chapter which applied bloc analysis to study small group behavior in the early terms of the Warren Court and in the Michigan Supreme Court.[13] Ferguson, using similar methods, has made an exploratory study of the Supreme Court of Illinois.[14] All four of these writers based their work upon data consisting of dyadic agreement in voting. All agree that the sets of judges who comprise the bench of relatively large appellate courts characteristically partition themselves into dissenting blocs that reflect the polarization of these courts into liberal, moderate, and conservative subsets.

The chapter by Ulmer in this volume differs in two important respects from these earlier attempts to study small group behavior in courts. His study of the Michigan Supreme Court is based upon opinion rather than voting data, and focuses upon leadership within the court as a small group, rather than upon the identification of cluster blocs within the court. He also uses dominance matrices, a technique of analysis recently developed in group dynamics[15] that does not appear previously to have been used in work on judicial behavior.

Several political scientists, reflecting the influence of the post-World War II revival of the Bentleyan orientation to political processes as a field of interaction among interest groups, have emphasized the importance of viewing judicial cases within the context of broader patterns of political conflict. Seen from this point of view, a "judicial case" begins in underlying conflict among social groups (for whom discrete individuals may be spokesmen and in whose name they may act); hence it is essential to examine the wellsprings of precedent political interaction out of which a lawsuit arises, as one stage—and merely one stage—of a continuing process. Similarly, what happens *after* a court, or the last in sequence of a set of courts in a hierarchy of judicial review, announces a "final" decision in a case, is of at least equal importance to the resolution of the conflict between the real parties to the dispute as is anything that occurs during the judicial phase of the controversy. This approach defines the judiciary as a party to the group struggle; and of course this implies that considerable attention should be given to the attempts of suitors to manipulate the judiciary by use of such means as selective entrée to preferred courts and judges, "lobbying" through the coalitional support of *amici curiae,* and planting propaganda in the form of articles in law journals. This perspective is best exemplified in a teaching monograph by Jack Peltason and a paper by Clement E. Vose.[16] The most substantial empirical applications are found in two recent books by these same authors.[17]

Two chapters in the present volume represent, in part, extensions of the political process approach. Jacob and Vines would recapture the state courts from the legalists, and restore them to the fold as an appropriate and important object of political inquiry, by viewing and by studying state judges as parts of the American political system. Torgersen discusses the career patterns of Norwegian judges with a similar concern for the role of judges within the Norwegian political system.

One of the most prominent elements in traditional constitutional scholarship has been the production of biographies of Supreme Court justices—Beveridge's *Marshall,* Swisher's *Taney,* Fairman's *Miller,* and Mason's *Brandeis* and *Stone,* to mention only a few of the best and better-known works. Such writings long had been part of the stock in trade of the public law teacher, but until very recently no attempt had been made systematically to analyze the diverse biographical sources, using them as a source of data on the social background of the justices and their place in the social structure. Schmidhauser did this in an article published in 1959.[18] The obvious next step would be to correlate background characteristics of judges with their decision-making behaviors, in an attempt to discover the extent to which, and the ways in which, the socialization and adult social conditioning of judges affect their voting and opinion-writing choices. Some preliminary work in this direction has been undertaken by Nagel.

Schmidhauser's work also has resulted in the stimulation of foreign scholars, as exemplified in Torgersen's paper, which, however, also reflects another important stimulus: the program of the Institute for Social Research in Oslo, an organization whose members have been in close contact with American social psychologists during the past decade. In connection with a much broader study of personnel changes among Norwegian elites, Vilhelm Aubert, Professor of Sociology of Law at the University of Oslo and an associate of the Institute, has collaborated with Torgersen and Karl Tangen on an extensive study of social mobility and other socio-economic attributes of Norwegian judges from 1814 until World War II. Torgersen draws upon both this Institute study and Schmidhauser's article in a paper which deals comparatively with the judges of the Norwegian and the American supreme courts.

Reference should, perhaps, also be made to two other recent approaches which, although the subject of some comment,[19] thus far at least have not appeared to be as influential in stimulating the work of other researchers. Kort's initial efforts at mathematical prediction of Supreme Court decisions, in an article which was not concerned with theoretical considerations, subsequently was subjected to extended critique by an econometrician who discussed in some detail aspects of both behavioral and statistical theory relevant to the empirical operations that Kort had performed upon his data.[20] Thus, it should be noted that Kort's article in the present volume represents a considerable refinement in method over his initial study, and more importantly, is articulated (as the earlier article was not) to a recognized body of behavioral and statistical theory. Schubert's work with game theory[21] constitutes one of the very few attempts that have been made to relate judicial behavior to economic theory, methods, and models of rational choice proc-

esses.[22] With the exception, however, of Schubert's reformulation with up-
dated data of one of these game models,[23] no other work along these lines
appears to have been forthcoming.

In addition, there have been two approaches that have appeared so
recently that any attempt at appraisal would be in both cases premature, and
also, in the latter case, unseemly. They ought, however, to be mentioned in
a chronicle of recent research approaches in the study of judicial behavior.
The first of these consists of drawing large samples of judges and using correlational techniques in association with statistical tests of significance in
order to measure the relationship between socio-economic traits, and performance in relation to selected variables of choice behavior. Stuart S. Nagel
has written a doctoral dissertation on this subject and recently has published several related articles in which he has reported his findings.[24] James
F. Herndon also has written a dissertation,[25] using similar methods, in which
he discusses some of the same questions as Nagel. The second approach
consists of Schubert's psychometric model of the Supreme Court,[26] which
represents an attempt to transcend the unidimensional theory and models,
and of linear methods, which characterize (not unreasonably, and certainly
not unnaturally) research in judicial behavior thus far. His psychometric
theory defines a multidimensional space in which the interrelationships
among case stimuli and judicial respondents can be measured as a function
of judicial attitudes toward several key variables, such as civil liberties,
economic liberalism, and governmental fiscal authority. Methodologically,
this involves the use of Guttman scaling and factor analysis. Conceivably,
Schubert's method for positioning in factorial space points, each of which
symbolizes the syndrome of attitudes of a justice, and Kort's method as
developed in this volume—which could be used to position cases in factorial
space, although he does not so use it—might be joined in a model that
would make possible the prediction of future decisions of a court.[27] But
such a development appears at the time of this writing to be merely a
possibility, not a very high probability; and it would have to come several
years in the future, if at all.

II

It may be of some help, in guiding the reader to the use of the papers in
this volume, to suggest some of the communalities which several among
them share. The attitudinal variable discussed by the majority of the studies
is liberalism. This is dealt with, in the most general terms, by Nagel. Civil
liberties are discussed by Kort, Tanenhaus, Aubert, and Schubert. Economic
liberalism is a theme for Spaeth and Kort. The relationship between judicial
behavior and political party affiliations is explored by Jacob and Vines,
Ulmer, and Torgersen. Ulmer and Schubert study group interaction; Jacob
and Vines, and Torgersen deal with the relationship between judiciaries
and larger political systems. The influence upon judicial decision-making of
a traditional factor in legal analysis, *stare decisis,* is of specific concern to
Kort and Schubert. Aubert studies court-martial trials in Norwegian culture,

and Schubert analyzes appellate judicial review of the decisions of courts-martial in the United States. The method of content analysis of judicial opinions is a basic tool for Aubert, Kort, and Schubert.

Three of the chapters (Jacob and Vines, Ulmer, and Nagel) focus upon the behavior of judges of American state courts; Aubert and Torgersen afford a basis for cross-cultural comparisons by drawing upon data relating to the Norwegian court system; while the other four chapters all are concerned with the United States Supreme Court. Thus, although some will feel that the imbalance in the direction of a preoccupation with researching the American Supreme Court so typical of earlier writings in public law also characterizes the present collection of studies, a majority of these chapters, at least, are focused elsewhere.

In terms of the content of the data analyzed, a majority of these chapters (Aubert, Kort, Schubert, Spaeth, and Ulmer) examine decisions of courts on the merits of the substantive issues presented, while one chapter (Tanenhaus) analyzes only jurisdictional decisions. The remaining three studies examine background factors, either in the psychology of individual judges (Nagel), the sociology of their socio-economic traits (Torgersen), or in the political milieu in which courts function (Jacob and Vines). Aubert, Kort, and Ulmer focus primarily upon opinion behavior, while making incidental use of related voting data; Schubert, Spaeth, and Tanenhaus work essentially with voting behavior, while making incidental use of opinion data. Of the remaining three authors, Nagel analyzes the results of a questionnaire survey that he conducted; Torgersen analyzes the results of a systematic compilation of biographical data on judicial personnel; and Jacob and Vines survey the published literature in two fields, that of state government, insofar as this relates to the judiciary, and that of judicial behavior, insofar as this relates to state courts.

And finally, there are three major, and different, emphases which characterize the interdisciplinary bridges manifest in the contributions that follow. The chapters by Jacob and Vines, Aubert, and Torgersen are written primarily from the point of view of political sociology, those by Tanenhaus and Kort are essentially concerned with the statistical prediction of decisions, and the other chapters all embrace perspectives drawn from social psychology.

NOTES

1. Anna Haddow, *Political Science in American Colleges and Universities* (New York: Appleton-Century, 1939); Martin Landau, "On the Use of Metaphor in Political Analysis," *Social Research,* Vol. 28 (Autumn, 1961), pp. 348-49.

2. To recall their names is to call the roll of former presidents of the American Political Science Association: although not limited to the following, they are surely exemplified by Henry Jones Ford, Charles A. Beard, Edward S. Corwin, Robert E. Cushman, Charles Grove Haines, and Carl Brent Swisher. I am indebted to my colleague, Professor Samuel Krislov, for having sharpened my perception of this point.

3. The close link between the substantive and methodological content of Pritchett's book and more recent developments in the theory of judicial behavior is demonstrated in Glendon Schubert, "A Solution to the Indeterminate Factorial Resolution of Thurstone and Degan's Study of the Supreme Court," *Behavioral Science,* Vol. 7 (October, 1962), pp. 448-458.

4. C. Herman Pritchett, *The Roosevelt Court: A Study in Judicial Politics and Values, 1937-1947* (New York: Macmillan, 1948), p. xi.

5. Heinz Eulau, Samuel J. Eldersveld, and Morris Janowitz, *Political Behavior: A Reader in Theory and Research* (Glencoe: The Free Press, 1956), pp. 7-8, 24-31; Robert A. Dahl, "The Behavioral Approach," *American Political Science Review*, Vol. 55 (December, 1961), p. 763; Heinz Eulau, "Political Science," in Bert F. Hoselitz (ed.), *A Reader's Guide to the Social Sciences* (Glencoe: The Free Press, 1959), p. 107.

6. Dahl, *op. cit.*, pp. 764-66.

7. Eulau, Eldersveld, and Janowitz, *op. cit.*

8. "The Uses and Limitations of Social Science Methods in Analyzing Judicial Behavior" (Washington, D. C., American Political Science Association, September 7, 1956; mimeographed).

9. Glendon Schubert, *Quantitative Analysis of Judicial Behavior* (Glencoe: The Free Press, 1959), chap. 5; Ulmer, "Supreme Court Behavior and Civil Rights," *Western Political Quarterly*, Vol. 13 (June, 1960), pp. 288-311, and "Scaling Judicial Cases: A Methodological Note," *American Behavioral Scientist*, Vol. 4 (April, 1961), pp. 31-34.

10. (London: Routledge and Kegan Paul, 1954), chap. 4.

11. *Civil Liberties and the Vinson Court* (Chicago: University of Chicago Press, 1954).

12. Eloise C. Snyder, "The Supreme Court as a Small Group," *Social Forces*, Vol. 36 (March, 1958), pp. 232-38.

13. *Quantitative Analysis of Judicial Behavior*, chap. 3.

14. Edward Ferguson III, "Some Comments on the Applicability of Bloc Analysis to State Appellate Courts," a paper read at the Midwest Conference of Political Scientists (May, 1961; mimeographed).

15. John R. P. French, Jr., "A Formal Theory of Social Power," chap. 38 in Dorwin Cartwright and Alvin Zander (eds.), *Group Dynamics: Research and Theory*, 2nd ed. (Evanston: Row, Peterson, 1960), especially pp. 740-742.

16. Jack W. Peltason, *Federal Courts in the Political Process* (New York: Random House, 1955); Clement E. Vose, "The Impact of Pressure Groups on Constitutional Interpretation," a paper read at the Annual Convention of the American Political Science Association (Chicago: September 8, 1954; mimeographed).

17. J. W. Peltason, *Fifty-eight Lonely Men: Southern Federal Judges and School Desegregation* (New York: Harcourt, Brace & World, 1961); and Clement E. Vose, *Caucasians Only: The Supreme Court, the NAACP, and the Restrictive Covenant Cases* (Berkeley: University of California Press, 1959).

18. "The Justices of the Supreme Court: A Collective Portrait," *Midwest Journal of Political Science*, Vol. 3 (1959), pp. 1-57.

19. Charles Winick, Israel Gerver, and Abraham Blumberg, "The Psychology of Judges," chap. 6 in Hans Toch (ed.), *Legal and Criminal Psychology* (New York: Holt, Rinehart, and Winston, 1961), p. 138; and Richard R. Fagen, "Some Contributions of Mathematical Reasoning to the Study of Politics," *American Political Science Review*, Vol. 55 (December, 1961), pp. 898-99.

20. Fred Kort, "Predicting Supreme Court Decisions Mathematically: A Quantitative Analysis of the Right to Counsel Cases," *American Political Science Review*, Vol. 51 (March, 1957), pp. 1-12; and Franklin M. Fisher, "The Mathematical Analysis of Supreme Court Decisions: The Use and Abuse of Quantitative Methods," *American Political Science Review*, Vol. 52 (June, 1958), pp. 321-28, and "On the Existence and Linearity of Perfect Predictors in 'Content Analysis'," *Modern Uses of Logic in Law*, Vol. 1 (March 1960), pp. 1-9. Cf. Reed C. Lawlor, "Prediction of Supreme Court Decisions," in *Proceedings of the Second National Law and Electronics Conference*, Lake Arrowhead, California, May, 1962 (Albany: Matthew Bender, in press).

21. "The Hughberts Game" focuses on conflict over power among the justices of the Supreme Court during the "Court-packing" crisis of the 1936 term; "The Certiorari Game" discusses the manipulation of jurisdictional decisions in order to establish policy control in F.E.L.A. cases. See *Quantitative Analysis of Judicial Behavior*, chap. 4.

22. Apparently, the neglect is general, rather than specific to judicial behavior. For a commentary on the recent literature most relevant to the study of political behavior,

concluding (*inter alia*) that "political scientists have tended to ignore" this body of theory, see William H. Riker, "Voting and the Summation of Preferences: An Interpretive Bibliographical Review of Selected Developments during the Last Decade," *American Political Science Review,* Vol. 55 (December, 1961), p. 911; and cf. Riker's recent book, *The Theory of Political Coalitions* (New Haven: Yale University Press, 1962).

23. Schubert, "Policy without Law: An Extension of the Certiorari Game," *Stanford Law Review,* Vol. 14 (March, 1962), pp. 284-327.

24. "Judicial Characteristics and Judicial Decision-Making" (Evanston: Northwestern University, Ph.D. dissertation, 1961); "Political Party Affiliation and Judges' Decisions," *American Political Science Review,* Vol. 55 (December, 1961), pp. 843-50; and other articles cited in the bibliography to this volume.

25. James F. Herndon, "The Relationship between Partisanship and the Decisions of State Supreme Courts," University of Michigan, Ph.D. dissertation in political science, listed in *American Political Science Review,* Vol. 53 (1959), p. 900.

26. Schubert: *op. cit. supra* (Note 3); "A Psychometric Model of the Supreme Court," *American Behavioral Scientist,* Vol. 5 (November, 1961), pp. 14-18; "Psychometric Research in Judicial Behavior," *Modern Uses of Logic in Law,* Vol. 2 (March, 1962), pp. 9-18; "The 1960-61 Term of the Supreme Court: A Psychological Analysis," *American Political Science Review,* Vol. 56 (March, 1962), pp. 90-107; and "Psychometric Analysis of Judicial Behavior: The 1961 Term of the Supreme Court," *Law and Contemporary Problems,* Vol. 28, No. 1 (Winter, 1963).

27. Cf. Harold D. Lasswell, "Current Studies in the Decision Process: Automation versus Creativity," *Western Political Quarterly,* Vol. 8 (1955), pp. 398-99.

PART ONE

SOCIAL PSYCHOLOGY AND JUDGES

Leadership in the Michigan Supreme Court

S. SIDNEY ULMER

THE ROLE OF LEADERSHIP in small groups, its development, and its characteristics have received considerable attention from sociologists and others engaged in small group research.[1] Yet, though collegial courts may be defined sociologically as small problem-solving groups, the identification and study of leaders in such groups has been seemingly neglected by students of American judicial processes.[2] It is not difficult to suggest a reason for such a research decision. It is primarily due to the nature of the research situation which confronts one interested in the matter. While small group scholars have created a number of interesting devices and techniques for the study of the group leader, the minimal condition for the use of such devices is access to the inner recesses of intragroup relationships. As a result, much more has been done with experimental groups than with such real life groups as operating collegial courts. Such courts must be studied as groups at longer range, with less information about and less cooperation from group members than one can depend upon in experimental situations.

In working with courts, it becomes necessary to adapt old methods to new conditions or, in many cases, to create new ways and means of revealing intragroup relations. One who would study leadership on a collegial court faces, at the outset, what are clearly substantial obstacles. The "purple curtain" that hides much of the doings of courts of law is no accident. By design, great care is taken to safeguard deliberations leading to decision, and the conference room of the collegial court especially is considered inviolate. Such practices are neither arbitrary nor superfluous, since an important function of obscuring decisional processes is to sustain the myth of judicial objectivity

I wish to express appreciation to my colleague Charles Press for reading and commenting on portions of this paper and to Ernest Riddle for assistance in collecting some of the data used in the analysis. In addition I am indebted to Associate Justices George Edwards and Thomas Kavanagh of the Michigan Supreme Court, each of whom read one or more parts of my manuscript. Their comments and suggestions served to clarify my own thoughts about the Court and in some instances enabled me to avoid possible error. Of course they share no responsibility for, nor do they necessarily agree with, the tentative conclusions I have reached.

13

which permeates the American judicial system.[3] The Michigan Supreme Court[4] does not differ from the United States Supreme Court and other state and federal courts, in its desire to protect the privacy of the conference, and to cloak in secrecy the proceedings leading to decision. Attempts of most courts along this line have been highly successful in spite of occasional leaks and indiscretions, and the publication of certain judicial commentary.

A second problem facing one interested in leadership in a collegial court is one that plagues all who focus on "leadership" as a concept. Various definitions and conceptualizations are almost continually being offered. Sometimes leadership is equated with power or influence, sometimes with position; sometimes it is related to situation, sometimes to personality or the charismatic qualities of a personality. And even if we can agree on a definition of leadership, we have difficulty in deciding how its qualities or characteristics may be identified and measured.[5]

In spite of all this, however, attempts to specify the leaders in a judicial decision-making group who have influenced their colleagues as well as a court's decisional output are worthwhile. If such leaders are successfully identified, their ideological and legal positions acquire added meaning. Where the judgeship is a political position—appointive or elective—knowledge of the influential incumbent is of importance to the appointing agency, or the party or group which normally sponsors candidates for judicial office. Finally, for practicing lawyers, information about the power or influence structure of a collegial court is of some value in predicting the judicial response to the fact stimuli presented in particular cases. The formulation of the lawyer's brief and the nature of his argument may very well be influenced by such data.

In examining interaction patterns among the justices of a collegial court, it is not implausible to think that some members of the court will be more influential than others: that this group, like others, will develop leaders. Our problem is that of identification. Some small group research has suggested that leaders tend to be bigger and brighter than other group members; other studies indicate that the leader displays better personality adjustment than his followers, or that he tends to give more information and make more frequent interpretations about a given situation than those with whom he interacts. Such research has exemplified two general approaches—a focus on "traits" or on "behavior."

The trait approach has received marked attention over the years. Such traits as psychosexual appeal and intelligence have been suggested as possible universal traits of leaders, and long lists of suggested traits have been compiled. The difficulty with such lists, however, is that only about 5 per cent of the discovered traits are common to four or more investigations.[6] This is not to argue that certain minimal abilities may not be required of all leaders. It is simply to say that a focus on and a comparison of the behavior patterns of the members of a group may be more fruitful, given our present limited ability to conceptualize and measure personality traits.

Looking at behavior, we do not expect to find leaders associated with constant behavior patterns. Such an approach is much too rigid and is not justified by our present knowledge in this area. Research to date seems to show (1) that leadership is a set of qualities and capabilities possessed in varying degrees by all group members and (2) that the degree to which a particular group member is a leader will vary with the group situation. We shall define leadership as *a process of exerting influence on that behavior, in an organized group, which leads to the establishment and achievement of goals.* This definition includes all leadership exerted in the group. It does not specify how the influence is exercised, nor is it concerned with the multiple subtleties of "power play" in organized problem-solving groups. Neither does it suggest that only one group member is the leader. From our definition, any justice of the Michigan Supreme Court may be studied to determine his influence in the group. This means that the possibility of all members of a collegial court exerting influence in varying degrees is not ruled out.

Since this flexible view associates leadership with situation, the proper analytical approach is first to identify the general situation, subsequently breaking it down into contextual components. The measure of leadership or influence in general will be the mean of the influence exerted in varying degrees in a large number of particular situations. Those working with small groups agree that evidence of influence takes several general forms. Thus, some weight has been given to such things as the rate at which a group member initiates behavior or is the recipient of behavior from others, the extent to which members of a group attempt problem delineation and volunteer solutions, and the relative quantity of verbal expression in problem-solving sessions. It seems agreed that the ratios of supportive/nonsupportive behavior received and given by group members are often probative in the study of group influence structure.[7]

One interested in identifying "leaders" in group situations, however, must be careful lest an "element" in a leadership situation be mistaken for the whole. That is to say, the ability of the leader to influence the behavior of others in terms of specified goals may be based on many factors and may be indicated in a number of different ways. In working with a collegial court—a situation characterized by a relative lack of information about the inner workings of the group—caution is obviously dictated. It is essentially the problem of the forest whose outer edge can only suggest what lies beyond, or that of the mountain whose peak alone is visible above the cloudy mists. What we see in such situations is less than what is hidden, and the visible indicators may, in fact, give false clues to the total situation. For who can tell whether the rocky peak tops a forested base or how extensive an area the forest itself covers?

Thus it cannot be emphasized too much that the type of empirical material available on collegial courts is, in the last analysis, a rather crude indicator of what we seek—influence structure in the group. Such data, when summarized and analyzed, reveal only one element among many that would have to be considered if one would identify, in any full sense, the degree of leadership exercised by each member of a judicial group. In the present study we do not suggest that the delineation, in all its panoply, of the many facets of judicial leadership on the Michigan Supreme Court is possible.

On the other hand, data establishing support/nonsupport ratios (SNR) among the justices of that court may not be safely ignored. Quite the contrary, it is suggested that such data are evidence which ought to be included in any attempt to outline influence structure in such a group.

In examining the extent to which the justices of the Michigan Supreme Court support or fail to support (oppose) each other, we cannot concern ourselves solely with interagreement patterns among the votes cast by members of this collegial court. There will always be instances in which the agreement in votes is coupled with disagreement in the opinion or rationale for the vote. Where voting data is relied upon, the focus is upon a situation in which the judge must vote with the majority or dissent. In either case a certain amount of agreement with colleagues is built into the situation. This is likely to distort the research conclusions. For such agreement does not necessarily reflect the choice of a justice to agree with another or with another's position. A judge, as perceived by his colleagues, is not only a physical entity existing in space; he also represents a set of attitudes and values. While the attraction of one justice for another may be influenced by the physical attributes of the first, we believe such considerations to be of minimal significance. In this paper we are concerned with the attraction power of each judge's attitudes and values for every other judge in the Michigan Supreme Court.

A consideration of agreement and disagreement in opinions permits somewhat sharper analysis than voting data provides. For a *conscious* decision either to agree with some opinion, write an opinion, or merely agree or disagree in result must be made by the judge in each case. Thus, if we observe a justice agreeing with the opinions of another justice we may infer that the attitudes and values of the first have some attraction for the second. The strength of such an inference will depend upon the number of cases on which the agreement/disagreement ratios are based. In the present case opinion analysis has an additional advantage, because opinion assigning procedures in the Michigan Supreme Court present a choice-making situation that lends itself to the kind of inquiry we are posing.

Like those in many other state courts, the procedures used in the Michigan Court differ from those of its federal counterpart. In the United States Supreme Court the opinion "for the Court" (normally supported by a majority of votes) is written by assignment. That is, the Chief Justice (if in the majority) or the senior associate justice in the majority decides who is to be the author of the Court's opinion. In the Michigan Supreme Court a different system is used. Each judge on the Michigan Supreme Court is given a number, and individual cases are assigned to justices by number on a rotation basis. Several days before argument is set on a case the judge takes his case home for study. At 8:30 A.M. on the day set for argument a conference is held, at which time the judge assigned the case reports to his colleagues. He states the facts in the dispute and the propositions of law the court is to decide. At this point no opinion is expressed. Each judge merely presents the case assigned to him. Argument follows later that same day. After the morning and afternoon arguments by counsel, a conference convenes at 3:00 P.M., the cases are discussed further, and oral opinions may be expressed; but no vote is taken at that time.

The justice to whom the case is assigned writes an opinion for the case, which is circulated among the other justices at least ten days prior to a conference set for the decision. At the same time any other justice may write an opinion if he chooses to do so. On conference day justices as a group review all the opinions written, having previously done so individually. If differences can be reconciled, an unanimous opinion results; otherwise, all opinions are circulated for signature. No formal vote is taken. The writer signs first and the opinion goes around the table at which justices sit according to number. The majority opinion, in a given case, is simply the one obtaining a majority of the signatures. Authors of majority opinions, therefore, are not known until the process of suggestion and compromise that precedes decision is completed. Justices of the court are free to support or oppose any opinion and often do so, not knowing whether the opinion will ultimately be a dissent, a concurrence, or the opinion of the court.

I

We shall now examine the extent to which the eight Michigan judges supported the opinions of each other in the period 1958-1960. Although two judges may agree with each other most of the time, this alone does not reveal who is influencing whom. It is necessary to devise a measure that will distinguish each justice from those with whom he is paired. An inter-individual solidarity index using opinion data enables us to overcome, in part, this difficulty.[8] Such an index has been compiled for the Michigan

TABLE 1

Inter-Individual Solidarity Index, Michigan Supreme Court, 1958-1960

Targets	INITIATORS							
	Ka	Vo	De	Sm	Ca	Ed	Bl	Ke
Kavanagh		76	80	85	81	88	83	77
Voelker	81		60	90	59	86	99	63
Dethmers	66	65		75	99	77	72	95
Smith	78	79	63		57	81	84	64
Carr	63	58	100	66		70	61	100
Edwards	61	68	66	76	65		70	65
Black	75	84	48	77	44	68		55
Kelly	60	53	86	63	91	61	62	

Supreme Court and is based on opinion behavior in 500 cases covering the defined period.[9] These data are presented in Table 1. The entry for each justice is based on the formula

$$\text{ISI} = \frac{aij}{aij + dij} \times 100$$

where aij is the number of supportive acts originated by the ith individual (the initiator) and directed toward the jth individual (the target); dij is the number of nonsupportive acts originated by the ith individual and directed toward the jth individual. In this case the supportive act is the agreement of the ith individual with an opinion written by the jth individual (be it a majority, concurring, or dissenting opinion), and the nonsupportive act is the failure of the ith individual to agree with an opinion written by the jth individual. The range of the index is from 0 (perfect nonsupport) to 100 (perfect support).

The index does not show equal reciprocal support for any of our dyads. Dethmers and Carr come closest to a mutual exchange with support/nonsupport ratios of 100 and 99, respectively. Republican Carr is also perfectly supported by the other Republican member of the court. In terms of comparative support, Smith received more support than he gave from Edwards, Kelly, and Black; Edwards received more than he gave from Black and Kelly; Kavanagh received more from Smith, Edwards, Dethmers, Black, Kelly, and Carr. The remaining justices who received more support in opinions than they gave were Dethmers from Smith, Edwards, Black, Kelly, and Voelker; Kelly from Black; Carr from Smith, Edwards, Dethmers, Black, and Kelly; and Voelker from Smith, Edwards, Kavanagh, Black, Kelly, and Carr. Thus the number of justices from whom each justice received more support in opinions than he gave would be as follows: Kavanagh—six, Voelker —six, Dethmers—five, Carr—five, Smith—three, Edwards—two, Kelly—one. Black was the only justice who gave more support than he received to every other member of the group.

The solidarity index not only furnishes valuable information about the relationships between pairs of justices but also enables us to speculate concerning influence structure in the court. The ISI entry for each of our judges can be viewed as a rating assigned by the judges to each other. In some respects the rating is similar to a sociometric choice or a generalization of such choices. By comparing these ratings we may infer something about influence structure in the group. In Table 2 the columnar entries of each justice are rank ordered from one through seven. The sums of rows of these rankings may be used as one indication of the relative influence of each

TABLE 2

ISI Ranks, Michigan Supreme Court, 1958-1960

INITIATORS

Targets	Ka	Vo	De	Sm	Ca	Ed	Bl	Ke	Σ Rows	Average Rank
Ka		3	3	2	3	1	3	3	18	1
Vo	1		6	1	5	2	1	6	22	2
De	4	5		5	1	4	4	2	25	3.5
Sm	2	2	5		6	3	2	5	25	3.5
Ca	5	6	1	6		5	7	1	31	5.5
Ed	6	4	4	4	4		5	4	31	5.5
Bl	3	1	7	3	7	6		7	34	7
Ke	7	7	2	7	2	7	6		38	8

judge in the group as a whole. The data indicate that a judge's position may be determined by the fact that he has a weak relationship with all his colleagues, that he has a strong position with all other justices, or that he is strong with some and weak with others when it comes to receiving support for and giving support to the written opinions produced by members of the tribunal.

This matrix suggests that Kavanagh may exercise leadership most often and Kelly least often among members of the group. In the case of Kavanagh support is across the board. The political party variable seems to be of some consequence, although its impact is affected by individual considerations. Kavanagh, for example, seems the most attractive Democrat for Republicans, exhibiting at the same time strong appeal for his fellow Democrats. For Kelly, however, the situation is different. His low standing is a result of the fact that five Democrats on the court rank him in position six or seven. The two Republicans treat him much better giving a second position in both cases. While Kelly seems to be the least attractive Republican to Democrats, Black is the least attractive Democrat for Republicans as a group. And the most attractive Republican for the Democratic members of the court seems to have been Chief Justice Dethmers.

Taking Democrats as a group, we find not Kavanagh but Voelker as the justice given the greatest support for his opinions. As shown in Table 3,

TABLE 3

ISI Ranks for Democratic Justices

	INITIATORS						
Targets	Vo	Ka	Sm	Bl	Ed	Σ Rows	Average Rank
Vo		1	1	1	2	5	1
Ka	3		2	3	1	9	2.5
Sm	2	2		2	3	9	2.5
Bl	1	3	3		6	13	4
Ed	4	6	4	5		19	5

only Smith and Voelker assign a ranking of one, two, three, four, to the other four Democrats. This suggests that the political party variable may be more crucial for them than for the other Democratic members, each of whom manage to rank at least one Republican above a Democrat.

For the Republicans the most supported judge is Carr who appears relatively weaker in the court as a whole because the Democrats all prefer

TABLE 4

ISI Ranks for Republican Justices

	INITIATORS				
Targets	Ca	De	Ke	Σ Rows	Average Rank
Ca		1	1	2	1
De	1		2	3	2
Ke	2	2		4	3

Dethmers to him. He is ranked first by both Dethmers and Kelly. As Table 4 shows, no Republican ranks a Democrat above a Republican in this support chart.

II

As a leadership indicator our solidarity table suffers from the fact that it is limited primarily to the first-order relationships between pairs of justices. Although the data in Tables 2, 3, and 4 give evidence bearing on the relative support between any pair of justices, no inference concerning the relationships beyond the first order can be drawn. Support may be given, of course, not directly but through a third justice, or through a fourth, fifth, or sixth justice in some cases. A support index not only should take this into consideration, but also should assign different weights to the relationships depending upon the order class into which a particular relationship falls. The problem here can be approached through the use of the sociometric matrix—a special class of matrices sometimes used for the analysis of power relations. Support relations between any pair of judges in a collegial court will be symmetrical rather than asymmetrical as a result of group structure. But such a relationship can be conceptualized as asymmetrical if, for any pair, we think in terms of the difference in the degree to which members of a court support each other over time.[10]

A relationship between support relations and inter-individual influence is not difficult to establish. It is not unreasonable to assume that a justice finds those he supports attractive. The basis of the attraction could be similarity of values, intellectual brilliance, or other more exotic factors. But regardless of its composition, or our knowledge of it, the fact remains that a justice who supports another is attracted to that other. And a justice who attracts others will inevitably exert influence upon them. Thus, for present purposes, we shall equate relative support with relative influence or leadership.

Such reasoning does not, of course, eliminate the many difficulties associated with the analysis of influence relations. The power theorists have polished every facet of this many-sided problem. We need not belabor their work, but a comment on the most obvious weakness of the approach used here is warranted. The weakness is, of course, that we are viewing an influence relationship in a dyad on a single dimension, whereas such relations are often thought to be multidimensional. Since influence relations may vary with subject matter, some writers have suggested the necessity for a separate index for each area. According to them, such operationalizations tend to be *ad hoc* and not subject to generalization. The best answer to this criticism is that an index defined in terms of subject matter also is, inevitably, characterized by the same weakness. That is, each reveals a structure based on particular observations or variables. As applied to judicial data, the statement that Justice X is supported by Justice Y in Workman's Compensation cases 65 per cent of the time does not differ in type from the statement that Justice A is supported by Justice B in 65 per cent of the cases generally. The study of influence in this paper proceeds from the belief that a general analysis is a necessary prelude to more refined studies.

In terms of our definition, Table 1 indicates that Black and Dethmers each exert some influence on the other. But if we consider the difference in the entry for Black and that for Dethmers, it is probable that Dethmers is the more influential member in the relationship. Likewise, Dethmers seems more influential with Smith, and Smith more influential with Black. Asymmetrical relationships of this type may be depicted by means of directed-line graphs. The directed-line graph (digraph) in Figure 1 sketches the situation just outlined.[11]

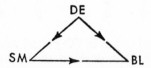

Figure 1. Directed-line graph of dominance relations in a three-member group.

Figure 1 portrays Dethmers as the most influential member of this particular triad, since he is dominant (i.e., receives more support than he gives) over Smith and Black. Smith is second, since he is dominant over Black; and Black is weakest, since he is dominated by Dethmers and Smith but is himself dominant over neither. However, when studying a large number of relationships the directed-line graph becomes cumbersome, particularly for portraying in various orders the relations being studied. Such a graph becomes very difficult to perceive visually when applied to all members of the Michigan Supreme Court. Nevertheless, by careful study of such a graph it should be possible to see all the relationships involved. This graph would show that Smith has a first-order dominance over Edwards, Black, and Kelly, a second-order dominance over Black, Kelly, and Black, and a third-order dominance over Black. For more highly supported members of the court the various relations become quite complex.

To simplify our problem we may resort to the dominance matrix. This is a square matrix having 0 and 1 as entries. The rows and columns are labeled with the symbols representing the various justices of the Michigan Supreme Court. An entry of 1 in a cell indicates that the justice in the row of that cell has a higher relative support/nonsupport ratio (SNR) than the justice in the column of that cell. An entry of 0 means the opposite.

Table 5 is a dominance matrix for the Michigan Supreme Court derived from the data of Table 1. This matrix we shall call Matrix D. It shows the first-stage SNR relationships between each pair on the court. The second-order relationships may be derived from the square of the first matrix (or from D^2), the third-order from D^3, the fourth-order from D^4 and so on. A leadership indicator may be derived from a dominance matrix by the summation of the row for each justice. If this is done for the first-order matrix, the resulting rank order is close to that derived in Table 2 ($\rho = 0.91$; significant at 0.01). We wish to derive, however, a SNR ranking that takes

TABLE 5

Dominance Matrix D: First-Order Relationships

TARGETS

Initiators	Vo	Ka	De	Ca	Sm	Ed	Ke	Bl	∑ Row	Average Rank
Vo	0	1	0	1	1	1	1	1	6	1.5
Ka	0	0	1	1	1	1	1	1	6	1.5
De	1	0	0	0	1	1	1	1	5	3.5
Ca	0	0	1	0	1	1	1	1	5	3.5
Sm	0	0	0	0	0	1	1	1	3	5
Ed	0	0	0	0	0	0	1	1	2	6
Ke	0	0	0	0	0	0	0	1	1	7
Bl	0	0	0	0	0	0	0	0	0	8

into consideration additional stages in the paired relationships. One possibility would be to define relative SNR position as the sum of the rows in D, D^2, D^3, . . . D^n. Such an approach, however, would assign equal weight to all stages of support. But it is more plausible to assign greater weight to the first-stage summation, the next greatest weight to the second-stage summation, next to the third stage, and so on. Thus, we may establish a general SNR structure by the formula

$$D + \frac{D^2}{2} + \frac{D^3}{3} + \cdot\cdot\cdot + \frac{D^n}{n}.$$

As this procedure is carried out it is possible that the rank order will vary from one stage to the next. The question then arises, at what point is the series to be cut off? In this case, we continued the series until the rank order was (1) free of ties and (2) the same for three successive stages. In the present instance these criteria were satisfied for

$$S = D + \frac{D^2}{2} + \frac{D^3}{3} + \frac{D^4}{4} + \frac{D^5}{5} + \frac{D^6}{6}.$$

The resulting rank order is given in Table 6.

TABLE 6

Weighted Summary Matrix S for Matrices D-D⁶

TARGETS

Initiators	Vo	Ka	De	Ca	Sm	Ed	Ke	Bl	∑ Rows	Average Rank
Vo	0	1.91	2.46	2.65	6.16	9.11	17.96	23.16	63.41	1
Ka	1.56	0	2.40	2.38	4.21	8.15	13.48	20.88	53.06	2
De	1.50	1.35	0	1.76	4.54	6.31	10.89	19.15	45.50	3
Ca	1.06	1.03	1.50	0	3.59	5.32	8.60	13.48	34.58	4
Sm	0	0	0	0	0	1	1.50	2.33	4.83	5
Ed	0	0	0	0	0	0	1	1.5	2.5	6
Ke	0	0	0	0	0	0	0	1	1	7
Bl	0	0	0	0	0	0	0	0	0	8

A number of relational statements can be derived from Table 6. The row entries for each justice might be interpreted from right to left as the degree of influence exerted by the row justice on each justice with whom he intersects. Read in reverse, the entries reflect the degree of relative support given the row justice by each intersecting justice. The column entries might be interpreted as indicating the degree to which the column justice had influence exerted upon him. The sum of the columnar entries, of course, produces a rank order which is the reciprocal of that derived from summing the rows. Thus, if high row sums indicate strength, high column sums indicate weakness. Finally, it should be noted that the S matrix possesses scalar properties. That is, reading the rows from left to right, the justice who exerts influence on the highest rank justice with whom he intersects will exert a continually increasing degree of influence on each subsequent justice in the row. Likewise, from the columns, a justice who is influenced by the highest ranked justice with whom he intersects will be influenced less by each subsequent justice down the ranks.

Several exceptions to these generalizations may be noted. Kavanagh exerted slightly more influence on Dethmers than on Carr; Dethmers exerted more on Voelker than on Kavanagh; and Carr exerted more on Voelker than on Kavanagh. Otherwise, perfect row consistency is evident. The only exception to the columnar generalization is Smith, who was influenced by Dethmers to a greater degree than by the higher ranking Kavanagh.

The rank order derived from matrix S correlates with that of matrix D at 0.989 (significant at 0.01), indicating little change after taking into consideration all six stages. The additional analysis did, however, (1) establish the degree of deviation introduced by relationships past the first order and (2) eliminate the two ties which were present in the D matrix ranking.

Finally, we should note the possibility that the rankings may be spurious since they are based on support differentials for 36 pairs without taking into consideration the degree of difference involved. The use of the dominance matrix required that dominance be stipulated for one member of each pair. This requirement ruled out the possibility of what might be called an indifference relationship in some of our dyads. Is it therefore possible that such a limitation has led to a distorted conclusion, and if so, to what degree? In order to treat this problem it is necessary to specify whether a paired relationship exhibits significant or insignificant support differentials. For present purposes, we have considered the deviation of the observed SNR from the expected SNR significant if it could occur by chance less than five times in a hundred. Dominance was then specified only for those relationships in which a deviation of sufficient magnitude was observed.

Figure 2 is a directed-line graph (or digraph) depicting the dominance structure for this limited case. The similarity between the ordered pairs in the general analysis and the order pairs for the limited case is easily perceived from Figure 2. A modified SNR may be computed directly from the data of Table 7 without resort to matrix multiplication. The ordered relations do not extend beyond the second stage. Thus, we may assign 1 to a justice for each justice he dominates in the first stage and ½ for each

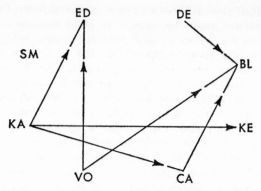

Figure 2. Digraph of dominance structure for most differentiated pairs.

justice he dominates in the second stage. Likewise, we may subtract 1 for each instance in which a justice is dominated in the first stage and ½ for each instance in the second stage. SNR_1 is the difference between these two computations—a modified SNR retaining, however, the same weight for similar classes of observation. Since the rank correlation between Tables 6 and 7 is 0.95 (significant at 0.01 level), the failure to consider the magnitude of support differentials seems to have been inconsequential.

TABLE 7

Complete Dominance Matrix for Significantly Differentiated Pairs, Michigan Supreme Court, 1958-1960

Justices	I. DIRECT DOMINANCE ORDER		II. REVERSE DOMINANCE ORDER		III. SNR_1	
	1st Stage	2nd Stage	1st Stage	2nd Stage	(I—II)	Rank
Ka	3	½	0	0	3½	1
Vo	2	0	0	0	2	2
De	1	0	0	0	1	3
Ca	1	0	1	0	0	4.5
Sm	0	0	0	0	0	4.5
Ke	0	0	1	0	−1	6
Ed	0	0	2	0	−2	7
Bl	0	0	3	1	−3½	8

III

At this point we have completed the development of several overlapping indicators of influence structure in the Michigan Supreme Court. In building these indicators, we did not distinguish between majority opinions on the one hand and dissenting and concurring opinions on the other. Yet the majority opinion has an appeal for the judge of a collegial court which the other types of opinions lack. That is, the majority opinion alone serves as a vehicle through which the ideological and legal preferences of the writer may be incorporated into the jurisprudence of the land. For it is the majority opinion that tends to control the direction and development of the law in specified subject matter areas. It is the majority opinion that furnishes the principal rationale for court decsions and spells out its implications for those who may subsequently find themselves in similar situations.

In the case at hand it is useful to make the distinction discussed above in order to relate our indicators more closely to reality. For one may reasonably ask whether the rank orders associated with our eight judges have any empirically establishable consequences? One such consequence can be illustrated by focusing on majority opinions. For the support patterns analyzed do affect the opportunities for each individual judge to make his own attitudinal or legal preferences the "law of the land." Since every opinion written by a Michigan Supreme Court justice is a prospective majority opinion,[12] the percentage of his total opinion output which becomes majority opinions is a modified reflection of the types of support patterns analyzed in this paper.

These percentages have been computed for each judge and are presented in column 5 of Table 8. The column reflects the fact that those justices with high relative support in all opinions were most successful in attracting

TABLE 8

Final Ranking of Justices Derived from Four Indices

	INDICES					
Justices	ISI	SNR	SNR_1	Majority Opinions*	Σ Rows	Final Ranking
Ka	1	2	1	1 (97%)	5	1
Vo	2	1	2	2 (90%)	7	2
De	3.5	3	3	3 (84%)	12.5	3
Sm	3.5	5	4.5	4 (82%)	17	4
Ca	5.5	4	4.5	6 (71%)	20	5
Ed	5.5	6	7	5 (77%)	23.5	6
Ke	8	7	6	7 (70%)	28	7
Bl	7	8	8	8 (66%)	31	8

*Figures in parentheses represent the percentage of a judge's total opinion output that became majority opinions.

majority support for their opinions. This means that those justices were most effective in creating the opportunities for controlling the development and direction of the law. The two exceptions to our generalization were Carr and Edwards whose reversed positions on the majority index suggest disproportionate SNR's in concurring and dissenting opinions. It appears that Carr had a higher relative ratio and Edwards a lower relative ratio in concurring and dissenting opinions than in majority opinions.

IV

As a result of the foregoing analysis, what can be said concerning leadership or influence in the Michigan court? We cannot specify an all-purpose influence rank for each of our eight justices on the basis of the data presented here. We have, after all, dealt with only one aspect of the many-faceted subject of leadership. And our indicators have been structured in general terms. That structure cannot be expected to remain the same in all situations; if different conditions or situations are specified the results are likely to be affected. Other caveats may be necessary. The following are suggested:

1. We have assumed that each judge is trying to write a majority opinion in every case. Other motivations may affect our analysis. (For example, a judge's opinion may be an appeal to certain groups for their electoral support.)

2. We have assumed that every judge is industrious. Yet it is possible that some judges are lazy and write only in "easy cases," apart from those cases that are assigned to them.

3. We have assumed that each judge is trying to persuade others to his point of view—i.e., he is trying to "lead." Yet, some judges may be "majority prone" and engage in what Robert Dahl calls "chameleon" behavior.

4. We have not distinguished between assigned cases and nonassigned cases, nor between particular subject matter areas, nor between different periods of time. Such considerations may lead to variant results.

5. We have not weighted support and nonsupport differently for unlike types of opinions. To do so would undoubtedly lead to a variant result.

Our design, however, was intended to be exploratory and suggestive, rather than exhaustive. Consistent with such an aim, the results of the investigation would seem to offer a limited set of inferences in view of the evidence we have compiled and the absence of evidence to the contrary. As a hypothesis, we suggest that the relative degree of leadership or influence exercised by members of the Michigan Supreme Court in the period studied is described in Table 8. Our data, though limited, are consonant with this description. Thus, this hypothesized structure may serve as a point of departure for more refined analyses which seek to transcend the unidimensional focus characterizing our approach. If this structure can be validated, the following observations would seem significant:

1. Although the Michigan Supreme Court was composed of five Democrats and three Republicans in the defined period, the Democratic justices do not appear to have exercised influence in the same proportion. Instead of finding the first five positions occupied by Democrats and the last three by Republicans, we find Democrats and Republicans interspersed along the entire length of the support continuum. Thus, while a Democrat (Kavanagh) appears to have been most influential, a Democrat (Black) appears to have been least influential.

2. The justice ranked first (Kavanagh) is on record as favoring the continuation of the present system of selecting personnel for the court. This suggests that he perceived himself sufficiently effective with the kind of men such processes send to the court. His high ranking tends to validate such a perception.

3. The justice ranked last (Black) is on record as opposing the continuation of the present method of choosing Michigan Supreme Court

justices. If he perceives himself as insufficiently effective with the kind of men nominated and elected under present procedures, his low ranking tends to validate such a perception.

4. Finally, the Chief Justice, who is often thought of as the leader of courts of last resort, occupies the third position in the Michigan Court. We have previously noted that the Chief Justice in Michigan is chosen by the associate justices of his court. The finding here may imply the preference of the majority for a Chief Justice with a modicum of those qualities usually associated with leadership. Our data are consistent with such a contention.

NOTES

1. Dorwin Cartwright and Alvin Zander (eds.), *Group Dynamics* (Evanston, Ill.: Row, Peterson, 1960), and A. Paul Hare, Edgar F. Borgatta, Robert F. Bales, (eds.), *Small Groups* (New York: Knopf, 1955). A brief summary of developments in this area is Michael S. Olmsted, *The Small Group* (New York: Random House, 1959).

2. See, however, Glendon Schubert, *Quantitative Analysis of Judicial Behavior* (Glencoe: The Free Press, 1959), pp. 16, 141-42, 209-10; S. Sidney Ulmer, "The Analysis of Behavior Patterns on the United States Supreme Court," *Journal of Politics*, Vol. 22 (Nov., 1960), 629, 636-40, "Homeostatic Tendencies in the United States Supreme Court" in S. Sidney Ulmer (ed.), *Introductory Readings in Political Behavior* (Chicago: Rand, McNally, 1961), pp. 176-77; and see especially David J. Danelski, "The Influence of the Chief Justice in the Decisional Process" (paper delivered at the meeting of the American Political Science Association, 1960).

3. Another is to prevent a determination of the amount of time being devoted to each case or issue. For enlightening comments on the importance of time see: Robert H. Jackson, *The Supreme Court in the American System of Government* (Cambridge, Mass.: Harvard University Press, 1958), pp. 14-16; William O. Douglas, "The Supreme Court and Its Case Load," *Cornell Law Quarterly*, Vol. 45 (Spring, 1960), 401-14; comment of Justice Harlan, concurring, in *Reid* v. *Covert*, 354 U.S. 1, pp. 65-66.

4. The Michigan Supreme Court is composed of eight justices elected on a nonpartisan ballot for eight-year terms. The Chief Justice is elected by the justices from among their number. Nomination for office is by political party convention and the party affiliation of the candidate is well advertised during each election campaign. In the period covered in this study the Court was composed of Smith, Edwards, Kavanagh, Black, and Voelker (Democrats) and Dethmers, Carr, and Kelly (Republicans). Souris (Democrat) replaced Voelker near the end of the period and participated in too few cases to warrant inclusion.

5. Cf. Herbert Simon, "Notes on the Observation and Measurement of Power," *Journal of Politics*, Vol. 15 (1953), 500-16; Maurice A. Ash, "An Analysis of Power, with Special Reference to International Politics," *World Politics*, Vol. 3 (1951), 218-32; Alvin W. Gouldner (ed.), *Studies in Leadership* (New York: Harper, 1950), pp. 21-35.

6. Gouldner, *op. cit. supra* (note 5).

7. For a development of this idea, see Robert F. Bales, *Interaction Process Analysis: A Method for the Study of Small Groups* (Cambridge, Mass.: Harvard University Press, 1950).

8. The idea is adapted from Bales, *op. cit. supra* (note 7).

9. Specifically the cases covered are those reported from 352 *Michigan Reports* 019 through 359 *Michigan Reports* 680.

10. This is, of course, only one of the possible metrics in terms of which relative influence could be measured. The relationship here is in essence what James March refers to as a "third possible metric," defined as "more adoptions than rejections or more rejections than adoptions." "Measurement Concepts in the Theory of Influence," *Journal of Politics*, Vol. 19 (May, 1957), 202-206.

11. See: John G. Kemeny, J. Laurie Snell, and Gerald L. Thompson, *Introduction to Finite Mathematics* (Englewood Cliffs, N.J.: Prentice Hall, 1956), pp. 307-12; and Dorwin Cartwright and Frank Harary, *Structural Models: An Introduction to the Theory of Directed Graphs* (New York: Prentice-Hall, in press).

12. Of course, there may be exceptions to this generalization, since a justice may write to satisfy some psychological need to dissent, or to appeal to a voting public, or for other reasons.

Off-the-Bench
Judicial Attitudes

STUART S. NAGEL

SINCE 1959, AT LEAST THREE ARTICLES and one book have been published with titles indicating that they deal with the attitudes of some segment of the American judiciary.[1] However, these studies are concerned only with the on-the-bench attitudes of judges as manifested in judicial decisions. As yet no study seems to have been made of the more general attitudes of the American judiciary.[2] This chapter offers some findings in this area based on a questionnaire survey conducted by the author.

1. The Questionnaire

Appendix 3 at the end of this chapter shows both sides of the questionnaire[3] which was mailed in 1960 to the 313 state and federal supreme court judges who had occupied the bench in 1955, according to the listing in the *Directory of American Judges.*[4] Each questionnaire had a different identification number typed on its last line so that the responses of the judges who replied could be correlated with their judicial decisions or their background characteristics.

The questionnaire was designed to determine the degree of liberalism of the respondent. "Liberalism," as used in this study, refers to a viewpoint associated with the interests of the lower or less privileged economic or social groups in a society and, to a lesser extent, with acceptance of long-run social change. The term "conservative," on the other hand, is used primarily to refer to a viewpoint associated with the interests of the upper or dominant groups in a society, and with resistance to long-run social

---

This paper was prepared as part of a study of judicial backgrounds and attitudes conducted with a grant from the Social Science Research Council. After this chapter had gone to press, the writer completed a closely related paper entitled "Judicial Attitudes and Those of Legislators and Administrators," presented at the annual meeting of the American Political Science Association, 1962. The paper (available on request) contains data with regard to the comparative findings of a survey of all three sets of political decision-makers.

change.[5] Since liberalism is used here as a variable concept, one cannot really be considered a liberal or a conservative in an absolute sense, but only as more, less, or equally liberal or conservative in comparison with someone else. The liberalism-conservatism attitude was chosen over other attitudinal or personality characteristics because it seemed to represent the frame of mind most likely to account for why some judges vote one way and some judges another way in many nonunanimous cases.

Various studies have shown that liberalism is composed of or correlated with a number of sub-attitudes.[6] These sub-attitudes (given here in alphabetical order) include: (1) approval of marital and family planning, (2) criminal rehabilitationism and tolerance of deviant behavior, (3) "democraticness" (i.e., advocacy of majority rule and tolerance of deviant beliefs), (4) ethnic equalitarianism, (5) internationalism and pacifism, (6) naturalism as contrasted to supernaturalism, (7) sex equalitarianism, and (8) working class and socialistic sympathy.

The 24 items in the questionnaire were taken with slight changes from among the 40 items in a liberalism inventory devised by Hans Eysenck.[7] The Eysenck liberalism inventory was chosen for the following reasons:

1. It has items relating to all eight of the sub-attitudes of liberalism.

2. It has been subjected to a factor analysis that determined that all the items were measuring the same underlying factor.[8]

3. It provides for the Likert method of scoring, which is easy for respondents and test interpreters to handle.[9]

4. Its items are worded relatively concisely, unambiguously, and maturely.

5. It clearly distinguished British Socialists and Communists on the one hand from British Conservatives and Fascists on the other hand as a test of its validity.

6. It is relatively free from being time-bound or culture-bound in its terms.

7. It has enough items to produce a meaningful scale.

8. It has some items worded in a liberal direction and some in a conservative direction.

9. It has a high internal consistency between its items as measured by a split-half reliability coefficient.[10]

None of the other proposed liberalism inventories have all these advantages.[11]

The 40 items were reduced to 24 in order to have a less bulky questionnaire and thereby presumably a higher rate of response. The particular 24 items selected were chosen in such a way that there would be three items for describing each of the eight sub-attitudes, anticipating that correlations would be made between each sub-attitude and the decisional behavior of the judges (as well as between the over-all attitude of liberalism and their decisional behavior). The particular three items chosen to represent each sub-attitude were those three items which had the highest correlation with the factor of liberalism.[12] Slight changes were made in the wording of some of the items that seemed somewhat ambiguous or out of date, or not quite appropriate in the United States. However, changes in phraseology were kept to a minimum so that Eysenck's extensive research with the original inventory could be related to the results obtained with the derived questionnaire.[13] According to the Eysenck method of scoring, a liberal by definition expresses agreement with items 2, 4, 5, 6, 8, 9, 13, 14, 17, 21, and 23, and disagreement with items 1, 3, 7, 10, 11, 12, 15, 16, 18, 19, 20, 22, and 24; a conservative would be expected to respond in the opposite way.

Of the 313 state and federal supreme court justices, 119 answered the questionnaire, and all but one of the 119 questionnaires were usable. Of the 194 remaining judges, 38 are known to have died between 1955 (when the *Directory* was published) and 1960 when the questionnaire was sent out, 20 wrote back but failed to answer the questions, and 136 failed to reply.[14] Two of the 119 responding judges completed and returned the questionnaire with the identification number disfigured beyond recognition, but their responses were still usable in the distribution tables (Tables 1, 2, and 3), although not in the correlation table (Table 4).

2. The Structured Responses

Table 1 shows the distribution of the judges' answers for each question-naire item. For ease in reading, the table also groups the items into the sub-attitudes previously mentioned. The sub-attitudes are arranged in order of their relevance to the factor of liberalism as measured by the correlation coefficients which each component item had with the factor of liberalism in Eysenck's study. An *L* or *C* after each item indicates whether the item is worded in a liberal or a conservative direction. The percentage of response in the category closest to the mean for each item is in bold face.[15] The average response to ten of the items was conservative (i.e., disagreeing with a liberal-worded item or agreeing with a conservative-worded one), to seven of the items the average response was neutral, and to seven of the items the average response was liberal (i.e., agreeing with a liberal-worded item or dis-agreeing with a conservative-worded one). The items to which the judges responded in a conservative or neutral direction, however, were the items that had a relatively higher correlation with Eysenck's factor of liberalism-con-servatism.

To get a more meaningful idea of how liberal or how conservative are the state and federal supreme court judges who responded, it is helpful to compare their scores with those of some analogous group. Among the varied groups to whom Eysenck administered his questionnaire, the group of British Conservative Party members may be deemed the closest counter-parts of the American judges. The questionnaire scores of this group, which consisted of 250 middle-class members of the Conservative Party, are com-pared with those of the American judges in Table 2. An analysis of the respective responses and the nature of the questionnaire items to which they pertain reveals that the American judges were more liberal than the British Conservatives on 13 items, that the British Conservatives were more liberal on 10 items, and that both groups had identical percentages on one item.

TABLE 1
Distribution of the Judges' Responses to Each Questionnaire Item

	PERCENTAGE OF THE 118 JUDGES INDICATING**					
QUESTIONNAIRE ITEM*	Strong Disagree-ment	Mild Disagree-ment	Neu-trality	Mild Agree-ment	Strong Agree-ment	Average Re-sponse
I. Socialistic Sympathy						
2. Laws favor rich (L)	35	48	8	6	3	C
9. Have more collectivism (L)	33	39	16	9	3	C
15. Nationalization means stagnation (C)	3	8	4	55	31	C
II. Internationalism and Pacifism						
3. War is inherent (C)	14	47	5	28	5	N
5. Abandon some sovereignty (L)	22	30	8	30	10	N
10. Conscientious objectors are traitors (C)	31	53	7	8	2	L
III. Criminal Rehabilitationism						
4. Criminal treatment is too harsh (L)	21	40	19	16	4	C
18. Spare rod, spoil child (C)	6	21	6	51	18	C
23. Abolish death penalty (L)	24	36	6	26	8	N
IV. Religiosity						
6. Sunday observance is old-fashioned (L)	32	45	12	8	3	C
11. Go back to religion (C)	7	17	10	41	25	C
16. Have religion in schools (C)	20	38	10	26	5	N
V. Ethnic Equalitarianism						
1. Colored are inferior (C)	13	38	13	29	8	N
12. Discourage miscegenation (C)	3	7	3	46	42	C
20. Jews are too powerful (C)	19	58	13	6	3	L
VI. Family Planning						
14. Make divorce laws easier (L)	25	51	9	11	3	C
17. Premarital sex permissible (L)	38	39	8	13	2	C
22. Make birth control illegal (C)	36	47	5	9	3	L
VII. Faith in Democracy						
8. Have unrestricted discussion (L)	13	30	9	35	14	N
13. Have more controversy on radio (L)	3	22	11	47	17	L
24. Have education test for voting (C)	16	38	8	23	14	N
VIII. Sex Equalitarianism						
7. Give men more sex freedom (C)	33	47	8	11	2	L
19. Women are inferior to men (C)	26	47	9	14	3	L
21. Have equal pay for both sexes (L)	4	19	7	54	15	L

*See Appendix 3 for the exact wording of each questionnaire item.
**The mean response to each item is closest to the category for which the percentage of response is set in bold face.

TABLE 2

Comparison of the American Judges with a Sample of British Conservatives

Questionnaire Item*	Percentage of the 118 Judges Indicating Agreement	Percentage of the 250 British Tories Indicating Agreement	Differ- ence	Judges More Conserva- tive
I. Socialistic Sympathy				
2. Laws favor rich (L)	9	27	18	Yes
9. Have more collectivism (L)	12	3	9	No**
15. Nationalization means stagnation (C)	86	86	0	—**
II. Internationalism and Pacifism				
3. War is inherent (C)	33	67	34	No
5. Abandon some sovereignty (L)	40	32	8	No
10. Conscientious objectors are traitors (C)	10	28	18	No
III. Criminal Rehabilitationism				
4. Criminal treatment is too harsh (L)	20	39	19	Yes
18. Spare rod, spoil child (C)	69	56	13	Yes
23. Abolish death penalty (L)	34	30	4	No
IV. Religiosity				
6. Sunday observance is old-fashioned (L)	11	36	25	Yes
11. Go back to religion (C)	66	65	1	Yes
16. Have religion in schools (C)	31	66	35	No**
V. Ethnic Equalitarianism				
1. Colored are inferior (C)	37	42	5	No
12. Discourage miscegenation (C)	88	77	11	Yes
20. Jews are too powerful (C)	9	65	59	No
VI. Family Planning				
14. Make divorce laws easier (L)	14	33	19	Yes
17. Premarital sex is permissible (L)	15	35	20	Yes
22. Make birth control illegal (C)	12	22	10	No
VII. Faith in Democracy				
8. Have unrestricted discussion (L)	49	75	26	Yes
13. Have more controversy on radio (L)	64	67	3	Yes
24. Have education test for voting (C)	37	55	18	No
VIII. Sex Equalitarianism				
7. Give men more sex freedom (C)	13	44	31	No
19. Women are inferior to men (C)	17	40	23	No
21. Have equal pay for both sexes (L)	69	68	1	No

*See Appendix 3 for the exact wording of each questionnaire item.
**A comparison of these items in the British version of the questionnaire (quoted in note 13) with the text of the corresponding items of Appendix 3 shows the greater moderation of the American version regarding collectivism and religious education.

Thus, the average American state and federal supreme court judge seems to be about as liberal as the average middle-class member of the British Conservative Party, to the extent that the data presented are representative of the two groups.[16]

The American judges seem to be more conservative than the British middle-class Tories in matters concerning marital and family planning, criminal rehabilitation, collectivism, and faith in democracy; whereas the American judges appear to be more liberal than the British middle-class Tories in matters concerning internationalism-pacifism, sex equalitarianism, ethnic equalitarianism, and religiosity. The item on which the American judges were most liberal compared to the British group was item 20, "The Jews have too much power and influence in this country"; and the items on which the American judges were the most conservative were items 6 and 8 dealing with Sunday observance and unrestricted freedom of discussion.

Table 3 shows which items provoked the most similarity and the least similarity in the responses of the judges. The degree of similarity is measured by the difference between the percentage of disagreement and the percentage of agreement on each item. The greater the difference (e.g., 100 per cent

TABLE 3

Attitudinal Items Provoking Most and Least Similarity in Responses of the Judges

Items	Percentage of Disagreement	Percentage of Agreement	Degree of Similarity
Provoking the Most Similarity			
12. Discourage miscegenation (C)	10	88	78
15. Nationalization means stagnation (C)	11	86	75
2. Laws favor rich (L)	83	9	74
10. Conscientious objectors are traitors (C)	84	10	74
22. Make birth control illegal (C)	83	12	71
Provoking the Least Similarity			
8. Have unrestricted discussion (L)	43	49	6
5. Abandon some sovereignty (L)	52	40	12
1. Colored are inferior (C)	51	37	14
24. Have education test for voting (C)	54	37	17
23. Abolish death penalty (L)	60	34	26

and 0 per cent), the greater the similarity of responses. The greatest degree of similarity was present on item 12: nearly all the judges favored discouraging marriages between white and colored people. The lowest degree of similarity was present on item 8: the judges were about evenly divided on whether or not they favored "unrestricted" freedom of discussion. With regard to the broader categories, the highest average degree of similarity of response was present among the items relating to working-class and socialistic sympathy, whereas the lowest average degree of similarity was present among the items relating to faith in democracy.

3. The Open-Ended Responses

Some of the most interesting responses to the attitudinal questionnaires were not the pluses and minuses, but rather the unsolicited comments that many of the judges made. For example, one respondent, who was no longer a judge, felt compelled to mention in quite vigorous language that his electoral defeat was due to the fact that he refused to bow to extremist segregation forces within his Southern state. Another judge wrote: "There is nothing confidential about my answers. They indicate moreover why I was, on the bench, in continual disagreement with my brothers, [and] was glad to quit." Some judges praised the study by saying such things as "It is heartening to know that those with money are interested in these important matters, and it is a pleasure for me to cooperate." Another enthusiastic judge said: "Although I am no longer a judge on the . . . Supreme Court, I have made an attempt to respond to the statements being solicited by you in your most interesting research project. I trust you may have the cooperation of all the judges in this very important undertaking." A few judges, however, disapproved of the study. One simply wrote back, "What a lot of hog-wash!" and another said, "This is about as asinine as any questionnaire I have received."

A variety of reasons were given by the judges who gave reasons for not answering the questionnaire. Some of them offered the irrelevant reason that they were no longer judges. Some judges objected to the way the questions were worded. Still others thought the subject matter was too controversial. A few said it was their policy never to answer questionnaires. One judge said, "I do not care to have my qualifications or ability measured by any IBM apparatus or any other mechanical device."

Some of the judges answered the questionnaires that were sent them but expressed doubts as to whether any correlation would be found between their answers and their judicial decisions. For instance one judge said: "I have strong beliefs on questions 9 [dealing with the desirability of collectivism and the TVA, on which he placed a double negative] and 15 [dealing with the undesirability of nationalization, on which he placed a double positive], but doubt if they could ever influence my decisions as a judge. This is because under my philosophy of constitutional law, this is a matter for the legislatures and Congress and not the courts."

Many of the comments on specific items were also quite interesting. For instance, judges who volunteered comments on the divorce item mainly indicated that they felt divorce proceedings were overly legalistic regardless of whether a divorce is easy or difficult to obtain. Such comments were typified by the judge who said, "I do think there is need of a new approach to the problem with the view of utilizing the religious, psychiatric, social and medical resources of the community to the end that divorce might be prevented and the adversary nature of present proceedings eliminated." Some humorous comments were made on item 17 on whether couples should find out if they are sexually suited before marriage. One judge quipped "As the Indian said when he met the mermaid, 'How'," and another said: "Would not that be great. Hell, no." In a more serious vain one respondent said, "If they love each other and are suitable in other particulars, sex will take care of itself." On whether birth control should be made illegal (item 22), one Catholic judge commented, "I have indicated a negative answer because there are methods of birth control that in any system of ethics are permissible"; whereas two Protestant judges who made comments on this item said, "Effective birth control methods should be made available to all people" and "Birth control . . . should be encouraged among poverty-stricken, congested persons."[17]

The prevailing comments to item 4 on punishment versus rehabilitation are typified by a quotation from one judge, who said: "Criminals are not all sick; whenever they are, effort should be made to cure them. But there is too much maudlin sympathy for cold, calculating characters a la Chessman." Reactions to "spare the rod and spoil the child" (item 18) ranged from "use kindness and love" to "there is a very great duty on all parents and persons connected with the raising of children to lead them in the right direction and where necessary use effective disciplinary measures." Two of the four judges making comments on the death penalty favored its abolition only if life imprisonment was not subject to parole. A third judge said, "the death penalty should be abolished except possibly for the commission of a second murder after conviction for the first."

Item 8 on unrestricted discussion raised more comments than any other item did, but most of the comments merely mentioned the need to allow exceptions for "defamation," "filth," "treasonable matter," and in one case "blasphemy." One judge offered a novel conservative free speech standard by stating, "I would not permit discussion in literature, press, or on the stage of topics that I would not want to have discussed in my home." Concerning item 13 on the desirability of more political discussion on radio and television, one judge felt moved to declare: "I would not extend discussion by professional commentators or agitators. We have enough of that now." With regard to intelligence and education tests for voting (item 24), one judge indicated that the tests would have to be weighted because "a poorly-educated intelligent person may be a more capable voter than the educated dumbbell."

On the inferiority of colored people (item 1), two judges agreed only as to Negroes and not as to other races. Two judges said there might be no differences if equality of opportunity was present. Other judges offered some dubious anthropological observations such as "There are no known uncivilized white people, whereas the same cannot be said of various portions of other colors" and "They [Negroes] are a younger race." Item 12 on discouraging interracial marriage had a higher percentage of agreement than any other item, but one respondent possibly summed up the feelings of many of the judges by commenting that "I am against marriage between white and colored people although I am an agitator for equal rights of both types of peoples." No comments at all were made with regard to the substance of item 20 on whether Jews have too much power.

Most of the comments addressed to item 3 (on whether war is inherent) dealt with what the respondent meant by war. Comments addressed to other items also frequently dealt with definitions of terms. As a study in contrasts, one judge commented on item 5 by saying, "If peace ever becomes permanent there must be some merging of national sovereignty in an effort to overcome the inherent tendency of the human race to participate in violent conflict." Another judge, however, said, "I strenuously object to the surrender of any part of our sovereignty because it will not bring peace to the world but will destroy then the most perfect government of human relations, economically, socially, and morally that ever existed." The same judge who expressed the latter opinion on the partial relinquishment of sovereignty also said in response to item 10 that "A genuine conscientious objector . . . has a warped mind and doesn't appreciate the fact that his religious freedom would perish if the government for which he refuses to fight did not safeguard that right to him."

Concerning Sunday observance (item 6) one judge indicated that he favored "church participation" but not "ridiculous blue laws." Other judges objected to the implication in the item that there was much of any Sunday observance left to decrease. Item 11, on going back to religion, moved one judge to write: "We must come back to religion in order to combat communism. The godless philosophy of communism is the greatest threat to our civilization today." Whereas, on the same item another judge wrote, "Although I am an active member of the . . . Church, I do not think that the hope of the world depends on going back to religion." Concerning religious education in the schools (item 16), one judge declared that "Based upon the thinking of today when honor men in our oldest and perhaps outstanding universities write articles in their law journals that both the Bible and Federal Constitution are out of date today, something must be done to instill in the minds of our children at an early age the precepts of Christianity. It is the hope of the world."

On whether men should be permitted greater sexual freedom than women (item 7), the only two judges who made comments both expressed the opinion that this was ordained by nature. A few judges commented on item 19 that woman were the equals of men in intelligence but not in organizing ability or vice versa. With regard to equal pay for men and women in the same work, one judge noted, "This bothers me—so long as we make the man legally responsible for his family, he will probably have to have some economic advantage."

The items relating to working-class sympathy and collectivism, like the items relating to religiosity, aroused many strongly worded comments. On whether laws favor the rich as against the poor (item 2), one judge stated, "If there is any difference, present laws favor the poor," while another judge observed that the laws favor neither group but the "administration and application often does [favor the rich]." Whether there should be more collectivism like the TVA (item 9) provoked such comments as "incompatible with democracy," "costing us billions annually," and "managerial inefficiency." On the other hand, one of the judges commented, "I do not

wish to be understood to be opposed to collectivism under the right circumstances." And a judge from one of the states benefiting from the TVA
wrote this dissent: "I feel you misuse 'collectivism' in reference to TVA.
The word now connotes a Russian type, where the individual is forced into
a unit. TVA and the other public power projects are no more socialistic
than the Post Office. They are something the private power people were
not willing to do and could never have done well." Relevant to item 15 on
nationalization, one judge who is admittedly active in the John Birch Society
exclaimed, "God forbid that this government shall ever become socialistic."
Another judge, however, lent some balance to what seemed in general to be
predominantly conservative comments by stating, "Some nationalization will
not [lead to inefficiency, bureaucracy, and stagnation]."

4. Causes of the Conservatism
of Judicial Attitudes

An analysis of the responses to each questionnaire item shown in Table
1, a comparison of the responses with those of a group of 250 middle-class
Tories in Table 2, and a review of the prevailing supplementary comments
seem to suggest that the off-the-bench attitudes of the supreme court
judiciary are in general fairly conservative. Of course, it is possible that the
sample of 118 judges in the survey included a disproportionate number of
conservatives. But the facts suggest that quite the opposite situation obtained.
For various reasons, if the sample of 1955 judges was weighted in any direction, it was disproportionately liberal. For one thing, at least 38 of the
judges in the sample died between 1955 (the year when the *Directory of
American Judges* was published) and 1960 (the year when the attitudinal
questionnaires were mailed) and thus in effect excluded themselves from
the sample. These excluded judges were probably among the more conservative judges in the sample of 313 since these judges were the older judges,
and older judges tend to be more conservative than younger judges both in
their decisions and their attitudes.[18] For another thing, there is evidence to
indicate that when socio-economic factors are held constant, respondents to
questionnaires tend to be more liberal-oriented than do nonrespondents.[19]

It also throws some light on the nature of the respondents to note that
38 per cent of the nonrespondents were Southerners, that is, judges from
the slaveholding states of 1860 plus Oklahoma. As might be expected, an
analysis of the completed questionnaires showed that the responses of the
Southern judges were in general significantly more conservative than the
responses of the Northern judges. In addition, if the average supreme court
judge really does tend to be more conservative than the average American,
and the judges themselves are aware of this, then some of the judges might
consciously or subconsciously upgrade the liberalism of their responses so
as to reduce the correlations between their responses and their judicial decisions that the letter accompanying the questionnaires told them were going
to be made.[20] Finally it should be noted that, given the sample of 118
judges, the chance probability is less than 5 out of 100 that the average

response to any item could deviate from the true average by more than 10 per cent.[21]

Why might supreme court judges be a more conservative group than the general public or officials in the legislative and administrative branches of government? There may be several operative factors here. First of all, supreme court judges are always drawn from the ranks of lawyers, whereas legislators and administrators may come from a variety of occupational backgrounds.[22] Being a lawyer may correlate with conservatism because lawyers tend to come from families of above-average income[23] and also tend to be well-to-do themselves.[24] Over 80 per cent of the responding judges said their fathers had been professional men, businessmen, or farm owners.[25] As lawyers, the judges themselves tended to belong to the higher-salaried legal ranks of prosecuting attorneys and corporation lawyers.[26] The 313 supreme court judges themselves had an average salary of $16,000 per year in 1955.[27] The constant reliance on precedents characteristic of lawyers in a common-law system may also account for some of their conservatism.[28]

In addition to economic and occupational factors, it should be noted that the 313 judges had a high average age of 63,[29] and advanced age is positively and significantly correlated with increased conservatism on the bench. Furthermore, their ethnic characteristics (race, religion, and ancestral nationality) were heavily weighted in the direction of those ethnic characteristics associated with high socio-economic status and with attitudinal conservatism.[30] The group affiliations of the judges also appeared to be much more conservative on the average than might be expected of state legislators or Congressmen, but these affiliations are probably made precisely because of the judges' conservative attitudes and do not generally operate as value-shaping factors except in a reinforcing sense.[31] Their relatively long tenure and (frequently) appointment rather than election may also make the judges less sensitive to popular opinion and thereby more conservative.

5. Decisional Effects of the Conservatism of Judicial Attitudes

A high degree of conservatism on the part of the American judiciary would have no particular significance if the values of judges had no bearing on the decisions they reach. In order to determine whether there is a relationship between judicial attitudes and judicial decision-making, each judge was given a liberalism score. This score was based on the total of the liberalism scores he received for each item after the items were weighted in terms of the correlation that each item had with the factor of liberalism in Eysenck's study.[32] The median liberalism score was 109 on a scale that ranged from 41 to 195. Twenty-two of the supreme courts of 1955 had at least one judge who scored above 109 and at least one judge who scored below 109. On these courts, as is shown in Table 4, the *low-scoring* (under 109) judges in their nonunanimous decisions of 1955 tended to vote for the *prosecution* in criminal cases, for the *business concern* in business regulation cases, for the party being sued (generally an *insurance company*) in motor vehicle

TABLE 4

How the Decisions of (1) Judges with Liberalism Scores at or below 109 Differ from Those of (2) Judges with Liberalism Scores above 109

(Using the nonunanimous cases of the state and federal supreme courts of 1955 on which both groups are represented)

Decision Score (percentage of judgments, for whom, in what types of cases)	Number of Judges Involved		Percentage of Group 1 Judges Above Their Court Average	Percentage of Group 2 Judges Above Their Court Average	Direction of the Differ- ence
	Group 1	Group 2			
For the defense in criminal cases	22	23	27%	57%	Positive
For the administrative agency in business regulation cases	16	16	38	75	Positive
For the injured party in motor vehicle accident cases	16	20	44	60	Positive
For the employee in employee injury cases	20	20	45	50	Positive

accident cases, and for the *employer* in workmen's compensation cases slightly more than did the high scoring (over 109) judges.[33] There were too few diversely responding judges involved in cases of other types for meaningful comparisons.[34]

Correlations were also made between responses to specific items and various decisional propensities. For example, there was a high and statistically significant correlation between *disagreeing* with item 4 ("Our treatment of criminals is too harsh; we should try to cure, not to punish them") and being above the average of one's court with regard to the proportion of times one voted for the *prosecution* in criminal cases.[35] Off-the-bench judicial attitudes thus do seem to correlate in a meaningful way with on-the-bench judicial decisions.[36] If judges are more conservative than legislators, administrators, and the general public, it can be expected that their conservatism will be reflected in their decision-making.

6. Proposals for Decreasing the Effect of Judicial Attitudes

It is the purpose of this section of the study to attempt to test empirically three proposals designed to decrease the effect of judicial attitudes in judicial decision-making. These are the three proposals: (1) require judicial experience as a prerequisite to a state or federal supreme court judgeship; (2) abandon the custom of wearing robes by the judiciary; and (3) require evidence of legal scholarship as a prerequisite to being a judge. Is it possible to determine whether judges operating under these devices tend to vote contrary to their off-the-bench attitudinal positions more than judges who do not operate under them?

As has been indicated, there was a statistically significant correlation between agreeing with the opinion expressed in item 4 ("Our treatment of criminals is too harsh; we should try to cure not to punish them") and being above the average of one's court with regard to the proportion of times one voted for the defense in criminal cases. A judge who *agreed* with the statement and yet was *below* the average of his court in the number of times he voted for the defense thus seemed to be voting contrary to his value position with regard to criminal law, as was a judge who *disagreed* but was *above* the court average in voting for the defense. Therefore it seems a logical question to ask if those judges who voted contrary to their value position have anything in common. Do they perhaps have more judicial experience or more scholarly backgrounds, or are they more likely to be members of courts where judicial robes are worn than judges who voted in accordance with their value position?

The United States Congress has considered, but failed to pass, legislation that would require a certain minimum of judicial experience of all justices appointed to the United States Supreme Court.[37] The rationale offered for such legislation is, of course, that judges with such judicial experience will be less likely to be influenced by their personal values and will be more technically competent. A possible consequence of such legislation is a more conservative judiciary—at least to the extent that the more years a judge has been on the bench, the older he is likely to be; and the older a judge is, the more conservative he is likely to be. This result may be the real motive of the proponents of such legislation, though if so, it does not affect the validity of their rationale one way or the other.

No attempt has been made to measure the technical competence of judges in this paper, but something can be said about the degree of correlation between judicial experience and judicial objectivity. The judicial experience of the state and federal supreme court judges in our sample as of the beginning of 1955 ranged from no prior service to one jurist who had been serving as a judge on various courts for 48 years. The average judge in the group of 313 had 17 years of judicial experience. The first row of Table 5 shows the degree to which the respondents' judicial experience correlated with a voting record contrary to their value position in criminal cases. The relationship is slightly negative, in that a greater percentage of judges with low judicial experience voted contrary to their value position than did judges with high judicial experience. The correlation is so slight, however, that from this table one can largely agree with Justice Frankfurter's statement that "the correlation between prior judicial service and fitness for the functions of the Supreme Court is zero,"[38] at least so far as fitness refers to exercising judicial restraint by keeping personal values out of legal decisions.

Some legal scholars, such as the late Jerome Frank, have theorized that the wearing of robes encourages the public to think of judges as being different from ordinary humans in their ability to suppress their personal attitudes.[39] Such a public image of the judiciary supposedly enables judges

TABLE 5

Relationship between Being a Judge with Certain Qualifications and Being a Judge Who Voted Contrary to His Value Position

Group 1	Group 2	Number of Judges Involved		Percentage Who Voted Contrary to Their Value Position		Direction of the Difference
		Group 1	Group 2	Group 1	Group 2	
Judges with 17 years or less judicial experience	Judges with more than 17 years judicial experience	33	29	39%	31%	Negative
Judges who wear robes	Judges who do not wear robes	52	11	37	18	Negative
Judges who have not been honored as scholars	Judges who have been honored as scholars	49	12	37	33	Negative

to inject their personal attitudes into decisions with less fear of being detected. On eight state supreme courts (Arizona, Arkansas, Kentucky, Missouri, North Dakota, Oklahoma, South Dakota, and Texas), the judges do not wear robes; on 38 state supreme courts and the United States Supreme Court the judges do wear robes; and for two state supreme courts (Pennsylvania and Rhode Island) this information is not available at the time this is written.[40] The second row of Table 5 shows the relationship between being a judge who does not wear robes and being a judge who voted contrary to his value position in criminal cases. The table tends to indicate that there is a negative correlation between not wearing robes and suppressing personal attitudes. The negative correlation, however, is not large enough to be statistically significant below the 0.05 level of chance probability.

Attempts to raise the scholarly competence of members of the bench may result in judges who can move the docket along faster, who can spot legal issues with greater facility, and who can more readily muster precedents and legal arguments to support their decisions. However, there is no real evidence that such judges would be more objective. A non-lawyer would probably be more likely to resort to personal preferences as opposed to legal rules than would a lawyer in deciding a case. But assuming that all judges are lawyers, there is probably no correlation between scholarliness and objectivity.

Some indications of scholarliness used as criteria in this study include (1) election to the Order of the Coif, which is conferred upon graduating law school students who have established extremely high scholastic records, (2) election to Phi Beta Kappa, which is the liberal arts equivalent of the Coif, (3) graduation cum laude from law school, and (4) election to the editorial board of a law school review. Sixty jurists, or approximately 20 per cent of the 1955 state and federal supreme court judges, indicated they had received such scholarly honors in response to the request for this information in the *Directory of American Judges;* 220, or approximately 70 per cent, did not indicate having received such honors; and 32 failed to respond to the *Directory* questionnaire. The last row of Table 5 shows the relationship between being a judge who had received at least one of these scholarly honors and being a judge who voted contrary to his value position in criminal cases. This relationship, in view of its slightly negative character, tends to show that there is no significant correlation between scholarly competence and objectivity.

Other reforms have been proposed to promote judicial objectivity, but they cannot be tested here because no American jurisdiction has adopted them. These proposals include psychoanalysis of judges,[41] self-analysis by judges,[42] special interrogatories by lawyers to judges concerning their decisions,[43] and special qualifying examinations and training.[44] A civil code system or a system more fully oriented to stare decisis, by decreasing judicial discretion, might also decrease judicial subjectivity, but the rigidities introduced by the cure might be worse than the subjectivities of the disease. Some reforms have been proposed to promote judicial objectivity which also cannot be tested in this study because they are applicable mainly to trial courts and lower appellate courts. These proposals include facilitating appeals, making it easier to get a change of venue or a change in the judge, having multiple-judge trial courts so the decision is the product of several minds, and requiring written opinions to justify the decisions reached. Some proposals for decreasing judicial subjectivity are particularly relevant to decreasing partisan political influences on judicial decisions. These include gubernatorial appointment, nonpartisan ballots, and long tenure. Their effect on decreasing background-decisional correlations was discussed in a recent article.[45]

7. Conclusions

In summary, the off-the-bench attitudes of state and federal supreme court judges seem to be fairly conservative, as indicated both by their responses to structured questions and by their volunteered comments. Since there were very few federal supreme court judges in the sample, this conclusion applies primarily to state supreme court judges.

The judicial conservatism revealed in the study can probably be largely attributed to factors of class, family background, pre-judicial occupations, training, age, and ethnic characteristics. And the conservative off-the-bench attitudes seem to be reflected in the decisions reached by these jurists. This is seen in the fact that judges who made more conservative responses to the questionnaire also tended to decide for the prosecution in criminal cases, for the business firm in business regulation cases, for the defendant in auto accident cases, and for the employer in workmen's compensation cases.

Judges who have had many years of judicial experience seem to inject their values into their decisions just as much as judges with few years of judicial experience. Judges who do not wear robes seem to inject their values into their decision just as much as judges who do wear robes. Nor is judicial subjectivity a result of lack of judicial scholarship. Brilliant or not so brilliant, as Jerome Frank emphasized 30 years ago, all judges are human.[46] They thus have values which are shaped by their backgrounds and which are manifested in their decisions.

NOTES

1. Harold Spaeth, "An Approach to the Study of Attitudinal Differences as an Aspect of Judicial Behavior," *Midwest Journal of Political Science,* Vol. 5 (1961), 165-80; Joseph Tanenhaus, "Supreme Court Attitudes toward Federal Administrative Agencies," *Journal of Politics,* Vol. 22 (1960), 502-24; John P. Reid, "The Reformer and the Precision: A Study in Judicial Attitudes," *Journal of Legal Education,* Vol. 12 (1959), 157-81; and Arnold Paul, *Conservative Crisis and the Rule of Law: Attitudes of Bar and Bench, 1887-1895* (Ithaca, N.Y.: Cornell University Press, 1960).

2. Some questionnaire studies have been published involving judges' attitudes toward relatively narrow issues. The *U.S. News and World Report* (October 24, 1958, pp. 36-37), asked 351 federal district and circuit court judges whether they agreed or disagreed with the 1958 report of the Conference of State Chief Justices, which was critical of various trends in United States Supreme Court decisions. Of the 109 judges who cooperated with *U.S. News* by answering yes or no to the single question posed to them, 54 per cent indicated yes they did agree with the report. William Keefe asked 41 elected judges on the Pennsylvania courts which of various types of judicial selection they preferred. Of the 26 judges who responded, 76 per cent preferred partisan election, 17 per cent preferred nonpartisan election, and only 7 per cent preferred a modified system of gubernatorial appointment. William J. Keefe, "Judges and Politics: The Pennsylvania Plan of Judge Selection," *University of Pittsburgh Law Review,* Vol. 20 (1959), 621-31.

3. See Appendix 1 for the cover letter that accompanied the questionnaire and for the reminder letter which was sent to nonrespondents approximately six weeks after the initial mailing.

4. Charles Liebman (ed.), *Directory of American Judges* (Chicago: American Directories, 1955).

5. Robert MacIver, *The Web of Government* (New York: Macmillan, 1951), pp. 215-216.

6. Hans Eysenck, *Psychology of Politics* (London: Routledge and Kegan Paul, 1954); W. A. Kerr, "Correlates of Political-Economic Liberalism-Conservatism," *Social Psychology,* Vol. 20 (1944), 61-77; and G. B. Vetter, "What Makes Attitudes and Opinions Liberal or Conservative," *Journal of Abnormal and Social Psychology,* Vol. 47 (1947), 125-30.

7. Eysenck, *op. cit. supra* (note 6), pp. 122-24. Portions of the questionnaire are reproduced with the kind permission of Routledge and Kegan Paul, Publishers, London, England.

8. Factor analysis is explained in J. P. Guilford, *Psychometric Methods* (New York: McGraw-Hill, 1954), pp. 470-536.

9. Likert scoring is explained in Bert F. Green, "Attitude Measurement" in Gardner Lindzey (ed.), *Handbook of Social Psychology* (Reading, Mass.: Addison-Wesley, 1954), Vol. I, pp. 351-53. It involves responding to attitudinal statements by indicating whether the respondent disagrees strongly, disagrees mildly, neither disagrees or agrees, mildly agrees, or strongly agrees. Some Likert-type questionnaires provide for three, seven, or some other number of responses rather than the five used by Likert.

10. Split-half reliability is explained in J. P. Guilford, *Statistics for Psychology and Education* (New York: McGraw-Hill, 1956) pp. 435-60. It involves determining the correlation between responses to the odd-numbered items and the responses to the even-numbered items.

11. Other liberalism questionnaires include those in the following list. The numbers in parentheses after each reference indicate the advantages of the Eysenck questionnaire, as listed in the text, which were especially lacking. Theodore Adorno, "Political-Economic

Conservatism Scale," *The Authoritarian Personality* (New York: Harper, 1950) (#1, 7, 6); Bernard R. Berelson, Paul F. Lazarsfeld and William McPhee, "Economic Liberalism Scale," *Voting* (Chicago: University of Chicago Press, 1954) (#7, 6); Richard Centers, "Conservatism-Radicalism Scale," *Psychology of Social Classes* (Princeton: Princeton University Press, 1949) (#6, 3, 7, 4); John G. Darley and Walter J. McNamara, "Economic Conservatism Scale," *Minnesota Personality Scale* (New York: Psychological Corp., 1949) (#1, 6, 4); W. A. Kerr, *Tulane Factors of Liberalism-Conservatism* (New Orleans: Psychometric Affiliates, 1946) (#3, 4, 8); Theodore F. Lentz, *Conservatism-Radicalism Opinionnaire* (St. Louis: Character Research Association, 1935) (#1); Theodore Newcomb, "Political-Economic Progressivism (PEP) Scale," *Personality and Social Change* (New York: Dryden Press, 1943) (#6, 4, 2); Milton Rokeach, "Left-Right Opinionation (L.O.-R.O.) Scale," *Political and Religious Dogmatism*, Psychological Monograph Series No. 425 (1956) (#4); and G. B. Vetter, "Liberalism-Conservatism Scale," in "The Measurement of Liberalism-Conservatism," *Journal of Abnormal and Social Psychology*, Vol. 25 (1930), 153-62 (#4, 6).

12. These correlation coefficients (Eysenck refers to them as factor saturations) correlating each item with the factor of liberalism are given in column 5 on p. 129 of Eysenck, *op. cit.* The highest correlation coefficients are those represented by the largest number regardless of the positive or negative sign of the number.

13. The most significant changes related to toning down the items favorable to socialism so as to get a more diverse response from an American sample. Thus, item 9 originally read, "Ultimately, private property should be abolished and complete socialism introduced," and item 15 originally read, "The nationalization of the great industries is likely to lead to inefficiency, bureaucracy, and stagnation." Item 16, which expressed a sentiment favorable toward church and state coordination, also was toned down, since it originally read, "It is right and proper that religious education in schools should be compulsory."

14. Two of these 136 judges sent completed questionnaires back too late to be included in the analysis. For a complete list of the judges who responded to the questionnaire, see Stuart S. Nagel, *Judicial Characteristics and Judicial Decision-Making* (Ann Arbor: University Microfilms, 1962). For a discussion of the statistical reliability of such a sample size, see note 21 *infra* and the accompanying text.

15. The average response to each item was calculated by (1) assigning a score from 1 through 5 to each of the five possible responses, (2) multiplying each score by the frequency of its occurrence, (3) summing the products from step 2, and (4) dividing the sum from step 3 by 118.

16. A survey with the same questionnaire applied to a comparable sample of state and federal legislators and administrators was completed after this chapter had gone to press. It indicated that, in general, the administrators seem to be the most liberal, especially if economic and first amendment issues are emphasized; the legislators, next; and the judges, the most conservative of the three sets of political decision-makers. (Substance of a paper entitled "Judicial Attitudes and Those of Legislators and Administrators," presented at the American Political Science Association, Washington, D.C., September, 1962.)

17. The religious affiliation of these judges is indicated in the *Directory of American Judges*.

18. Sixty-seven years was the average age in 1955 of the 38 judges who were known to have died between 1955 and 1960, whereas sixty-two years was the average age of the other 275 judges in the sample. Thirty-seven of the supreme courts of 1955 had at least one judge who was over age 65 (the upper-third age group of the total sample) and at least one judge who was under age 60 (the lower third). On these courts the older judges (over 65), in their nonunanimous decisions of 1955, tended to vote for the business concern in the administrative regulation of business cases, for narrowing free speech in free speech cases, for management in labor-management cases, and for the creditor in creditor-debtor cases more than did the younger judges (under 60). And they did so to an extent statistically significant below the 0.05 level of chance probability. In other types of cases, there was a generally similar relationship between being an older judge and voting for what we consider to be the conservative position (although not to a

statistically significant extent). The older judges also generally made more conservative responses to the questionnaire than did their younger colleagues on the same court.

19. See Lee G. Burchinal, "Personality Characteristics and Sample Bias," *Journal of Applied Psychology,* Vol. 64 (1960), 172-74; Lester Milbrath, "Latent Causes of Liberalism-Conservatism and Party Identification" (Evanston: Northwestern Political Behavior Program, 1960; mimeographed); and Arthur Couch and Kenneth Keniston, "Yeasayers and Naysayers: Agreeing Response Set as a Personality Variable," *Journal of Abnormal and Social Psychology,* Vol. 60 (1960), 169.

20. See the cover letter in Appendix 1.

21. Margaret J. Hagood and Daniel O. Price, *Statistics for Sociologists* (New York: Holt, 1952), pp. 279-94 and Mildred Parten, *Surveys, Polls and Samples: Practical Procedures* (New York: Harper, 1950), pp. 290-330.

22. Data mentioned in this paragraph on the pre-judicial occupations, age, ethnic characteristics, and pressure group affiliations of the 313 judges were determined by consulting Charles Liebman (ed.), *The Directory of American Judges* (Chicago: American Directories, 1955); Wheeler Sammons (ed.), *Who's Who in America* (Chicago: Marquis Publishers, 1954-58); *Martindale-Hubbell Law Directory* (Summit, N.J.: Martindale-Hubbell, Inc., 1955); and Elsdon C. Smith, *Dictionary of Family Names* (New York: Harper, 1956).

23. William Miller, "American Lawyers in Business and Politics: Their Social Backgrounds and Early Training," *Yale Law Journal,* Vol. 60 (1951), 66-76.

24. In 1954, the average gross income of nonsalaried lawyers was $16,719, with a net (after overhead) of $10,258. Maurice Liebenberg, "Income of Lawyers in the Post-War Period," *Survey of Current Business,* Vol. 36 (December 1956), 29. The average income of salaried lawyers was slightly higher. *Ibid.*

25. The attitudinal questionnaire shown in Appendix 3 asked each judge what his father's main occupation was. Thirty-three per cent of the respondents said their fathers were professional men, 30 per cent said government officials, business proprietors, or executives; and 29 per cent said farmers. Only 23 per cent said clerical employees, skilled or unskilled workers, or farm laborers. The total is more than 100 per cent because some judges gave more than one occupation for their fathers. It is well to remember that in the 1890's (the decade in which the average respondent was born) only 5 per cent of the labor force was composed of professional men and only 6 per cent were government officials, business proprietors, and executives, while 63 per cent of the labor force was composed of clerical employees, skilled or unskilled workers, and farm laborers. Donald Matthews, *The Social Background of Political Decision-Makers* (New York: Random House, 1954). Compare John R. Schmidhauser, "The Justices of the Supreme Court: A Collective Portrait," *Midwest Journal of Political Science,* Vol. 3 (Feb., 1959), 6-13, 45, 48-49; and Ulf Torgersen, "The Role of the Supreme Court in the Norwegian Political System," Chap. 8 of this volume.

26. Of the few judges who indicated a legal specialty in the *Directory,* 24 said their specialty was corporation law, but only one said his specialty was labor law. Likewise 121 mentioned having been a prosecutor, but none mentioned having done criminal defense work.

27. Council of State Governments, *The Book of the States* (Chicago: The Council of State Governments, 1956). The relation between wealth and conservatism is discussed in Richard Centers' *Psychology of Social Classes* (Princeton: Princeton University Press, 1949).

28. Jerome Frank, *Courts on Trial* (Princeton: Princeton University Press, 1949), pp. 262-89.

29. The median age of members of both legislative houses of every state was 48.4 years in 1935. Harvey Walker, *The Legislative Process: Lawmaking in the United States* (New York: Ronald Press, 1948), p. 149. Fifty-two years was the most frequent age of the federal executives serving on a high enough level to be worthy of inclusion in Jerome Rosow's *American Men in Government* (Washington: Public Affairs Press, 1949), p. xvii.

30. S. Nagel, "Ethnic Affiliations and Judicial Propensities," *Journal of Politics,* Vol. 24 (1962), 92-110.

31. Not even one judge indicated that he was a member of a liberal organization like

the Americans for Democratic Action, the American Civil Liberties Union, the National Lawyers Guild, or the American Veterans Committee. On the other hand, many judges indicated they were members of conservative organizations like the Sons of the American Revolution, the American Bar Association, the American Legion, and various business groups.

32. See Appendix 2 for a description of the scoring system used.

33. The attitude-behavior correlations, however, were not based on enough judges nor were the correlations large enough to be statistically significant below the .05 level of chance probability.

34. The results are approximately the same if one compares (1) judges who scored above their own court's liberalism median with (2) judges who scored below their own court's liberalism median, instead of comparing judges who scored above 109 with judges who scored below 109.

35. See Stuart S. Nagel, "Judicial Backgrounds and Criminal Cases," *Journal of Criminal Law, Criminology and Police Science* Vol. 53 (Sept., 1962), 333-39.

36. The personal attitudes of legislators, however, correlate much more highly with their roll-call behavior, although party and constituency pressures may sometimes conflict with their personal attitudes. See Warren Miller and Donald Stokes, "Policy Preferences of Congressional Candidates and Constituents," a paper presented at the annual meeting of the American Political Science Association, 1961.

37. See, for example, "The Smathers Bill" at 102 *Congressional Record* (Part 6) 84th Congress, 2nd Session, April 30, 1956, p. 7277.

38. Felix Frankfurter, "The Supreme Court in the Mirror of Justices; Nature of Its Functions and Qualifications for their Exercise," *Vital Speeches,* Vol. 23 (May 1, 1957), 436.

39. Frank, *op. cit. supra* (note 28), pp. 254-61.

40. Council of State Governments, *The Courts of Last Resort of the Forty-Eight States* (Chicago, 1950), Table 3.

41. Theodore Schroeder, "The Psychological Study of Judicial Opinions," *California Law Review,* Vol. 6 (June 1918), 89-113.

42. Harold Lasswell, "Self-Analysis and Judicial Thinking," *International Journal of Ethics,* Vol. 40 (April 1930), 342-62.

43. Frank, *op. cit. supra* (note 28), pp. 423, 141-43.

44. *Ibid,* pp. 247-53.

45. Stuart S. Nagel, "Political Party Affiliation and Judges' Decisions," *American Political Science Review,* Vol. 55 (1961), 843-50.

46. Jerome Frank, "Are Judges Human?" *University of Pennsylvania Law Review,* Vol. 80 (1931), 17.

Appendix 1. The Cover Letter and Reminder Letter Sent to the Judges

Stuart S. Nagel
Harris Hall 105

NORTHWESTERN UNIVERSITY
Evanston, Illinois

The Honorable John A. Doe   March 4, 1960
Justice of the Supreme Court of Arizona
Home address
Hometown, Arizona

My dear Justice Doe:

I am conducting a nationwide research project on the influence of judicial backgrounds
and attitudes on judicial decisions. The project involves recording on IBM cards many
of the background and attitudinal characteristics of the 312 federal and state supreme
court justices who, including yourself, were serving in 1955. The acquittal granted
percentages, divorce granted percentages, and other decisional percentages for 1955
of the 312 justices are also being recorded. The IBM cards will be statistically processed to determine what, if any, judicial characteristics tend to go with high or low
decisional percentages of different kinds. Such information will be of considerable
value in my subsequent testing of proposals designed to decrease the influence of
background and attitudinal factors on decisions.

I have been able to find considerable background information on all 312 justices from
the Directory of American Judges (which has been published only for 1955 judges) and
from the Martindale-Hubbell Law Directory. I have also been able to find considerable decisional information on all 312 justices from the federal and state court reports.
In order to obtain the attitudinal information and just one additional background item,
I am sending a copy of the enclosed standardized questionnaire to you and each of the
312 justices from which various attitudinal positions can be determined when combinations of the responses are analyzed.

This research is being conducted with a grant from the Political Theory and Legal Philosophy Committee of the Social Science Research Council. My qualifications in this
area include an LL.B. from Northwestern, membership in the Illinois and federal bar,
a Ph.D. in political science to be awarded this August, and membership in the Judicial Administration Section of the ABA. Upon completing this study, I intend to follow
a career of teaching and doing research in the fields of judicial administration and constitutional law.

I shall greatly appreciate your filling out the questionnaire. No identification of the
attitudes of specific judges will be made in the published study, and your answers
will be kept completely confidential. The questionnaire will only take about five
minutes to complete. You may make any comments you wish to make on the back of
the questionnaire. A stamped self-addressed envelope is enclosed for your convenience in mailing it back to me. Whether or not you fill out the questionnaire, I shall
be happy to send you a summary of the results of the project when it is completed.

Gratefully yours,

SN:jn   Stuart S. Nagel

Stuart S. Nagel
Harris Hall 105
NORTHWESTERN UNIVERSITY
Evanston, Illinois

April 19, 1960

The Honorable John A. Doe
Justice of the Supreme Court of Arizona
Home address
Hometown, Arizona

My dear Justice Doe:

On approximately March 14, a copy of the enclosed letter, questionnaire, and return envelope was sent to you. Your unsigned questionnaire has not as yet been returned. I would, therefore, greatly appreciate your returning it in the enclosed envelope with as many answers as you would like to make. I have already received a high percentage of returns from your fellow 1955 State and Federal Supreme Court Justices.

Some of the returns have included volunteered comments like the following: "Although I am no longer a Judge of the . . . Supreme Court, I have made an attempt to respond to the statements being solicited by you in your most interesting research project. I trust you may have the cooperation of all the Judges in this very important undertaking." I shall be looking forward to receiving your questionnaire.

Very sincerely yours,

Stuart S. Nagel

SN/jn

Appendix 2. Scoring the Questionnaire

The method used for scoring a completed questionnaire is fairly simple. First the response to each item is scored. Then the sum of the item scores is determined to give the respondent a total liberalism score. Table 6 shows how the responses for each item are scored. Instead of the double minus, single minus, etc., system of recording answers, sometimes respondents use "no" and "yes" to indicate direction and an exclamation mark or words like "definitely" to indicate emphasis. These substitutes can be easily translated by the scorer into the plus and minus system.

The scoring of Table 6 is designed in such a way that the more liberal a response to an item is, the higher the response is scored; and the less liberal a response to an item is, the lower the response is scored. Items worded in a liberal direction (e.g., item 8) are scored in an ascending

TABLE 6

Scoring of Questionnaire Responses for Each Questionnaire Item

(Table entries represent scores for responses to items)

Questionnaire Item*	Responses:				
	$--$	$-$	0	$+$	$++$
1. Colored are inferior (C)	8	7	5	3	2
2. Laws favor rich (L)	2	3	5	7	8
3. War is inherent (C)	9	8	5	2	1
4. Criminal treatment is too harsh (L)	1	2	5	8	9
5. Abandon some sovereignty (L)	1	2	5	8	9
6. Sunday observance is old-fashioned (L)	1	2	5	8	9
7. Give men more sex freedom than women (C)	7	6	5	4	3
8. Have unrestricted discussion (L)	3	4	5	6	7
9. Have more collectivism (L)	1	2	5	8	9
10. Conscientious objectors are traitors (C)	8	7	5	3	2
11. Go back to religion (C)	8	7	5	3	2
12. Discourage miscegenation (C)	9	8	5	2	1
13. Have more controversy (L)	2	3	5	7	8
14. Make divorce laws easier (L)	2	3	5	7	8
15. Nationalization means stagnation (C)	9	8	5	2	1
16. Have religion in schools (C)	9	8	5	2	1
17. Premarital sex is permissible (L)	1	2	5	8	9
18. Spare rod, spoil child (C)	8	7	5	3	2
19. Women are inferior (C)	7	6	5	4	3
20. Jews are too powerful (C)	9	8	5	2	1
21. Have equal pay for both sexes (L)	2	3	5	7	8
22. Make birth control illegal (C)	8	7	5	3	2
23. Abolish death penalty (L)	1	2	5	8	9
24. Have education test for voting (C)	7	6	5	4	3

*See Appendix 3 for the exact wording of each item.

direction (e.g., 3, 4, 5, 6, 7) for ascending responses (i.e., — —, —, 0, +, ++); whereas items worded in a conservative direction (e.g., item 24) are scored in a descending direction (e.g., 7, 6, 5, 4, 3) for ascending responses.

Items with a 34567 or a 76543 scoring are those items which Eysenck found had correlation coefficients with the factor of liberalism of +0.01 to +0.24; items with a 23578 or 87532 scoring are those items which had correlation coefficients with the factor of liberalism of +0.25 to +0.49; and items with a 12589 or 98521 scoring are those items which had correlation coefficients with the factor of liberalism of +0.50 to +0.74. This weighting system, although not used by Eysenck or other psychometricians, seemed desirable in order to take into consideration the fact that some of the items are more important components of liberalism than others, and also the fact that the importance of an item to a factor can be measured by correlation coefficients.

Appendix 3. The Questionnaire

Below are given 24 statements which represent widely-held opinions on various social questions selected from speeches, books, newspapers, and other sources. They were chosen in such a way that most people are likely to agree with some and disagree with others. After each statement please record your completely confidential personal opinion regarding the statement, using the following system of marking:

++ if you strongly agree with the statement.
+ if you agree on the whole but not strongly.
0 if you cannot decide for or against or if you think the question
      is worded in such a way that you cannot give an answer.
− if you disagree on the whole but not strongly.
−− if you strongly disagree.

Opinion Statements

Your Frank Opinion

1. Colored people are innately inferior to white people. _____

2. Present laws favor the rich as against the poor. _____

3. War is inherent in human nature. _____

4. Our treatment of criminals is too harsh; we should try to cure, not to punish them. _____

5. In the interests of peace, we must give up part of our national sovereignty. _____

6. Sunday-observance is old-fashioned, and should cease to govern our behavior. _____

7. It is right that men should be permitted greater sexual freedom than women by society. _____

8. Unrestricted freedom of discussion on every topic is desirable in the press, in literature, and on the stage. _____

9. More collectivism, like the TVA, should be introduced into our society. _____

10. Conscientious objectors are traitors to their country, and should be treated accordingly. _____

11. Only by going back to religion can civilization hope to survive. _____

12. Marriages between white and colored people should be greatly discouraged. _____

13. There should be far more controversial and political discussion over the radio and television. _____

14. Divorce laws should be altered to make divorce easier. _____

15. Nationalization in any industry is likely to lead to inefficiency, bureaucracy, and stagnation. _____

Opinion Statements

16. It is right and proper that non-sectarian religious education in schools should be compulsory.

    _____

17. Men and women have the right to find out whether they are sexually suited before marriage.

    _____

18. The principle "Spare the rod and spoil the child" has much truth in it, and should govern our methods of bringing up children.

    _____

19. Women are not the equals of men in intelligence and organizing ability.

    _____

20. The Jews have too much power and influence in this country.

    _____

21. Differences in pay between men and women doing the same work should be abolished.

    _____

22. Birth control, except when medically indicated, should be made illegal.

    _____

23. The death penalty is barbaric, and should be abolished.

    _____

24. Only people with a definite minimum of intelligence and education should be allowed to vote.

    _____

Your father's main occupation (a possibly relevant background item not published in the directories)_____

Correlation number (for IBM computer purposes)_____

Civilian Control
and Stare Decisis
in the Warren Court

GLENDON SCHUBERT

IN THE POPULAR IMAGE of the United States Supreme Court, the justices rise to their noblest stature and perform their highest function when they exercise judicial review over acts of Congress and the President. Although no disquietude is occasioned, and there appears to be no popular awareness, when a majority of the justices *upholds* the constitutionality of national statutes, there are always some observers who view with alarm when the Court, within a relatively short period of time, decides a series of cases dealing with the same basic issue and declaring acts of Congress to be *un*constitutional.

Political scientists, who are in a position to take a somewhat more dispassionate view of the Court's work and task,[1] may question whether judicial review of national statutes is in fact a major activity of the Court, at least in quantitative terms.[2] In any case, the "constitutional crisis" of 1958-59 —in contrast to that of 1937—was a direct result of the Court's activities in *interpreting* national statutes and in invalidating *state* statutes.[3] Another distinguishing aspect of the 1958-59 "crisis" was that, unlike the 1937 controversy, in which liberals attacked the Court for its defense of classical economic theory and private property rights,[4] it was the conservatives who attacked the Court for its defense of civil rights and liberties. The latter circumstance is unique in the history of the Court and the nation, for reasons that Pritchett has explained:

The New Deal drive had largely spent its force in Congress by 1938, which was just when the Court began to feel the liberalizing effect of its new members. During the next decade or so the Court was for almost the first time in our national experience more liberal than Congress or the country. There was consequently no reason for the Court to exercise any restraining influence upon congressional use of regulatory powers. . . . In the recent controversy, . . . liberals . . . believed the Court was under attack because, for the first time in its history, it was basing itself on liberal principles and undertaking to defend the freedoms of the First Amendment against illiberal, misconceived, fundamentally unconstitutional legislation or legislative action.[5]

If we take Pritchett's interpretation and treat it as a hypothesis, the question arises why there has been, during the quarter of a century that has elapsed since 1937, such a dearth of adverse judicial review of federal legislation, assuming the libertarian orientation of the Court alleged by Pritchett and others. Certainly, the lack of such cases does not reflect a commensurate lack of opportunity for the Court. The period of which we speak includes the usual quota of anti-civil liberties legislation that characteristically marks the endeavors of Congress in prosecuting a major war; it also encompasses a postwar period which has been denominated the "Cold War," and was for a time symbolized by the transient but menacing symbol of the late Senator McCarthy, and in which there has been substantial national legislation that has tended to repress civil rights and liberties.

Pritchett's argument is that the Court was able substantially to realize its libertarian goals by relying less upon judicial review and more upon the alternative technique of statutory interpretation. This explanation does, undoubtedly, have some validity. But the fact remains that during a period of almost two decades, thus including both the Roosevelt and Vinson Courts, only three scattered and relatively minor decisions emerged: *Tot* v. *United States,* 319 U.S. 463 (1943); *United States* v. *Lovett,* 328 U.S. 303 (1946); and *United States* v. *Cardiff,* 344 U.S. 174 (1952). Only the second of these decisions attracted much public attention; and none of them is considered to be a landmark case in constitutional law. In all three decisions, however, the Court did uphold claims of constitutional civil rights.

In dramatic contrast, the Warren Court, within a span of half a dozen years beginning in 1955, has in seven cases struck down various sections of the Uniform Code of Military Justice of 1950 and a section of the Nationality Act of 1940, in which the basic question for decision was the extension of military law and trial by courts-martial to include civilian defendants and civilian rights.[6] Although the Chief Justice remarked, in the opinion for a plurality of the Court accompanying the decision upholding the most extreme libertarian claim (and therefore resulting in the closest voting margin of the cases in this set), that "the ordeal of judgment" must be approached "cautiously" when the Court thus exercised the power of judicial review,[7] it is not unreasonable, against the background that has been sketched, to infer that the Warren Court has manifested exceptional zeal in its defense of constitutional claims against military control over civilian rights.

I

Since the inference stated—that the Warren Court has undertaken a zealous defense of civilian rights against Congressional attempts to expand the system of military control—is not the only one that might be drawn from, nor the only interpretation that might be based upon, the data examined thus far, this inference and other possible alternatives must be deduced from differing theories which purport to explain the Supreme Court's decision-making behavior. The legal scientist, like the political scientist or the psychologist or any other behavioral scientist, therefore has an obligation to articulate precisely the theoretical model of judicial behavior in terms of which he proposes to observe, to measure, to analyze, and to interpret a set of real-life events such as a series of decisions of a court. It will have been more or less obvious—depending upon one's degree of sophistication in socio-psychological theory—to readers of this chapter that the implicit model for studying such a variable as "judicial hostility towards military control" or "a justice's libertarian attitude toward civil liberty claims" is that of the attitude scale.[8]

Attitudinal scaling of judges constitutes a relatively new development in legal research. Although other techniques of collecting the raw data (such as interview or questionnaire surveys) are commonly employed in the investigation of social attitudes by social psychologists,[9] most of the exploratory studies of recent years have sought to measure judicial attitudes *indirectly* by examining voting data for split decisions of the United States Supreme Court.[10] Such research is premised upon the general stimulus-response model of modern psychometrics and, more specifically, upon the concept of the cumulative scale developed during World War II by Guttman and his associates.[11] The Guttman scale is linear and one-dimensional, and it assumes that an attitude can properly be conceptualized as a continuous variable that ranges over a continuum. Within any segment of the continuum, points lying near one end of the segment can be identified as more positive, and points near the other end of the segment as more negative, depending upon how the variable has been defined and how directionality has been attributed to the continuum. It is postulated that as one discerns discrete points moving along the continuum in the direction that has been defined as positive, such points are measures of the increasingly affirmative and intense attitude toward the variable that an individual might possess. Correspondingly, different points might be conceived of as questions of increasing "difficulty" that might stimulate an affirmative response from an individual whose ideal-point was located at least as far along the continuum in the stipulated direction as the questions asked. The scale is "cumulative" in the sense that an individual would be assumed to respond affirmatively until the question asked corresponds to a stimulus-point that is located beyond (in a more extreme position on the continuum than) his own ideal-point; to this and to all questions even more extreme, he would respond negatively. Thus, if an individual respondent's attitude toward a given variable were perfectly consistent, he would respond affirmatively to all questions up to a critical point, and he would respond negatively to all questions that were more extreme than his ideal-point. Thus, a group of individuals, responding to a series of questions corresponding to a set of stimulus-points on the continuum, might be represented by a set of ideal-points on the same continuum. Different individuals in the group might, therefore, respond differently to the various questions (stimuli) and still be perfectly consistent in their respective individual attitudes. To the extent that an individual responds inconsistently to a series of questions that are answered consistently by other members of the same group, one might infer that the inconsistent respondent was committing perceptual errors, or that he had not yet "made up his mind" about the value to which the questions relate.

A Supreme Court justice is an individual, and a case before the Court for decision can be conceptualized as asking the justice to respond by his vote on the merits, signifying his attitude toward the major value or values at stake in the decision. Certainly, it is not prima facie unreasonable to suggest that the seven recent cases dealing with judicial review of courts-martial jurisdiction were testing the individual attitudes of the justices toward a basic value in our constitutional system: civil supremacy over the military (or, stated reciprocally, civilian freedom from military control). Under such an assumption, the articulation, as judicial opinion behavior, of language which directs attention to other issues than the scale variable, is not necessarily to be construed as evidence that the case is viewed as multivariate by the justices who associate themselves with such language; the model requires that the analyst examine the consistency of voting behavior, rather than the consistency of opinion behavior (as appears to be so frequently done in traditional legal analysis) as the basis for inferences about the attitudes of the justices toward the scale variable under investigation.

The number of cases in this particular set is insufficient to permit the construction of a scalogram, even though the sample of seven includes all of the relevant decisions of the Court. (Older cases are not relevant, in terms of the model that we are using, because the personnel of the Warren Court did not participate in the earlier decisions which might, from a legal point of view, be deemed to be relevant as precedents.) A minimum of at least ten decisions in which two or more justices dissented would be required for the construction of a judicial scalogram.[12] It is possible, nevertheless, to arrange the voting data provided by the available cases in the form of a scalogram; however, one would necessarily have considerably less confidence in inferences based upon such a quasi-scale[13] than would be the case if a larger sample of decisions on this subject were presently available for analysis.

II

Table 1 is a quasi-scale of the Court's final decisions on the merits in the first three cases in our sample. It should be noted that these decisions, declaring acts of Congress unconstitutional, appeared in successive terms of the Court. (The middle case consisted of two separate cases that were joined for common final disposition in the 1956 Term, although in the previous term each had received what appeared then to be a separate decision on the merits, as we shall see in greater detail below; for purposes of the present analysis, the two cases will be considered as one, as has been done thus far in this chapter, when reference is made to the later decision of the 1956 Term only.)[14] From the point of view of scale theory—although not, we should note, from the point of view of some alternative theories of judicial decision-making—it is only a coincidence that the ordering of the cases corresponds to their chronological ordering. Since the cases and votes are in

TABLE 1

Decisions of the Warren Court Declaring Unconstitutional Acts of Congress Extending Court-Martial Jurisdiction over Civil Rights (1955-1957 Terms)[15]

Justice	*Toth v. Quarles,* 350 U.S. 11 (1955)	*Reid v. Covert,* 354 U.S. 1 (1957)	*Trop v. Dulles,* 356 U.S. 86 (1958)
Bl	('+')	('+'	('+'
Do	(+)	(+	(+
Wa	(+)	(+	('+'
Br	*	(+	('+'
Wh	*	NP	(+
Fr	(+)	('+'	'—')
Ha	(+)	('+'	—)
Cl	(+)	'—')	—)
Mi	—)	*	*
Re	'—')	*	*
Bu	—)	—)	—)
Voting Division	6-3	6-2	5-4

LEGEND	Justices
+ = a vote in favor of holding the statute unconstitutional	Bl Black
	Br Brennan
— = a vote against holding the statute unconstitutional	Bu Burton
	Cl Clark
' ' = wrote opinion	Do Douglas
	Fr Frankfurter
( ) = joined in the opinion of the Court	Ha Harlan
(= concurring opinion	Mi Minton
) = dissenting opinion	Re Reed
	St Stewart
* = not seated at the time of this decision	Wa Warren
NP = seated but not participating in this decision	Wh Whittaker

an ordinal relationship, however, scale theory suggests certain inferences and predictions that we might not otherwise be in a position to see or to make.

As Table 1 indicates, the justices are, in effect, partitioned among four subsets, corresponding to their ranks or scale scores. Black, Warren, Douglas, Brennan, and Whittaker all would receive the maximal scale score of 3, since each voted affirmatively in the most "difficult" or marginal case, *Trop* v. *Dulles*. But we can also partition further this subset of five justices, according to the degree of confidence that we would place in the scale score assigned to these individuals. Clearly, we should have most confidence in the scoring of Black, Warren, and Douglas, because we have three observations of the voting behavior of each of them, since each participated in the decision of all three cases; and we should put less confidence in Brennan's score, and least in Whittaker's. By the same reasoning, we should have substantial confidence in assigning Frankfurter and Harlan a scale score of 2, Clark a score of 1, and Burton a score of 0; our lesser confidence in the scores of 0 for Reed and Minton is inconsequential, since their retirement from the Court (and replacement by Brennan and Whittaker) subsequent to the decision in *Toth* v. *Quarles* effectively removed them from consideration as relevant factors in the disposition of any other cases in our sample.

Although, as a matter of fact, the Court could not have formed majorities favorable to the claim of civil right in *Toth* and *Covert* without the support of Frankfurter and Harlan, the quasi-scale suggests that if Whittaker had voted in *Covert* and if both Brennan and Whittaker had participated in *Toth* (in lieu of Reed and Minton), minimal favorable majorities would have been formed *irrespective* of Frankfurter's and Harlan's attitudes toward, and votes in, these cases. That is to say, despite our lesser confidence in having correctly identified the underlying attitudes of Brennan and Whittaker toward the basic policy problem of military control over civilians, it seems more probable than not that each would have voted in favor of the claim of civil right had he participated. The votes of Clark and Burton, on the other hand, were not essential, in either fact or theory, to assure a favorable decision in these particular cases; but the fact that Clark did vote favorably to the civil right claim in the "easiest" of these cases, *Toth,* indicates that he was more sympathetic to the principle of civilian control than were Burton, Reed, and Minton. In fact, the quasi-scale, based as it is upon such a small and inadequate sampling of the attitudes of the justices of the Supreme Court upon this issue, really provides us with more information about Frankfurter, Harlan, and Clark than about any of the other justices.

Let us assume an infinite extension of our underlying attitudinal continuum, in both directions. There is some sociological and anthropological evidence that in other societies and cultures, opinions on the subject of military control over civilians, both pro and con, are much more extreme than the range of positions commonly accepted within American society today. Furthermore, the segment of the continuum which includes American lawyers is doubtless a narrower segment than that for American society as a whole; and the justices' ideal-points doubtless lie on a subsegment of the "legal" segment of the continuum. The point is that the range of the continuum within which disagreement among Supreme Court justices can occur, with consequent split decisions of the Court, is probably a very narrow segment of the total continuum. Although this point may well be "self-evident," it seems desirable to articulate it, in view of the considerable volume of passionate criticism of the Court which either states or assumes that the Court always is in disagreement, and generally by a 5-4 margin. More sophisticated observers are well aware that the Court is unanimous in over 90% of its decisions in each term; they also understand that the Court's division in over half of the decisions that it makes after oral argument and on the merits is a reflection of the value conflicts explicit in the questions (cases) that the Court, by a process of self-selection, undertakes to resolve. Conflict among spokesmen for different values on the Court is as real as it is earnest. However, it is well to remember that this conflict takes place within a milieu whose communication context is such that the value conflict among the justices is magnified, and the essential homogeneity of values common to the justices as a group[16] tends to be overlooked.

Returning to our quasi-scale, we can now say that the stimulus-points corresponding to these three cases are bunched more or less closely together, somewhere in the middle of the relatively narrow subsegment (of the extended continuum) which includes the ideal-points of all the justices who participated in these three decisions. Somewhere not too far to the left of *Toth* is a stimulus-point or question which, if it had been asked of the Court, would have evoked favorable responses from Burton, Reed, and Minton, as well as from their brethren. Somewhere immediately to the right of *Trop* lies a question which the Court would—given its present composition—answer unfavorably to the claim of civil right; and somewhat further to the right there lie an infinity of questions to all of which the Court would respond, and with increasing vehemence, unanimously in the negative—although most of these latter questions are so extreme that they could never survive jurisdictional screening and so would not appear upon the Supreme Court's dockets for oral argument and decision on the merits of the substantive issues presented.

On the basis of this assumption about the relatively narrow subsegment of the continuum of military control over civilians, within which *Toth, Covert,* and *Trop* are hypothesized as being located, it has been suggested recently that:

It is most reasonable to assume that if another case should come along, asking the Court to support a libertarian claim *more extreme* than that of *Trop,* the liberal bloc might be hard pressed to keep Whittaker in the fold, or to attract Stewart, even assuming (as seems warranted) that Stewart's attitudes on this issue are likely to be more liberal than those of the man he replaced, who was the Court's anchor man in defense of the military. Indeed, the liberal bloc might well have to face up to the defection of Brennan, as in [*Perez* v. *Brownell,* 356 U.S. 44 (1958)]. Even Warren refused to associate himself with the Black-Douglas concurrence in *Trop*; and from all appearances, only those two justices considered the military-control-over-civilian-rights angle to bear a sufficiently important relationship to this case to justify discussion. It seemed most likely, on the basis of the data shown in Table [1], that the Court's trend toward curtailing military control over civil rights had come to an end, and that any case similar to but less deprivational than *Trop* would find the libertarians, as on many other issues of constitutional policy that come before the Supreme Court for decision, exercising the traditional right of dissent.[17]

The above statement, which I wrote for use in an undergraduate text, is not sufficiently precise to be useful for present purposes. Moreover, it is clear that three cases are far too few to justify any statements about a "trend." Nor is it valid to assume that, simply because the chronological sequence in which these three cases arose coincided with their scalar order, such a coincidence could be expected to hold for any future case that might arise. Of course, the assumption explicit in the qualification that the next case to come along should be "similar to but less deprivational than *Trop*" is equivalent, from the point of view of scale theory, to the statement that such a case should raise "a libertarian claim *more extreme* than that of *Trop.*"

It is possible to restate the prediction, more precisely, as follows: If the next case (or cases) which the Court accepts for decision raises a question (or questions) for which the corresponding stimulus point lies on the segment of the underlying continuum bounded by *Covert* and *Trop,* the Court's decision will be favorable to the claim of civil right; and if the stimulus point lies in the segment which is bounded determinately by *Trop* and indeterminately by the Court's jurisdictional tolerance to entertain the issue—and the latter point would almost certainly be more extreme than Brennan's ideal-point (since at least four votes are required for a favorable jurisdictional decision)—then the case might be decided either favorably or unfavorably, depending upon the extremity of the libertarian claim. Stated in this form, the prediction is sufficiently precise to be tested empirically by an examination of the decisions of the Court in the next cases to arise in fact, an event which occurred in the 1959 Term. A test of the prediction should prove to be valuable as a means for affording insight into the utility of cumulative-scale theory and analysis as an approach to the understanding, as well as the prediction, of Supreme Court decision-making behavior.

III

Since the placement on the scale of the next cases to arise is critical to the testing of the prediction, it is necessary now to turn to the raw data provided by the earlier cases themselves. In the absence of a more sophisticated system of content analysis than is attempted in the present chapter,[18] the kind of question about the underlying scale variable that a case asks can best be determined by examining the facts of the case and the questions deemed relevant to decision by the participating justices. This, in turn, requires that opinion data and behavior, as well as voting data and behavior, be observed.

The first case in our sample to arise, *Toth* v. *Quarles,* 350 U.S. 11 (1955), does not require extended consideration. A discharged serviceman and veteran of the Korean War was arrested at his place of employment by military police and swiftly and secretly spirited out of the country and flown to Korea, where he stood trial by court-martial on a murder charge arising out of events that occurred in Korea during his prior and expired term of military service. The survival of military jurisdiction over the defendant, for such an offense, was explicitly authorized by statutory language in the then recently adopted Uniform Code of Military Justice of 1950, which in turn was intended to overrule the Court's decision in *United States* ex rel *Hirshberg* v. *Cooke,* 336 U.S. 210 (1949).[19] Now it was the Court's turn again, and as Table 1 shows, a clear majority of six justices, including Frankfurter and Harlan and Clark, joined in Black's opinion for the Court overruling Congress on this issue. Since the three dissenters agreed that the basic question for decision was whether civilians within the United States could be taken overseas for trial by court-martial, we have no further interest in the minority opinion in the *Toth* case; neither the votes nor the specific views articulated by any of the three dissenting justices would be relevant to the testing of our prediction, since all of the dissenters left the Court before a test could be made.

The second case, *Reid* v. *Covert,* 354 U.S. 1 (1957), involves more complex consideration. In effect—although not, of course, in form—the Court was overruling itself in this decision, since almost exactly a year earlier, the Court had decided precisely the same issue in the opposite way by its decisions in *Kinsella* v. *Krueger,* 351 U.S. 470 (1956), and *Reid* v. *Covert,* 351 U.S. 487 (1956). The defendants in these cases, Dorothy Krueger Smith and Clarice Covert, were accompanying civilian dependents of military personnel. Each had shot and killed her respective spouse at an overseas American military base; each was tried and convicted of murder, by a court-martial as explicitly authorized by the Uniform Code of Military Justice. Existing statutory and executive law made no provision for an alternative forum in which the defendants could be brought to trial. As Table 2 indicates, the Court's initial decision was 3-5 against the defendants. A bare majority of the Court, conceivably aware of the imminent retirement of Minton (and possibly that of Reed, as well), ramrodded the decision through at the very close of the Term. And it did so over the protests of a maximal minority of four justices, all of whom voiced their regret at the unseemly haste with which the majority was disposing of a major issue of constitutional policy. Frankfurter went so far as to refuse to participate in the decision, and explicitly on the grounds of inadequate time for proper judgment.

Petitions for rehearing were filed during the summer vacation, and only a couple of weeks after Minton's retirement in October, the Court took the highly unusual step of granting the petition, and of scheduling the cases for reargument. Table 2 shows that most of the justices voted on the question of rehearing precisely the same, as would be expected, as they had voted on the merits five months earlier: Douglas, Black, and Warren voted for the defendants; Clark, Reed, and Burton voted against them. The former majority lost one vote when Brennan's nonparticipation took the place of Minton's negative vote; and the former minority gained a vote when Frankfurter's reservation was transformed into an affirmative vote in favor of rehearing— although this, too, was a perfectly consistent action for Frankfurter to take,

TABLE 2

The Three Decisions in the Covert-Krueger Cases
(1955 and 1956 Terms)[20]

	Kinsella v. Krueger, 351 U.S. 470, and Reid v. Covert, 351 U.S. 487 (June 11, 1956)	Reid v. Covert, and Kinsella v. Krueger, 352 U.S. 901 (November 5, 1956) [On petition for rehearing]	Reid v. Covert, and Kinsella v. Krueger, 354 U.S. 1 (June 10, 1957) [On rehearing]
Bl	'+')	+	('+'
Do	'+')	+	(+
Wa	'+')	+	(+
Br	*	NP	(+
Fr	R	+	('+'
Ha	(−)	+	('+'
Mi	(−)	*	*
Re	(−)	−	*
Bu	(−)	−	−)
Cl	('−')	−	'−')
Wh	*	*	NP
Voting Division	3-5	5-3	6-2
	Con	Pro	Pro

LEGEND

+ = a vote in favor of the defendants	) = dissenting opinion
− = a vote against the defendants	* = not seated at the time of this decision
' ' = wrote opinion	NP = seated but not participating in this decision
( ) = joined in the opinion of the Court	R = vote reserved until a later time
(= concurring opinion	

considering the stated basis for his reservation. But if this had been all, the motion for rehearing would have been denied, at least in a decision announced at this time,[21] by an equally divided court. The really critical event was Harlan's change of vote and, as he subsequently confessed,[22] of attitude toward the question presented by these cases.

In the subsequent decision on the merits in the following June, the majority was further enlarged, and the new minority further diminished, as a consequence of Brennan's affirmative vote and Reed's retirement. Thus by this process of conversion and replacement of personnel a minority of three grew to a new majority of six, and a former majority of five shrank to a minority of two, all in less than a year. And yet, the available evidence suggests that of the ten justices who participated in one or more of the decisions in this series of cases, only one—Harlan—voted inconsistently or changed his attitude toward the policy question at issue. Clark certainly had not changed his mind; his dissenting opinion in 1957 restated the argument of what had been his opinion for the Court in 1956, and with considerably less vehemence and more graciousness than has been manifested by certain other justices in similar situations where the interval between the announcement of their opinions for the Court and an overruling decision was even greater.[23]

The core of the new majority was provided by Black, Douglas, Warren, and Brennan, whose opinion disputed the authority of Congress to vest in courts-martial jurisdiction to try civilians already overseas for nonmilitary offenses. The other two affirmative votes were provided by Frankfurter and Harlan, who attempted to introduce a new variable into the case: a distinction between capital and noncapital offenses, a policy norm which they apparently were trying to import from the state right-to-counsel decisions of the Court.[24] Both the Black-Douglas-Warren-Brennan group and Clark and Burton in dissent explicitly rejected as spurious the purported distinction between capital and noncapital offenses; all six of these justices were agreed that such a rule was not a relevant criterion of judgment for these cases. As a result, the Court was partitioned in two different ways in its second decision on the merits in the Covert-Krueger cases (see Table 3).

TABLE 3

Voting and Opinion Response in the Second Covert-Krueger Decision

		Acceptance of the Capital Offense Distinction:		
		No	Yes	
	Majority	Bl, Do, Wa, Br	Fr, Ha	6
Vote on the Merits:				
	Minority	Cl, Bu		2
		6	2	

The third case in Table 1, *Trop* v. *Dulles*, 356 U.S. 86 (1958), also produced a split majority. The principal opinion, as in *Reid* v. *Covert*, was joined in by only four justices; otherwise the two decisions were more distinguished by their differences than by their similarities. Trop was a soldier who had deserted in time of war and in an overseas theater of action. He was subsequently apprehended, tried, and convicted by a court-martial on a lesser charge than the capital offense for which he might have been required to stand trial. As part of his punishment, Trop, a native-born American, was deprived of his United States citizenship, as the court-martial was explicitly authorized to do by the Nationality Act of 1940. So the question now was not, as in the two earlier decisions, whether court-martial jurisdiction could be extended to include civilian defendants on trial for nonmilitary offenses. In *Trop* the court-martial had exercised its unquestioned rightful jurisdiction over a military defendant who had committed a military offense for which it might, upon a judgment of conviction, have decreed capital punishment. The question in *Trop* was whether Congress could properly authorize such a court-martial to impose the lesser punishment of expatriation.

A minimal majority of five justices agreed that it would be unconstitutional to permit this lesser punishment, and presumably it would make no difference whether the sentence of expatriation had been uttered by a court-martial or a civilian court, at least to some members of the five-justice majority. The Warren opinion, in which Black, Douglas, and Whittaker joined, seemed to rest on the premise that expatriation is not a permissible form of punishment, since it is cruel and unusual and contrary to the Eighth Amendment. Black and Douglas, however, wrote a brief concurrence in which the virtue of civilian control over the military was emphasized, while Brennan, who dissociated himself from either the Warren or the Black opinion, took the less extreme position that expatriation is not a permissible form of punishment *under the war power.*[25]

A single dissenting opinion, authored by Frankfurter in behalf of Harlan and Clark and Burton as well as himself, took issue with all three positions that had been advanced by justices in the majority, and emphasized—as the losers always do in decisions invalidating Congressional and executive actions—the importance of judicial restraint. Frankfurter and Harlan had no qualms about the imposition of a "lesser" form of punishment in a capital case; and they obviously considered the distinction between capital and noncapital offenses, which they had pushed unsuccessfully in *Reid* v. *Covert,* to be irrelevant in the present case where no one questioned the right of a military court to impose capital punishment upon a military defendant who commits perhaps the most serious of all offenses against military law. Clark and Burton, who had dissented in *Reid* v. *Covert,* of course dissented against a favorable response to this even more extreme libertarian claim.

To summarize, an examination of the facts and opinion data for the *Toth, Covert,* and *Trop* cases corroborates the assignment of positions in the quasi-scale of Table 1 on the basis of cumulative-scale theory and the voting data. *Toth* presents the strongest civil liberty claim, and *Trop* raises the weakest (or most extreme) libertarian claim; and both the opinion and the voting responses of the justices correspond to the increasing "difficulty" of the questions raised by these cases for decision. We can also summarize, on the basis of the data provided by these three cases, the expected future behaviors of the justices in any related cases that might arise subsequent to *Trop.*

In terms of scale theory, we have no further interest in Minton, Reed, and Burton, since all of them had retired by the opening of the October 1958 Term, and hence a knowledge of their attitudes could be of no help in predicting what the Court would decide in subsequent cases. We are interested in Stewart, but we can say nothing about his attitude toward the scale variable, since he joined the Court too late[26] to participate in any of the three decisions for which we have information. A majority of five justices (Black, Douglas, Warren, Brennan, and Whittaker) can be expected—though with varying degrees of confidence—to vote favorably to any libertarian claim less extreme than that of *Trop*. In the case of more extreme claims, we should expect (on the basis of the *opinion* data) Black and Douglas to support more extreme claims than the other three. However, we cannot (on the basis of the *voting* data) differentiate among the ideal-points of these five justices, except in terms of confidence levels and other than to say that all five are located to the right of the *Trop* stimulus-point on the continuum, because in terms of our quite limited information, all five justices must be assigned the same rank or scale score. We should, of course, expect Frankfurter, Harlan, and Clark to vote against any claim more extreme than *Trop*'s, and we should expect Frankfurter and Harlan to favor a claim falling between *Toth* and *Covert,* and Clark to reject a claim falling between *Covert* and *Trop*. But we cannot predict Clark's vote in a case lying between *Toth* and *Covert,* nor those of Frankfurter and Harlan in a case lying between *Covert* and *Trop*.

Assuming that all justices participate in the decision, there are four possibilities:

1. In a case less extreme than *Toth,* eight justices should vote favorably, but Stewart's vote would be indeterminate.

2. In a case more extreme than *Toth* but less extreme than *Covert,* seven justices should vote favorably, but Clark's and Stewart's votes would be indeterminate.

3. In a case more extreme than *Covert* but less extreme than *Trop,* five justices should vote favorably and Clark should dissent, but the votes of Frankfurter, Harlan, and Stewart would be indeterminate.

4. In a case more extreme than *Trop,* three justices (Frankfurter, Harlan, and Clark) should reject the claim, and six votes (Black, Douglas, Warren, Brennan, Whittaker, and Stewart) would be indeterminate. We could predict that any case less extreme than *Trop* would be decided favorably; but we could not predict the decision in any case more extreme than *Trop*.

Since all three of the cases on the quasi-scale involved trials by courts-martial for capital offenses, but only the first two involved *civilian* defendants —and any claim in behalf of a *civilian* defendant against trial by court-martial might logically be considered to present a stronger civil liberty claim than that of a *military* defendant invoking a civil right—we might expect any case raising a question about the constitutional civil rights of *civilian* defendants to lie to the left of *Trop* on the scale. Moreover, since Frankfurter and Harlan had postulated an explicit distinction between capital and noncapital offenses, we might expect that, *at least for these two justices,* a case raising a question about court-martial trial of a civilian defendant for a noncapital offense necessarily would fall between *Covert* and *Trop* on the quasi-scale. (Translated into psychological language, we should say that five justices— Black, Douglas, Warren, Brennan, and Clark—would perceive *no difference* in the locus of the stimulus-point of such a case and that of *Covert;* Frankfurter and Harlan would perceive the stimulus-point of the new case to be located to the right of the stimulus-point of *Covert* on the continuum; but we cannot say whether Whittaker and Stewart would perceive the difference, since neither had as yet revealed his attitude toward this question.) We can, therefore, refine our expectations regarding possibility 3 to this extent: If a case should arise involving the court-martial trial of a civilian defendant for a noncapital offense, the decision should be favorable to the defendant's claim and the voting division of the Court should be 5-4 or 6-3 (in view of the uncertainty about Stewart) with Frankfurter, Harlan, and Clark in dissent; and if another case should arise involving the court-martial trial of a civilian defendant for a capital offense, the decision should be favorable to the defendant's claim and the voting division of the Court should be 7-2 or 8-1, with Clark (and possibly Stewart, too) in dissent. Such a prediction is based, of course, upon the assumption that all of the justices would perceive to be relevant one major independent variable—*Civilian/Military Control*—and that at least two of the justices also would perceive to be relevant a second independent variable—*Capital/Noncapital Offense*.[27]

IV

It was not long after *Trop* that the Court decided a series of cases in which questions were raised that furnished an appropriate test of our "refined" predictions for both alternative circumstances that might arise under what we have called possibility 3. On January 18, 1960, the Court decided seriatim four cases[28] that centered on the following questions: Can Congress authorize trial by court-martial of the following persons:

1. Civilian *dependents* for *noncapital* offenses?
2. Civilian *employees* for *capital* offenses?
3. Civilian *employees* for *noncapital* offenses?

The first question is consistent with our expectations, and we ought to expect our prediction to hold for the decision of the case, *Kinsella* v. *Singleton,* 361 U.S. 234, in which this question was raised. But the second and third questions have introduced a new and unanticipated independent variable—*civilian dependent/employee.* In effect, the major independent variable, *civilian/military control,* has now been further subdivided, as follows:

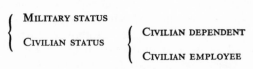

The voting data, of course, provide no information about what effect (if any) might be produced by the recognition, on the part of any or all of the justices, of this new variable as a relevant consideration. The opinion data indicate that it would be improbable, but possible, for the remaining justices who participated in *Covert* to attach much weight to this new variable. Certainly we should not expect, if the cases are perceived by the justices as falling between *Covert* and *Trop* on the continuum, that this new distinction would have sufficient effect to change the predicted favorable votes of Black, Douglas, Warren, and Brennan, or the predicted unfavorable vote of Clark. Indeed, if the new variable were to be perceived as relevant by any of the justices, the most likely candidates would be Stewart and Whittaker, who were uncommitted[29] by any previous votes or expression of opinion, and whose attitudes, therefore, could be assumed to be most flexible (i.e., least definitely structured) and most open to advocacy and persuasion on this issue.

If we view the *Covert* case as the most directly relevant precedent for the decisions made in January, 1960, we might array the cases, with the question that each raised, as follows:

(0) *Reid* v. *Covert*, 354 U.S. 1 — Civilian *dependent, capital* offense
(1) *Kinsella* v. *Singleton*, 361 U.S. 234 — Civilian *dependent, noncapital* offense
(2) *Grisham* v. *Hagan*, 361 U.S. 278 — Civilian *employee, capital* offense
(3) *McElroy* v. *Guagliardo*, 361 U.S. 281 — Civilian *employee, noncapital* offense
(3) *Wilson* v. *Bohlender*, 361 U.S. 281 — Civilian *employee, noncapital* offense

The cases and questions might then be considered to fall in a fourfold table (Table 4).

TABLE 4

Stimuli Attributes in the Court-Martial Decisions of the 1959 Term

| | Civilian Status: | |
	Dependent	Employee
Offense: Capital	0	2
Noncapital	1	3

We can now see that the most directly relevant precedent, *Covert* (0), did not provide an unambiguous predictor for any of the four new cases, because of the uncertain effect that might be produced if there were general recognition among the justices of the presence of a new independent variable (civilian status). As it turned out, however, only the two uncommitted justices (Stewart and Whittaker) were attracted by the government's suggestion of this new variable, with the result that the stimuli (1-3) evoked the responses from the justices shown in Table 5.

In other words, Black, Douglas, Warren, Brennan, and Clark voted for the defendants on all three questions (in all four cases); this majority was joined by Whittaker and Stewart, over the dissents of Frankfurter and Harlan, when the defendant was a civilian *dependent* but the offense was *noncapital;* the same majority group of five was joined by Frankfurter and Harlan, over

TABLE 5

Voting Response in the Court-Martial Decisions of the 1959 Term

		Civilian Status:		
		All	*Dependents Only*	
Offenses:	All	Bl, Do, Wa Br, Cl	Wh, St	7
	Capital Only	Fr, Ha		2
		7	2	

the dissents of Whittaker and Stewart, when the offense was *capital* but the defendant was a civilian *employee;* while Frankfurter, Harlan, Whittaker, and Stewart all dissented against the decision of the majority five, upholding the claims of defendants who were civilian *employees* accused of *noncapital* offenses.

V

We can now examine the results of the test of our so-called "refined" prediction; that is, we can compare our prediction, based upon cumulative-scale theory and the data available prior to January, 1960, with the decisions made by the Court at that time. The results are given in Table 6.

TABLE 6

A Test of a Scale-Theory Prediction of the Court-Martial Decisions of the 1959 Term

Question	Prediction	Result	Errors
(1) Civilian Dependent, Noncapital Offense			
outcome:	pro	pro	
division:	6–3 or 5–4	7–2	1 vote
dissenters:	Fr, Ha, Cl (St?)	Fr, Ha	Cl
(2) Civilian Employee, Capital Offense			
outcome:	pro	pro	
division:	7–2 or 8–1	7–2	
dissenters:	Cl (St?)	Wh, St	Cl, Wh
(3) Civilian Employee, Noncapital Offense			
outcome:	pro	pro	
division:	5–4 or 6–3	5–4	
dissenters:	Fr, Ha, Cl (St?)	Fr, Ha, Wh, St	Cl, Wh

The Court's decisions were all favorable to the civil liberty claimants, as expected; and six justices—Black, Douglas, Warren, Brennan, Frankfurter, and Harlan—voted precisely as we had predicted. We were in error about Whittaker's vote in the second and third questions; but Whittaker (and, of course, Stewart also) voted *consistently* in terms of the unpredicted new variable, which also accounts for our failure to predict accurately Whittaker's responses. The really surprising error is our failure to predict Clark's vote in any of the decisions on these three questions; to which should be added the further shock of discovering that Clark wrote the majority opinion for all four cases!

One possible inference might be that Clark, like Harlan in the various decisions in the Covert-Krueger cases, had changed his *attitude* toward the major independent scale variable—military control over civilians. However, this seems unlikely in view of the fact that Clark's votes in these decisions appear as *inconsistencies* in a cumulative scale of all civil liberties cases for the 1959 Term, and particularly when one takes into consideration that on such a scale Clark ranked at the bottom of the Court in support of civil liberties claims with only one other pro-civil liberty vote, in a split decision, during the entire term.[30] But if Clark did not change his attitude toward the question of military control over civilians, how are we to account for our failure to predict his voting in these cases?

VI

As we have done before in this article, we can turn to the opinion data to complement the insights that we can derive from the voting data. Such a task is considerably facilitated, in this instance, by the circumstance that Clark wrote the opinion of the Court for all four of these cases. An examination of Clark's opinions reveals a perfectly clear and unambiguous reliance upon yet another new independent variable: the time-honored common-law principle of stare decisis. Both opinions for the majority in *Covert,* said Clark, agreed that trial by court-martial of *civilian dependents* in *capital* cases, in time of peace, is unconstitutional. (This is Clark's first major premise, which we shall call, for convenience, P-I). Moreover, a clear majority of six justices (i.e., Black, Douglas, Warren, and Brennan, from the majority; and the two dissenters, Clark and Burton) agreed, said Clark, that the purported distinction between capital and noncapital offenses (urged by Frankfurter and Harlan in concurrence) was spurious and irrelevant. (This is Clark's second major premise, which we shall call P-II.) Therefore, Clark reasoned, P-I + P-II require a favorable response to question (1); that is, *Covert* applies as a precedent to civilian dependents in both capital and noncapital cases, in time of peace. Also, P-I requires a favorable response to question (2); that is, *Covert* applies as a precedent to both civilian *dependents* and *employees,* in capital cases, in time of peace. And of course, the favorable responses to questions (1) and (2) necessarily require, in turn, a favorable response to question (3). That is, *Singleton* and *Grisham—Covert* is not mentioned in Clark's opinion for *Guagliardo* and *Wilson*—apply as precedents to civilian *employees*, in *noncapital* cases, in time of peace. This is the precise logic of Clark's opinions; and this is the precise sequence in which the questions and cases were decided.

The opinion data also confirmed what is implicit in Table 5, namely, that by January, 1960, the Court was *unanimous* on the issue that had created such unusually great dissension and caused difficulty in reaching a final decision that would stick only three and a half years earlier: the unconstitutionality of trial by court-martial of *civilian dependents* in *capital* cases. This post hoc unanimity was accompanied, however, by disagreement among the justices on several other related issues, as our analysis of the *civilian status, capital offense,* and now yet a third variable *stare decisis* has demonstrated; so there was no net gain in consensus on the Court.

We are led to conclude that our prediction, based upon scale theory, of the court-martial decisions of the 1959 Term, was very substantially validated by the empirical data. The voting "errors" of Clark and Whittaker can be readily explained by the presence of two additional independent variables that were not present in the *Covert* decision. Of course, one might well have anticipated, from the point of view of Austinian positivism, that *stare decisis* might become an important, or at least a relevant, factor in the decision of a set of cases for which a recent precedent existed. The major error in our prediction must be attributed to our failure to include such a traditional legal variable as *stare decisis* within the frame of reference deemed relevant.

Of course, this suggests the necessity for a more complex system of analysis and an extended frame of reference which can accommodate both the externally oriented (e.g., *civilian/military control, civilian dependent/employee, capital/noncapital offense*) and the internally oriented (e.g., *stare decisis*) values of the justices. An investigation of the interrelationships among all of these socio-psychological variables would be an obvious next step.

It is not possible, with such a small sample, to carry out the suggested multivariate analysis, but we can suggest briefly, in general terms, the theory and method which would lead to a solution of this problem. Once it is recognized that more than one variable is present, there is no reason to assume that the voting preferences of the justices will be transitive,[31] and that the data will fit the model of the one-dimensional cumulative scale. Clearly, the data for the court-martial decision of the 1959 Term do *not* scale consistently in one dimension.[32] It is easy to demonstrate, however, that these same data—and that for the *Covert* case, as well—can be accommodated in two dimensions. For this purpose, we shall use an individual compensatory composition model.[33] We assume, as before, that the stimulus-points of cases and the ideal-points of justices are located in the same joint space, but the space now is considered to be a plane instead of a line. Therefore, instead of lying upon a linear continuum, a stimulus-point representing a case is located at the end of a vector, the origin of which is the conjuncture of the two orthogonal reference axes which define the dimensionality of the space. Assuming that our court-martial cases are correlated with the major scale variable for *one* dimension (*civilian/military control*), we can assume that this dimension will be our abscissal axis; and we shall assume that the ordinal axis represents the *stare decisis* variable.

The extended vectors for the stimulus-points of cases may also be conceptualized as oblique axes representing the subvariables *offense* and *status*; and we shall call such axes "scale axes," because each represents a continuum along which the attitudes of the justices might be arrayed, together with other possible (potential) cases not included within our very small empirical sample. We shall assume that the question of the *status* of defendants is more closely correlated, in the minds of the justices, with the general question of *civilian control;* while the degree of the *offense* with which the defendant is charged is more closely correlated with judicial attitudes toward *stare decisis*. The *status* of civilians becomes increasingly marginal in the positive direction of this scale axis; thus, it requires a more positive attitude towards *status* to uphold the claims of employees to be exempt from trial by court-martial than it does to uphold the equivalent claims of dependents. Similarly, successively more trivial *offenses* would lie near the positive terminus of the scale axis; while capital offenses would fall near the other end in the opposite direction of this axis.

Covert might be assumed to fall directly upon, and to have a high negative correlation with, the *civilian control* reference axis. This is equivalent to saying that, since *Covert* was quite literally unprecedented, insofar as concerns the *status* and *offense* variables, it should be assumed to have a zero loading upon (*i.e.*, to be statistically independent of) the *stare decisis* reference axis.

Singleton ought to lie on a scale axis that will intercept the differential attitudes of the justices toward the question whether courts-martial can try civilian dependents for less serious *offenses;* and in view of *Covert,* it might well be considered that this issue will sample more of judicial attitudes toward *stare decisis* than toward *civilian control*. *Grisham,* on the other hand, raises the question of a more extreme claim of civilian *status*, and we have hypothesized that the justices are likely to view this as more of an issue of *civilian control* than of *stare decisis*. The remaining two cases, *Guagliardo* and *Wilson,* combine the questions of *offense* and *status* so we ought logically to assume that these cases will lie on an axis that is the centroid (or arithmetic mean) of the *offense* and *status* scale axes.

The location of the ideal-points of the justices in the space that we have postulated will depend upon their attitudes toward the reference axis variables, *civilian control* and *stare decisis*. These judicial ideal-points will project (orthogonally, of course) upon both the reference axes and the oblique scale axes. It is assumed that, if the projection upon an axis from a justice's ideal-point equals or exceeds (in the positive direction) the locus of the stimulus-point on that axis, then the justice will respond positively (vote favorably) to the defendant's claim in the case; and if the locus of the stimulus-point exceeds the projection from the judicial ideal-point, he will reject the defendant's claim (and, in these particular cases, dissent). The decision in a case depends, naturally, upon whether the projections from a majority of the judicial ideal-points exceed the stimulus-point of the case;[34]

or, in other words, whether the attitudes of a majority of the justices are such that they accept the defendant's claim.

Figure 1 demonstrates how it is possible, in psychometric theory, to reconcile the seeming inconsistencies in the voting data for these cases if we expand the frame of reference to two dimensions. The two most recent cases, which raised the most extreme claim, were disposed of by a common decision, and they are represented, accordingly, by a single stimulus-point.

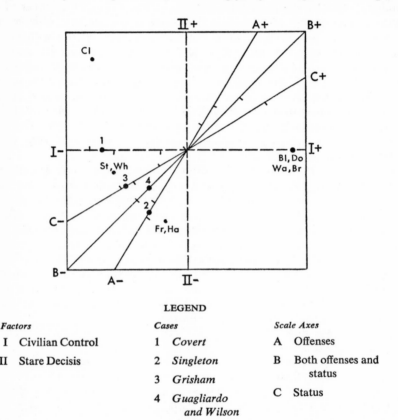

LEGEND

Factors		Cases		Scale Axes	
I	Civilian Control	1	Covert	A	Offenses
II	Stare Decisis	2	Singleton	B	Both offenses and status
		3	Grisham	C	Status
		4	Guagliardo and Wilson		

Figure 1. Judicial attitudes toward *civilian control* and *stare decisis* in the court-martial decisions of the 1956 and 1959 terms.

Justices Black, Douglas, Warren, and Brennan all are represented by the same ideal-point, since we cannot distinguish whatever differences in attitude they may have entertained, in terms of the data of these particular cases. Similarly, Frankfurter and Harlan are represented by a single point, as are also Whittaker and Stewart.

It is easy to see, from their respective projections, how Whittaker and Stewart would accept *Singleton* but not *Grisham,* while Frankfurter and Harlan would do the opposite, and all four of these justices would dissent in

Guagliardo-Wilson. Whittaker and Stewart—who did not participate in the decision of *Covert*—have enough regard for *stare decisis* that, notwithstanding their slight sympathy for *civilian control,* they feel bound to accept the claims of civilian dependents irrespective of the degree of the *offense* with which they are charged. However, their regard for *stare decisis* is not great enough to permit them to compensate for their tolerance of military control when the question is one of extending the *Covert* precedent to cover a more marginal category of civilians. And contrariwise, it was Frankfurter's and Harlan's relatively low respect for *stare decisis,* notwithstanding their relatively higher sympathy for *civilian control,* that required them to dissent in three of the four court-martial cases of the 1959 Term, thus persisting in the concurring (and unique) views that they had expressed in the precedential *Covert* decision. The four libertarians all have such high sympathy for *civilian control* that their neutral attitude toward *stare decisis* is no bar to their enthusiastic acceptance of all claims raised in these cases.

The most important demonstration, however, is with regard to Clark: Figure 1 explains why Clark, whose sympathy for *civilian control* was so slight that he dissented in *Covert,* nevertheless compensated for this deficiency with an exceptionally high loading on *stare decisis,* which required him to support the four libertarian justices and even to supply the critical fifth vote to form a favorable majority in *Guagliardo-Wilson.*

And so it is that attitudinal analysis of the justices, now on a multivariate basis, has suggested the necessity for an even more complex theoretical model of judicial behavior. In measuring judicial attitudes, we must be concerned not only with the externally oriented values which represent the recurrent issues of law and policy raised before the Court for decision; we must also be concerned with the internally oriented values which represent the institutional identifications of the justices with the Court, its customs and traditions, and their attitudes toward each other as members of the same small decision-making group.

NOTES

1. See Robert A. Dahl, "Decision-Making in a Democracy: The Role of the Supreme Court as a National Policy-Maker," *Journal of Public Law,* Vol. 6 (1957), 286; S. Sidney Ulmer, "Judicial Review as Political Behavior: A Temporary Check on Congress," *Administrative Science Quarterly,* Vol. 4 (1960), 426.

2. Glendon Schubert, *Quantitative Analysis of Judicial Behavior* (Glencoe: The Free Press, 1960), chap. 2, and *Constitutional Politics: The Political Behavior of Supreme Court Justices and the Constitutional Policies that They Make* (New York: Holt, Rinehart and Winston, 1960), pp. 174-75, 188-90.

3. C. Herman Pritchett, *Congress versus the Supreme Court, 1957-1960* (Minneapolis: University of Minnesota, 1961), pp. 11-14, 119-21.

4. Alpheus T. Mason, *The Supreme Court: Vehicle of Revealed Truth or Power Group, 1930-1937* (Boston: Boston University Press, 1954); and Pritchett, *The Roosevelt Court: A Study in Judicial Politics and Values, 1937-1947* (New York: Macmillan, 1948), pp. 2-9.

5. Pritchett, *op. cit. supra* (note 3), pp. 9, 123.

6. *Toth* v. *Quarles,* 350 U.S. 11 (1955); *Reid* v. *Covert,* 354 U.S. 1 (1957); *Trop* v. *Dulles,* 356 U.S. 86 (1958); *Kinsella* v. *Singleton,* 361 U.S. 234 (1960); *Grisham* v.

76   GLENDON SCHUBERT

Hagan, 361 U.S. 278 (1960); *McElroy* v. *Guagliardo,* 361 U.S. 281 (1960); and *Wilson* v. *Bohlender,* 361 U.S. 281 (1960). Cf. *Kinsella* v. *Krueger,* 351 U.S. 470 (1956); and *Reid* v. *Covert,* 351 U.S. 487 (1956). For a typical legalistic analysis of the role of *stare decisis* in these cases, see Robert Girard, "The Constitution and Court-Martial of Civilians Accompanying the Armed Forces—A Preliminary Analysis," *Stanford Law Review,* Vol. 13 (1961), 461-521, esp. 495-99. In the unrelated case of *Bolling* v. *Sharpe,* 347 U.S. 497 (1954), the Warren Court declared unconstitutional several acts of Congress authorizing racial segregation in public schools in the District of Columbia. This also, of course, was a pro-civil liberty decision; but, unlike the courts-martial cases that followed, the nominal scope of the national legislation at issue was local rather than nationwide, or, indeed, international.

7. *Trop* v. *Dulles,* 356 U.S. 86, 104 (1958).

8. For a general discussion, see Warren S. Torgerson, *Theory and Methods of Scaling* (New York: Wiley, 1958).

9. See the special issue edited by Daniel Katz, "Attitude Change," *Public Opinion Quarterly,* Vol. 24, No. 2 (Summer, 1960), and references cited therein. See also Hans J. Eysenck, *The Psychology of Politics* (London: Routledge and Kegan Paul, 1954).

10. For a detailed explanation of the theory and method of one-dimensional cumulative scale analysis of judicial votes, see Schubert, *Quantitative Analysis, op. cit. supra* (note 2), chap. 5. For other examples of recent empirical applications of scale analysis of judicial votes, see Ulmer, "Scaling Judicial Cases: A Methodological Note," *American Behavioral Scientist,* Vol. 4 (April, 1961), 31; "The Analysis of Behavior Patterns on the United States Supreme Court," *Journal of Politics,* Vol. 22 (1960), 629-653; and "Supreme Court Behavior and Civil Rights," *Western Political Quarterly,* Vol. 13 (1960), 288-311.

11. The basic reference is Samuel Stouffer, *et al., Measurement and Prediction,* Vol. 4 of Studies in Social Psychology in World War II, (Princeton: Princeton University Press, 1950).

12. Schubert, *Quantitative Analysis, op. cit. supra* (note 2), pp. 279-80; and Torgerson, *op. cit. supra* (note 8), p. 324.

13. A different concept of "quasi-scale" is discussed in Torgerson, *ibid.*

14. *Reid* v. *Covert,* 354 U.S. 1 (1956 Term); *Kinsella* v. *Krueger,* 351 U.S. 470, and *Reid* v. *Covert,* 351 U.S. 487 (1955 Term).

15. Table 1 is reproduced from Schubert, *Constitutional Politics, op. cit. supra* (note 2), p. 205. Permission granted by the publisher.

16. For some persuasive evidence in support of this proposition, see "Homeostatic Tendencies in the United States Supreme Court," in Ulmer (ed.), *Introductory Readings in Political Behavior* (Chicago: Rand McNally, 1961), pp. 173-78. Ulmer shows that Kendall's W, an index of multiple ordinal concordance, is significantly high and positive for the decision-making of the Supreme Court throughout the period from 1888-1958, with the single exception of 1941-45. The exceptional period of discordance is, of course, that of the Stone Court; and the exceptionally high rate of disagreement among the justices, under Stone's leadership, has been pointed out by many observers, including Stone's biographer: Mason, *The Supreme Court from Taft to Warren* (Baton Rouge: Louisiana State University Press, 1958), pp. 154-55.

17. Schubert, *Constitutional Politics, op. cit. supra* (note 2), pp. 204, 206. Emphasis added.

18. Cf. Stuart S. Nagel, "Weighting Variables in Judicial Prediction," *Modern Uses of Logic in Law,* Vol. 60S, 94-95; Fred Kort, "The Quantitative Content Analysis of Judicial Opinions," *Political Research: Organization and Design,* Vol. 3 (March, 1960), 11, and chap. 9, *infra;* Schubert, "The Study of Judicial Decision-Making as an Aspect of Political Behavior," *American Political Science Review,* Vol. 52 (1958), 1007.

19. *Hirshberg* had invalidated an administrative regulation embodying the same policy, on the ground that the regulation was in conflict with the statutory language contained (then) in the Articles of War. See Schubert, *The Presidency in the Courts* (Minneapolis: University of Minnesota Press, 1957), p. 181.

20. Table 2 is reproduced from Schubert, *Constitutional Politics, op. cit. supra* (note 2), p. 152. Permission granted by the publisher.

21. See the statement by Mr. Justice Jackson in *Jewell Ridge Coal Corp.* v. *Local No. 6167, U.M.W.*, 325 U.S. 879-98 (1945) (concurring opinion).

22. Mr. Justice Harlan in *Reid* v. *Covert*, 354 U.S. 1, 65 (1957) (concurring opinion).

23. See, e.g., Mr. Justice Frankfurter in *West Virginia State Board of Education* v. *Barnette*, 319 U.S. 624, 646 (1943) (dissenting opinion); and Mr. Justice Roberts in *Smith* v. *Allwright*, 321 U.S. 649, 666, 669-670 (1944) (dissenting opinion).

24. See Schubert, *Quantitative Analysis, op. cit. supra* (note 2), pp. 322, 333.

25. Mr. Justice Brennan in *Trop* v. *Dulles*, 356 U.S. 86, 105 (1958) (concurring opinion).

26. Mr. Justice Stewart replaced Mr. Justice Burton at the beginning of the 1958 Term.

27. A third independent variable, *war/peace*, is referred to in Clark's opinions in the two decisions on the merits in the Covert-Krueger cases, but this variable obviously would be of no help in prediction until a case arises under circumstances that at least some of the justices would consider to be those of a time of war.

28. *Kinsella* v. *Singleton*, 361 U.S. 234; *Grisham* v. *Hagan*, 361 U.S. 278; and *McElroy* v. *Guagliardo* and *Wilson* v. *Bohlender*, 361 U.S. 281.

29. From a psychological, although not perhaps from a legal, point of view.

30. In "Scaling Judicial Cases: A Methodological Note," *American Behavioral Scientist* Vol. 4 (April, 1961), 31, 32, Ulmer presents a scalogram that includes these same cases, which he computed independently on the basis of his own data. Ulmer's scale indicates (and incorrectly, in the judgment of the present writer) inconsistent votes for Clark *only* on questions (2) and (3), thus attributing inconsistent votes to Frankfurter and Harlan (instead of to Clark) on question (1). As our analysis has demonstrated, it is much less plausible to attribute inconsistency to Frankfurter and Harlan than to Clark in these court-martial decisions of the 1959 Term. But is interesting to note that of a total of eight inconsistent votes reported by Ulmer for all civil liberties decisions of the 1959 Term, five—or almost two-thirds of the total inconsistencies—occurred in these four court-martial cases. This agrees with the present writer's findings. Cf. the perplexity of two expositors of the military point of view toward these decisions: "The switch of Justice Clark presents something of a mystery. . . . The attitudes [he] conveyed (if not the words used) in [*Covert, Guagliardo* and *Wilson*] fail to square. One can only conclude that he did indeed have a change of heart, but the opinion casts little light on his reasons." Captain John C. Ries and Captain Owen S. Nibley, "Justice, Juries, and Military Dependents," *Western Political Quarterly*, Vol. 15 (1962), p. 441n.22.

31. See William H. Riker, "Voting and the Summation of Preferences: An Interpretive Bibliographical Review of Selected Developments during the Last Decade," *American Political Science Review*, Vol. 55 (December, 1961), 900-911.

32. See note 30, *supra*.

33. This concept is defined in Torgerson, *op. cit. supra* (note 8), pp. 345-59; and for an extended explanation of the theory, see Clyde Coombs, *The Theory of Data* (Wiley, in press), chap. 12.

34. For a more extended development of this theory of judicial decision-making, see Schubert: "A Psychometric Model of the Supreme Court," *American Behavioral Scientist*, Vol. 5, No. 3 (November 1961), 14-18; "Psychometric Research in Judicial Behavior," *Modern Uses of Logic in Law*, Vol. 2, No. 3 (March, 1962), pp. 9-18; "The 1960-61 Term of the Supreme Court: A Psychological Analysis," *American Political Science Review*, Vol. 56 (March, 1962), pp. 90-107; "A Solution to the Indeterminate Factorial Resolution of Thurstone and Degan's Study of the Supreme Court," *Behavioral Science*, Vol. 7 (October, 1962), pp. 448-58; and "Psychometric Analysis of Judicial Behavior: The 1961 Term of the Supreme Court," *Law and Contemporary Problems*, Vol. 28, No. 1 (Winter, 1963).

Like the present chapter, the latter article also discusses problems of prediction, but with a significant difference. This chapter has dealt with logical prediction under conditions of certain knowledge, while the article deals with the prediction of events that have not yet occurred—with prediction under conditions of uncertainty.

Warren Court
Attitudes Toward Business:
The "B" Scale

HAROLD J. SPAETH

THIS CHAPTER is an analysis of the decision-making of the Warren Court in the business regulation cases decided during the 1953-1959 Terms. Previous research has demonstrated for the 1960 Term the existence of an E scale, in which the justices' behavior is motivated by attitudinal responses to the value "economic liberalism."[1] The purpose of this chapter is to focus upon attitudes toward regulation of business (the B scale), which is one of the two major components of economic liberalism. In particular, this study is concerned with specifying the voting behavior of the justices in business cases, the relationship of their behavior to that manifest in the E scale, and the interrelationships of response in the subcomponents of the B scale. The method employed in analyzing the Court's behavior is cumulative (Guttman) scale theory.

I

The content of the E scale extends to all formally decided cases[2] of the 1953-1959 Terms in which either an issue involving labor unions or one concerning regulation of business or business activities was present. The variable tested, economic liberalism, is defined as pro-union (as distinct from members of labor unions, for in a conflict between a union and union members, the economic liberal supports the union), pro-competition, and anti-business. Except in cases where labor unions are involved, the universe of items *excludes* all personal injury and admiralty actions, internal revenue cases, suits involving individuals in a nonbusiness capacity, and items decided

This study was made possible by a grant from the University of Detroit Research Council. My graduate assistant, Miss Ildikó Cserneczky, assisted in the identification and collection of the relevant data.

primarily on the basis of diversity of citizenship or judicial power, as evidenced by the opinions of the various justices.[3]

In Figure 1 and subsequent figures, a consistent vote in support of the scale variable is denoted by the symbol +, and a consistent vote antipathetic to the scale variable by −. The symbol / indicates an inconsistent vote. If the / appears above a given justice's breakpoint, the inconsistent vote is anti-economic liberalism; if below, it is pro-economic liberalism. Blank spaces in a justice's column indicate nonparticipation by reason of nonmembership on the Court at the time the item was decided. An asterisk signifies nonparticipation during incumbency. Scale scores are simple functions of scale position, with the latter determined by the justice's last consistent positive vote. Where nonparticipation occurs between the last consistent positive vote and the first consistent negative vote of a justice, his scale position is fixed at the mean of the nonparticipation or nonparticipations. Since it is just as likely that a justice might have voted positively as negatively in these items, probability theory warrants placement of the breakpoint at the mean. Numbers in the column to the left of the array of votes refer to the listing of cases in the appendix. Those which are in heavy type involve labor unions; the others are the business regulation cases. Identification of a single row of votes by more than one case number denotes several items decided by an identical scale type (voting alignment). In tabulating totals, scale position, and scale score, each case is counted. Scale scores are computed by use of the formula $s = (\frac{2p}{n}) - 1$, where s equals a justice's scale score, p his scale position, and n the number of cases in the scale. Scale scores may range from 1.00 to −1.00; the more extreme the response of a justice to the variable of economic liberalism, the closer his approximation to ±1.00. Depending upon his scale score, a justice may be classified, in terms of his response to economic liberalism, as strongly pro (+1.00 to +0.60), pro (+0.59 to +0.20), neutral (+0.19 to −0.19), anti (−0.20 to −0.59), or strongly anti (−0.60 to −1.00).

The coefficients appearing at the bottom of each figure measure the degree of consistency in the set of votes that is being scaled. R is Guttman's coefficient of reproducibility. An R between 0.90 and 1.00 is considered evidence of unidimensionality, i.e., that response to a single variable motivates voting behavior in the scaled set. S is Menzel's coefficient of scalability.[4] An S of 0.60 to 0.65 or higher is considered evidence that set consistency is not spuriously inflated by the presence of extreme marginal distributions of either cases or justices. In applying S to Supreme Court decision-making, it is virtually certain that the distribution of justices will be more extreme than the distribution of the cases. Case division tends to average out about 6-3—i.e., with two majority votes for every dissenting vote. It is usual, however, for most justices to divide their votes more extremely than this. In the E scale, for example, only six of the thirteen justices show a ratio approximating 2:1 or less (Brennan, Clark, Stewart, Minton, Reed, and Burton), while in the B scale only four of the justices have so nearly equal a distribution (Stewart, Minton, Reed, and Burton).

Figure 1 illustrates the E scale. Because of the large number of cases decided in response to the variable of economic liberalism, considerations of space preclude inclusion of items which are noncomputable by Guttman theory. Consequently, those items with only a single dissent (except one which is analogized to the cases with a 2-7 marginal split) do not appear in Figure 1; they are contained in all of the other figures, however. There were 34 such noncomputable items decided during the 1953-59 terms, of which 21 were pro-E decisions, 13 anti-E. They are included in the computation of scale positions, scale scores, and total votes for justices in Figure 1. We have then a total of 144 nonunanimous E items decided by the Court during the first seven terms of the Warren Court. In addition, there were 97 E items decided unanimously, 76 pro-E, 21 anti-E.[5] The grand total of 241 E items accounts for approximately one-third of the Warren Court's formally decided cases during the seven terms analyzed here.

On the basis of scale scores, the justices span a broad spectrum of response to the value of economic liberalism. As a group, the Court inclined toward support of economic liberalism. Seven of the thirteen justices score positively; six of these seven were incumbent at the time of this writing. In terms of the nonunanimous E decisions, 87 of 144, or 60 per cent, were decided pro-E. Douglas, Black, Warren, and Brennan—who are generally considered to be the most liberal over-all—occupy the highest positions on the E scale, with the first three all scoring higher than $+0.55$ on the E scale and in Figures 2 through 7 as well. Clark, noted for his lack of sympathy for civil liberties, is ranked fifth in Figure 1, with a score that marks him as an economic liberal. At the extreme right are Whittaker, Harlan, and Frankfurter; with the exception of Harlan's -0.11 in Figure 4, the highest score any of these three justices achieves in any of the seven scales presented is $-.39$. Frankfurter's placement as a marginal anti-economic liberal (and almost within the *strongly* anti-economic liberal category) might be considered somewhat surprising, given his involvement with the New Deal and other earlier social and economic reforms. In the 142 nonunanimous E items in which he participated, he cast a liberal vote proportionately less frequently (20 per cent) than any other member of the Court except Whittaker, whose proportion also was 20 per cent, and Jackson, who voted $E+$ in only 12 per cent of the 17 cases in which he participated. Given Frankfurter's over-all response to E, particular attention will be paid to his attitudes in business cases involving state and administrative agency action regulating business, since he is reputed to be deferential to states and to administrative expertise.

Between the six most liberal justices and the three most conservative are found all four of the nonincumbent justices (at the time of this writing) of the Warren Court: the neutral Minton and Reed, and the anti-liberal Burton and Jackson. Inasmuch as Jackson participated in only one term of the Warren Court, any evaluation of his response to E must be considered to be quite tentative. Some reservations may also be entered with regard to Stewart's neutral scale score. Apart from Jackson, he cast fewer votes than any of the other justices during the period under analysis. Furthermore, intermingled among his 13 liberal votes (out of a total of 39 cast)

Figure 1. The E Scale

Case Nos.[a] / Justices	Do	Bl	Wa	Br	Cl	St	Mi	Re	Bu	Ja	Fr	Ha	Wh	Totals
Scale Positions	139	128	116	99	90	78	76	64	47	31	30	28	14	
Scale Scores	0.93	0.78	0.61	0.38	0.25	0.08	0.06	−0.11	−0.35	−0.57	−0.58	−0.61	−0.81	
147	/	+	+	+	+	+					/	+	/	7–2
96, 97	+	+	+	+	+					/	+	+	−	7–2
57	+	+	+	+	+	/					+	+	−	7–2
58	/	+	+		+		+	/	+		+	+		7–2
122	+	+	+	+	+	/					+	+	−	7–2
80	+	+	+	+	+	+					/	+	−	7–2
83	+	+	+	+	+	/					+	−	/	7–2
59	/	+	+		+		+	+	+		+	−		7–2
3	+	+	+		+		/	+	+	+	−			7–2
25	+	+	+		+		+	+	+	−	−			7–2
49, 60, 63	+	+	+		+		+	+	+	−	−			7–2
32	+	+	+	*	+			+	+		−	−		6–2
110	+	+	+	+	+				+		−	−	/	7–2
54	/	+	+		+		+	+	+		−	*		6–2
22	/	+	*		+		+	+	+		−	−		5–3
27	+	+	+	/			+	+	+		−	−		6–3
32	+	+	+		+		/	+	+		−	−		6–2
15	+	+	+		+		/	+	+		−	*		6–2
21	+	+	+		+		/	+	+		−	−		6–3
73	+	+	+	/	+			+	+		−	−		6–3
85	+	/	+	+	+				+		−	−	/	6–3
101	+	+	+	+	*				+		−	−	−	5–3
102	+	+	+	+	+				+		−	−	−	6–3
34, 50	+	+	+		+		+	+	−		−			6–2
62	+	+	+		+		+	+	−		−	−		6–3
80	+	+	+	+	+				−		/	−	−	6–3
99	+	+	/	+	+				−		/	−	/	6–3
106, 109	+	+	+	+	+				−		−	−	/	6–3
114, 120	+	+	+	+	+	*					−	−	−	5–3
126	+	+	+	+	+	*					−	−	/	6–2
70	+	/	+	+	/	+					/	/	−	6–3
75, 142, 144	+	+	+	+	+	+					−	−	−	6–3
76, 123	+	+	+	+	+	/					−	/	−	6–3
27	/	+	+	/			+	+	−	*	/			5–3
44	+	+	+		+		/	−	−		/	/		6–3
46	+	+	+		+		+	−	−		−	*		5–3
61	/	+	+		+		+	−	−		/	−		5–4
75	+	+	+	+	+				−		−	−	*	5–3
49	+	+	+	+	/			/			−	−	−	5–4
81	+	+	+	+	*				−		−	*	*	4–2
78, 82, 98, 104, 105	+	+	+	+	+				−		−	−	−	5–4
39	+	+	+	/	+				−		−	−	/	5–4
116	/	/	+	+	+	+					−	/	−	5–4

Figure 1. The E Scale (continued)

Case Nos.[a] (Justices)	Do	Bl	Wa	Br	Cl	St	Mi	Re	Bu	Ja	Fr	Ha	Wh	Totals
127	+	+	+	+	/	+					−	−	−	5–4
133	+	+	+	+	+	−					*	−	−	5–3
78	+	+	+	+	/	−					−	/	−	5–4
146, 149, 151, 156, 157	+	+	+	+	+	−					−	−	−	5–4
45, 56	+	+	+		+		−	/	−		−	−		5–4
132	+	+	+	/	+	−					−	−		4–5
19, 20	+	+	+		+		−	−	−	−	−	−		4–5
92, 93, 94	+	+	+	+	−					−	−	−	−	4–5
77	+	+	+	+	−	−					−	−	−	4–5
69	/	+	+	*	−				−	−		−	−	2–6
71	/	+	+	+	−	−					−	−	−	3–6
9	/	+	+		*		−	−	−	*	−			2–5
10	+	+	+	−			−	−	−	−	−	−		3–6
13	+	+	+	−			−	−	−		−	*		3–5
23, 28	+	+	+	−			−	−	−		−			3–6
64	+	+	+	*			−	−	−		−	*		3–4
74	+	+	+	−	*		−	−			−	−		3–5
34	+	+	+	−	−		−	−			−	−		3–6
44, 76	+	+	+	−	−				−		−	−	*	3–5
46, 53, 55	+	+	+	−	−				−		−	−	−	3–6
50, 51	+	*	+	−	−				−		−	−		2–6
115	+	+	+	−	*	−					−	−		3–5
60, 66, 67	+	+	+	−	−	−					−	−		3–6
82	+	+	+	−	−	−					−	*	−	3–5
1	+	+	−		−		−	−	−	−	/			3–6
63	+	+	−	−	−	−					/	−	−	3–6
16	+	+	−		−		/	*	−	*	−			3–4
18	+	*	−		*		/	−	/	−	−			3–4
5	*	+	+				−	−	−	−	−	−	−	1–7
4, 14	+	+	−				−	−	−	−	−	−	−	2–7
9	+	+	−				−	−	−	−	*	−		2–6
11	+	+	−				−	−	−	−	−	*		2–6
54	+	+	−	−		−					−	−	−	2–7
124, 150	+	+	−	−	−	−					−	−	−	2–7
2	/	−	−		−		−	/	/		−	−		2–7
6, 7	+	−	−		−		/	−	−	−	−			2–7
														506–446
Totals[b]	120-23	116-19	113-29	60-28	82-54	13-26	24-28	28-28	35-64	2-15	29-113	31-75	16-64 / 669-566	

$$R = 1 - \frac{73}{952} = 0.923 \qquad S = 1 - \frac{92}{331} = 0.722$$

LEGEND

+ = pro-economic liberalism vote   / = inconsistent vote

− = anti-economic liberalism vote   * = not participating

[a] As listed in the appendixes. Case numbers in bold face type are *W* scale; others are *B* scale.
[b] Respondent totals include *all* nonunanimous *E* scale cases.

are five illiberal inconsistencies. Because of this, plus Schubert's finding that he ranked seventh in the 1960 term with a score of —0.40,[6] it is not unlikely that Stewart is at present considerably less liberal in his response to E than during his first two terms on the Court.

Substantiation of the presence of E as a variable dominating much of the Court's behavior not only establishes the fact of significant continuity in the decision-making in E-scale items, but it also provides additional evidence that the Court's decision-making is reducible to a small number of variables. How small a number is graphically shown by Schubert in his analysis of decision-making in the 1960 term. Using only three major variables—a C scale (civil liberties), an E scale (economic liberalism), and an F scale (fiscal authority)—he scaled 91 per cent of the Court's decisions.[7]

II

The E scale contains two major components: labor union cases and those involving regulation of business. These two subsets (Figures 2 and 3) are exhaustive of the items contained in the E scale. The labor union scale is designated here as the W scale, the business regulation scale as the B scale.[8]

Both subsets produce acceptable coefficients of reproducibility and scalability, with those on the W scale appreciably higher than those on the B scale. Indeed, the coefficient of scalability on B is lower than that on E (0.697 in comparison with 0.722), while the reproducibility coefficient is virtually identical for both B and E. After the set of E cases has been partitioned into the B and W subsets, a total of five E inconsistencies disappear, all of which are in W cases: Minton's votes in Nos. 15 and 21, Burton's in No. 49, Clark's in No. 78, and Stewart's in No. 76.

Figure 2. The W Scale

Case Nos.	Scale Scores →	1.00	0.84	0.61	0.12	-0.06	-0.10	-0.10	-0.18	-0.18	-0.33	-0.41	-0.45	-0.73	
	Scale Positions →	51	47	41	28½	24	23	23	21	21	17	15	14	7	
	Justices →	Do	Bl	Wa	Br	Cl	Bu	Re	St	Ja	Mi	Fr	Ha	Wh	Totals
2		/	+	+		+	+	+		+	+	+			8-1
8		+	/	+		+	+	+		*	+	+			7-1
25		+	+	+		+	+	+			+	/	*		7-1
40, 41, 42		+	*	+	+	+	+					/	+	+	7-1
74		+	+	+	+	+			*			/	+	+	7-1
59		+	+	*	+	+			*			*	+	−	5-1
72, 79		+	+	+	+	+			+			+	+	−	8-1
85, 86		+	*	+	+	+			+			+	+	−	7-1
57		+	+	+	+	+			/			+	+	−	7-2
80		+	+	+	+	+			+			/	+	−	7-2
83		+	+	+	+	+			/			+	−	/	7-2
32		+	+	+	*	+	+	+				−	−		6-2
27		+	+	+		/	+	+			+	−	−		6-3

Figure 2 continued on page 85

Figure 2. The W Scale (continued)

Case Nos. Justices	Do	Bl	Wa	Br	Cl	Bu	Re	St	Ja	Mi	Fr	Ha	Wh	Totals
15	+	+	+		+	+	+			−	−	*		6–2
21	+	+	+		+	+	+			−	−	−		6–3
70	+	/	+	+	/			+			/	/	−	6–3
75	+	+	+	+	+			+			−	−	−	6–3
76	+	+	+	+	+		−				−	/	−	6–3
49	+	+	+	+	/	+				−	−	−		5–4
39	+	+	+	/	+	−				−	−		/	5–4
78	+	+	+	+	−			−			−	/	−	5–4
77	+	+	+	+	−			−			−	−	−	4–5
71	/	+	+	+	−			−			−	−	−	3–6
13	+	+	+		−	−	−				−	−	*	3–5
23, 28	+	+	+		−	−	−			−	−	−		3–6
34	+	+	+	−	−	−	−				−	−		3–6
44	+	+	+	−	−	−					−	−	*	3–5
46, 53, 55	+	+	+	−	−	−					−	−	−	3–6
50, 51	+	*	+	−	−	−					−	−	−	2–6
60, 66, 67	+	+	+	−	−			−			−	−	−	3–6
82	+	+	+	−	−			−			−	*	−	3–5
1	+	+	−		−	−	−		−	−	/			3–6
63	+	+	−		−	−		−			/	−	−	3–6
4	+	+	−		−	−	−		−	−	−			2–7
9	+	+	−		−	−	−	*	−	−				2–6
11	+	+	−		−	−	−			−	−	*		2–6
54	+	+	−	−	−	−					−	−	−	2–7
6, 7	+	−	−		−	−	−		−	/	−			2–7
37	+	−	−	−	−	−					−	−	*	1–7
68	+	−	−	−	−			−			−	−	−	1–8
														230–208
Totals	49-2	38-6	40-10	19-16	21-30	11-19	7-10	7-12	1-4	6-9	11-39	14-25	6-26	230-208

$$R = 1 - \frac{19}{324} = 0.941 \qquad S = 1 - \frac{26}{118} = 0.780$$

LEGEND

+ = pro-labor union vote	/ = inconsistent vote
− = anti-labor union vote	* = not participating

Not only does the B scale contain a higher proportion (66 per cent) of the E inconsistencies than does W (51 per cent) in relation to its portion of E cases—61 inconsistencies in 93 items, as compared with 26 in 51 items; B also contains the bulk of the E-scale items containing multiple inconsistencies. There are 11 multiple inconsistency cases in B, containing 28 inconsistent votes. In W, there are only three items with more than a single inconsistency. Eight inconsistencies appear in these three items.

Figure 3. The B Scale

	Do	Bl	Wa	Br	Cl	St	Mi	Re	Bu	Ja	Fr	Ha	Wh	Totals
Scale Scores	0.89	0.74	0.61	0.51	0.40	0.16	0.13	−0.10	−0.40	−0.66	−0.68	−0.70	−0.85	
Scale Positions	88	81	75	70	65	54	52½	42	28	16	15	14	7	
Case Nos. / Justices	Do	Bl	Wa	Br	Cl	St	Mi	Re	Bu	Ja	Fr	Ha	Wh	*Totals*
35	/	+	+		+		+	+	+		+			7–1
41	/	*	+		+		+	+	+		+	+		7–1
66, 67	/	+	+	*	+			*	+		+	+		6–1
87, 90	+	+	+	+	+				+		/	+	+	8–1
100	/	+	+	+	+				+		+	+	+	8–1
117	+	+	+	+	+	*					+	+	−	7–1
143	+	+	+	+	+	+					+	+	−	8–1
147	/	+	+	+	+	+					/	+	/	7–2
96, 97	+	+	+	+	+				/		+	+	−	7–2
58	/	+	+		+		+	/	+		+	+		7–2
122	+	+	+	+	+	/					+	+	−	7–2
59	/	+	+		+		+	+	+		+	−		7–2
3	+	+	+		+		/	+	+	+	−			7–2
25	+	+	+		+		+	+	+		−	−		7–2
49, 60, 63	+	+	+		+		+	+	+		−	−		7–2
110	+	+	+	+	+				+		−	−	/	7–2
54	/	+	+		+		+	+	+		−	*		6–2
22	/	+	*		+		+	+	+		−	−		5–3
32	+	+	+		+		/	+	+		−			6–2
73	+	+	+	/	+			+	+		−	−		6–3
85	+	/	+	+	+				+		−	−	/	6–3
101	+	+	+	+	*				+		−	−	−	5–3
102	+	+	+	+	+				+		−	−	−	6–3
34, 50	+	+	+		+		+	+			−	−		6–2
62	+	+	+		+		+	+			−	−	−	6–3
80	+	+	+	+	+				−		/	−	−	6–3
99	+	+	/	+	+				−		/	−	/	6–3
106, 109	+	+	+	+	+				−		−	−	/	6–3
123	+	+	+	+	+	/					−	/	−	6–3
126	+	+	+	+	+	*					−	−	/	6–2
142, 144	+	+	+	+	+	+					−	−	−	6–3
114, 120	+	+	+	+	+	*					−	−	−	5–3
27	/	+	+	/			+	+	−	*	/			5–3
44	+	+	+		+		/	−	−		/	/		6–3
46	+	+	+		+		+	−	−		−	*		5–3
61	/	+	+		+		+	−	−		/	−		5–4
75	+	+	+	+	+				−		−	−	*	5–3
81	+	+	+	+	*				−		−	*	*	4–2
Five cases[a]	+	+	+	+	+				−		−	−	−	5–4
116	/	/	+	+	+	+					−	/	−	5–4
127	+	+	+	+	/	+					−	−	−	5–4
133	+	+	+	+	+	−					*	−	−	5–3
Five cases[b]	+	+	+	+	+	−					−	−	−	5–4

Figure 3. The B Scale (continued)

Case Nos. Justices	Do	Bl	Wa [a]	Br	Cl	St	Mi	Re	Bu	Ja	Fr	Ha	Wh	Totals
45, 56	+	+	+		+		−	/	−		−	−		5–4
132	+	+	+	/	+	−					−	−	−	4–5
19, 20	+	+	+		+		−	−	−	−	−			4–5
92, 93, 94	+	+	+	+	−			−			−	−	−	4–5
69	/	+	+	*	−			−	−		−	−		2–6
9	/	+	+		*		−	−	−	*	−			2–5
10	+	+	+		−		−	−	−	−	−			3–6
64	+	+	+		*		−	−	−		−	*		3–4
74	+	+	+	−	*			−	−		−	−		3–5
76	+	+	+	−	−			−			−	−	*	3–5
115	+	+	+	−	*	−			−		−	−	−	3–5
16	+	+	−		−		/	*	−	*	−			3–4
18	+	*	−		*		/	−	/	−	−			3–4
5	*	+	−		−		−	−	−	−	−			1–7
14	+	+	−		−		−	−	−	−	−			2–7
124, 150	+	+	−	−	−	−					−	−	−	2–7
2	/	−	−		−		−	/	/	−	−			2–7
38, 42	+	−	−		−		−	−	−		−	*		1–7
88, 108	+	−	−	−	−			−			−	−	−	1–8
135	+	−	−	−	*	−					−	*	−	1–6
140	+	−	−	−	−	−					−	−	−	1–8
6, 21	−	−	−		−		−	/	−	−	−			1–8
52	−	−	−		−		−	−	−		/	−		1–8
55	−	−	−		−		−	−	−		−	/		1–8
84	−	/	−	−	−			−			−	−	−	1–8
														439–358
Totals	71-21	78-13	73-19	41-12	61-24	6-14	18-19	21-18	24-45	1-11	18-74	17-50	10-38	439-358

$$R = 1 - \frac{49}{628} = 0.922 \qquad S = 1 - \frac{61}{201} = 0.697$$

LEGEND

+ = anti-business vote   / = inconsistent vote
− = pro-business vote   * = not participating

[a]Case Nos. 78, 82, 98, 104, 105.
[b]Case Nos. 146, 149, 151, 156, 157.

One plausible explanation for the multiple inconsistency cases might be that in the B scale cases other variables in addition to economic liberalism are manifest. Examination reveals the presence of such multi-issue factors: six involve the existence or exercise of state regulatory power (Nos. 27, 61, 85, 99, 123, and 147), with three of these items (Nos. 27, 85, and 99) possessing the added distinction of being among the five nonunanimous B cases in which support of business and the exercise of state regulatory power *coincide*.[9] If we assume that for most justices the attitude of favoring state regulatory power coincides with an attitude of relative lack of sympathy for laissez faire, and vice-versa, it is easy to see that such justices experience no conflict when state power and business claims are opposed to each other. But when they coincide in a given case, choice between them is inescapable; and one possible explanation for the inconsistencies in this small subset of cases is that the state power variable was dominant for justices voting inconsistently, with anti-business justices voting deferentially to state regulatory power, while normally pro-business justices—the economic conservatives such as Frankfurter and Whittaker—voted against state regulatory power.

Of the remaining five *B* items containing more than a single inconsistency, only one appears clearly multivariate. No. 116 presented a criminal offense under I.C.C. regulations. Two of the three inconsistencies herein were votes by Black and Douglas, who were forced to choose between supporting economic or civil libertarianism. The latter proved dominant, causing their response to *E* to be negative. No. 2 may perhaps be conceived as a multivariate item, at least for the three justices voting inconsistently. The case involved the application of the Sherman Act to professional baseball, and this item, along with two of the other three antitrust cases (Nos. 32 and 73) involving professional athletics, contains five of the inconsistent votes cast in the nonunanimous antitrust cases. These inconsistencies may be due to attitudes toward professional athletics and/or the authority (or lack thereof) which *Federal Baseball Club* v. *National League,* 259 U.S. 200 (1922), has as a precedent. In the remaining 14 nonunanimous antitrust items, only two inconsistent votes appear.[10] Of the other three items with multi-inconsistencies, one (No. 18) concerned disagreement between the majority and minority over the nature of the issue before the Court for decision.

Two justices, Douglas and Frankfurter, together produced over 40 per cent (36 of 87) of the total inconsistencies in the two component scales. Douglas was much more inconsistent in *B* than in *W;* while Frankfurter was high in inconsistencies in both scales. Warren, on the other hand, cast only one inconsistent vote out of a total of 142 participations in both scales—and here he voted in support of California, like a true native son of the Golden West.[11] Burton and Reed were perfectly consistent in their *W* scale responses, while together they account for ten inconsistent responses to the *B* scale.

In responding to the variable of economic liberalism in the *W* and *B* components of *E,* the justices concord highly in rank as Table 1 shows. Rank position in *B* is unchanged from that in *E,* while *W* shows shifting only among those in the middle ranks (6–10); indeed, the rank order, for those who remain incumbents in early 1962, is identical for all three scales, except for Stewart. This demonstrates the high positive correlation between the attitudes of most justices toward labor and business; the rank correlation (τ) between *B* and *W* is $+0.857$, which is highly significant $(P < 0.0001)$. In other words, the interconsistency of these two sets of attitudes is sufficiently high that we can readily combine them to comprise a single set of attitudes toward the paravariable, economic liberalism.

TABLE 1

Concordance of Attitudes toward Business Regulation, Labor Regulation, and Economic Liberalism

Justices	SCORE ON			RANK ON		
	B Scale	W Scale	E Scale	B Scale	W Scale	E Scale
Do	0.89	1.00	0.93	1	1	1
Bl	0.74	0.84	0.78	2	2	2
Wa	0.61	0.61	0.61	3	3	3
Br	0.51	0.12	0.38	4	4	4
Cl	0.40	−0.06	0.25	5	5	5
St	0.16	−0.18	0.08	6	8½	6
Mi	0.13	−0.33	0.06	7	10	7
Re	−0.10	−0.10	−0.11	8	6½	8
Bu	−0.40	−0.10	−0.35	9	6½	9
Ja	−0.66	−0.18	−0.57	10	8½	10
Fr	−0.68	−0.41	−0.58	11	11	11
Ha	−0.70	−0.45	−0.61	12	12	12
Wh	−0.85	−0.73	−0.81	13	13	13

$C = 0.966 \quad P < 0.001$

The only attitudinal differences of sufficient magnitude to bring about rank order changes in W (apart from the two pairs of ties) are Stewart's and Minton's relative antipathy toward labor unions, in comparison to the attitudes of these justices toward B. Brennan and Clark are also conspicuously more sympathetic to business regulation than to labor unions, while the opposite is true of Burton, Jackson, Frankfurter, and Harlan, although the rank order of all of these justices with respect to each other is the same on both scales. Also noteworthy are the extremity of the views of Douglas, Black, and Whittaker, and the consistency of the manifest attitudes of Warren and Reed, in both scales.

In both the W and B scales, the division between pro and con cases coincides almost precisely with Clark's breakpoint, since Clark is the fifth most liberal justice on both scales. It is not too much to say that on issues of economic liberalism, as Clark went, so went the Court. The proportion of pro decisions in both scales reflects, therefore, Clark's significantly greater sympathy for the regulation of business than for labor unions: two-thirds of the B scale cases were decided as pros, while the Court reached a liberal result in only half of the W items (Table 2). The influence of the less extreme justices in determining the outcome of split decisions is further attested to by the fact that there were more B than W pros, notwithstanding the circumstance that the two most liberal justices, like the five least liberal ones, all show relatively greater sympathy for labor unions than for governmental regulation of business. However, the difference in the proportions of pro decisions for the two scales is reduced when unanimous decisions also are taken into consideration (Table 2). The proportion of pro decisions, for both split and unanimous cases, is 70 per cent for B and 63 per cent for W; both are high, but the difference is now only 7 per cent instead of 18 per cent. The tendency to decide all B cases liberally is highly statistically significant ($P<0.001$), while the corresponding but lesser tendency for W cases is also significant ($P<0.020$).

Before turning to the subcomponents of B, a final point should be noted. In Guttman theory, the normal expectation is that inconsistent responses will tend to congregate in the vicinity of the respondents' breakpoints, with intensity of feeling strongest at the tails of the scale, the first principal component of which is conceived of as (mathematically speaking) having a U or J shape.[12] The expectation, then, is that intensity of attitude in the tails will strongly reinforce *consistency* in voting in the tails. In none of our

TABLE 2

Proportion of Pro-Liberal Decisions and Number of Split and Unanimous Decisions, B, W, and E Scales

	B	W	E
Split	0.67 / 93	0.49 / 51	0.60 / 144
Unanimous	0.76 / 62	0.83 / 35	0.78 / 97
Total	0.70 / 155	0.63 / 86	0.68 / 241

scales, however, does this prove true. Inconsistencies are not grouped about the justices' "zone of indecision," while intensity in the tails is apparently no more pronounced than in the remainder of the scales. In the E scale, only two inconsistencies fall within four votes of the justices' breakpoints: Whittaker's vote in No. 147 and Frankfurter's in No. 80. These two votes also appear as inconsistencies in the B and the W scale respectively. As for the outer ranges of the scale, 49 per cent of the E inconsistencies occur in items with less than three dissents. In the W and B subsets, 50 and 51 per cent, respectively, of the inconsistent votes are found in items with less than three dissents.[13]

There is no apparent difference, in terms of subject categories, between cases in the middle and those in the tails of the E scale. It would appear that, at least for this sample of economic liberalism cases, if Supreme Court justices *do* feel more intensely about their responses in cases where the division of the Court is one-sided, there is no consequent reinforcement of their attitudes toward the value to a sufficient degree to increase the *consistency* of their responses. In lieu of an adequate psychological explanation, we can, however, suggest the possibility that there may be a *sociological* factor which causes the justices to compensate for their personal indecision in the center range of the scale by affiliating with the blocs with which they are normally aligned. Whether or not this be true requires identification of such blocs, a task which has not been undertaken in this study.

In any event, even if such blocs do exist, their presence would not explain the numerous inconsistencies in the tails. By way of a final hypothesis, reference may be had to Douglas' cryptic remark that "the right to dissent is the only thing that makes life tolerable for a judge of an appellate court."[14] If such compulsion should be shown to mark the behavior of members of the Court, it would be sensible to assume that release would be sought in cases in which the compulsive vote was not crucial to the outcome of the decision.

III

In the remainder of this chapter attention is focused upon two values which, from a legalistic standpoint, are generally considered to be significant in judicial decision-making: considerations of federalism and deference to administrative agency decision-making. We concern ourselves first with considerations of federalism.

The specific question we ask is whether or not there is a difference in the attitudes of the justices toward the control of business activity by national as distinguished from state law? In order to answer this question, it is necessary first of all to partition the 93 B-scale items into state and national subsets. Five cases that involve both state and national control must be removed (Nos. 16, 27, 42, 104, and 105). Inspection of the remaining B-scale items reveals cases in which there is governmental action (a) in opposition to business and (b) in support of business. The bulk of the items are those in which government action is opposed to business. Indeed, there are too few cases involving either state or national regulation in support of business to allow scaling them.[15] Hence, in order to focus as sharply as possible upon the federalism variable, three cases (Nos. 22, 85, and 99) in which state regulatory action supports business interests must be excluded. Similarly, 14 national regulatory action cases also must be excluded: nine items in which national action supports business (Nos. 44, 49, 56, 76, 87, 88, 106, 115, and 140), and five cases in which the government is not a party (Nos. 14, 46, 78, 82, and 146). This leaves us with 18 state items and 53 national items in which regulation is opposed to business.

Since the data allow us to compare only those differences in attitudes toward state and national regulation in opposition to business, we can say nothing about: (a) differences in attitudes toward state control when in support and when in opposition to business; (b) differences in attitudes toward national control when in support and when in opposition to business; or (c) differences in attitudes toward state and national control in support of business. What can be compared—differences in attitudes toward state and national regulation in opposition to business—is presented in Figures 4 and 5. Figure 4 is the state subset, Figure 5 the national.

In the pair of subscales, attitudes toward business remain dominant. The R and S coefficients are higher for both subscales than for the B scale. The court upheld a slightly lower percentage of the state cases in which state regulation opposed business (61 per cent) than was true for the national government's anti-business regulatory efforts (68 per cent).[16] Since the Court is more deferential to national than to state regulation of business, and there is a high positive correlation between the state and national sub-scales ($\tau = +.693$, $P<0.00076$), states' rights sentiments can be considered to have no more than a slight influence upon the attitudes of some individual justices in cases where there is opposition between state regulation and business interests.

Figure 4.　State Regulation of Business

Case Nos.	Scale Scores:													
	0.78	0.67	0.56	0.44	0.39	0.17	-0.11	-0.11	-0.11	-0.44	-0.67	-0.72	-1.00	
	Scale Positions:													
	16	15	14	13	12½	10½	8	8	8	5	3	2½	0	
	Justices: Do	Bl	Wa	Cl	Br	Mt	Ha	Re	Bu	Fr	St	Ja	Wh	Totals
143	+	+	+	+	+		+			+	+		−	8–1
147	/	+	+	+	+		+			/	+		/	7–2
96, 97	+	+	+	+	+		+	/	+				−	7–2
122	+	+	+	+	+		+			+	−		−	7–2
25	+	+	+	+		+		+	+	−		−		7–2
54	/	+	+	+		+	*	+	+	−				6–2
123	+	+	+	+	+		+		−		−		−	6–3
126	+	+	+	+	+		−			−	*		/	6–2
61	/	+	+	+		+	−	−	−	/				5–4
98	+	+	+	+	+		−		−	−	−			5–4
19, 20	+	+	+	+	−		−	−	−		−			4–5
10	+	+	+	−	−		−	−	−		−			3–6
150	+	+	−	−	−		−		−		−		−	2–7
38	+	−	−	−		−	*	−	−		−			1–7
21	−	−	−	−		−		/	−	−		−		1–8
84	−	/	−	−	−		−		−	−			−	1–8
														87–72
Totals	13-5	16-2	14-4	13-5	8-2	3-5	6-5	3-5	2-10	5-13	2-3	0-5	2-8	87-72

$$R = 1 - \frac{9}{124} = 0.927 \qquad S = 1 - \frac{11}{40} = 0.725$$

LEGEND

+ = pro-state regulation, anti-business vote　　　　　　　− = anti-state regulation, pro-business vote

The three most extreme anti-business justices (Douglas, Black, and Warren) occupy the extreme liberal positions in both Figure 4 and Figure 5, Whittaker, the most extreme pro-business of all the members of the Warren Court, occupies the lowest position on both scales. The most pronounced shifts in rank order were those of Harlan, who—alone among the justices—showed considerably more sympathy for state than for national regulation, and Reed, Stewart, and Jackson, all of whom appeared to be more tolerant of national regulation. But Harlan's higher score on Figure 4 results exclusively from his $E+$ vote in No. 123—a multiple inconsistency case in the B scale, where this vote of Harlan's is one of the inconsistencies. And Reed's advance from an eighth place tie in Figure 4 (he was also ranked eighth in the B scale) to fifth position in the national scale is due solely to a single vote in a national case, No. 45, and this vote appears as an inconsistency in the B scale. Similarly, Stewart's low score on the state subscale is the result of only two votes (in Nos. 122 and 123), both of which appear as inconsistencies in the B scale. Jackson's higher scale score on the national scale is also the result of a single vote (in No. 3), although this was Jackson's only anti-business vote in the set of B cases. Clearly, we are justi-

Figure 5. National Regulation of Business

Case Nos.	Scale Scores 0.89	0.77	0.66	0.57	0.43	0.40	0.13	0.04	0.02	−0.36	−0.66	−0.70	−0.77	Totals
Scale Positions	50	47	44	41½	38	37	30	27½	27	17	9	8	6	
Justices	Do	Bl	Wa	Br	Re	Cl	St	Mi	Ja	Bu	Fr	Ha	Wh	
35	/	+	+		+	+		+		+	+			7–1
41	/	*	+		+	+		+		+	+	+		7–1
66, 67	/	+	+	*	*	+				+	+	+		6–1
90	+	+	+	+		+				+	/	+	+	8–1
100	/	+	+	+		+				+	+	+	+	8–1
117	+	+	+	+		+	*			+	+	−		7–1
58	/	+	+	/		+		+		+	+	+		7–2
59	/	+	+		+	+		+		+	+	−		7–2
3	+	+	+		+	+	/		+	+	−			7–2
60, 63	+	+	+		+	+		+		+	−	−		7–2
110	+	+	+	+		+				+	−	−	/	7–2
32	+	+	+		+	+	/			+	−			6–2
73	+	+	+	/	+	+				+	−	−		6–3
101	+	+	+	+		*				+	−	−	−	5–3
102	+	+	+	+		+				+	−	−	−	6–3
34, 50	+	+	+		+	+		+		−	−			6–2
62	+	+	+		+	+		+		−	−	−		6–3
80	+	+	+	+		+				−	/	−	−	6–3
109	+	+	+	+		+				−	−	−	/	6–3
142, 144	+	+	+	+	+	+				−	−	−		6–3
114, 120	+	+	+	+	+	*				−	−	−		5–3
75	+	+	+	+	+					−	−	−	*	4–2
81	+	+	+	+	*					−	−	*	*	4–2
116	/	/	+	+		+	+			−	/	−		5–4
127	+	+	+	+		/	+			−	−	−		5–4
133	+	+	+	+	+	−				*	−	−		5–3
Four cases[a]	+	+	+	+	+	−				−	−	−		5–4
45	+	+	+		+	+	−			−	−	−		5–4
132	+	+	+	/	+	−				−	−	−		5–4
92, 93, 94	+	+	+	+	−					−	−	−	−	4–5

Figure 5 continued on page 94

Figure 5. National Regulation of Business (continued)

Case Nos. / Justices	Do	Bl	Wa	Br	Re	Cl	St	Mi	Ja	Bu	Fr	Ha	Wh	Totals
69	/	+	+	*	−	−				−	−	−		2–6
9	/	+	+		−	*		−	*	−	−			2–5
64	+	+	+		−	*		−		−	−	*		3–4
74	+	+	+	−	−	*				−	−	−		3–5
18	+	*	−		−	*		/	−	/	−			3–4
5	*	+	−		−	−		−	−	−	−			1–7
124	+	+	−	−		−	−			−	−		−	2–7
2	/	−	−	/	−			−	−	/	−			2–7
108	+	−	−	−		−				−	−	−	−	1–8
135	+	−	−	−	*	−					−	*	−	1–6
6	−	−	−	/	−			−	−	−	−	−		1–8
52	−	−	−		−	−		−		−	/	−		1–8
55	−	−	−		−	−		−		−	−	/		1–8
														254–194
Totals	38-14	44-7	44-9	24-6	14-9	34-12	4-8	10-10	1-4	18-20	10-42	9-31	4-22	254-194

$$R = 1 - \frac{21}{349} = 0.940 \qquad S = 1 - \frac{30}{113} = 0.735$$

LEGEND

+ = pro-national regulation, anti-business vote

− = anti-national regulation, pro-business vote

aCase Nos. 149, 151, 156, 157.

fied in reposing very little confidence in changes in scale scores and shifts in rank that are functions of votes in only one or two cases—and particularly is this so when such votes appear to be inconsistent in the scale for the combined set of *B* cases.

It is interesting to note that greatest support for state regulation of business is provided by Clark, plus the so-called "judicial activists"—Douglas, Black, Warren, and Brennan. As a group, these five justices supported state action in all but 18 of their 82 votes in Figure 4. Strongest support came from Black and Brennan. The former upheld state business regulation in 89 per cent of his votes, Brennan in 80 per cent. Even though (as we assume) the votes of these justices were dominantly motivated by their attitudes toward business, rather than by states' rights considerations as such, the fact remains that their votes *did* support state regulation to a much greater extent than the votes of any of the other Warren Court justices. Consequently, we may conclude that the rather indiscriminate use of Douglas, Black, Warren, and Brennan as *bêtes noires* by states' rights critics of the Court is not supported by either their behavior or that of their colleagues where state regulation of business is concerned.

Conversely, the failure of Frankfurter to manifest greater support for state regulation appears rather anomalous, given his reputed concern for considerations of federalism. Only five of his 18 Figure 4 votes supported state action—an anti-state ratio exceeded only by Burton, Whittaker, and Jackson. Although Frankfurter may be states' rights oriented when business interests are *not* present, when there is conflict between state regulations and support of business interests, Frankfurter votes in favor of business.

IV

We turn our attention now to the business cases involving regulation by national administrative agencies. Since we no longer are concerned with national-state differences, nor are we distinguishing—at least initially—between government opposition to business and nongovernmental opposition or governmental support, the 19 cases deleted from the national sample (Figure 5) may be restored.[17]

The first question we may ask is whether there is a difference in judicial attitudes toward business depending upon whether the trial adjudicator was a lower federal court or an administrative agency of the national government? To ask this question, Nos. 16, 27, 42, 104, and 105, which involve both state and national regulation, must be added to the administrative subset. The resulting scales reveal not only that business attitudes remain dominant, but also that the rank order of the justices in the two scales correlates highly ($\tau = +0.909$, $P = 0.00003$).[18] Consequently, it is clear that there is no difference of any importance between Supreme Court attitudes toward business in cases which arise in the lower federal courts, and in ones which arise in administrative agencies.

Further analysis of the 35-item set of cases involving regulation by the lower federal courts allows us to partition these into two exhaustive sub-subsets: the 17 items that concern application of the antitrust laws and the 18 that do not.[19] Again business attitudes dominate: the antitrust items produce an R coefficient of 0.950 and an S of 0.720; the non-antitrust cases an R of 0.948 and an S of 0.763. Rank correlation for the two sets of scale scores is also high ($\tau = +0.872$, $P = 0.00005$). In these two scales, Douglas, Black, Warren, Brennan, and Clark scored more anti-business than any other members of the Court; while Frankfurter, Harlan, and Whittaker were most pro-business. These justices were also the most anti- and pro-business, respectively, in the administrative agency subset. Hence, our finding remains negative: there is no significant difference in attitudes toward business whether cases arising in the lower federal courts involve application of the antitrust laws or not.

The remainder of our analysis concentrates upon attitudes in the administrative agency cases. The question we ask is the counterpart of the question asked about the federalism variable; namely, do the attitudes of the justices vary depending upon whether or not national administrative agencies have acted in opposition to or in support of business? To answer the question, the 37 agency cases are partitioned into separate sets containing the 23 cases in which agency action opposed business (Figure 6), and the 14 cases in which agency action supported business (Figure 7). As the coefficients reveal, business attitudes continue to dominate; attitudes toward administrative agency decision-making have no greater influence than do considerations of federalism.

In keeping with its anti-business orientation, the Court upheld 78 per cent

Figure 6. Administrative Agency Decision-Making
in Opposition to Business

Scale Scores	0.91	0.91	0.87	0.87	0.74	0.65	0.39	0.30	-0.09	-0.22	-0.39	-0.39	-0.57	
Scale Positions	22	22	21½	21½	20	19	16	15	10½	9	7	7	5	
Case Nos.[a] / Justices	Do	Mt	Bl	Br	Wa	Cl	Re	St	Ja	Bu	Fr	Ha	Wh	Totals
35	/	+	+		+	+	+			+	+			7–1
41	/	+	*		+	+	+			+	+	+		7–1
66, 67	/		+	*	+	+	*			+	+	+		6–1
100	/		+	+	+	+				+	+	+	+	8–1
117	+		+	+	+	+		*			+	+	–	7–1
58	/	+	+		+	+	/			+	+	+		7–2
60, 63	+	+	+		+	+	+			+	–	–		7–2
34, 50	+	+	+		+	+	+			–	–			6–2
80	+		+	+	+	+				–	/	–	–	6–3
114	+		+	+	+	+	*			–	–	–	–	5–3
144	+		+	+	+	+		+		–	–	–	–	6–3
127	+		+	+	+	/		+		–	–	–	–	5–4
151, 156, 157	+		+	+	+	+		–		–	–	–	–	5–4
132	+		+	/	+	+		–		–	–	–	–	4–5
94	+		+	+	+	–		–		–	–	–	–	4–5
16	+	+	+		–	–	*		*	–	–			3–4
18	+	+	*		–	*	–		–	/	–			3–4
55	–	–	–		–	–	–			–	–	/		1–8
														126–67
Totals	16–7	9–1	20–1	10–1	20–3	18–4	6–3	2–5	0–1	9–5	8–15	7–11	1–10	126–67

$$R = 1 - \frac{6}{137} = 0.956 \qquad\qquad S = 1 - \frac{12}{43} = 0.721$$

LEGEND

+ = pro-agency, anti-business vote   [a]Bold-face cases are I.C.C.
− = anti-agency, pro-business vote

of the anti-business agency decisions as compared with but 43 per cent of the pro-business agency decisions. When unanimously decided items are included, 80 per cent of the anti-business agency decisions were upheld by the Court. This contrasts with a mere 26 per cent of all the pro-business agency decisions. Complementing this picture is the fact that when the Court does

Figure 7. Administrative Agency Decision-Making
in Support of Business

Case Nos.[a]	Scale Scores	1.00 Do	0.57 Bl	0.57 Wa	0.14 Cl	0.14 Br	0.00 Ja	−0.29 St	−0.43 Re	−0.43 Mi	−0.43 Wh	−0.71 Bu	−0.86 Ha	−1.00 Fr	Totals
	Scale Positions	14	11	11	8	8	7	5	4	4	4	2	1	0	
87		+	+	+	+	+					+	+	+	−	8–1
49		+	+	+	+				+	+		+	−	−	7–2
106		+	+	+	+	+				+	−	−	−	/	6–3
27		/	+	+	/	*			+	+	+	−	−	−	5–3
44		+	+	+	+	+			+	−	−	−	/	/	6–3
104, 105		+	+	+	+	+					−	−	−	−	5–4
56		+	+	+	+	+			/		−	−	−	−	5–4
69		/	+	+	−	*		−			−	−	−	−	2–6
76		+	+	+	−	−					*	−	−	−	3–5
115		+	+	+	*	−			−		−		−	−	3–5
42		+	−	−	−				−		−	−	*	−	1–7
88		+	−	−	−				−		−	−	−	−	1–8
140		+	−	−	−			−			−	−	−	−	1–8
															58–63
Totals		12-2	11-3	11-3	7-6	4-4	0-0	0-2	3-3	2-3	2-5	2-10	2-10	2-12	58-63

$$R = 1 - \frac{7}{86} = 0.919 \qquad S = 1 - \frac{7}{31} = 0.774$$

LEGEND

+ = anti-agency, anti-business vote   [a]Bold-face cases are I.C.C.
− = pro-agency, pro-business vote

vote to reverse agency decision-making, it overturns pro-business agency decisions much more frequently than those which are anti-business. Of the thirteen reversals in Figures 6 and 7, eight (62 per cent) reversed pro-business agency action. The proportion increases to 68 per cent when unanimous decisions are added. Examination of the various justices' votes in Figures 6 and 7 shows Douglas to be most active in seeking to reverse agency decision-making, with 19 of his 37 votes being cast for reversal. Next to Douglas stands Frankfurter, who voted to reverse on 17 occasions. But unlike Douglas, Frankfurter's votes for reversal show an unusually high degree of consistency: 15 of his 17 votes (88 per cent) were directed at reversing an *anti*-business agency decision. By comparison, only 63 per cent of Douglas' reversal votes were directed at pro-business agency decisions. Indeed, only Black was more extreme than Frankfurter in his votes for reversal, but in the opposite direction, of course, with eleven of twelve (92 per cent) being directed against *pro*-business agency actions. Black also voted for reversal only two-thirds as often as did Frankfurter.

Although Frankfurter is staunchly restraint-oriented in those relatively few cases in which the propriety of exercising Supreme Court power appears in isolation from economic liberalism and civil liberties values,[20] his voting behavior in the cases involving administrative agency regulation of business is hardly compatible with the image his apologists would have us accept, of which the following statement is characteristic:

Justice Frankfurter does indeed have a "scale of values." He leans heavily toward the view that basic policy issues should be left for the politically responsible agencies of government.[21]

TABLE 3

Judicial Support of National Administrative Agency Decision-Making

Justices*	I. Agency Pro-Business Ratio Anti-Agency	N	II. Agency Anti-Business Ratio Pro-Agency	N	III. Agency Deference Ratio (II–I)
Do	0.86	14	0.70	23	−0.16
Bl	0.79	14	0.95	21	+0.16
Wa	0.79	14	0.87	23	+0.08
Br	0.50	8	0.91	11	+0.41
Cl	0.54	13	0.82	22	+0.28
St	0.00	2	0.29	7	+0.29
Mi	0.40	5	0.90	10	+0.50
Re	0.50	6	0.67	9	+0.17
Bu	0.17	12	0.64	14	+0.47
Fr	0.14	14	0.35	23	+0.21
Ha	0.17	12	0.39	18	+0.22
Wh	0.29	7	0.09	11	−0.20

*Jackson is not included, since he participated in only one of these cases. The other justices are listed in the rank order in which they voted against business in the combined set of 37 agency cases.

Table 3 specifies the degree to which deference to agency decision-making appears to influence the attitudes of the various justices toward business. The data in Column I of Table 3 is drawn from the justices' response in Figure 7, and the ratios measure the extent to which the justices reject the *pro*-business decision-making of the administrative agencies. As Column I reveals, the anti-business justices were least supportive, voting most frequently for reversal of the agencies' pro-business decisions. At the other extreme, Frankfurter, Harlan, and Whittaker—in keeping with their pro-business attitudes— were very much in agreement with the agencies in the items scaled in Figure 7. Whittaker's higher anti-agency ratio than those of his conservative colleagues is reflected in his advance in rank position in Figure 7 above Burton, Harlan, and Frankfurter. Whittaker's shift, however, hinges upon a single vote, in No. 106, where his anti-business vote had heretofore appeared as an inconsistency.

In support of anti-business agency decisions, the picture is reversed. Column II of Table 3 shows that the anti-business liberals are considerably more in agreement with agencies than their pro-business colleagues. However, Minton also deferred to anti-business agency decisions in nine of his 10 votes; he is the only justice whose ranking in Figure 6 is grossly at variance with his response in the other subsets of the B scale. Except for Figure 6, his attitude toward business fell in the neutral response category. But in Figure 6 he scores extremely anti-business, tied with Douglas for first rank with a score of $+0.91$, although his shift in rank is based upon his votes in only two cases, Nos. 16 and 18, which appeared as inconsistencies in the B scale (Figure 3). Only in the voting of Minton, Burton, and Brennan do we find evidence in Column III of marginally significant deference to agency decision-making.[22] Of some interest is the fact that the two justices at the opposite ends of the scale in Figure 6—Douglas and Whittaker—both show, in Column III, slight *negative* deference to agencies. It seems doubtful, however, that such small differences should be attributed to anything other than chance variation, given the exceptionally strong orientation of both of these justices toward the B value, although in Douglas' case an obvious *statistical* explanation lies in his five solo dissents in favor of business and against agencies—all of which votes appear as inconsistencies—as shown in Figure 6.[23] These inconsistencies do not, of course, affect Douglas' high score on that scale.

To this point, our analysis of the administrative agency cases has focused upon the effects resulting from agency support of and opposition to business. We now propose to divide the 37 agency items into those involving the Interstate Commerce Commission and those involving the other agencies. We do this to determine whether differences in attitudes toward the agencies themselves have a significant effect upon attitudes toward business.[24] However, not only do business attitudes dominate (in the I.C.C. subset, the R coeffi-

TABLE 4

Judicial Support of I.C.C. and Other Agencies' Decision-Making

Justices	I. *I.C.C.* Ratio Pro-I.C.C.	N	II. *Other Agencies* Ratio Pro-Agencies	N	III. *Deference to I.C.C.* (I–II)
Do	0.32	19	0.67	18	−0.35
Bl	0.50	18	0.82	17	−0.32
Wa	0.47	19	0.78	18	−0.31
Br	0.60	10	0.89	9	−0.29
Cl	0.61	18	0.76	17	−0.15
St	0.50	2	0.50	6	0.00
Mi	0.67	6	0.89	9	−0.22
Re	0.43	7	0.75	8	−0.32
Ja	0.00	1	—	0	—
Bu	0.75	16	0.64	11	+0.11
Fr	0.74	19	0.33	18	+0.41
Ha	0.72	18	0.33	12	+0.39
Wh	0.56	9	0.11	9	+0.45

cient is 0.926 and S is 0.755; in the non-I.C.C. set, R is 0.953 and S is 0.724), but attitudes toward the I.C.C. and other agencies vary less than when, as in Table 3 and in comparing Figures 6 and 7, differences between agency support and nonsupport of business is examined. As between the I.C.C. and non-I.C.C. subsets, the τ coefficient is $+0.733$, and $P = 0.00050$; while between the scales of Figures 6 and 7, τ is $+0.622$ and $P = 0.00298$.

In keeping with the well-known pro-business orientation of the I.C.C.,[25] the pro-business justices as a group are most deferential to it, as Table 4 reveals.[26] Least deferential are the liberals. The latter, however, manifested far greater deference to the decision-making of the other agencies than did the conservatives, since the other agencies are much more anti-business oriented than the I.C.C.

V

Our analysis has shown that a single politically defined value dominated the voting behavior of the Warren Court justices in the 155 cases regulatory of business that were formally decided during the 1953-1959 Terms. That is, the justices' attitudes toward business were shown to be part of a larger value, defined as economic liberalism, in which the liberally-oriented justice is anti-business, pro-competition, and pro-union. Clark was the Court's equipoise, with Douglas, Black, Warren, and Brennan occupying positions to his left. Most conservative were Frankfurter, Harlan, and Whittaker. In its decision-making, the Court was shown to be liberally oriented—somewhat more so in its regulation of business than of labor unions.

The impact of other values upon the operation of business sentiment—i.e., considerations of federalism, deference to courts versus administrative agencies of the national government, antitrust and non-antitrust cases, attitudes toward the I.C.C. as opposed to the other national administrative agencies regulating business, and deference to administrative expertise—was demonstrated to be very small. Judicial choice in these cases continued to hinge upon the justices' attitudes toward business. Attitudes other than business sentiment produced some effects in the response of individual justices in only a few isolated instances: Harlan reacted favorably to states' rights sentiment, and Stewart adversely; while Minton showed deference to administrative expertise.

In conclusion, the scaling of the business regulation cases, and the confirmation that these are a subset of the larger variable of economic liberalism, provides further evidence that the great bulk of the Court's decision-making may be reducible to a small number of attitudinal variables. Earlier work in this direction includes the present writer's scaling of the judicial power cases of the Warren Court through the end of the 1960 Term,[27] Ulmer's scaling of the civil liberties decisions of the 1956-1959 Terms,[28] and Schubert's scaling of civil liberties and economic liberalism cases as well as those dealing with monetary conflicts of interest between private individuals and government.[29]

If, as seems likely, further application of psychometric techniques of analysis should demonstrate that the Court does render virtually all its decisions on the basis of the operation of a very few basic attitudes, extensive reinterpretation may be required of the standard explanations of Supreme Court decision-making. Repercussions stemming from psychometric analyses should do no damage to the reputation and prestige of the Court, however. For, psychologically speaking, a basic function of law is to meet the need of man for a feeling of stability in the flux of life. Thus if the individual members of the Court are shown to behave with rigorous consistency in response to a few basic variables, representing a set of public policy dimensions, a condition of stability much more deeply rooted than mere adherence to decisional precedent controls the decision-making of the justices.

NOTES

1. Glendon Schubert, "The 1960-1961 Term of the Supreme Court: A Psychological Analysis," *American Political Science Review*, Vol. 56 (March, 1962), 90-107.

2. I define "formally decided" cases as all those appearing in the first part of the *U.S. Reports* (i.e., antecedent to p. 801 or p. 901 of each volume) which were orally argued. Where a number of cases are gathered together under one opinion of the Court, the case is counted as one formally decided item, provided that each participating justice voted the same way in all of the combined cases. Where one or more justices distinguished between the cases by concurring in some and dissenting in the remainder, the cases are counted compatibly with the smallest whole number necessary to account for the variant behavior of the justice or justices involved.

3. My definition of the E scale appears to be identical with that of Schubert (*op. cit. supra*, note 1), except for his inclusion of workmen's disability compensation cases.

4. Herbert Menzel, "A New Coefficient for Scalogram Analysis," *Public Opinion Quarterly*, Vol. 17 (1953), 268-80.

5. Unanimously decided E items are indicated by an asterisk in the listing in the appendices.

6. Schubert, *op. cit. supra* (note 1), 100.

7. *Ibid.*, 102.

8. In constructing these scales, as well as the subscales of B, the cases are arrayed in the order in which they appear in the E scale.

9. The other two are Nos. 16 and 22, each of which contains a single inconsistency. The five items combined include a total of 10 inconsistencies.

10. Douglas' vote in No. 9, and Whittaker's in No. 109.

11. Cf. Warren's patently inconsistent and anti-civil libertarian vote in the search-and-seizure case, *Irvine* v. *California*, 347 U.S. 128 (1954). Of course, Warren had been attorney general of the State of California before he became its governor.

12. Warren S. Torgerson, *Theory and Methods of Scaling* (New York: Wiley, 1958), pp. 336-38; Edward A. Suchman, "The Intensity Component in Attitude and Opinion Research," in Samuel A. Stouffer, *et al.*, *Measurement and Prediction*, Vol. 4 of Studies in Social Psychology in World War II (Princeton: Princeton University Press, 1950), pp. 213-76.

13. Cases with fewer than three dissents comprise 50 per cent of the E items, 53 per cent of the W items, and 48 per cent of those in B. Hence, about half of the cases in each scale have less than three dissents; and on each scale, inconsistencies are equally divided between cases with one or two dissents and those with three or four dissents.

14. William O. Douglas, *America Challenged* (Princeton: Princeton University Press, 1960), p. 4.

15. Guttman theory requires a minimum of ten computable items in a scale. See Glendon Schubert, *Quantitative Analysis of Judicial Behavior* (Glencoe: The Free Press, 1959), pp. 279-80.

16. This difference becomes more pronounced when unanimous decisions are considered. The Court upheld only 9 of the 17 state anti-business items, as compared with 27 of the 33 national cases in which regulation opposed business interests. Over-all, state action in opposition to business was upheld 57 per cent of the time, while national action in opposition to business was upheld 73 per cent of the time.

17. Nos. 16, 27, 42, 104, and 105, which involved both national and state control; Nos. 44, 49, 56, 76, 87, 88, 106, 115, and 140, in which national action supported business; and Nos. 14, 46, 78, 82, and 146, in which the national government was not a party.

18. The scales have not been reproduced. There are 35 items involving regulation by the national judiciary: Nos. 90, 59, 3, 110, **32, 73, 101,** 102, **62, 109, 120, 142,** 46, 75, 78, **81,** 82, 116, **133,** 146, 149, 45, **92, 93, 9, 64, 74, 5,** 14, **124, 2,** 108, 135, 6, and 52. Thirty-seven cases involve regulation by administrative agencies. These are arrayed in Figures 6 and 7. The judiciary set produces an R of 0.949 and an S of 0.746; the agencies an R of 0.928 and an S of 0.709. Of the judicial items, 63 per cent were decided anti-business, as compared with 70 per cent of the agency cases. No meaningful difference occurs when unanimously decided cases are included: 14 of 17 unanimous judicial regulation cases were decided anti-business, as compared with 23 of the 26 agency items.

19. The 17 antitrust cases are the ones whose numbers are in bold face type in footnote 18; the other 18 cases in the judicial list are not antitrust. Of the antitrust items, 53 per cent were decided anti-business by the Court, as were 72 per cent of the non-antitrust cases. This discrepancy disappears, however, when unanimously decided items are included. All eight antitrust items were decided anti-business, for a cumulative percentage of 68 per cent. Only six of nine non-antitrust unanimous decisions were anti-business, for a cumulative percentage of 70 per cent.

20. Harold J. Spaeth, "Judicial Power as a Variable Motivating Supreme Court Behavior," *Midwest Journal of Political Science,* Vol. 6 (1962), 59-62.

21. Wallace Mendelson, "Communications to the Editor," *American Political Science Review,* Vol. 55 (1961), 884.

22. Using Fisher's exact probability test for Minton and Brennan and chi square for Burton, the statistical probability, that the observed differences between columns I and II are significant, ranges, for these three justices, between 0.07 and 0.09. The probability is considerably higher than .10 for all other justices in the table.

23. Three of the five cases involve issues of governmental fiscal authority; Douglas' votes in these three cases would not appear as inconsistent on Schubert's F scale (note 1, *infra*), which suggests that for Douglas, at least, the issue of fiscal authority dominated the issue of economic liberalism in these cases.

24. There are 19 nonunanimous I.C.C. items; these case numbers are in bold-face type in Figures 6 and 7. The other 18 cases arrayed in Figures 6 and 7 involve the other administrative agencies. Ten of the 19 I.C.C. items were decided pro-business by that agency. By comparison, only 4 of the 18 non-I.C.C. agency cases were decided pro-business by the agencies concerned. Among the unanimous decisions 4 of 6 were decided pro-business by the I.C.C., as compared with only 5 of 20 by the other agencies. Adding together both unanimous and nonunanimous decisions, the I.C.C. decided 56 per cent (14 of 25) pro-business, while the other agencies decided only 24 per cent (9 of 38) pro-business.

25. Cf. C. Herman Pritchett, *The Roosevelt Court; A Study in Judicial Politics and Values, 1937-1947* (New York: Macmillan, 1948), p. 190.

26. The differences between columns I and II are statistically significant for Douglas (chi square, $P < 0.05$) and Frankfurter (chi square, $P < 0.01$), and they are marginally significant for Black and Harlan (chi square, $P < 0.10$) and Whittaker (Fisher, $P = 0.066$).

27. Spaeth, *op. cit. supra* (note 20), pp. 54-82.

28. S. Sidney Ulmer, "Supreme Court Behavior and Civil Rights," *Western Political Quarterly,* Vol. 13 (1960), 288-311; "The Analysis of Behavior Patterns on the United States Supreme Court," *Journal of Politics,* Vol. 22 (1960), 647-652; and "Scaling

Judicial Cases: A Methodological Note," *American Behavioral Scientist,* Vol. 4 (April 1961), 31-34.

29. Schubert, *op. cit. supra* (note 1). As noted above, Schubert found that response to the variables of civil liberties, economic liberalism, and fiscal power motivated behavior in "91 of the 99 split decisions of the 1960 Term . . . 91 per cent of the decisions of the term." *Ibid.* In an earlier study, Schubert also found the F.E.L.A. items to be scalable. *Op. cit. supra* (note 15), pp. 290-297. Schubert now considers the latter to be part of the *E* scale.

Appendix A. Formally Decided Labor Union Cases, 1953-1959 Terms

Note: An asterisk following the case indicates that the decision was unanimous.

1. N.L.R.B. v. Local Union, 346 U.S. 464 (1953)
2. Howell Chevrolet Co. v. N.L.R.B., 346 U.S. 482 (1953)
3. Garner v. Teamsters, 346 U.S. 485 (1953)*
4. Radio Officers' Union v. N.L.R.B., 347 U.S. 17 (1954)
5. United States v. Binghamton Construction Co., 347 U.S. 171 (1954)*
6. United States v. Employing Plasterers Assn., 347 U.S. 186 (1954)
7. United States v. Employing Lathers Assn., 347 U.S. 198 (1954)
8. Capital Service v. N.L.R.B., 347 U.S. 501 (1954)
9. United Workers v. Laburnum Corp., 347 U.S. 656 (1954)
10. Brooks v. N.L.R.B., 348 U.S. 96 (1954)*
11. Westinghouse Salaried Employees v. Westinghouse Corp., 348 U.S. 437 (1955)
12. Weber v. Anheuser-Busch, 348 U.S. 468 (1955)*
13. Clothing Workers v. Richman Brothers, 348 U.S. 511 (1955)
14. Maneja v. Waialua Agricultural Co., 349 U.S. 254 (1955)*
15. Mitchell v. C. W. Vollmer, 349 U.S. 427 (1955)
16. N.L.R.B. v. Warren Co., 350 U.S. 107 (1955)*
17. Teamsters v. N.Y.N.H.&H. R. Co., 350 U.S. 155 (1956)*
18. Steiner v. Mitchell, 350 U.S. 247 (1956)*
19. Mitchell v. King Packing Co., 350 U.S. 260 (1956)*
20. N.L.R.B. v. Coca-Cola Bottling Co., 350 U.S. 264 (1956)*
21. Mastro Plastics v. N.L.R.B., 350 U.S. 270 (1956)
22. United States v. Ryan, 350 U.S. 299 (1956)*
23. United States v. Green, 350 U.S. 415 (1956)
24. Mitchell v. Budd, 350 U.S. 473 (1956)*
25. Mine Workers v. Arkansas Flooring Co., 351 U.S. 62 (1956)
26. N.L.R.B. v. Babcock & Wilcox Co., 351 U.S. 105 (1956)*
27. N.L.R.B. v. Truitt Mfg. Co., 351 U.S. 149 (1956)
28. U.A.W. v. Wisconsin Board, 351 U.S. 266 (1956)
29. Railway Employes v. Hanson, 351 U.S. 225 (1956)*
30. Leedom v. Mine, Mill, and Smelter Workers, 352 U.S. 145 (1956)*
31. Amalgamated Meat Cutters v. N.L.R.B., 352 U.S. 153 (1956)*
32. N.L.R.B. v. Lion Oil Co., 352 U.S. 282 (1957)
33. Pennsylvania R. Co. v. Rychlik, 352 U.S. 480 (1957)*
34. United States v. U.A.W., 352 U.S. 567 (1957)
35. Railroad Trainmen v. C.R.&I. R. Co., 353 U.S. 30 (1957)*

36. N.L.R.B. v. Teamsters, 353 U.S. 87 (1957)*
37. Benz v. Compania Naviera Hidalgo, 353 U.S. 138 (1957)
38. United States v. Carter, 353 U.S. 210 (1957)*
39. Office Employes Union v. N.L.R.B., 353 U.S. 313 (1957)
40. Textile Workers v. Lincoln Mills, 353 U.S. 448 (1957)
41. General Electric Co. v. Local 205, 353 U.S. 547 (1957)
42. Goodall-Sanford v. Textile Workers, 353 U.S. 550 (1957)
43. California v. Taylor, 353 U.S. 553 (1957)*
44. Teamsters v. Vogt, 354 U.S. 284 (1957)
45. Conley v. Gibson, 355 U.S. 41 (1957)*
46. Youngdahl v. Rainfair, 355 U.S. 131 (1957)
47. N.L.R.B. v. U.M.W., 355 U.S. 453 (1958)*
48. Borg-Warner Corp. v. N.L.R.B., 356 U.S. 342 (1958)*
49. N.L.R.B. v. Borg-Warner Corp., 356 U.S. 342 (1958)
50. Machinists v. Gonzales, 356 U.S. 617 (1958)
51. U.A.W. v. Russell, 356 U.S. 634 (1958)
52. Lewis v. N.L.R.B., 357 U.S. 10 (1958)*
53. Carpenters' Union v. N.L.R.B., 357 U.S. 93 (1958)
54. N.L.R.B. v. United Steelworkers, 357 U.S. 357 (1958)
55. N.L.R.B. v. Avondale Mills, 357 U.S. 357 (1958)
56. Hotel Employees v. Leedom, 358 U.S. 99 (1958)*
57. Mitchell v. Lublin, McGaughy, 358 U.S. 207 (1959)
58. Hotel Employees v. Sax Enterprises, 358 U.S. 270 (1959)*
59. Teamsters v. Oliver, 358 U.S. 283 (1959)
60. United States v. Embassy Restaurant, 359 U.S. 29 (1959)
61. San Diego Unions v. Garmon, 359 U.S. 236 (1959)*
62. Mitchell v. Kentucky Finance Co., 359 U.S. 290 (1959)*
63. Felter v. Southern Pacific Co., 359 U.S. 326 (1959)
64. Plumbers' Union v. Door County, 359 U.S. 354 (1959)*
65. N.L.R.B. v. Cabot Carbon Co., 360 U.S. 203 (1959)*
66. Pennsylvania R. Co. v. Day, 360 U.S. 548 (1959)
67. Union Pacific R. Co. v. Price, 360 U.S. 601 (1959)
68. United Steelworkers v. United States, 361 U.S. 39 (1959)
69. Mitchell v. Oregon Frozen Foods, 361 U.S. 231 (1960)*
70. Mitchell v. DeMario Jewelry, 361 U.S. 288 (1960)
71. Oil Workers Union v. Missouri, 361 U.S. 363 (1960)
72. Arnold v. Ben Kanowsky, 361 U.S. 388 (1960)
73. N.L.R.B. v. Deena Artware, 361 U.S. 398 (1960)*
74. Lewis v. Benedict Coal Corp., 361 U.S. 459 (1960)
75. N.L.R.B. v. Insurance Agents' Union, 361 U.S. 477 (1960)
76. N.L.R.B. v. Drivers Local Union, 362 U.S. 274 (1960)
77. Mitchell v. H. B. Zachry, 362 U.S. 310 (1960)
78. Telegraphers v. C.&N.W. R. Co. Co., 362 U.S. 330 (1960)
79. Marine Cooks v. Panama Steamship Co., 362 U.S. 365 (1960)
80. Machinists Local v. N.L.R.B., 362 U.S. 411 (1960)
81. Communications Workers v. N.L.R.B., 362 U.S. 479 (1960)*
82. De Veau v. Braisted, 363 U.S. 144 (1960)
83. Locomotive Engineers v. M-K-T R. Co., 363 U.S. 528 (1960)
84. United Steelworkers v. American Mfg. Co., 363 U.S. 564 (1960)*
85. United Steelworkers v. Warrior & Gulf, 363 U.S. 574 (1960)
86. United Steelworkers v. Enterprise Corp., 363 U.S. 593 (1960)

Appendix B. Formally Decided Business Regulation Cases,
1953-1959 Terms

Note: An asterisk following the case indicates that the decision was unanimous.

 1. A.T.&S.F. R. Co. v. Public Utilities Commission, 346 U.S. 346 (1953)*
 2. Toolson v. New York Yankees, 346 U.S. 356 (1953)
 3. Wilko v. Swan, 346 U.S. 427 (1953)
 4. General Protective Comm. v. S.E.C., 346 U.S. 521 (1954)*
 5. Theatre Enterprises v. Paramount, 346 U.S. 537 (1954)
 6. United States v. Lindsay, 346 U.S. 568 (1954)
 7. Western Air Lines v. C.A.B., 347 U.S. 67 (1954)*
 8. Delta Air Lines v. Summerfield, 347 U.S. 74 (1954)*
 9. Partmar Corp. v. Paramount Corp., 347 U.S. 89 (1954)
10. Kern-Limerick v. Scurlock, 347 U.S. 110 (1954)
11. Michigan-Wisconsin Pipe Line Co. v. Calvert, 347 U.S. 157 (1954)*
12. United States v. Employing Plasterers Assn., 347 U.S. 186 (1954)†
13. United States v. Employing Lathers Assn., 347 U.S. 198 (1954)†
14. Mazer v. Stein, 347 U.S. 201 (1954)
15. Walters v. City of St. Louis, 347 U.S. 231 (1954)*
16. F.P.C. v. Niagara Mohawk Power Co., 347 U.S. 239 (1954)
17. F.C.C. v. American Broadcasting Co., 347 U.S. 284 (1954)*
18. St. Joe Paper Co. v. A.C.L. R. Co., 347 U.S. 298 (1954)
19. Miller Brothers v. Maryland, 347 U.S. 340 (1954)
20. Railway Express Agency v. Virginia, 347 U.S. 359 (1954)
21. Franklin Natl. Bank v. New York, 347 U.S. 373 (1954)
22. Brownell v. Singer, 347 U.S. 403 (1954)
23. United States v. Borden Co., 347 U.S. 514 (1954)*
24. Allen v. Grand Central Aircraft Co., 347 U.S. 535 (1954)*
25. Braniff Airways v. Nebraska Board, 347 U.S. 590 (1954)
26. Secy. of Agriculture v. United States, 347 U.S. 645 (1954)*
27. Phillips Petroleum Co. v. Wisconsin, 347 U.S. 672 (1954)
28. Castle v. Hayes Freight Lines, 348 U.S. 61 (1954)*
29. Watson v. Employers Liability Corp., 348 U.S. 66 (1954)*
30. Moore v. Mead's Fine Bread Co., 348 U.S. 115 (1954)*
31. United States v. Shubert, 348 U.S. 222 (1955)*
32. United States v. Intl. Boxing Club, 348 U.S. 236 (1955)
33. United States v. Guy W. Capps, Inc., 348 U.S. 296 (1955)*
34. S.E.C. v. Drexel & Co., 348 U.S. 341 (1955)
35. United States v. California Eastern Line, 348 U.S. 351 (1955)
36. Williamson v. Lee Optical Co., 348 U.S. 483 (1955)*
37. F.P.C. v. Colorado Interstate Gas Co., 348 U.S. 492 (1955)*
38. Natural Gas Co. v. Panoma Corp., 349 U.S. 44 (1955)
39. Society for Savings v. Bowers, 349 U.S. 143 (1955)*
40. Lawlor v. Natl. Screen Service, 349 U.S. 322 (1955)*
41. F.C.C. v. Allentown Broadcasting Co., 349 U.S. 358 (1955)
42. F.P.C. v. Oregon, 349 U.S. 435 (1955)
43. Rex Trailer Co. v. United States, 350 U.S. 148 (1956)*
44. Secy. of Agriculture v. United States, 350 U.S. 162 (1956)
45. United States v. Twin City Power Co., 350 U.S. 222 (1956)

46. Shields v. A.C.L. R. Co., 350 U.S. 318 (1956)
47. United Gas Pipe Line Co. v. Mobile Gas, 350 U.S. 332 (1956)*
48. F.P.C. v. Sierra Pacific Power Co., 350 U.S. 348 (1956)*
49. United States v. Contract Steel Carriers, 350 U.S. 409 (1956)
50. General Stores Corp. v. Shlensky, 350 U.S. 462 (1956)
51. Doud v. Hodge, 350 U.S. 485 (1956)
52. Murdock Acceptance Corp. v. United States, 350 U.S. 488 (1956)
53. Werner Machine Co. v. Director of Taxation, 350 U.S. 492 (1956)*
54. Intl. Harvester v. Goodrich, 350 U.S. 537 (1956)
55. Frozen Food Express v. United States, 351 U.S. 40 (1956)
56. East Texas Motor Lines v. Frozen Food Express, 351 U.S. 49 (1956)
57. Dixie Carriers v. United States, 351 U.S. 56 (1956)*
58. American Airlines v. North American Airlines, 351 U.S. 79 (1956)
59. General Box Co. v. United States, 351 U.S. 159 (1956)
60. United States v. Storer Broadcasting Co., 351 U.S. 192 (1956)
61. Offutt Housing Co. v. County of Sarpy, 351 U.S. 253 (1956)
62. United States v. McKesson & Robbins, 351 U.S. 305 (1956)
63. D.&R.G.W. R. Co. v. Union Pacific R. Co., 351 U.S. 321 (1956)
64. United States v. du Pont, 351 U.S. 377 (1956)
65. Brownell v. Chase Natl. Bank, 352 U.S. 36 (1956)*
66. United States v. Western Pacific R. Co., 352 U.S. 59 (1956)
67. United States v. C.&O. R. Co., 352 U.S. 77 (1956)
68. Nelson v. New York, 352 U.S. 103 (1956)*
69. United States v. I.C.C., 352 U.S. 158 (1956)
70. Miller v. Arkansas, 352 U.S. 187 (1956)*
71. United States v. Howard, 352 U.S. 212 (1957)*
72. F.T.C. v. Natl. Lead Co., 352 U.S. 419 (1957)*
73. Radovich v. Natl. Football League, 352 U.S. 445 (1957)
74. United States Gypsum v. Natl. Gypsum, 352 U.S. 457 (1957)
75. United States v. Union Pacific R. Co., 353 U.S. 112 (1957)
76. Alleghany Corp. v. Breswick & Co., 353 U.S. 151 (1957)
77. C.A.B. v. Hermann, 353 U.S. 322 (1957)*
78. B.&O. R. Co. v. Jackson, 353 U.S. 325 (1957)
79. S.E.C. v. Louisiana P.S.C., 353 U.S. 368 (1957)*
80. Pan-Atlantic Steamship Co. v. A.C.L. R. Co., 353 U.S. 436 (1957)
81. United States v. du Pont, 353 U.S. 586 (1957)
82. Smith v. Sperling, 354 U.S. 91 (1957)
83. Swanson v. Traer, 354 U.S. 114 (1957)*
84. West Point Grocery Co. v. Opelika, 354 U.S. 390 (1957)
85. Morey v. Doud, 354 U.S. 457 (1957)
86. Black v. Magnolia Liquor Co., 355 U.S. 24 (1957)*
87. Schaffer Transportation Co. v. United States, 355 U.S. 83 (1957)
88. American Trucking Associations v. United States, 355 U.S. 141 (1957)
89. McGee v. Intl. Life Insurance Co., 355 U.S. 220 (1957)*
90. United States v. N.Y.N.H.&H. R. Co., 355 U.S. 253 (1957)
91. C.M.St.P.&P. R. Co. v. Illinois, 355 U.S. 300 (1958)*
92. Nashville Milk Co. v. Carnation Co., 355 U.S. 373 (1958)
93. Safeway Stores v. Vance, 355 U.S. 389 (1958)
94. F.T.C. v. Standard Oil Co., 355 U.S. 396 (1958)
95. Moog Industries v. F.T.C., 355 U.S. 411 (1958)*
96. United States v. Detroit, 355 U.S. 466 (1958)
97. United States v. Township of Muskegon, 355 U.S. 484 (1958)

98. Detroit v. Murray Corp., 355 U.S. 489 (1958)
99. P.U.C. of California v. United States, 355 U.S. 534 (1958)
100. Nelson v. United States, 355 U.S. 554 (1958)
101. Northern Pacific R. Co. v. United States, 356 U.S. 1 (1958)
102. Denver Union Stockyard Co. v. Producers Livestock Assn., 356 U.S. 282 (1958)
103. Panama Canal Co. v. Grace Line, 356 U.S. 309 (1958)*
104. County of Marin v. United States, 356 U.S. 412 (1958)
105. P.S.C. of Utah v. United States, 356 U.S. 421 (1958)
106. Federal Maritime Board v. Isbrandtsen Co., 356 U.S. 481 (1958)
107. Rainwater v. United States, 356 U.S. 590 (1958)*
108. United States v. McNinch, 356 U.S. 595 (1958)
109. United States v. Proctor & Gamble, 356 U.S. 677 (1958)
110. United States v. Eureka Mining Co., 357 U.S. 155 (1958)
111. Societe Internationale v. Rogers, 357 U.S. 197 (1958)*
112. Ivanhoe Irrigation District v. McCracken, 357 U.S. 275 (1958)*
113. F.T.C. v. Natl. Casualty Co., 357 U.S. 560 (1958)*
114. F.H.A. v. The Darlington, 358 U.S. 84 (1958)
115. United Gas Pipe Line Co. v. Memphis Light, 358 U.S. 103 (1958)
116. United States v. A&P Trucking Co., 358 U.S. 121 (1958)
117. American Trucking Associations v. Frisco Transportation Co., 358 U.S. 133 (1958)
118. Flemming v. Florida Citrus Exchange, 358 U.S. 153 (1958)*
119. Alaska v. American Can Co., 358 U.S. 224 (1959)*
120. Intl. Boxing Club v. United States, 358 U.S. 242 (1959)
121. United States v. RCA, 358 U.S. 334 (1959)*
122. Railway Express Agency v. Virginia, 358 U.S. 434 (1959)
123. Portland Cement Co. v. Minnesota, 358 U.S. 450 (1959)
124. Kelly v. Kosuga, 358 U.S. 516 (1959)
125. Allied Stores v. Bowers, 358 U.S. 522 (1959)*
126. Youngstown Sheet & Tube v. Bowers, 358 U.S. 534 (1959)
127. S.E.C. v. Variable Annuity Life Insurance Co., 359 U.S. 65 (1959)
128. Service Storage & Transfer v. Virginia, 359 U.S. 171 (1959)*
129. Klor's v. Broadway-Hale Stores, 359 U.S. 207 (1959)*
130. Melrose Distillers v. United States, 359 U.S. 271 (1959)*
131. F.T.C. v. Mandel Brothers, 359 U.S. 385 (1959)*
132. T.I.M.E. v. United States, 359 U.S. 464 (1959)
133. Beacon Theatres v. Westover, 359 U.S. 500 (1959)
134. Bibb v. Navajo Freight Lines, 359 U.S. 520 (1959)*
135. United States v. Atlantic Refining Co., 360 U.S. 19 (1959)
136. F.T.C. v. Simplicity Pattern Co., 360 U.S. 55 (1959)*
137. Safeway Stores v. Oklahoma Retail Grocers Assn., 360 U.S. 334 (1959)*
138. Atlantic Refining Co. v. P.S.C. of New York, 360 U.S. 378 (1959)*
139. United States v. Seaboard Air Line R. Co., 361 U.S. 78 (1959)*
140. M.&St.L. R. Co. v. United States, 361 U.S. 173 (1959)
141. Phillips Chemical Co. v. Dumas School Dist., 361 U.S. 376 (1960)*
142. United States v. Parke, Davis & Co., 362 U.S. 29 (1960)
143. Scripto v. Carson, 362 U.S. 207 (1960)
144. F.T.C. v. Travelers Health Assn., 362 U.S. 293 (1960)
145. Union Pacific R. Co. v. United States, 362 U.S. 327 (1960)*
146. Miller Music Corp. v. Daniels, 362 U.S. 373 (1960)
147. Huron Portland Cement Co. v. Detroit, 362 U.S. 440 (1960)
148. Md. & Va. Milk Producers Assn. v. United States, 362 U.S. 458 (1960)*
149. United States v. Republic Steel, 362 U.S. 482 (1960)

150. Rohr Aircraft v. County of San Diego, 362 U.S. 628 (1960)
151. F.T.C. v. Broch & Co., 363 U.S. 166 (1960)
152. Pennsylvania R. Co. v. United States, 363 U.S. 202 (1960)*
153. Texas Gas Transmission Corp. v. Shell Oil Co., 363 U.S. 263 (1960)*
154. F.T.C. v. Anheuser-Busch, 363 U.S. 536 (1960)*
155. American Trucking Associations v. United States, 364 U.S. 1 (1960)*
156. Sunray Oil Co. v. F.P.C., 364 U.S. 137 (1960)
157. Sun Oil Co. v. F.P.C., 364 U.S. 170 (1960)

†This case contains both a business regulation and labor union issue. Inasmuch as it fits more compatibly into the W scale, the case is not counted as part of the business regulation universe per se.

PART TWO

STATISTICAL PREDICTION AND DECISIONS

The Supreme Court's Certiorari Jurisdiction: Cue Theory

JOSEPH TANENHAUS, MARVIN SCHICK, MATTHEW MURASKIN, and DANIEL ROSEN

1. Introduction

THE STATUTORY WRIT of certiorari, whose origin may be traced to the Circuit Courts of Appeals Act of 1891, did not become a major avenue of access to the United States Supreme Court until some 40 years ago. With the passage of the Webb bill in 1916 the discretionary writ of certiorari replaced the obligatory writ of error in many state decisions denying federal claims. This policy, which, as it were, replaced access by right with access by grace, was enormously extended, at the persistent urging of the Court itself, in the Judiciary Act of 1925.

The rationale for the public policy sanctioning the writ as the major source of the Court's business seems to consist of three propositions. First, the Court must not be required to undertake more work in any single term than it can dispose of conveniently. As Frankfurter and Landis have shown in their standard account of the development of the Court's business since 1789,[1] the continual growth of federal litigation (an unavoidable byproduct of changing activities in a rapidly expanding community) has repeatedly threatened to overwhelm the Court. Second, the Court must be in a position to attempt expeditious and authoritative rulings when cases and controversies of far-reaching importance fall within its jurisdiction. Third, the Court itself should be permitted wide discretion in seeking to satisfy the first and second propositions simultaneously.

The senior author would like to express his debt to the Social Science Research Council for its support of his Court studies and to the Ford Foundation for a Public Affairs Grant that made it possible for his associates to participate in this adventure. We would also like to indicate our indebtedness to Professor Glendon Schubert, whose penetrating commentaries on earlier versions of this report are reflected throughout.

Ever since the effects of the Judiciary Act came to be fully felt, certiorari has provided the bulk of the cases that go to oral argument each term. According to data reported by Schubert, for example, 465 cases were decided after oral argument during the 1953-1956 Terms.[2] Of these cases 76.6 per cent reached the Court via the certiorari route.[3]

Certiorari petitions[4] are of two types: those submitted *in forma pauperis,* which since 1947 have been placed on the Miscellaneous Docket, and other (not *in forma pauperis*) petitions, which go on the Appellate Docket. Applications of both kinds are very numerous. During the 1950-1959 terms, 695 appellate docket and 571 *in forma pauperis* petitions were disposed of, on the average, per term.

Appellate docket petitions for the writ are fairly standardized in format. They are printed documents, usually 10 to 30 pages in length, that must set forth the basis for the Court's jurisdiction, frame the questions presented for review, state the facts material to a consideration of those questions, and, in the words of the late Chief Justice Vinson, "explain why it is vital that the question involved be decided finally by the Supreme Court."[5] The opinions and judgments of the tribunals below, and any administrative agencies involved, are appended to the petitions, as well as at least one copy of the record. Respondents may counter with briefs in opposition seeking to show why certiorari should be denied, and petitioners may file supplementary briefs in reply. Individual copies of all these documents, with the frequent exception of copies of the record, go to each member of the Court. Most justices ask their clerks to prepare a memorandum on each application before attacking the documents themselves.

Applications *in forma pauperis* are very different in nature. Usually the petitioner submits but a single copy of a typewritten document prepared without legal assistance and without access to the complete record of his case. As a result the petitions follow no particular form, tend to contain much that is irrelevant, and omit materials essential for a thorough understanding of the facts and issues involved. When only a single copy of an application is filed, it goes to the Office of the Chief Justice. Its processing there seems to be as follows. The Chief's clerks prepare memoranda analyzing each application and send copies to every Justice. The petitions themselves tend to be circulated only if a prisoner's life is at stake or if some matter of particular interest and importance seems to be involved.

Both appellate docket and *in forma pauperis* petitions are handled in much the same way in conference. Every petition is placed on the agenda of at least one conference and will be discussed if even a single justice so desires. What makes the system manageable at all is that normally half of the appellate docket certioraris and an overwhelming majority of the *in forma pauperis* petitions receive little or no conference discussion. In fact, Chief Justice Hughes, in an effort to expedite the processing of certiorari applications, initiated a practice which has apparently been carried on by Chief Justices ever since. He prepared and circulated to the members of the Court before each conference a special list of petitions that in his judgment did not merit conference discussion. Only rarely did a justice exercise his right to have a petition removed from these "blacklists" and discussed.[6]

It has long been the practice of the Court to grant certiorari if as many as four justices so desire. If certiorari is granted, the Court may either decide the case on its merits on the basis of the documents in hand, or earmark it for argument in open court.

Although applications for certiorari provide a large share of the cases that go to oral argument, these successful applications make up only a small proportion of the total applications for discretionary review. The Administrative Office of the United States Courts reports that 6946 appellate docket applications for certiorari were disposed of during the 1950-1959 Terms.[7] Of these, 15.5 per cent were granted, ranging from a low of 13.0 per cent for 1953 to a high of 16.9 per cent for 1954. Petitions *in forma pauperis* for the 10-term period were almost as numerous: 5708. Only 4.1 per cent of these petitions were granted, however, ranging from a low of 1.9 per cent for 1953 to a high of 6.9 per cent for 1959. It must be noted, moreover, that the percentages of applications granted include a goodly number that were decided without going to oral argument.

Both the importance of certiorari as an avenue of access to the Court and the rather small proportion of certiorari applications granted have been widely known for many years. It is small wonder, then, that there has been a substantial interest in the standards the Court uses in evaluating applications for the writ.

2. Rule 19*

The most important official statement of the standards used by the Court in granting or denying certiorari is Rule 19. This Rule has has remained largely unchanged for more than three decades. Its opening sentences state:

A review on writ of certiorari is not a matter of right, but of sound judicial discretion, and will be granted only where there are special and important reasons therefor. The following, while neither controlling nor fully measuring the court's discretion, indicate the character of reasons which will be considered.

The reasons mentioned may be summarized as follows:

1. A Court of Appeals decides a point of local law in conflict with local decisions.

2. A Court of Appeals departs from or sanctions departure from the usual course of judicial proceedings.

3. A lower court ruling conflicts with a ruling of the Supreme Court.

4. A conflict in circuits exists.

5. An important question has been decided on which the Supreme Court has not yet ruled.

---

*Prior to the 1954 revision of the Court's Rules, the contents of Rule 19 were contained in Section 5 of Rule 38. For reasons of style both the old 38(5) and the new 19 will be referred to as Rule 19.

Other than Rule 19 there is only the group of rules on technical requirements such as format, the number of copies of documents to be submitted, and filing dates.

Analyses of the utilization of Rule 19 reveal that it does not constitute a very adequate explanation of the standards the Court uses in evaluating applications for certiorari. The first analyses were undertaken by Frankfurter and his associates for the 1934-1936 Terms.[8] Apparently these early studies had been prompted by Chief Justice Hughes' 1934 address to the American Law Institute in which he suggested that the Court would not be so deluged with frivolous petitions for the writ if lawyers paid more careful attention to the contents of the Rule.[9] Harper made an analysis roughly similar to Frankfurter's for the 1952 Term,[10] and we have followed suit for the 1956-1958 Terms. Our data appear in Table 1. While these analyses are not comparable in all respects, because of somewhat differing methods of data collection, they do warrant a number of conclusions about the Court's employment of the Rule.

For one thing, only rarely does the Court give any reason for refusing to grant the writ. In fact our data for the reasons for denying certiorari span the 1947-1958 Terms. On less than 40 occasions in a systematic sample of more than 3000 unsuccessful applications for the writ during those 12 Terms did the Court explain why it had denied certiorari. And then the most commonly offered explanation was that a petition had been dismissed on the motion of one or both parties. Another reason sometimes offered was that the application was not filed in time. It should be noted, what is more, that these are not Rule 19 explanations.

Explanatory comments in cases decided with opinion are more frequent. They appeared in about one case in three for the 1934-1936 Terms and in more than 66.8 per cent of the opinions of the Court during the 1956-1958 Terms. It might seem at first glance, then, that the widespread criticism of the Court for its failure to explain why certiorari was granted has been extraordinarily effective. More careful analysis substantially discounts any such conclusion. For as Table 1 shows, the reason offered in 20.1 per cent of the Court's opinions for the 1956-1958 Terms was simply "to decide the issue presented"—and this in reality is no different from offering no reason at all. Realistically, then, the Court gave reasons of the type mentioned in Rule 19 in only 46.7 per cent of its opinions during the 1956-1958 Terms. This is, to be sure, something of an increase over the 32.4 per cent for the 1934-1936 Terms. But the increase, while statistically significant at the 0.01 level of confidence ($X^2 = 11.65$), is not very impressive when one bears in mind the repeated scholarly pressures on the Court to disclose more fully its reasons for granting review.

The several analyses of the utilization of Rule 19 further disclose that the first three items on the list of five reasons summarized above are rarely cited. Only a conflict in circuits, the importance of the issue, or a combination of the two are referred to very often. Importance is cited somewhat more frequently than conflict in circuits. If one considers only cases in which Rule 19 reasons were actually given, importance alone was cited 48.5 per

TABLE 1

Reasons Offered by the Supreme Court for Granting Review in Certiorari Cases Decided after Oral Argument: 1956-1958 Terms*

REASON	1956 TERM		1957 TERM		1958 TERM		THREE-TERM TOTAL	
	N	Per Cent	N	Per Cent	N	Per Cent	N	Per Cent
1. None	28	31.4	43	43.9	21	23.1	92	33.1
2. To decide issue presented	12	13.5	12	12.2	32	35.2	56	20.1
3. Importance of issue	26	29.2	28	28.6	20	22.0	74	26.6
4. Importance and circuit conflict	13	14.6	4	4.1	5	5.5	22	7.9
5. Circuit conflict: actual	9	10.1	11	11.2	7	7.7	27	9.7
6. Circuit conflict: alleged	1	1.1	0	—	2	2.2	3	1.1
7. Conflict with Supreme Court	0	—	0	—	4	4.4	4	1.4
TOTAL:	89	99.9	98	100.0	91	100.1	278	99.9

*Opinions deciding more than one case have been counted only once.

cent of the time during the 1935-1936 Terms, 55.1 per cent during the 1952 Term, and 56.9 per cent during the 1956-1958 Terms. Using this same group of cases as a universe, conflict in circuits (whether alone or in combination with other reasons) was mentioned 40.6 per cent of the time during the 1935-1936 Terms, 40.0 per cent during the 1952 Term, and 40.0 per cent during the 1956-1958 Terms. The increase in the frequency of Rule 19 reasons cited in more recent terms, it thus appears, is almost entirely attributable to Reason 3, "the importance of the issue."

Although importance was officially cited more frequently than any other reason, it is not of much assistance in enabling students of the Court to understand the basis of its exercise of its certiorari jurisdiction. This is so because the Court has sedulously avoided providing any metric for determining what is or is not important—other than that which at least four justices wish makes it so.

Conflict in circuits is another matter. There has been, it is true enough, some controversy as to whether the Court has granted certiorari in every case of direct conflict without exception.[11] But there is no question but that a clear conflict in circuits usually leads to a grant of the writ. In fact universal recognition of the importance of this ground for access to the Court is reflected in the heroic efforts of skilled lawyers to work in some sort of conflict angle, however tenuous. A few terms back the Court seemed to be encouraging this practice by stretching the concept of conflict in circuits to cover sweeping ground.[12] "Alleged conflict," "apparent conflict," and "seeming conflict" began to be cited as reasons for granting certiorari. But during the 1956-1958 Terms such reasons were mentioned on only three occasions.

However, the most serious limitation of conflict in circuits as a satisfactory explanation for the way the Court exercises its certiorari jurisdiction is neither that sometimes square conflicts do not result in certiorari, nor that the Court sometimes stretches the concept to cover cases where the existence of direct conflict is most doubtful. Rather the most serious limitation of conflict of circuits as a key to the Court's certiorari behavior is that conflict is cited as a reason for granting certiorari in less than 20 per cent of the certiorari cases decided with full opinion: 14.3 per cent during the 1935-1936 Terms, and 18.7 per cent during the 1956-1958 Terms.

3. Other Analyses of Certiorari

Scholarly inquiry into the Court's exercise of its certiorari jurisdiction has by no means been confined to demonstrating the inadequacy of Rule 19. Some students, for example, have suggested things the Court might do to dispel some of the mystery shrouding its certiorari practice.[13] Others have employed their exegetical talents in developing their own glosses on the Rule.[14] A particularly good example is the one Stern and Gressman present in their *Supreme Court Practice*.[15]

Other students of certiorari have systematically assembled data in the hope of providing more substantial evidence about what the Court is really doing. Among the very best of these quantitative studies are the nine articles by Felix Frankfurter and his associates.[16] With commendable imagination they discussed the implications of the data they had systematically assembled on the growing number of petitions for certiorari, the court systems from which they originated, and the substance of the petitions granted and denied. Roughly comparable data are now published annually by the editors of the *Harvard Law Review*—without Frankfurter's penetrating analysis.[17] One might also mention in this connection the work of three students at the University of Pennsylvania Law School who systematically combed petitioners' and respondents' statements in all Appellate Docket petitions filed during the 1958 Term.[18] Although their report does not present the data they developed with much precision, it leaves one with a clearer notion of the materials with which the Court must work in exercising its certiorari jurisdiction.

A few students of certiorari have hypothesized standards not mentioned in Rule 19.[19] Some illustrations (occasionally restated perhaps with more precision than an author intended) follows.

The likelihood of a grant of certiorari increases if:

1. A large number of persons is affected by a decision.
2. A substantial amount of related litigation is pending or anticipated.

3. The decision below is incorrect or unjust.
4. A severe criminal penalty is involved.
5. The record in a criminal case is adequate.
6. A case came from a federal rather than a state court.
7. A respected judge dissented in the courts below.
8. A policy interest of at least four justices is involved.

Although such hypotheses as these are rather plentiful, only occasionally are efforts to test them made. Several studies which report such efforts deserve special mention. Reitz, in the course of presenting his own close analysis of 35 successful petitions submitted by state prisoners, discusses an important unpublished analysis by Radek and Spaniol of 1234 habeas corpus petitions brought by state prisoners to the Supreme Court during a period of two and one-half terms.[20] The Radek and Spaniol study shows that the chance of certiorari is much greater when the record is adequate than when it is not. Schubert, in a chapter of his recent book, *Quantitative Analysis of Judicial Behavior,* convincingly demonstrates that decisions to grant certiorari in Federal Employers Liability Act cases fulfill the requirements of one of his game theory models.[21] In another section of this same volume, he attempts with rather inadequate data to test two of the hypotheses in the above list (3 and 6).[22] Finally, Harper, in the first three articles in his "What the Supreme Court Did Not Do" series, was, not unexpectedly, able to demonstrate beyond challenge that the Court had been denying certiorari in quite a few cases in which Harper would have preferred to see it granted.[23]

Certainly the most striking aspect of research on the Court's certiorari practice is the slight attention given to theoretical considerations. Other than Schubert's game theory, which appears to us to have limited applicability, we are familiar with only one study which reflects a serious effort to develop some sort of theoretical or conceptual framework to account for the Court's behavior in exercising its certiorari jurisdiction. In an article printed in the *Hastings Law Journal,* Gibbs sets forth his theory of the mental processes employed by the justices in disposing of applications for the writ.[24] He contends that a petition is first examined for formal or jurisdictional defects. If a defect is present, the petition is denied; if no defect is apparent a justice must then decide whether granting the writ would be tactically inadvisable. If granting the writ would not be tactically unsound, a petition is then put into one of three groups: (*A*) "obviously important," (*B*) "obviously unimportant," or (*C*) neither. A Group *A* petition is automatically granted, a Group *B* petition automatically denied, and a Group *C* petition subjected to still a fourth test labelled the "tentative examination theory." At this fourth stage the justice studies the record and comes to a tentative conclusion about the correctness of the decision below. If he considers it correct, he votes to deny certiorari; if he thinks it incorrect, he votes to grant the writ.

Gibbs' theory is in our judgment unsatisfactory in two major respects: (1) he neither makes any attempt to test his theory nor does he indicate how it could be made operational and tested; and (2) it seems to require that substantially more time be devoted to certiorari petitions than the overworked justices can give them.

4. The Cue Theory

The theory that underlies our study, while similar in certain important respects to that of Gibbs, tries to overcome these inadequacies. We call our theory "the cue theory of certiorari." In constructing it we have proceeded from three assumptions, each of which is grounded in established knowledge. The first assumption, that Rule 19 does not provide a very satisfactory explanation for the Court's exercise of its certiorari jurisdiction, has already been discussed at length. Gibbs also makes this assumption.

Our second assumption is in direct conflict with the Gibbs theory. We assume that certiorari petitions are so sizable and so numerous that justices saddled with many other heavy obligations (e.g., hearing argument, attending lengthy conferences, doing necessary research, and drafting and redrafting opinions) can give no more than cursory attention to a large share of the applications for certiorari. Much has been written about the burdens of Supreme Court justices and the time pressure under which they must work.[25] These materials are widely known and require no restatement. There is only need to point out that Justice Douglas' recent Cornell speech does nothing to invalidate this second assumption. It may be true that the justices are not quite so pressed as they were 20 years ago, but very hard pressed indeed they remain.

Our third assumption is that a substantial share of appellate docket petitions for certiorari are so frivolous as to merit no serious attention at all. Chief Justice Hughes estimated that 60 per cent of the petitions for certiorari were of this character.[26] The usefulness of the earlier mentioned "blacklists" is additional evidence of the total lack of merit in many petitions, as are statements by other members of the Court.[27]

These three assumptions have led us to hypothesize that some method exists for separating the certiorari petitions requiring serious attention from those that are so frivolous as to be unworthy of careful study. We further hypothesized that a group of readily identifiable cues exists to serve this purpose. The presence of any one of these cues would warn a justice that a petition deserved scrutiny. If no cue were present, on the other hand, a justice could safely discard a petition without further expenditure of time and energy. Careful study by a justice of the petitions containing cues could then be made to determine which should be denied because of jurisdictional defects, inadequacies in the records, lack of ripeness, tactical inadvisability, etc., and which should be alloted some of the limited time available for oral argument, research, and the preparation of full opinions. Those remaining could then be disposed of by denying certiorari or by granting it and summarily affirming or reversing the court below.

A number of possible cues have occurred to us. These concern the parties seeking review, the reputations of the attorneys of record, the reputations of the judges who wrote the opinions below, several types of dissension (conflict in circuits, conflict in a given case within a court below, and conflict in a given case between the courts and agencies below), and subject matter.

Our limited resources permitted us to assemble the data necessary for testing only some of these.

Our justification for selecting the cues we did use for testing, and the methods employed both in collecting the requisite data and in testing hypotheses about the cues, will be discussed in detail in Sections V and VI of this chapter. But in general terms our approach has been to examine lower court reports for the presence of selected cues and then determine whether the incidence of writs granted was in fact greater (to a statistically significant degree) when cues were present than when they were not.

We were able to develop in advance of data processing no theoretical or empirical bases for hypothesizing about the relative importance of the several cues, the interrelationships among them, or their usefulness as predictors of what the Court will do with certiorari petitions containing given characteristics. These matters are nonetheless explored on pages 127 to 129, both because of their intrinsic interest and because they can yield new hypotheses for subsequent testing.

5. Technical Problems and Procedures

Plans for this analysis of the Supreme Court's exercise of its certiorari jurisdiction grew out of the conceptual framework for a broader study of Supreme Court behavior. This framework has already appeared in print and need not be restated here.[28]

The data used in this study were drawn from the published records of the United States Supreme Court and the lower courts and administrative agencies in which the cases were litigated. No use was made of the certiorari documents themselves. A codebook was used in assembling the data for a systematic sample of applications for review for the 1947-1958 Terms. Since both the codebook and sample were prepared for several purposes in addition to this study, something needs to be said in detail about each.

The sample was drawn as follows: Every fifth petition was coded for the ten terms 1947-1951, 1953-1955, and 1957-1958, and every petition for the two terms 1952 and 1956, with the exception of:

1. Original docket entries
2. Petitions for change of counsel, permission to submit amicus briefs or additional briefs and statements, postponement of consideration, etc.
3. Applications for rehearing
4. Entries on the Miscellaneous Docket other than petitions for certiorari carrying lower court citations

When two or more applications for review arose from a single lower court decision, each was counted separately. We should also point out that initial disposal only was coded; amended decisions and rulings were ignored.

The sampling design was established for purposes largely unrelated to this study, but the size of the sample was not. A sample as large as this one (more than 3500 cases) was deemed necessary because we were committed in this study to test with nominal data several independent variables, not all of which can be dichotomized. This meant, of course, a heavy reliance on cross-tabulation—a technique notorious for its appetite in consuming cases. In fact the original design called for coding the 1948 Term in the same manner as the 1952 and 1956 Terms, and for larger samples than one case in five from several of the other terms. However, those persistent inhibitors of overly ambitious research projects, time and money, forced us to modify our initial sampling plans.

An indication of the extent to which the sample mirrors the universe can be gained from Table 2. The differences between the sample and universe are slight and fall well within the usual limits of sampling error.

TABLE 2

Appellate Docket Certiorari Cases Disposed of during 1947-1958 Terms: Comparison of Study Sample and Actual Universe

	GRANTED		DENIED		TOTAL	
	N	Percentage	N	Percentage	N	Percentage
Universe	1279	15.7	6860	84.3	8139	100.0
Sample	445	16.9	2186	83.1	2631	100.0

The codebook, like the sample, was designed for several purposes besides this study. A draft of the codebook was prepared in the spring of 1959 by the senior author with the assistance of Mr. Dan Nimmo of Vanderbilt University. Revisions were made in the course of a graduate seminar later that year.

Data coded included case name and citation, docket and docket number, court immediately below and citation to it, agreement within the court immediately below, agreement among the courts and agencies below, parties involved, mode of application for review, disposition by the Supreme Court, exceptions taken by individual justices to the Supreme Court's handling of the case, and subject matter. Several of these classifications required more than 50 mutually exclusive categories.

No difficulties were experienced in using some classifications, such as the citations, courts below, and agreement within and among lower courts. Certain others proved more troublesome. We found it necessary to expand and refine some subject matter and party categories even after hundreds of cases had been coded.

Emending the categories after coding had begun increased the danger of unreliability even though we undertook all the coding ourselves. To compensate for this danger, most of the first 1500 cases coded were subsequently checked by a second coder. In addition, all problem cases in the entire sample—about one in six—were coded at least twice, and many were coded three times. After the data had been punched into IBM cards and verified, they were machine-processed for internal consistency, and the errors thereby uncovered were corrected. As a result of these measures we believe that all systematic errors that might have affected this analysis were removed. Whatever errors remain are, we think, random and do not exceed 1 per cent for any one of the variables to be used.

6. Hypotheses and Data

The cue theory of certiorari maintains that the justices of the Supreme Court employ cues as a means of separating those petitions worthy of scrutiny from those that may be discarded without further study. If the theory is valid, it should follow that:

Proposition I: Petitions that contain no cues will be denied.
Proposition II: Petitions that contain one or more cues will be studied carefully, and 25 to 43 per cent of them granted.

We estimate the percentage of petitions which contain cues and which are granted in the following manner. Previously cited statements by the members of the Court lead us to believe that 40 to 60 per cent of the appellate docket petitions have some merit, and therefore receive more or less careful attention. Since, furthermore, the Court grants the writ in 15 to 17 per cent of all appellate docket petitions, those granted should constitute from 25 per cent to 43 per cent of all meritorious certioraris.[29]

It hardly needs to be said that we cannot expect to find the requirements of the cue theory completely fulfilled, if only because not all the hypothesized cues have been included in our analysis. But if we have accounted for most of the major cues, these requirements should be fairly well satisfied. At the very least we should find a sizable and statistically significant correlation between the presence of one or more cues and the granting of certiorari. Before this relationship can be measured, however, it is necessary to determine whether each of the several possible cues about which we have collected data can properly be regarded as a cue. One method of doing this is to take cases involving none of the hypothesized cues and compare them in turn with those cases containing a given cue but no other. If a given cue is present, the likelihood of certiorari should be greater (to a statistically significant degree) than when none of the cues is involved. Whenever this turns out in fact to be the case, we shall accept it as satisfactory evidence that the hypothesized cue does exist. Because the large number of petitions involved causes rather small differences to produce large chi squares, we have set the confidence level necessary to accept an hypothesis at 0.001.

The hypothesis concerning the several cues we wish to test may be stated as follows:

A. Party as a Cue. When the federal government seeks review, but no other cue is involved, the likelihood of certiorari is greater (to a statistically significant degree) than when other parties seek review and no other cue is involved.
B. Dissension as a Cue. When dissension has been indicated among the judges of the court immediately below, or between two or more courts and agencies in a given case, but no other cue is involved, the likelihood of certiorari is greater (to a statistically significant degree) than when no such dissension is present and no other cue is involved.

C. Civil Liberties Issues as Cues. When a civil liberties issue is present, but no other cue is involved, the likelihood of certiorari is greater (to a statistically significant degree) than when no civil liberties issue is present and no other cue is involved.

D. Economic Issues as Cues. When an economic issue is present, but no other cue is involved, the likelihod of review is greater (to a statistically significant degree) than when no economic issue is present and no other cue is involved.

We turn now to our reasons for selecting each of these hypotheses for testing, the procedures used in classifying the petitions, and the data we have developed.

HYPOTHESIS A: PARTY AS A CUE.

This hypothesis finds some support in the literature. Frankfurter and Landis, in two of their early articles, observed that the Solicitor General speaks with special authority.[30] They pointed out that during the 1929 and 1930 Terms the federal government was extremely successful in having certiorari granted when it was appellant and denied when it was respondent. More recently Justice Harlan and the authors of a law review note made similar observations.[31]

There are several reasons why the position of the federal government may be regarded as an important cue. For one thing, many of the persons who prepare petitions for certiorari are sorely lacking in the required expertise.[32] This is decidedly not the case with the Solicitor General's staff and the other government attorneys who practice before the Court. They have the talent, the resources, and the experience fully to exploit the strong aspects of their own cases, and in reply briefs to expose the most glaring weaknesses of their opponents. We do not mean to imply that government attorneys are grossly unfair in seeking or opposing writs of certiorari. In fact we place credence in the widely circulated gossip that when a clerk or justice wants to get to the nub of a complex case in a hurry he turns to the government's brief. Still, it is surely not invidious to suggest that government attorneys generally turn their assets to the government's advantage.

Another consequence of the government lawyers' expertise is its tendency to prevent them from deluging the Court with applications that they know the Court has no interest in reviewing.

Still another reason why the petitions for review submitted by the lawyers for the government tend to be meritorious is that only rarely are they under pressure to carry cases to the Court solely to satisfy a client who insists upon leaving no stone unturned in his search for vindication. Nor is the government lawyer tempted to pursue a case regardless of merit in the hope that he may gain the prestige of having argued once before the highest court in the land.

Finally, we suspect that the Court's deference for the opinions of the executive branch tends to make it especially solicitous of the government's judgment that particular cases do or do not warrant review.

The data used to test Hypothesis *A* appear in Table 3. We have included in the group of cases "federal government favors review" not only those

TABLE 3
Party as a Cue

	CERTIORARI GRANTED		CERTIORARI DENIED		TOTAL	
	N	Percentage	N	Percentage	N	Percentage
Federal Government Favored Certiorari; Cue Involved	8	47.1	9	52.9	17	100.0
No Cues Involved	39	5.8	637	94.2	676	100.0
TOTAL:	47	6.8	646	93.2	693	100.0

$$\phi = +0.25 \qquad X^2 = 44.72 \qquad P < 0.001$$

in which the United States and its agencies and officials were petitioners, but also others if they clearly indicated that review should be granted—e.g., official declarations that review would not be opposed, and cases in which the federal government intervened on the side of the appellant. Cases involving the District of Columbia and the territories were not included unless a federal judge was a party. Cases dismissed for technical reasons, such as the petitioner withdrawing the case or mootness, and cases for which data on the parties were inadequate have been excluded from the analysis altogether.

The data reveal that when the federal government favored review and no other cue was involved the writ was issued 47.1 per cent of the time. On the other hand, when all other parties sought review, and no other cue was involved, only 5.8 per cent of the petitions were granted. Since these differences are statistically significant at the .001 level of confidence, Hypothesis A is confirmed. We accept these data as satisfactory evidence that party is a cue.

HYPOTHESIS B: DISSENSION AS A CUE.

Hypothesis B was formulated to determine whether dissension may be regarded as a cue. By dissension we mean disagreement among the judges in the court immediately below (one or more concurring opinions, dissenting votes, or dissenting opinions) or disagreement between two or more courts and agencies in a given case. We have employed the term dissension rather than conflict to avoid any possible confusion between the concept we are testing and conflict in circuits. We have not sought to test conflict in circuits, not because we do not regard it as an important cue, but because there was no systematic way to assemble the necessary data without going to the certiorari papers themselves. And this we were not in a position to do.

The justification for deciding to test dissension as a cue was suggested by Chief Justice Vinson when he said: "Our discretionary jurisdiction encompasses, for the most part, only the borderline cases—those in which there is a conflict among the lower courts or widespread uncertainty regarding problems of national importance."[33] When lower court judges and quasi-judicial administrators disagree strongly enough officially to reveal their differences, petitions for certiorari concerned with these disagreements are, we think, bound to be studied closely by the members of the highest appellate tribunal in the land. This feeling was buttressed by an examination of the certiorari cases decided with full opinion during the 1947-1958 Terms. At least 52 majority opinions during that period contained specific references to dissension within the court immediately below.

Table 4 contains the data used to test Hypothesis B. All appellate docket

TABLE 4

Dissension as a Cue

	CERTIORARI GRANTED		CERTIORARI DENIED		TOTAL	
	N	Percentage	N	Percentage	N	Percentage
Dissension only cue present	37	12.8	253	87.2	290	100.0
No cues involved	39	5.8	637	94.2	676	100.0
TOTAL:	76	7.9	890	92.1	966	100.0

$$\phi = +0.12 \qquad X^2 = 13.69 \qquad P < 0.001$$

applications for certiorari were included, except the handful decided on the technical grounds referred to just above.

The data disclose that 12.8 per cent of the petitions in which dissension, but no other cue, was present were granted. As earlier noted, certiorari was granted in only 5.8 per cent of the petitions without any cue at all. While the phi coefficient shows that the correlation between the presence of dissension and the grant of certiorari is rather weak, these differences are significant at the .001 level of confidence, and Hypothesis B is confirmed. We accept these data as satisfactory evidence that dissension is a cue.

HYPOTHESES C AND D: CIVIL LIBERTIES AND ECONOMIC ISSUES AS CUES.

Hypotheses C and D were formulated to determine whether certain types of subject matter can be regarded as cues. They will be considered together.

The supposition that subject matter is a major ingredient of what the Court refers to as "important" has been made so frequently that hypothesizing it as a cue needs no special justification. In fact, much data about subject matter appear in the literature. Petitions for certiorari granted and denied have been classified by subject matter by Frankfurter and his associates for the 1929-1938 Terms, by Harper for the 1952 Term, and by the editors of the *Harvard Law Review* for all terms since 1955.[34]

We settled upon two subject matter groups (with four subcategories each) as the most likely to attract the interest of the justices when scanning the mountainous piles of certiorari papers. In the civil liberties group we included petitions pertaining to (1) alien deportation, (2) racial discrimination, (3) military justice, and (4) miscellaneous civil liberties.[35] Our second group, economic issues, contain (5) labor, (6) regulation of economic life, (7) financial interest of the federal government, and (8) benefit and welfare legislation. Some of these categories are self-explanatory; others require a comment.

Miscellaneous civil liberties includes church-state relations, permits and licenses for the use of the streets and parks, postal and movie censorship, state and local censorship of reading matter, loyalty oaths, problems arising from the investigations of legislative committees, disbarment proceedings, regulation of occupations and professions, picketing—free speech, and right to work litigation. The financial interest of the federal government includes excise, gift, income, and excess profit tax cases, and government contract disputes in time of peace and war. The benefit and welfare category refers to litigation concerned with civil service rights, wage statutes, the Federal Employers Liability Act, seamen and longshoremen welfare legislation, servicemen's benefits, workmen's compensation, social security legislation, tort claims, agricultural benefit regulations, and unemployment insurance. About 1 per cent of the applications for certiorari could not be classified with satisfactory precision because insufficient data were available. These cases have been omitted from the analysis.

Table 5 contains the data used to test the civil liberties issue hypothesis (Hypothesis C). These data show that about one petition in every three con-

TABLE 5

Civil Liberties Issue as a Cue

	CERTIORARI GRANTED		CERTIORARI DENIED		TOTAL	
	N	Percentage	N	Percentage	N	Percentage
Civil Liberties Issue Only Cue Present	57	32.9	116	67.1	173	100.0
No Cues Involved	39	5.8	637	94.2	676	100.0
TOTAL:	96	11.3	753	88.7	849	100.0

$$\phi = +0.35 \qquad X^2 = 101.46 \qquad P < 0.001$$

taining a civil liberties cue, but no other, was granted. The differences between the treatment of petitions with civil liberties cues and petitions without any cues are significant at the 0.001 level of confidence. Hypothesis C is therefore confirmed, and we accept these data as satisfactory evidence that the presence of a civil liberties issue constitutes a cue.

The data used to test Hypothesis D (economic issue as a cue) appear in Table 6. As the contents of this table make clear, the likelihood of review when only an economic issue is present is not much greater than when no cue at all is involved. The phi coefficient shows that the correlation between the presence of an economic issue and the grant of certiorari is only slightly positive. Nor can a chi square of the magnitude attained be regarded as impressive for an N of nearly 1400 cases. Hypothesis D is not confirmed, and we cannot regard the presence of an economic issue as a cue.

TABLE 6

Economic Issue as a Cue

	CERTIORARI GRANTED		CERTIORARI DENIED		TOTAL	
	N	Percentage	N	Percentage	N	Percentage
Economic Issue Only Cue Present	59	8.5	637	91.5	696	100.0
No Cues Involved	39	5.8	637	94.2	676	100.0
TOTAL:	98	7.1	1274	92.9	1372	100.0

$\phi = +0.05$ $X^2 = 4.11$ $0.05 < P < 0.01$

Now that we have determined that party, dissension, and civil liberties issues are cues we can return to the two propositions set forth on page 121. We then pointed out that if the cue theory were valid, it should follow that: *(Proposition I)* petitions which contain no cue will be denied, and *(Proposition II)* petitions which contain one or more cues will be studied carefully and 25 to 43 per cent of them granted. Data giving some indication of the extent to which these propositions are satisfied by the data in our sample appear in Table 7.

TABLE 7

Petitions Containing One or More Cues and Petitions Containing No Cue Compared

	CERTIORARI GRANTED		CERTIORARI DENIED		TOTAL	
	N	Percentage	N	Percentage	N	Percentage
One or More Cues	337	27.5	889	72.5	1226	100.0
No Cues	98	7.1	1274	92.9	1372	100.0
TOTAL:	435	16.7	2163	83.3	2598	100.0

$\phi = +0.27$ $X^2 = 192.20$ $P < 0.001$

Table 7 makes it quite evident that the requirements of *Proposition II* are satisfied. Of the petitions containing at least one cue, 27.5 per cent were granted. In addition, the petitions containing cues constituted 47.2 per cent of all appellate docket petitions. This falls within the estimate that 40 to 60 per cent of all appellate docket petitions contain some merit.

Proposition I is not fully supported, since 98 petitions containing no cues (7.1 per cent) were granted. But these 98 deviant cases do not in our judgment invalidate the cue theory, since all hypothesized cues have not been tested. Our judgment is reinforced by reading the opinions of the Court in those deviant cases decided with full opinion. In 19 instances the Court specifically pointed to a conflict in circuits, a cue we were unable to test. In one case, the Court pointed to dissents by intermediate appellate judges, and in another to the fact that the federal government did not oppose review. Still another case had civil liberties overtones which had been missed when the case was coded. More painstaking analysis would, we are convinced, still further reduce the number of deviant cases not readily accounted for by the cue theory.

We feel justified in concluding, therefore, that the cue theory of certiorari is valid.

7.

As indicated in the third paragraph on page 119, we had no theoretical or empirical bases for hypothesizing in advance of data processing about the interrelationships among the several cues and their usefulness as predictors of what the Court will do with sets of certiorari petitions containing given characteristics.

Insofar as the cue theory itself is concerned, the relative magnitude of the correlations between established cues and the grant or denial of certiorari (outcome) is of no particular consequence. All the cue theory requires is that the presence of a cue is enough to insure that a petition for certiorari will be studied with care. Hence, the presence of more than one cue, or for that matter the fact that one established cue may be more or less strongly correlated with outcome than another, will not alter the likelihood that a petition will be scrutinized. However, these relationships do have enough intrinsic interest to warrant analysis.

In testing Hypotheses A, B, and C, ϕ coefficients were computed and included in the appropriate tables. The correlation between outcome and party was $+0.25$, outcome and dissension $+0.12$, and outcome and civil liberties $+0.35$. But these correlations are not very adequate measures of the relationship between the individual cues and outcome because cases containing more than one cue were not taken into account. A more satisfactory method for determining the magnitude of the association between outcome and any given cue, when all other cues are held constant, is to compute the portion of the variance explained by each. The portion of the variance accounted for by a given cue is obtained by multiplying the coefficient of correlation between outcome and the cue by its standard partial regression (β) coefficient.

The β's were obtained by Doolittle's method and appear, together with the data necessary for their computation, in Table 8. Since only cases for which adequate information about all three cues were available could be utilized, the number of cases used in this analysis was 2293.

As the data in Table 8 show, 7.4 per cent of the variance is explained by the party cue, 3.9 per cent by the civil liberties cue, and 2.4 per cent by the dissension cue. In our sample, therefore, party was relatively three times as important as dissension and almost twice as important as civil liberties in explaining outcome. Since the several contributions to the variance are additive, one may quickly determine the relative importance of the several cues in combination. For example, party alone was slightly more important

TABLE 8

Multiple Correlation and Regression Data

		X_1	X_2	X_3	X_4
	x_1	...	0.28	0.17	0.19
	x_2	0.28	...	0.16	−0.03
Intercorrelations	x_3	0.17	0.16	...	−0.06
	x_4	0.19	−0.03	−0.06	...

		X_1	X_2	X_3	X_4
$\overline{M}$		0.176	0.076	0.401	0.116
σ		0.379	0.266	0.490	0.319

$\beta_2 = 0.264$ $B_2 = 0.375$ $A = 0.076$

$\beta_3 = 0.140$ $B_3 = 0.108$

$\beta_4 = 0.206$ $B_4 = 0.245$

$r^2 1.234 = 0.138$

$(\beta_2)(\phi 12) = 0.074$

$(\beta_3)(\phi 13) = 0.024$ $r 1.234 = 0.37$

$(\beta_4)(\phi 14) = 0.039$ $x_1 = 0.375x_2 + 0.108x_3 + 0.245x_4 + 0.076$

LEGEND FOR VARIABLES

x_1 = Outcome (certiorari granted vs. certiorari denied) x_3 = Dissension

x_2 = Party (federal government favored certiorari vs. other cases) x_4 = Civil liberties issue

than dissension and civil liberties combined, and all three cues taken together account for nearly twice as much of the variance (13.7 per cent) as party taken alone.

However, these data on the percentage of the variance explained by the three cues, independently and in combination, do not in themselves enable us to predict the likelihood of certiorari grants in sets of cases containing various assumed proportions of cues. Such predictions are made possible by solving the regression equation $x_1 = B_2x_2 + B_3x_3 + B_4x_4 + A$, where outcome is the dependent variable (x_1) and the independent variables are party (x_2), dissension (x_3) and civil liberties issues (x_4). The equation and the data used in computing it appear in Table 8.

One can now substitute any set of means desired for the independent variables in the regression equation and solve for outcome. To illustrate, if in a given set of certiorari petitions the federal government sought review in 75 per cent, dissension was present in 50 per cent, and civil liberties issues were involved in 40 per cent, the following substitutions would be made:

$$x_1 = 0.375 \, (0.75) + (0.108) \, (0.50) + (0.245) \, (0.40) + 0.076.$$

Solving for outcome, $x_1 = 0.434$. Therefore, 43 per cent of the set of petitions will be granted.

Since our particular interest is to determine the predictive powers of the cues if every case in a set contains them in a given combination, we need to substitute 1.00 if we wish to include a cue and 0.00 if we wish to exclude it. For example, for a set in which every case contains all three cues, the following substitutions are made:

$$x_1 = (0.375) \ (1.00) + (0.108) \ (1.00) + (0.245) \ (1.00) + 0.076$$

Therefore, $x_1 = 0.804$, and 80 per cent of the petitions in the set will be granted. Similar substitutions provided the other results reported in Table 9.

TABLE 9

Predicted Percentages of Certiorari Petitions That Will Be Granted When All Cases in a Set Contain Indicated Cues

Party	CUES Civil Liberties	Dissension	Predicted Percentage of Certioraris to Be Granted
+	+	+	80
+	+	0	70
+	0	+	56
+	0	0	45
0	+	+	43
0	+	0	32
0	0	+	18
0	0	0	7

LEGEND

0 = absence of a cue in all cases in set   + = presence of a cue in all cases in set

We consider it important to re-emphasize that the relationships discussed in Section VII, unlike those in Sections IV-VI, were not hypothesized in advance of processing. As a result, we do not regard them as established, but only as useful bases for formulating hypotheses that need to be tested with fresh data.

Summary

Proceeding from assumptions based on what we consider to be established and relevant knowledge about the Supreme Court and its certiorari practice, we hypothesized the existence of a method of separating the petitions for certiorari requiring serious attention from those that are so frivolous as to be unworthy of careful study. We further hypothesized that a group of readily identifiable cues exists to serve this purpose. The presence of any one of these cues would warn a justice that a petition deserved scrutiny. If, on the other hand, no cue was present, a justice could safely discard a petition without further expenditure of time and energy. Careful study by a justice of the petitions containing cues could then be made to determine which should be denied because of jurisdictional defects, inadequacies in the records, lack of ripeness, tactical inadvisability, etc., and which should be allotted some of the limited time available for oral argument, research, and the preparation of full opinions. Those remaining could then be disposed of by denying certiorari, or by granting it and summarily affirming or reversing the courts below. This cluster of working hypotheses we labeled the cue theory.

Two propositions and four research hypotheses were developed to test the cue theory. Three of the hypotheses and both propositions were strongly enough supported by the data assembled to test them that we feel justified in considering the cue theory valid—at least until evidence is developed which casts doubt upon it.

We were not able to formulate in advance of data processing any useful hypotheses about interrelationships among the cues and the utility of the cues as predictors. These matters were, nevertheless, explored by means of multiple correlation and regression analysis. The results of this analysis provide the basis for formulating operational hypotheses that must be tested with fresh data.

NOTES

1. Felix Frankfurter and James M. Landis, *The Business of the Supreme Court: A Study in the Federal Judicial System* (New York: Macmillan, 1928).

2. Glendon Schubert, *Quantitative Analysis of Judicial Behavior* (Glencoe: The Free Press, 1959), pp. 40-41.

3. We are aware, of course, that the Supreme Court handles its obligatory jurisdiction in a rather discretionary manner.

4. The discussion of certiorari in the next few paragraphs is based on the standard sources, most of which are cited in Robert L. Stern and Eugene Gressman, *Supreme Court Practice*, 2nd ed. (Washington: BNA Incorporated, 1954), Chap. 4; Henry M. Hart, Jr., and Herbert Wechsler, *The Federal Courts and the Federal System* (Brooklyn: The Foundation Press, 1953), pp. 1394-1422; and in the notes *infra*.

5. Fred M. Vinson, "Work of the Federal Courts," a speech before the American Bar Association, 1949, reprinted in *Supreme Court Reporter*, Vol. 69, p. vi.

6. In addition to the standard accounts, see the unpublished study by Professor David J. Danelski, "The Influence of the Chief Justice in the Decisional Process of the Supreme Court," (1960, mimeographed), pp. 4-5.

7. *Annual Report of the Director of the Administrative Office of the United States Courts, 1960* (Washington: Government Printing Office, 1961), pp. 206-09.

8. Felix Frankfurter and Henry M. Hart, Jr., "The Business of the United States Supreme Court at October Term, 1933," *Harvard Law Review*, Vol. 48 (1934), 262 ff. [these data are not refined enough to be of much value]; Frankfurter and Hart, "The Business of the United States Supreme Court at October Term, 1934," *Harvard Law Review*, Vol. 49 (1935), 83; Frankfurter and Adrian S. Fisher, "The Business of the Supreme Court at the October Terms, 1935 and 1936," *Harvard Law Review*, Vol. 51 (1938), 595.

9. *Proceedings of American Law Institute*, Vol. 11 (1934), 313. The relevant passages are reprinted in Hart and Wechsler, *op. cit. supra* (Note 4), pp. 1395-96.

10. Fowler V. Harper and Arnold Leibowitz, "What the Supreme Court Did Not Do during the 1952 Term," *University of Pennsylvania Law Review*, Vol. 102 (1954), 439-48.

11. Cf. Robert L. Stern, "Denial of Certiorari Despite a Conflict," *Harvard Law Review*, Vol. 66 (1953), 465, with Edward T. Roehner and Sheila M. Roehner, "Certiorari—What Is a Conflict between Circuits?" *University of Chicago Law Review*, Vol. 20 (1953), 656.

12. See Harper and Leibowitz, *op. cit. supra* (Note 10), 444-45.

13. For example, Frankfurter and Hart, *op. cit., Harvard Law Review*, Vol. 48,

244; Louis L. Jaffe, "The Supreme Court, 1950 Term, *Harvard Law Review,* Vol. 65 (1951), 110; Harper and Leibowitz, *op. cit. supra* (Note 10), 451.

14. See, for example, works cited in Note 11, *supra.*

15. Pages 110-41.

16. The nine articles, several of which have been previously cited, appeared in the *Harvard Law Review* over the ten-year period 1929-1938.

17. The editors of the *Harvard Law Review* have published their data on all terms since 1948.

18. Note, "The Court, the Bar, and Certiorari at October Term, 1958," *University of Pennsylvania Law Review,* Vol. 108 (1960), 1160.

19. The relevant literature prior to 1954 is discussed by Harper and Leibowitz, *op. cit. supra* (Note 10), 447-50. See also Schubert, *op. cit. supra* (Note 2), pp. 37 ff.; Curtis R. Reitz, "Federal Habeas Corpus: Postconviction Remedy for State Prisoners," *University of Pennsylvania Law Review,* Vol. 108 (1960), 477 ff.; "Note," *University of Pennsylvania Law Review, op. cit. supra* (Note 18), 1171, 1215; Robert W. Gibbs, "Certiorari: Its Diagnosis and Cure," *Hastings Law Journal,* Vol. 6 (1955), 153.

20. Reitz, *op. cit. supra* (Note 19).

21. Schubert, *op. cit. supra* (Note 2), pp. 210 ff.

22. *Ibid.,* pp. 44-45, 55, 60, 66.

23. Fowler V. Harper and Alan S. Rosenthal, "What the Supreme Court Did Not Do in the 1949 Term—An Appraisal of Certiorari," *University of Pennsylvania Law Review,* Vol. 99 (1950), 293; Harper and Edwin D. Etherington, "What the Supreme Court Did Not Do during the 1950 Term," *University of Pennsylvania Law Review,* Vol. 100 (1951), 354; Harper and George C. Pratt, "What the Supreme Court Did Not Do during the 1951 Term," *University of Pennsylvania Law Review,* Vol. 101 (1953), 439. Reference might also be made to Simon Rosenzweig's "The Opinions of Judge Edgerton—A Study in the Judicial Process," *Cornell Law Quarterly,* Vol. 37 (1952), 149. Rosenzweig shows that the Court granted certiorari only 13 per cent of the time when Edgerton spoke for his court, and 60 per cent of the time when he dissented. Technically, Rosenzweig's work is not a study of certiorari at all, since his conclusion is that these data provide "a fair measure of the degree of his accuracy in his judgment of the Supreme Court's view of the law." However, his data suggest an alternative and somewhat more plausible explanation, i.e., that the Court respected Edgerton's opinions and tended to be guided by them.

24. Gibbs, *op. cit. supra* (Note 19).

25. See especially Henry M. Hart, Jr., "The Supreme Court, 1958 Term, Forward: The Time Chart of the Justices," *Harvard Law Review,* Vol. 73 (1959), 84; William O. Douglas, "The Supreme Court and Its Case Load," *Cornell Law Quarterly,* Vol. 45 (1960), 401; Frankfurter and Landis, "The Business of the Supreme Court at October Term, 1929," *Harvard Law Review,* Vol. 44 (1930), 1; and Schubert, *op. cit. supra* (Note 2), pp. 26 ff.

26. In a letter to Burton K. Wheeler, March 21, 1937, reprinted in Hart and Wechsler, *op. cit. supra* (Note 4), p. 1399.

27. For example, Harold H. Burton, "Judging Is Also Administration: An Appreciation of Constructive Leadership," *American Bar Association Journal,* Vol. 33 (1947), 1099; Vinson, *op. cit. supra* (Note 5), p. v; John M. Harlan, "Manning the Dikes," *Record of the Bar of the City of New York,* Vol. 13 (1958), 541.

28. Joseph Tanenhaus, "Supreme Court Attitudes Toward Federal Administrative Agencies," *Journal of Politics,* Vol. 22 (1960), 502, and *Vanderbilt Law Review,* Vol. 14 (1961), 473.

29. The lower range was set by assuming that (1) only petitions containing some merit have any chance of success, (2) 15 per cent of all petitions were granted, and (3) 60 per cent of all petitions contained some merit. If x equals the percentage of cases with merit granted, and N equals the total number of petitions filed, then $15N = (0.6N) (x)$, and $x = 25.0$. The upper range was set by assuming that (1) only petitions containing some merit have any chance of success, (2) 17 per cent of all petitions were granted, and (3) 40 per cent of all petitions contained some merit.

If x equals the percentage of cases with some merit granted, and N equals the total number of petitions filed, then $17N = (0.4N) (x)$, and $x = 42.5$.

30. Frankfurter and Landis, *op. cit., Harvard Law Review,* Vol. 44, 18-22; Frankfurter and Landis, "The Business of the Supreme Court at October Term, 1930," *Harvard Law Review,* Vol. 45 (1931), 281.

31. Harlan, *op. cit. supra* (Note 27), 548; "Note," *op. cit. supra* (Note 19), 1197.

32. "Note," *op. cit. supra* (Note 19), 1217.

33. Vinson, *op. cit. supra* (Note 5), pp. ix-x.

34. See *Harvard Law Review,* 1955 to present.

35. We decided at the outset not to include applications for review by criminal defendants in the civil liberties category even though the allegation of a deprivation of constitutional rights is usually involved. Our reason for the decision was our belief that such petitions tend to be so completely frivolous that the justices will ignore them unless some other cue is present.

Content Analysis
of Judicial Opinions
and Rules of Law

FRED KORT

MANY RULES OF LAW make the decisions of cases dependent on unspecified combinations of specified circumstances. Although such rules of law are by no means limited to the field of American constitutional law, it is, nevertheless, understandable that rules of constitutional interpretation which have this characteristic will readily attract attention. Indeed, the fair trial rule, which has been used by the Supreme Court of the United States in determining for state criminal procedure the requirements of the due process clause of the Fourteenth Amendment, is such a rule of law. It states that some combinations of the personal circumstances of the defendant (the petitioner before the Supreme Court) and of the procedural circumstances of the case constitute a denial of due process and, therefore, call for a decision in favor of the petitioner. Furthermore, it states that other combinations of such circumstances do not amount to a denial of a constitutional right and, therefore, cannot by themselves preclude a decision against the petitioner. This rule speci-

I wish to express my appreciation for the opportunity of initially preparing this study under the Law and Behavioral Science Fellowship program of the University of Chicago Law School. Among the many people on the staff of the University of Chicago Law School to whom I am indebted for their assistance, primary credit must be given to Fred L. Strodtbeck and Lee H. Hook for proposing the method of analysis employed in this study. A summary of an earlier version of this study appeared in *PROD* (now published as *The American Behavioral Scientist*), Vol. 3 (March 1960), 11-14. The results which are reported here have been obtained through computations performed on the IBM 7090 at the Computation Center of the Massachusetts Institute of Technology. I wish to express my appreciation for the generous allocation of free computer time by the Center. Moreover, I am indebted to James M. Sakoda, Brown University, and Lester M. Hyman, University of Connecticut, for extensive consultations on problems in programing. All errors and inadequacies in this study are, of course, my responsibility.

fies a general set of circumstances, but it does not specify which combinations of circumstances will lead to one result and which combinations will lead to the opposite result. Accordingly, in the "involuntary confession" cases—one area to which this rule has been applied—the Court has stated that whether or not a confession used to convict an accused in a state criminal proceeding is coerced (and therefore constitutes a denial of due process in violation of the Fourteenth Amendment) depends in each case on the combination of controlling circumstances.[1]

Likewise, in the "right to counsel" cases, another area in which the fair trial rule has been used, the Court has stated that whether or not the lack of counsel in a state criminal proceeding constitutes a denial of due process must be determined in each case on the basis of the controlling circumstances.[2] In judicial action which does not involve constitutional issues, similar patterns can be noted. For example, in reviewing administrative decisions in workmen's compensation cases, state appellate courts have followed the rule that the award or the denial of compensation must be decided on the basis of the particular combination of circumstances under which the injury occurred.[3]

The object of the present study is to provide a quantitative formulation of rules of law which have the indicated characteristic. Since such rules are found primarily in the form of case law,[4] i.e., in the context of those parts of judicial opinions that are most relevant to the decisions under the concept of *ratio decidendi,* this study utilizes content analysis as a quantitative method for the interpretation of judicial decision-making.[5] More specifically, the proposed quantitative formulation is directed at that part of the rule of law which refers to various possible combinations of the specified set of circumstances. Each combination of circumstances represents the facts of the case to which the rule of law is applied, as these facts purport to be perceived by a majority of the deciding court. The quantitative formulation in question will attempt to weight numerically each possible combination of circumstances. Furthermore, since any decision of a case within the framework of a rule of law represents an application of the rule to a particular combination of circumstances, the proposed method also will provide a weight for each decision. It will thus be possible to make a precise and exhaustive distinction between different combinations of circumstances—a distinction not made in the conventional verbal statement of the rule of law.

The method will be applied to the involuntary confession and right to counsel cases of the United States Supreme Court and to the workmen's compensation cases of the Supreme Court of Errors of Connecticut. The method is designed, however, to quantify *any* rule of law which makes the decisions of cases dependent on unspecified combinations of specified circumstances. An important condition, of course, is that there are enough cases for obtaining the necessary data. The present method differs in detail and technique from similar methods suggested in earlier studies,[6] but the objective of the research is the same, as the comparison to be made will demonstrate.

In the concluding section of this study, the purposes and implications of quantifying rules of law by the proposed method will be discussed.

1. The Method of Analysis

The model on which the analysis is based can be described in the following mathematical terms. The cases which are decided under the rules of law in question are represented by simultaneous equations. The decisions of the cases are regarded as a function of the combinations of circumstances in the cases. Accordingly, the circumstances of the cases are the independent variables in the equations, and the decisions are the dependent variable. It is possible, however, to restate the circumstances of the cases in terms of psychometric constructs called *factors*. On the basis of this restatement, the factors become the independent variables in the equations, and the decisions then are a function of the combinations of factors in the cases. Before a more detailed exposition of this model is given, some attention has to be devoted to the compilation of data which are necessary for performing the analysis.

The cases that constitute the sample for the analysis are identified by examining the issue in each case that might be relevant. In order to locate the cases that should be considered, it is not sufficient to rely on various *digest* systems. Frequently, digests do not contain references to all cases that might be relevant. It is necessary, therefore, to examine the index of every volume of court reports which cover the period under investigation. If the issue in a case indicates that the court is attempting to apply the rule of law which is the subject of the analysis, the case is included in the sample. If, on the other hand, the issue indicates that the court is concerned with a matter related to the rule of law in question, but not with the application of the rule itself, the case is excluded. For example, if the issue in an involuntary confession case indicates that the Supreme Court is trying to determine whether or not the combination of circumstances in the case amounts to an involuntary confession, the case is included in the sample. For in this situation the Court is attempting to apply the rule of law that defines the decision as a "function" of the combination of circumstances. If, on the other hand, the issue in an involuntary confession case is, for example, whether or not the proper instructions on the admissibility of the confession were given to the jury, the case is not included in the sample. For in this situation the Court is confronted with a question which does not involve the application of the rule of law under investigation. This procedure must be applied to every case for every rule of law which is examined in the framework of the analysis.

With the understanding that the circumstances of the cases are the *original* independent variables in a set of simultaneous equations, the shorter expression "variables" now will be used for referring to these circumstances. In each case, the variables are identified by relying on the *Opinion of the Court* (and not on concurring or dissenting opinions), for—as already has been noted—the analysis treats the decision of a case as a function of the combination of variables.[7] Accordingly, in each case the Opinion of the Court must be examined in order to determine which variables the Court *states* and *accepts* in reaching its decision. A list of these variables is prepared for each case.

At the same time, a list of the entire set of variables is prepared by using the list of variables in the first case which has been examined as the basis, and by adding to the list the new variables that are encountered in each case which is subsequently examined. The description of variables in these lists should approximate as closely as possible the language used by the court— again in order to satisfy the condition that the decisions of the cases are a function of the combinations of variables.

Grouped into categories, the variables in the involuntary confession cases, in the right to counsel cases, and in the Connecticut workmen's compensation cases are listed in Tables 1, 2, and 3, respectively. The titles and citations of these cases are listed in Tables 4, 5, and 6. The appearance of variables in each case is shown for the three groups of cases in Tables 7, 8, and 9, respectively. Each row of Tables 7, 8, and 9 represents a case. Each case can be identified by referring to its number in Tables 4, 5, and 6, respectively; it is designated by the same number in Tables 7, 8, and 9. Each column in Tables 7, 8, and 9 represents a variable, which can be identified by referring to its number in Tables 1, 2 and 3. A zero indicates that the variable is absent in the case; a 1 indicates that the variable is present in the case; a number larger than 1 signifies that the variable has as many manifestations in the case as the number indicates.

As listed in Tables 7, 8, and 9, the combination of variables indicated by each row represents the general set of circumstances relevant to each case. Some combinations of these variables lead to decisions in favor of the petitioner before the United States Supreme Court or the claimant of the workmen's compensation award ("pro" decisions). Other combinations of these variables lead to decisions against the petitioner or the claimant ("con" decisions).[8]

Which combinations produce one result and which combinations produce the opposite result? Of course, without resorting to quantification, it can be seen from the cases which constitute the sample for the analysis with what decisions some combinations of variables are associated. However, a qualitative treatment of this relationship has two limitations. First, it does not necessarily reveal whether or not the application of the rule of law under consideration exhibits a consistent pattern of judicial action. Secondly, assuming that a consistent pattern can be identified, it does not indicate what decisions a consistent application of the rule of law would require for combinations of variables that are not encountered in the cases of the sample. The aim of the present inquiry is to overcome these limitations by means of the proposed quantitative analysis.

As already noted, the object of the analysis is to weight the variables. This also will make possible the weighting of the decisions, which are based on the respective combinations of variables in the cases. But it also has already been pointed out that it is possible to restate the variables in terms of aggregational psychometric concepts called factors, and that the weight of a case then depends on the factors to which the variables can be reduced.

The method of reducing variables to factors is known as *factor analysis*. Since this method has found extensive application in psychology, it would

TABLE 1

Variables in the Involuntary Confession Cases*

Circumstances of Pressure:

1. Physical violence overtly designed to elicit a confession.
2. Physical violence *not* overtly designed to elicit a confession.
3. Nonviolent physical pressure, e.g., deprivation of food, sleep, or clothes, or long exposure to bright lights, etc., or any combination of these devices of pressure.
4. "Relay tactics" in questioning.
5. Protracted interrogation.
6. Verbal or mental coercion other than protracted interrogation, e.g., threat of physical violence, threat of arrest of relatives, statement by law-enforcing officers to the defendant that there is a threat of mob violence even though none actually might exist, false statement that accomplice has confessed, promise of leniency, or persuasion by a psychiatrist, or any combination of these devices of pressure.
7. Removal of the defendant to isolated places at night, for questioning.
8. Preceding admittedly coerced confession.
9. No other confession which is admittedly voluntary and indicative of the voluntary nature of the confession in question.
10. No formal presentation of charges prior to the challenged confession.
11. Delay in the formal presentation of charges.
12. Detention incommunicado.
13. An actually existing threat of mob violence, which the defendant notes without being made aware of it by law-enforcing officers.
14. No advice of the right to remain silent.
15. No advice of the right to counsel.
16. Request of consultation with counsel denied.
17. No consultation with counsel prior to the confession.

Personal Circumstances Indicative of the Inability to Resist Pressure:

18. Negro status.
19. Youth and concomitant immaturity.
20. Illiteracy, subnormal education, ignorance of English, mental incapacity, or limited contact with the prevailing culture pattern. (Multiple values if more than one manifestation.)
21. No previous experience in criminal proceedings, or unfamiliarity with criminal procedure in spite of such previous experience.

Possible Modifying Circumstance:

22. No evidence which, apart from the challenged confession, would be sufficient for a conviction.

---

*Although, in summarizing its position in the involuntary confession cases, the Court speaks of a category of variables designated as "power of resistance," it actually states these variables in the opinions of the various cases as variables indicative of the *lack* of the power of resistance. The group designation has been changed here accordingly. Certainly it is easier to identify the circumstances that obviously constitute a lack of the power to resist than circumstances that represent the power to resist. Moreover, from the viewpoint of the analysis such an identification is more advantageous, for "circumstances of pressure" and "lack of the power of resistance" are operative in the same direction, i.e., to the disadvantage of the defendant, whereas "circumstances of pressure" and "power of resistance" are operative in opposite directions. Note also that "Negro status" is a variable which the Court has strongly emphasized in the confession cases, but not in the counsel cases, as a relevant personal handicap of the defendant.

TABLE 2

Variables in the Right to Counsel Cases*

Gravity of the Crime:
1. Crime subject to capital punishment. (Where not identified, crime subject to noncapital punishment is implied.)

Personal Handicaps of the Defendant:
2. Youth and concomitant immaturity.
3. Illiteracy, subnormal education, ignorance of English, mental incapacity, or limited contact with the prevailing culture pattern. (Multiple values if more than one manifestation.)
4. No previous experience in court or unfamiliarity with court procedure in spite of previous convictions.

Phases of the Proceeding during Which Counsel Was Absent:
5. No assistance of counsel at the arraignment.
6. No assistance of counsel between the arraignment and the trial or the hearing on the plea of guilty.
7. No assistance of counsel at the trial or at the hearing on the plea of guilty.
8. No assistance of counsel at the time of sentencing.
9. No assistance of counsel at any other phase of the proceeding. (Multiple values if more than one manifestation.)

Denials of Counsel:
10. No advice of the right to counsel, no inquiry as to the desire to have counsel, no offer of counsel, or any combination of these deficiencies.
11. Request for assigned counsel denied.
12. Opportunity for consultation with own counsel denied.
13. No explicit waiver of the right to counsel.

Other Procedural Irregularities:
14. Detention incommunicado.
15. Detention and trial in a hostile environment or under inflammatory publicity.
16. Deception of the defendant by a distorted and misleading presentation of charges.
17. No explicit presentation of charges to the defendant.
18. Coercion or intimidation of the defendant to plead guilty.
19. Consequences of the plea of guilty not explained to the defendant.
20. Request of additional time for consultation with counsel and for the preparation of the defense denied.
21. Accelerated trial.
22. Procedural or substantive error during the trial or at the time of sentencing. (Multiple values if more than one manifestation.)

Complexity of the Issue:
23. Jurisdictional issue or complicated charges. (Multiple values if more than one manifestation.)

*The variables (circumstances of the cases) were referred to as "pivotal factors" in the earlier study of the right to counsel cases (Kort, *op. cit. infra*, note 6). In the present study, the term "factor" is reserved for a different concept, in accordance with accepted practice in the use of factor analysis. Variable 1 (gravity of the crime) is stated dichotomously, whereas in the earlier study a further differentiation among noncapital offenses was made, in accordance with the distinction which the Court emphasized in summarizing its position in *Uveges* v. *Pennsylvania, infra* (note 2). Correlation coefficients based on further differentiation of variable 1 did not produce meaningful factors, which suggests that the Court's distinction among noncapital offenses is significant only on a verbal, not on a decisional, level of action.

TABLE 3

Variables in the Connecticut Workmen's Compensation Cases

Nature of the Injury:
1. Alleged injury consists of a disease which could not have been revealed by an observable causative accident or act.
2. Alleged injury consists of a disease which is frequently encountered in the occupation of the employee.
3. Alleged injury consists of a disease which reasonably can be connected with the occupation of the employee.

Circumstances under Which an Accident or an Act Causing the Alleged Injury Occurred:
4. Accident or act occurred in the course of an activity permitted by the employer.
5. Accident or act occurred in the course of an activity conducive to efficient work.
6. Accident or act occurred in the course of an activity indispensable to the performance of the work.
7. Accident or act occurred on the premises of employment, in an area annexed to the place of employment, or in an area where the work normally is performed.
8. Accident or act occurred during an activity which did not involve unnecessary, self-imposed hazardous conduct, such as taking a "joy ride" on a conveyor belt for unloading coal.

Circumstances under Which the Alleged Injury Became Known:
9. Alleged injury became immediately apparent to the employee as a result of an accident.
10. Accident or act causing the alleged injury was observed by other persons.
11. Alleged injury became immediately apparent to other observers as a result of an accident or act.
12. Alleged injury was reported to the employer as soon as it became apparent to the employee.
13. Accident or act causing the alleged injury was brought to the attention of a physician.
14. Claim for compensation filed as soon as the alleged injury became apparent to the employee.

Physical Conditions of the Claimant Which Affect the Probability of an Injury Subject to Compensation:
15. Previous condition which contributes to the probability of an occupational disease, e.g., a person who is working in a tuberculosis sanitarium is regarded by the court as being especially prone to contact the disease at work if he was previously afflicted by the disease, even though he had been completely cured.
16. No known alternative cause of the injury and its consequences.

Evidence Derived from Expert Testimony:
17. Unanimous expert testimony in favor of the validity of the allegation made by the claimant.

Evidence Not Derived from Expert Testimony:
18. No contradictions in the evidence given by the claimant.
19. All evidence not derived from expert testimony in favor of the validity of the allegation made by the claimant.

be appropriate to give a simple hypothetical example in this area and then to draw the parallel to the problem under investigation. Assume that a group of students take 20 different tests, and that each student receives a score on each test. Assume, furthermore, that all tests measure—to different degrees—four main abilities, e.g., reading comprehension, arithmetical reasoning, spatial conception, and vocabulary. The tests may be called variables, and the abilities may be referred to as factors. If it can be determined to what extent each test measures each ability, it should be possible to restate each test score in terms of the degrees of the different abilities which it reveals, i.e., to restate the variables in terms of factors. Instead of the original 20 test scores, the performance of each student could then be restated as scores on the four factors which represent the four main abilities.[9] To what extent a variable (in this example, each test) is represented by a factor, i.e., the "factor loading" of the variable,[10] is determined in the course of one stage of factor analysis, which is called factoring. How the combinations of variables (in this example, the 20 test scores for each student) can be restated in terms of factors (in this example, the four main abilities) is the task of another stage of factor analysis, which is known as the estimation of factors.

By analogy, it can be said that—in the involuntary confession cases, in

TABLE 4

Involuntary Confession Cases

1. *Brown* v. *Mississippi,* 297 U.S. 278 (1936)
2. *Chambers* v. *Florida,* 309 U.S. 227 (1940)
3. *White* v. *Texas,* 310 U.S. 530 (1940)
4. *Lisbena* v. *California,* 314 U.S. 219 (1941)
5. *Ward* v. *Texas,* 316 U.S. 547 (1942)
6. *Ashcraft* v. *Tennessee,* 322 U.S. 143 (1944)
7. *Lyons* v. *Oklahoma,* 322 U.S. 596 (1944)
8. *Malinski* v. *New York,* 324 U.S. 401 (1945)
9. *Haley* v. *Ohio,* 332 U.S. 596 (1948)
10. *Watts* v. *Indiana,* 338 U.S. 49 (1949)
11. *Turner* v. *Pennsylvania,* 338 U.S. 62 (1949)
12. *Harris* v. *South Carolina,* 338 U.S. 68 (1949)
13. *Gallegos* v. *Nebraska,* 342 U.S. 55 (1951)
14. *Stroble* v. *California,* 343 U.S. 181 (1952)
15. *Brown* v. *Allen,* 344 U.S. 443 (1953)
16. *Stein* v. *New York,* 346 U.S. 156 (1953)
17. *Leyra* v. *Denno,* 347 U.S. 556 (1954)
18. *Fikes* v. *Alabama,* 352 U.S. 191 (1957)
19. *Thomas* v. *Arizona,* 356 U.S. 390 (1958)
20. *Payne* v. *Arkansas,* 356 U.S. 560 (1958)
21. *Ashdown* v. *Utah,* 357 U.S. 426 (1958)
22. *Crooker* v. *California,* 357 U.S. 433 (1958)
23. *Cicenia* v. *Lagay,* 357 U.S. 504 (1958)
24. *Spano* v. *New York,* 360 U.S. 315 (1959)
25. *Blackburn* v. *Alabama,* 361 U.S. 199 (1960)
26. *Culombe* v. *Connecticut,* 367 U.S. 568 (1961)

the right to counsel cases, in the Connecticut workmen's compensation cases, and in any other group of cases where the rule of law makes the decision dependent on unspecified combinations of a specified set of circumstances—each case is a counterpart of a student. Each circumstance (variable) is the counterpart of a test. Corresponding to the test scores, each circumstance can be represented by 1, if it is present in the case, or by 0, if it is absent in the case.[11] Furthermore, the circumstances of the cases might reveal common characteristics (factors), such as "tactic to keep the defendant ignorant of the proceeding against him" in the state criminal cases or "evidence directly relating the injury to the employment" in the workmen's compensation cases, which are analogous to the main abilities reflected in the various tests. These factors may or may not be similar to the legal categories in which the circumstances are placed by the court. For the classification of the circumstances in terms of these legal categories does not preclude relationships between circumstances which appear in different legal categories. As in the example involving the psychological tests, the variables can be restated in terms of factors. One purpose of this restatement is to achieve economy in the processing of data at the final stage of the analysis.[12] Another, even more important, purpose of this restatement is to take fully into account the mutual dependence or independence of the variables among each other.

On the basis of these considerations, three main stages in the analysis should be distinguished: (1) *factoring,* designed to reveal the factors and to show how each variable can be expressed in terms of these factors; (2) *estimation of the factors* in each case, i.e., the restatement of the combination of variables in each case in terms of the factors; (3) *weighting of the cases,* based on the respective combinations of factors. A consistent scale of case weights will distinguish between pro and con decisions. Each one of these stages of the analysis will now be demonstrated by their application to the three sets of cases: involuntary confession, right to counsel, and workmen's compensation.

1. FACTORING.

Hotelling's Iterative Method of Factoring, also known as the Principal Components, Principal Axes, or Principal Factors Method, has been used in this analysis to determine how each variable can be restated in terms of factors.[13]

Since the initial step in factor analysis is to obtain a correlation measure of the relationship between every pair of variables, the original correlation matrices[14] for the variables in the three groups of cases are shown in Tables 10, 11, and 12.[15] In view of the fact that the analysis is concerned with the presence or absence of variables (that is, a dichotomous distribution), the phi coefficient is used here as a correlation measure. It indicates the association or disassociation between every pair of variables, on the basis of the observations represented by the cases. Theoretically, the phi coefficient can range from $+1$ to -1, whereby $+1$ indicates the highest possible degree of association for a pair of variables, 0 indicates no association (mutual independence), and −1 indicates the highest possible degree of disassociation. Empirically, however, the phi coefficient seldom reaches these limits. It is in this connection that various limitations of the phi coefficient must be noted.

One limitation is that the more the ratio of the marginal frequencies of one variable differs from this ratio for the other variable, the more restricted is the range of the phi coefficient. For example, Table 10 shows that the correlation between variables 16 and 17 in the involuntary confession cases is −0.53. This is also the maximum negative limit (+0.16 is the maximum

TABLE 5

Right to Counsel Cases*

1. *Powell* v. *Alabama*, 287 U.S. 45 (1932)
2. *Avery* v. *Alabama*, 308 U.S. 444 (1940)
3. *Smith* v. *O'Grady*, 312 U.S. 329 (1941)
4. *Betts* v. *Brady*, 316 U.S. 455 (1942)
5. *Williams* v. *Kaiser*, 323 U.S. 471 (1945)
6. *Tomkins* v. *Missouri*, 323 U.S. 485 (1945)
7. *House* v. *Mayo*, 324 U.S. 42 (1945)
8. *White* v. *Ragen*, 324 U.S. 760 (1945)
9. *Rice* v. *Olsen*, 324 U.S. 786 (1945)
10. *Hawk* v. *Olson*, 326 U.S. 271 (1945)
11. *Canizio* v. *New York*, 327 U.S. 82 (1946)
12. *Carter* v. *Illinois*, 329 U.S. 173 (1946)
13. *De Meerleer* v. *Michigan*, 329 U.S. 663 (1947)
14. *Foster* v. *Illinois*, 332 U.S. 134 (1947)
15. *Gayes* v. *New York*, 332 U.S. 145 (1947)
16. *Marino* v. *Ragen*, 332 U.S. 561 (1947)
17. *Bute* v. *Illinois*, 333 U.S. 640 (1948)
18. *Wade* v. *Mayo*, 334 U.S. 672 (1948)
19. *Gryger* v. *Burke*, 334 U.S. 728 (1948)
20. *Townsend* v. *Burke*, 334 U.S. 736 (1948)
21. *Uveges* v. *Pennsylvania*, 335 U.S. 437 (1948)
22. *Gibbs* v. *Burke*, 337 U.S. 773 (1948)
23. *Quicksall* v. *Michigan*, 339 U.S. 660 (1950)
24. *Palmer* v. *Ashe*, 342 U.S. 134 (1951)
25. *Stroble* v. *California*, 343 U.S. 181 (1952)
26. *Chandler* v. *Fretag*, 348 U.S. 3 (1954)
27. *Massey* v. *Moore*, 348 U.S. 105 (1954)
28. *Herman* v. *Claudy*, 350 U.S. 116 (1956)
29. *Moore* v. *Michigan*, 355 U.S. 155 (1957)
30. *Crooker* v. *California*, 357 U.S. 433 (1958)
31. *Cicenia* v. *Lagay*, 357 U.S. 504 (1958)
32. *Cash* v. *Culver*, 358 U.S. 633 (1959)
33. *Hudson* v. *North Carolina*, 363 U.S. 697 (1960)
34. *McNeal* v. *Culver*, 365 U.S. 109 (1961)
35. *Reynolds* v. *Cochran*, 365 U.S. 525 (1961)

*The following cases are not included in the analysis: *In re Groban*, 352 U.S. 330 (1957); *Anonymous Nos. 6 & 7* v. *Baker*, 360 U.S. 287 (1959). These cases were treated by the majority of the Court as investigations, *not* as state criminal proceedings. Accordingly, the majority of the Court concluded that the considerations applicable to the right to counsel in state criminal proceedings were not controlling in these cases.

positive limit) which the phi coefficient can attain for the marginal frequencies of this pair of variables.[16] In such instances, this restriction prevents high associations or disassociations from being as pronounced as would be expected in terms of a $+1$ to -1 range. Since -0.53 is the highest negative value which the phi coefficient can reach within the given marginal frequencies, this value suggests that variables 16 and 17 in the involuntary confession cases are not so extremely disassociated as they are. To be sure, neither inferentially nor as a result of an inspection of Table 7 would one necessarily expect a high association between variables 16 and 17, i.e., between "request of consultation with counsel denied" and "no consultation with counsel prior to the confession." Logically speaking, one would say that a defendant whose request for consultation with counsel was denied probably had no earlier opportunity to consult with counsel. But a defendant who had no consulta-

TABLE 6
Connecticut Workmen's Compensation Cases*

1. *Whitney* v. *Hazard Lead Works*, 105 Conn. 512 (1927)
2. *Cishowski* v. *Clayton Mfg. Co.*, 105 Conn. 651 (1927)
3. *Guiliano* v. *O'Connell's Sons*, 105 Conn. 695 (1927)
4. *Kosik* v. *Manchester Construction Co.*, 106 Conn. 107 (1927)
5. *Norton* v. *Barton's Bias Narrow Fabric Co.*, 106 Conn. 360 (1927)
6. *Wilder* v. *Russell Library Co.*, 107 Conn. 56 (1927)
7. *Ryerson* v. *Bounty Co.*, 107 Conn. 370 (1928)
8. *Flanagan* v. *Webster & Webster*, 107 Conn. 502 (1928)
9. *Mossop* v. *Mossop*, 108 Conn. 148 (1928)
10. *Coffee* v. *Coffey Laundries, Inc.*, 108 Conn. 493 (1928)
11. *Taylor* v. *St. Paul's Universalist Church*, 109 Conn. 178 (1929)
12. *Ohmen* v. *Adams Brothers*, 109 Conn. 378 (1929)
13. *Mascika* v. *Connecticut Tool & Engineering Co.*, 109 Conn. 473 (1929)
14. *Stakonis* v. *United Advertising Corp.*, 110 Conn. 385 (1930)
15. *Galluzzo* v. *The State*, 111 Conn. 188 (1930)
16. *Smith* v. *Seamless Rubber Co.*, 111 Conn. 365 (1930)
17. *Judd* v. *Metropolitan Life Ins. Co.*, 111 Conn. 532 (1930)
18. *Lovallo* v. *American Brass Co.*, 112 Conn. 635 (1931)
19. *Lyons* v. *Fox New England Theatres, Inc.*, 112 Conn. 691 (1931)
20. *Bailey* v. *Mitchell*, 113 Conn. 721 (1931)
21. *Richardson* v. *New Haven*, 114 Conn. 389 (1932)
22. *De Martino* v. *New Haven*, 114 Conn. 519 (1932)
23. *Senzamici* v. *Waterbury Casting Co.*, 115 Conn. 446 (1932)
24. *Boulanger* v. *First National Stores, Inc.*, 115 Conn. 665 (1932)
25. *Plodzyk* v. *Connecticut Coke Co.*, 116 Conn. 297 (1933)
26. *McCormick* v. *Southern New England Ice Co.*, 118 Conn. 295 (1934)
27. *Northam* v. *Bunnell Transportation Co., Inc.*, 118 Conn. 312 (1934)
28. *Stier* v. *Derby*, 119 Conn. 44 (1934)
29. *McGrath* v. *Crane Co.*, 119 Conn. 170 (1934)
30. *Keeler* v. *Sears, Roebuck & Co.*, 121 Conn. 56 (1936)
31. *Kelliher* v. *New Haven Clock Co.*, 121 Conn. 528 (1936)
32. *Manacek* v. *George McLachlan Hat Co.*, 121 Conn. 541 (1936)
33. *Madeo* v. *I. Dibner & Brothers, Inc.*, 121 Conn. 664 (1936)

TABLE 6
(Continued)

Connecticut Workmen's Compensation Cases

34. *Covaleski* v. *Russell & Erwin Division, Amer. Hdw. Corp.*, 121 Conn. 708 (1936)
35. *Drouin* v. *Chelsea Silk Co.*, 122 Conn. 129 (1936)
36. *Savage* v. *St. Aeden's Church*, 122 Conn. 343 (1937)
37. *Nicotra* v. *Bigelow, Stanford Carpet Co.*, 122 Conn. 355 (1937)
38. *Furman* v. *National Dairy Products Corp.*, 123 Conn. 327 (1937)
39. *Ratushni* v. *Mutual Aid Unemployment Fund*, 123 Conn. 405 (1937)
40. *Sgritta* v. *Hertz Construction Co.*, 124 Conn. 6 (1938)
41. *Stulginski* v. *Waterbury Rolling Mills Co.*, 124 Conn. 355 (1938)
42. *Caraher* v. *Sears, Roebuck & Co.*, 124 Conn. 409 (1938)
43. *Johnson* v. *Wiese*, 125 Conn. 238 (1939)
44. *Reynolds* v. *Bider Dairy Co.*, 125 Conn. 380 (1939)
45. *Iliff* v. *Norwalk Tire & Rubber Co.*, 127 Conn. 248 (1940)
46. *Taylor* v. *M. A. Gamino Construction Co.*, 127 Conn. 528 (1941)
47. *Bakis* v. *Sidney Blumenthal & Co.*, 127 Conn. 717 (1941)
48. *Mulligan* v. *Oakes*, 128 Conn. 488 (1942)
49. *LeLenko* v. *Wilson H. Lee Co.*, 128 Conn. 499 (1942)
50. *Davis* v. *Goldie Motors, Inc.*, 129 Conn. 240 (1942)
51. *Richardson* v. *Pratt & Whitney Mfg. Co.*, 129 Conn. 689 (1943)
52. *Dennison* v. *Connecticut Good Humor, Inc.*, 130 Conn. 8 (1943)
53. *Burdick* v. *United States Finishing Co.*, 130 Conn. 454 (1943)
54. *Flodin* v. *Henry & Wright Mfg. Co.*, 131 Conn. 244 (1944)
55. *Carroll* v. *Westport Sanitarium*, 131 Conn. 334 (1944)
56. *Ruckgaber* v. *Clark*, 131 Conn. 341 (1944)
57. *O'Brien* v. *United States Aluminum Co.*, 131 Conn. 484 (1944)
58. *Winzler* v. *United Aircraft Corp.*, 132 Conn. 118 (1945)
59. *Puffin* v. *General Electric Co.*, 132 Conn. 279 (1945)
60. *Waters* v. *Service Oil Co.*, 132 Conn. 388 (1945)
61. *Kuharski* v. *Briston Brass Corp.*, 132 Conn. 563 (1946)
62. *Gesmundo* v. *Bush*, 133 Conn. 607 (1947)
63. *DiLauro* v. *Bassetti*, 133 Conn. 642 (1947)
64. *Shedlock* v. *Cudahy Packing Co.*, 134 Conn. 672 (1948)
65. *Katz* v. *Katz*, 137 Conn. 134 (1950)
66. *Willis* v. *Taylor & Fenn Co.*, 137 Conn. 626 (1951)
67. *Manfredi* v. *United Aircraft Corp.*, 138 Conn. 23 (1951)
68. *Harrison* v. *Armstrong Rubber Co.*, 138 Conn. 567 (1952)
69. *Smith* v. *State of Connecticut*, 138 Conn. 620 (1952)
70. *Stankewicz* v. *Stanley Works*, 139 Conn. 215 (1952)
71. *Henry Mund* v. *Farmers' Cooperative, Inc.*, 139 Conn. 338 (1952)
72. *Hughes* v. *American Brass Co.*, 141 Conn. 231 (1954)
73. *Marschner* v. *American Hardware Corp.*, 141 Conn. 742 (1954)
74. *Greenberg* v. *Electric Boat Co.*, 142 Conn. 404 (1955)
75. *Triano* v. *United States Rubber Co.*, 144 Conn. 393 (1957)
76. *D'Angelo* v. *Connecticut Light & Power Co.*, 146 Conn. 505 (1959)

*This table contains all applicable cases decided by the Supreme Court of Errors of Connecticut from 1927 to the present. The year 1927 was chosen as the starting date because of a major amendment to the Connecticut Workmen's Compensation Act in that year (Chapter 307, Public Acts of 1927). The information given in this table and in Table 9 was compiled by Fred Beckenstein, Department of Political Science, University of Connecticut.

tion with counsel prior to the confession did not necessarily make a request to have counsel. Table 7 supports this conclusion. In two-thirds of the cases in which a request for consultation with counsel was denied, the defendant had no opportunity to see counsel prior to the confession. But in five-sixths of the cases in which the defendant had no consultation with counsel prior to the confession, he apparently had not even made a request to have counsel. This example shows that the phi coefficient can be misleading if differences in the marginal frequencies are extreme.

Another limitation of the phi coefficient is that it does not account for multiple appearances of variables. Although this limitation does not have serious consequences for the analysis—only very few variables in the samples can have more than one manifestation in a case—it should be noted, nevertheless. Since the phi coefficient measures association or disassociation of variables in terms of a dichotomous distribution, it is concerned only with the presence or absence of variables on each observation (in each case), regard-

TABLE 7

Appearance of Variables in the Involuntary Confession Cases*

Cases**	1	2	3	4	5	6	7	8	9	10	11	12	13	14	15	16	17	18	19	20	21	22
1	1	0	0	0	0	1	1	0	1	1	1	1	0	1	1	0	1	1	0	1	1	1
2	0	0	1	0	1	0	0	0	1	1	1	1	1	1	1	0	1	1	1	1	1	1
3	0	0	1	0	1	0	1	0	1	1	1	1	0	1	1	0	1	1	0	1	1	1
4	0	0	1	0	1	0	0	0	1	0	1	0	0	1	0	1	0	0	0	0	1	0
5	0	1	0	0	1	0	1	0	1	1	1	1	1	1	1	0	1	1	0	1	1	1
6	0	0	1	1	1	0	0	0	1	0	1	1	0	1	1	0	1	0	0	0	1	1
7	0	0	0	0	0	0	0	1	0	1	1	0	0	0	1	0	1	0	0	0	0	0
8	0	0	1	0	0	0	0	0	1	1	1	1	0	1	1	1	1	0	0	0	1	0
9	0	0	1	1	1	0	0	0	1	1	1	1	0	1	1	0	1	1	1	1	1	0
10	0	0	1	1	1	0	0	0	1	1	1	1	0	1	1	0	1	0	0	0	1	0
11	0	0	0	1	1	1	0	0	1	1	1	1	0	1	1	0	1	0	0	0	1	0
12	0	0	0	1	1	1	0	0	1	1	1	1	0	1	1	0	1	1	0	1	1	0
13	0	0	0	0	0	0	0	0	0	1	1	1	0	1	1	0	1	0	0	2	1	0
14	0	1	0	0	0	0	0	0	1	1	1	1	0	1	1	0	1	0	0	0	0	0
15	0	0	0	0	0	0	0	0	1	1	1	1	0	0	1	0	1	1	0	1	1	0
16	0	0	0	1	1	0	0	0	1	1	1	1	0	1	1	0	1	0	0	0	0	0
17	0	0	1	0	1	1	0	1	1	1	1	0	0	1	1	0	1	0	0	0	1	1
18	0	0	0	0	1	0	0	0	1	1	1	1	0	0	0	0	1	1	0	2	0	1
19	0	1	0	0	0	0	0	0	1	0	0	0	1	0	0	0	1	1	0	0	0	0
20	0	1	0	0	0	1	0	0	1	1	1	1	1	1	1	0	1	1	1	2	1	0
21	0	0	0	0	0	0	0	0	1	1	1	1	0	0	0	1	1	0	0	0	1	0
22	0	0	0	0	0	0	0	0	1	1	1	1	0	1	1	0	1	1	0	0	0	1
23	0	0	0	0	0	0	0	0	1	1	1	1	0	1	1	1	1	0	0	0	1	1
24	0	0	1	0	1	1	0	0	1	0	0	0	0	0	0	1	0	0	0	2	1	0
25	0	0	0	0	1	0	0	0	1	0	0	1	0	0	0	0	1	1	0	1	0	1
26	0	0	0	0	0	1	0	0	1	1	1	0	0	1	1	0	1	0	0	3	0	0

*A zero signifies that the variable is absent in the case; any other number signifies that the variable is present, with as many manifestations as the number indicates.
**To identify a case refer to the corresponding number in Table 4.
†To identify a variable refer to the corresponding number in Table 1.

less of the number of times a variable might appear on an observation. For example, variable 20 in the involuntary confession cases, "illiteracy, subnormal education, etc.," can have multiple appearances in a case. But in computing its correlation with other variables, only one appearance can be counted, even in cases in which it has several manifestations. For counting more than one appearance would have the same effect on the computation of the phi

TABLE 8

Appearance of Variables in the Right to Counsel Cases*

Cases**	1	2	3	4	5	6	7	8	9	10	11	12	13	14	15	16	17	18	19	20	21	22	23
1	1	1	1	1	0	1	0	0	0	1	0	0	1	1	1	0	0	0	0	0	0	0	0
2	1	0	0	1	0	0	0	0	0	0	0	1	1	0	0	0	0	0	0	1	0	0	0
3	0	0	1	1	1	1	1	1	0	0	1	0	1	0	0	1	1	0	0	0	1	0	0
4	0	0	0	0	1	1	1	1	0	0	1	0	1	0	0	0	0	0	0	0	0	0	0
5	1	0	0	1	1	1	1	1	0	0	1	0	1	0	0	0	0	0	0	0	0	0	0
6	1	0	0	1	1	1	1	1	0	1	0	0	1	0	0	0	0	0	0	0	0	0	0
7	0	1	1	0	1	1	1	1	0	0	0	1	1	0	0	0	0	1	0	1	0	0	0
8	0	0	0	1	1	1	1	1	0	0	0	0	1	0	0	0	0	1	0	1	1	2	0
9	0	0	1	1	1	1	1	1	0	1	0	0	1	0	0	0	0	0	0	0	0	1	1
10	1	0	0	0	1	1	0	0	0	0	0	0	1	1	0	0	0	1	0	1	0	0	0
11	0	1	1	1	1	0	0	0	0	1	0	0	1	0	0	0	0	0	0	0	0	0	0
12	1	0	0	1	1	0	0	1	1	0	0	0	0	0	0	0	0	0	0	0	0	0	0
13	0	1	0	1	1	1	1	1	0	1	0	0	1	0	0	0	0	0	1	0	1	2	0
14	0	0	0	1	1	1	1	1	0	1	0	0	1	0	0	0	0	0	0	0	0	0	0
15	0	1	0	1	1	1	1	1	0	0	0	0	0	0	0	0	0	0	0	0	0	0	0
16	1	1	1	1	1	1	1	1	0	1	0	0	1	0	0	0	0	0	0	0	0	0	0
17	0	0	0	1	1	1	1	1	0	1	0	0	1	0	0	0	0	0	0	0	0	0	0
18	0	1	0	1	1	1	1	1	0	0	1	0	1	0	0	0	0	0	0	0	0	0	0
19	0	0	0	0	1	1	1	1	0	1	0	0	1	0	0	0	0	0	0	0	0	1	0
20	0	0	0	0	1	1	1	1	1	1	0	0	1	1	0	0	1	0	0	0	0	1	0
21	0	1	0	1	1	1	1	1	0	1	0	0	1	0	0	0	0	0	1	0	0	0	0
22	0	0	0	0	1	1	1	1	0	1	0	0	1	0	0	0	0	0	0	0	0	5	0
23	0	0	0	0	1	1	1	1	0	1	0	0	1	0	0	0	0	0	0	0	0	0	0
24	0	1	1	0	1	1	1	1	0	1	0	0	1	0	0	1	1	0	0	0	0	0	0
25	1	0	0	0	0	0	0	0	2	0	0	0	1	0	1	0	0	0	0	0	0	0	0
26	0	0	1	0	1	1	1	1	0	0	0	1	1	0	0	1	0	0	0	1	1	0	0
27	0	0	1	0	1	1	1	1	0	1	0	0	1	0	0	0	0	0	0	1	0	0	0
28	0	1	1	1	1	1	1	1	1	1	0	0	1	1	0	0	1	1	1	0	0	0	1
29	0	1	2	0	1	1	1	1	0	0	0	0	1	0	0	0	0	0	0	0	0	0	1
30	1	0	0	0	0	0	0	0	1	0	0	1	1	0	0	0	0	0	0	0	0	0	0
31	1	0	0	0	0	0	0	0	1	0	0	1	1	0	0	0	0	0	0	0	0	0	0
32	0	1	1	1	0	1	1	1	0	0	1	0	1	0	0	0	0	0	0	1	0	0	1
33	0	0	0	0	1	1	1	1	0	0	1	0	1	0	0	0	0	0	0	0	0	0	1
34	0	0	2	1	1	1	1	1	0	0	1	0	1	0	0	0	0	0	0	0	0	0	1
35	0	0	0	0	1	1	1	0	0	1	1	0	0	0	0	0	0	0	1	1	0	1	

*A zero signifies that the variable is absent in the case; any other number signifies that the variable is present, with as many manifestations as the number indicates.
**To identify a case refer to the corresponding number in Table 5.
†To identify a variable refer to the corresponding number in Table 2.

coefficient as adding observations to the sample which do not exist. To be sure, the multiple appearance of variables are taken into account in the computation of the factor estimates.

Aside from the limitations which can be attributed to the statistical properties of the phi coefficient, some correlations exhibit characteristics which are due to the nature of the variables. For example, Table 12 shows that variables 1, 2, and 3 in the workmen's compensation cases are negatively correlated with variables 4 to 11. Moreover, it shows that variables 4, 5, and 6 have high positive intercorrelations. These results must be explained

TABLE 9

Appearance of Variables in the Connecticut Workmen's Compensation Cases*

Cases**	1	2	3	4	5	6	7	8	9	10	11	12	13	14	15	16	17	18	19
1	0	0	0	0	0	0	0	1	1	0	1	1	0	1	0	1	1	1	1
2	1	1	1	0	0	0	0	0	0	0	0	1	0	1	0	1	0	1	1
3	0	0	0	1	0	0	0	1	1	1	1	1	1	1	0	1	1	1	1
4	1	0	1	0	0	0	0	0	0	0	0	1	0	1	1	0	0	1	0
5	1	0	0	0	0	0	0	0	0	0	0	1	0	1	1	0	0	1	0
6	0	0	0	1	1	0	1	1	0	1	0	1	0	0	0	0	1	1	1
7	0	0	0	1	1	1	1	1	1	0	0	1	0	1	0	1	1	1	1
8	0	0	0	1	1	1	1	1	1	1	1	1	1	1	0	1	1	1	1
9	0	0	0	1	1	1	0	1	0	1	0	1	1	1	0	1	1	1	1
10	0	0	0	1	0	0	1	0	0	1	0	1	0	1	1	0	0	1	0
11	0	0	0	1	1	1	1	1	1	1	1	1	1	1	0	1	1	1	1
12	0	0	0	1	1	1	1	1	1	1	1	1	1	0	1	0	1	1	1
13	0	0	0	1	0	0	1	1	1	1	1	1	1	1	0	1	1	1	1
14	0	0	0	1	1	1	1	1	1	1	1	1	1	1	0	1	1	1	1
15	1	0	0	0	0	0	0	0	0	0	0	1	0	0	0	0	0	1	1
16	0	0	0	1	0	0	1	1	0	1	0	1	1	1	0	1	1	1	1
17	0	0	0	1	1	1	1	1	1	1	1	1	0	1	0	1	1	1	1
18	0	0	0	1	1	0	1	1	1	1	1	1	1	1	0	1	1	1	1
19	1	0	0	0	0	0	0	0	0	0	0	0	0	1	1	0	0	1	0
20	1	0	0	0	0	0	0	0	0	0	0	1	1	1	1	0	0	1	1
21	0	0	0	1	1	1	1	1	1	0	0	1	0	1	1	0	0	1	1
22	0	0	0	1	1	1	1	1	0	0	0	0	1	1	0	1	1	1	1
23	1	0	0	0	0	0	0	0	0	0	0	1	0	1	0	0	0	1	1
24	0	0	0	1	1	1	1	1	1	0	1	1	1	1	0	1	1	1	1
25	0	0	0	1	1	1	1	1	1	0	0	1	0	1	1	0	0	0	0
26	0	0	0	1	1	0	1	1	1	0	1	1	0	1	0	1	1	1	1
27	0	0	0	1	1	0	1	1	1	1	1	1	1	1	0	1	1	1	1
28	0	0	0	1	1	1	1	1	0	1	1	1	0	1	0	1	0	1	1
29	1	1	0	0	0	0	0	0	0	0	0	1	0	1	1	0	0	0	0
30	0	0	0	1	1	1	1	1	1	1	1	1	1	1	0	1	1	1	1
31	0	0	0	1	1	1	1	1	1	1	1	1	1	1	0	1	1	1	1
32	1	0	1	0	0	0	0	0	0	0	0	1	0	1	1	0	0	1	1
33	1	0	0	0	0	0	0	0	0	0	0	1	0	1	0	0	1	1	0
34	1	1	0	0	0	0	0	0	0	0	0	1	0	1	1	0	0	1	1
35	0	0	0	0	0	0	0	0	1	1	1	1	1	1	0	1	1	1	1

TABLE 9
(Continued)

Appearance of Variables in the Connecticut Workmen's Compensation Cases

Cases**	1	2	3	4	5	6	7	8	9	10	11	12	13	14	15	16	17	18	19
36	0	0	0	1	1	1	1	1	1	0	0	1	1	1	1	0	0	1	0
37	0	0	0	1	1	1	1	1	1	1	1	1	1	1	1	0	0	1	1
38	1	0	0	0	0	0	0	0	0	0	0	1	0	1	1	0	0	1	1
39	1	0	0	0	0	0	0	0	0	0	0	1	0	1	1	0	0	1	0
40	0	0	0	1	1	1	1	1	1	1	1	1	1	1	0	1	0	1	1
41	0	0	0	1	1	0	1	0	1	1	1	1	0	1	0	1	1	1	0
42	0	0	0	1	1	0	1	1	1	0	1	1	1	1	0	1	1	1	0
43	0	0	0	1	1	1	1	1	1	1	1	1	1	1	0	1	1	1	1
44	0	0	0	1	1	1	1	1	0	1	0	1	1	1	0	1	0	1	1
45	0	0	0	1	0	0	1	1	1	1	1	1	1	1	0	1	1	1	1
46	0	0	0	1	1	1	1	1	1	1	1	1	1	1	0	1	1	1	1
47	1	0	0	0	0	0	0	0	0	0	0	1	1	1	1	0	0	1	1
48	0	0	0	1	0	0	0	1	1	1	1	1	0	1	0	1	0	0	1
49	1	0	1	0	0	0	0	0	0	0	0	0	1	0	1	1	1	1	1
50	0	0	0	1	0	0	0	1	1	1	1	1	1	1	0	1	1	1	1
51	1	0	0	0	0	0	0	0	0	0	0	1	0	1	1	0	0	1	0
52	0	0	0	0	0	0	1	1	1	1	1	1	1	1	0	1	1	1	1
53	0	0	0	1	1	1	1	1	0	0	0	1	0	1	1	0	0	1	0
54	0	0	0	0	0	0	0	0	1	1	1	1	0	1	0	1	1	1	1
55	0	0	0	1	1	1	1	1	1	0	0	1	0	1	0	1	1	1	1
56	0	0	0	1	1	1	1	1	1	1	1	1	1	1	0	1	1	1	1
57	0	0	0	1	1	1	1	1	1	1	1	1	1	1	1	0	0	1	1
58	1	0	0	0	0	0	0	0	0	0	0	1	0	1	1	0	0	1	0
59	0	0	0	1	1	0	1	1	1	1	1	1	1	1	0	1	1	1	1
60	0	0	0	1	1	1	1	1	1	1	1	1	1	1	0	1	1	1	1
61	0	0	0	1	1	1	1	1	1	1	1	1	1	1	0	1	1	1	1
62	0	0	0	1	1	1	1	1	1	0	0	1	1	1	0	1	1	1	1
63	0	0	0	0	0	0	1	0	1	1	1	1	0	1	0	1	1	1	1
64	0	0	0	0	0	0	1	0	1	1	1	1	1	1	0	1	1	1	0
65	0	0	0	1	1	1	1	1	1	1	1	1	1	1	0	1	1	1	1
66	0	0	0	0	0	0	1	0	1	1	1	1	0	1	0	1	1	1	0
67	0	0	0	1	1	1	1	1	0	0	0	1	0	1	1	0	0	0	0
68	0	0	0	1	1	1	1	1	1	1	1	1	0	1	0	1	0	1	1
69	1	1	1	0	0	0	0	0	0	0	0	1	0	1	1	1	1	1	1
70	0	0	0	1	1	1	1	1	1	0	0	1	1	1	0	1	0	1	0
71	0	0	0	1	1	1	1	1	1	0	0	1	0	1	1	1	1	1	1
72	0	0	0	1	1	1	1	1	1	0	0	1	0	1	0	1	1	1	1
73	1	0	0	0	0	0	0	0	0	0	0	1	0	1	1	0	0	1	0
74	0	0	0	1	1	1	1	1	0	1	0	1	1	1	0	0	0	1	1
75	0	0	0	1	1	1	1	1	0	0	0	0	0	0	1	0	0	1	1
76	0	0	1	0	0	0	0	0	0	1	0	0	0	0	0	0	0	0	0

*A zero signifies that the variable is absent in the case; any other number signifies that the variable is present, with as many manifestations as the number indicates.

**To identify a case refer to the corresponding number in Table 6.

†To identify a variable refer to the corresponding number in Table 3.

TABLE 10
Original Correlation Matrix for the Involuntary Confession Cases*

Variables

Variables	1	2	3	4	5	6	7	8	9	10	11	12	13	14	15	16	17	18	19	20	21	22
1		-0.08	-0.15	-0.11	-0.22	0.33	0.55	-0.06	0.06	0.10	0.07	0.11	-0.08	0.13	0.11	-0.11	0.06	0.23	-0.07	0.20	0.13	0.25
2			-0.31	-0.23	-0.25	-0.02	0.18	-0.12	0.12	-0.06	-0.18	-0.02	0.70	0.05	-0.02	-0.23	0.12	0.28	0.18	0.00	-0.18	-0.12
3				0.18	0.51	-0.08	-0.01	0.09	0.21	-0.26	0.01	-0.18	-0.09	0.31	0.02	0.18	0.40	-0.13	0.24	-0.08	0.48	0.09
4					0.51	0.08	-0.20	-0.16	0.16	0.04	0.20	0.30	-0.23	0.36	0.30	-0.30	0.16	-0.10	0.09	-0.18	0.17	-0.24
5						0.04	0.09	-0.02	0.31	-0.26	-0.09	0.04	-0.03	0.22	-0.14	-0.22	-0.27	0.17	0.09	0.15	0.22	0.26
6							0.05	0.15	0.18	0.08	-0.05	-0.28	-0.02	0.22	0.13	-0.13	-0.15	0.01	0.05	0.26	0.22	-0.12
7								-0.10	0.10	0.18	0.13	0.20	0.18	0.24	0.20	-0.20	0.10	0.42	-0.13	0.36	0.24	0.46
8									-0.46	0.14	0.10	-0.53	-0.12	-0.12	0.16	-0.16	0.08	-0.25	-0.10	-0.29	-0.12	0.07
9										-0.14	-0.10	0.18	0.12	0.12	-0.16	0.16	-0.08	0.25	0.10	0.00	0.12	0.23
10											0.74	0.43	-0.06	0.31	0.66	-0.20	0.59	0.02	0.18	0.10	0.10	-0.02
11												0.37	-0.18	0.54	0.66	-0.09	0.35	-0.18	0.13	-0.12	0.28	0.04
12													-0.02	0.23	0.35	-0.13	0.53	0.28	0.20	0.18	0.23	0.24
13														0.05	-0.02	-0.23	0.12	0.50	0.51	0.21	0.05	0.10
14															0.62	-0.02	0.12	-0.10	0.24	0.00	0.46	0.01
15																-0.35	-0.53	-0.08	0.20	0.00	0.23	0.06
16																	-0.53	-0.47	-0.20	-0.36	0.17	-0.06
17																		0.25	0.10	0.00	-0.19	0.23
18																			0.42	0.70	0.06	0.28
19																				0.36	0.24	-0.04
20																					0.17	0.16
21																						0.01
22																						

*To identify variables refer to Table 1.

TABLE 11

Original Correlation Matrix for the Right to Counsel Cases*

Variables

Variables	1	2	3	4	5	6	7	8	9	10	11	12	13	14	15	16	17	18	19	20	21	22	23
1		-0.19	-0.22	0.07	-0.55	-0.55	-0.71	-0.63	0.38	-0.11	-0.16	0.22	-0.12	0.17	0.39	-0.19	-0.23	-0.03	-0.19	0.00	-0.29	-0.29	-0.32
2			0.44	0.30	0.01	0.17	0.11	0.06	-0.17	0.14	-0.06	-0.17	-0.08	0.12	0.08	-0.01	0.12	0.12	0.42	-0.06	-0.17	-0.17	0.09
3				0.11	0.04	0.19	0.14	0.09	-0.19	0.08	0.06	-0.04	0.19	0.10	0.07	0.40	0.28	0.10	-0.02	0.06	0.12	-0.19	0.36
4					0.04	0.04	0.05	0.12	-0.19	0.20	0.17	-0.34	-0.23	-0.03	-0.02	-0.13	-0.03	-0.03	0.28	-0.12	-0.04	-0.04	0.03
5						0.60	0.66	0.72	-0.40	0.29	0.04	-0.40	-0.11	-0.08	-0.54	0.14	0.16	0.16	0.14	-0.15	0.21	0.21	0.04
6							0.84	0.72	-0.60	0.29	0.23	-0.40	0.22	0.16	-0.22	0.14	0.16	0.16	0.14	0.04	0.21	0.21	0.21
7								0.92	-0.48	0.26	0.27	-0.29	0.16	-0.23	-0.45	0.17	0.20	-0.02	0.17	-0.07	0.25	0.25	0.21
8									-0.34	0.20	0.25	-0.34	-0.12	-0.27	-0.49	0.15	0.18	-0.04	0.15	-0.11	0.23	0.23	0.27
9										-0.14	-0.23	0.20	-0.22	0.31	0.22	-0.14	0.31	0.08	0.13	-0.23	-0.21	0.25	0.25
10											-0.34	-0.44	0.24	0.19	0.01	-0.09	0.19	-0.17	0.32	-0.49	-0.14	0.32	-0.04
11												-0.23	0.12	-0.18	-0.12	0.10	0.04	-0.18	-0.15	-0.07	-0.04	-0.01	-0.04
12													0.11	-0.16	-0.11	0.13	-0.16	0.08	-0.14	0.53	0.20	-0.21	-0.20
13														0.09	0.06	0.08	0.09	0.09	0.08	0.12	0.11	0.11	0.29
14															0.30	-0.11	0.44	0.44	0.21	0.04	-0.16	0.08	-0.04
15																-0.08	-0.09	-0.09	-0.08	-0.12	-0.11	-0.11	0.12
16																	-0.08	-0.09	-0.09	0.10	0.40	-0.14	0.04
17																		0.15	0.21	-0.18	0.08	0.08	-0.12
18																			0.21	0.49	0.08	0.08	-0.15
19																				-0.15	0.13	0.13	0.04
20																					0.34	-0.04	0.10
21																						0.20	0.11
22																							-0.04
23																							

*To identify variables refer to Table 2.

in terms of the nature of the variables which are involved. Since variable 1 is a disease which "could not have been revealed by a causative accident or act," it is, of course, highly disassociated from any variable which refers to an accident or other causative act. Moreover, any other disease which possibly is an occupational disease would rarely be related to an accident. Consequently, the correlations of variable 1 with variables 4 to 11, each of which refers to an accident or similar act, are highly negative, and the correlations of variables 2 and 3 with variables 4 to 11 indicate at least some disassociation. Variables 4, 5, and 6 are cumulative variables. The presence of variable 6 implies the presence of variables 4 and 5, and the presence of variable 5 implies the presence of variable 4, but not vice versa. In other words, the fact that an activity is "indispensable for the performance of the work" implies that it is "conducive to efficient work" and is "permitted by the employer," and the fact that an activity is "conducive to efficient work" implies that it is "permitted by the employer," but not vice versa. Since these implications are not reciprocal, the three variables have to be identified separately. But their cumulative relationship imposes the condition that they are positively correlated.

Some correlations might appear to be contrary to intuitive expectations. For example, it might seem surprising that variable 8 in the involuntary confession cases, "preceding admittedly coerced confession," and variable 12, "detention incommunicado" are negatively correlated (see Table 10). Upon closer examination, however, the correlation coefficient of -0.53 becomes meaningful. It shows that law-enforcing officers who resort to detention incommunicado are not inclined to admit that any confession which they obtained was coerced.

The factor loadings for the variables in the three sets of cases, i.e., the measures of the degrees to which the variables are represented by factors, are listed in Tables 13, 14, and 15, respectively. The notations a_{j1}, a_{j2}, etc., represent the factor loadings of the variables, i.e., variable j ($j = 1, 2, \ldots, n$) has the factor loading a_{j1} on factor 1, a_{j2} on factor 2, etc. The notation h_j^2 represents the communality of the variable. The factor loadings are correlation measures, which indicate the degree of association or disassociation of variables with factors. They can range from $+1$ to -1. A factor loading of $+1$ indicates the highest possible degree of association of a variable with a factor, 0 indicates no association (mutual independence), and -1 indicates the highest possible degree of disassociation.

For example, in the right to counsel cases (Table 14), variable 7, "no assistance of counsel at the trial or at the hearing on the plea of guilty," has a relatively high loading on factor 1; it is positively associated with this factor, and it can be restated to a considerable degree in terms of this factor. The same observation can be made with regard to variable 5, "no assistance of counsel at the arraignment," variable 6, "no assistance of counsel between the arraignment and the trial or the hearing on the plea of guilty," and variable 8, "no assistance of counsel at the time of sentencing." It appears, therefore, that factor 1 can be characterized to a large extent as a factor that represents the deprivation of the defendant of the services of counsel during the main phases of the state criminal proceeding. On the other hand, variable 18, "coercion or intimidation of the defendant to plead guilty," has a loading of almost 0 on factor 1; in other words, it is virtually independent of factor 1, and it cannot be restated in terms of

TABLE 12
Original Correlation Matrix for the Connecticut Workmen's Compensation Cases*

Variables

Variables	1	2	3	4	5	6	7	8	9	10	11	12	13	14	15	16	17	18	19
1		0.41	0.39	-0.78	-0.64	-0.53	-0.78	-0.78	-0.70	-0.61	-0.56	0.00	-0.43	0.00	0.57	-0.57	-0.48	0.03	-0.28
2			0.37	-0.32	-0.26	-0.22	-0.32	-0.32	-0.28	-0.25	-0.23	0.06	-0.22	0.06	0.21	-0.06	-0.15	-0.18	0.01
3				-0.39	-0.32	-0.27	-0.39	-0.39	-0.35	-0.21	-0.28	-0.15	-0.28	-0.15	0.21	-0.08	-0.14	-0.12	-0.05
4					0.82	0.69	0.77	0.88	0.50	0.40	0.34	0.07	0.43	0.07	-0.36	0.40	0.29	0.02	0.31
5						0.83	0.77	0.77	0.44	0.21	0.24	0.02	0.38	0.02	-0.27	0.30	0.23	0.08	0.24
6							0.63	0.69	0.34	0.14	0.10	-0.02	0.34	0.10	-0.14	0.21	0.06	0.03	0.25
7								0.71	0.56	0.40	0.39	0.07	0.37	0.07	-0.36	0.40	0.35	0.14	0.18
8									0.56	0.34	0.39	0.07	0.48	0.07	-0.42	0.46	0.35	0.02	0.43
9										0.45	0.76	0.28	0.41	0.28	-0.50	0.64	0.57	0.10	0.29
10											0.71	0.13	0.48	0.01	-0.57	0.48	0.39	0.07	0.33
11												0.23	0.45	0.23	-0.57	0.64	0.54	0.15	0.34
12													0.11	0.47	-0.09	0.19	0.15	0.18	0.13
13														0.22	-0.38	0.40	0.35	0.25	0.33
14															0.04	0.31	0.15	0.18	-0.01
15																-0.74	-0.63	-0.15	-0.41
16																	0.76	0.24	0.44
17																		0.30	0.38
18																			0.32
19																			

*To identify variables refer to Table 3.

TABLE 13

Factor Loadings of Variables in the Involuntary Confession Cases*

j	a_{j1}	a_{j2}	a_{j3}	a_{j4}	a_{j5}	a_{j6}	a_{j7}	a_{j8}	a_{j9}	h_j^2
1	0.282	0.144	-0.031	0.609	-0.042	0.031	0.224	0.164	0.038	0.553
2	0.124	0.495	-0.329	-0.361	-0.188	0.319	-0.047	0.398	-0.105	0.807
3	-0.104	-0.150	0.731	-0.024	-0.204	0.064	-0.343	-0.112	-0.007	0.744
4	0.251	-0.368	0.439	-0.406	0.162	-0.335	0.287	0.226	-0.052	0.831
5	0.035	0.087	0.751	-0.126	0.005	-0.458	-0.172	0.087	-0.012	0.837
6	0.092	0.027	0.147	0.218	-0.450	-0.015	0.515	0.131	0.297	0.651
7	0.461	0.334	0.069	0.585	-0.034	0.040	-0.175	0.259	-0.237	0.829
8	-0.144	-0.329	-0.256	0.119	-0.586	-0.329	-0.319	-0.032	0.149	0.786
9	0.073	0.281	0.436	-0.036	0.287	0.173	0.051	0.296	0.436	0.667
10	0.682	-0.380	-0.321	0.062	-0.025	0.101	0.026	-0.201	0.150	0.790
11	0.597	-0.571	-0.029	0.058	-0.012	0.190	-0.114	-0.085	0.000	0.743
12	0.651	-0.013	0.050	-0.080	0.648	0.076	-0.004	-0.100	-0.059	0.872
13	0.233	0.636	-0.100	-0.376	-0.289	0.280	-0.223	0.090	0.022	0.830
14	0.572	-0.299	0.389	-0.057	-0.235	0.225	0.031	0.257	-0.124	0.759
15	0.723	-0.454	-0.080	-0.032	-0.203	0.052	-0.031	0.068	-0.026	0.787
16	-0.530	-0.192	0.134	0.213	0.255	0.560	-0.083	-0.137	0.138	0.805
17	0.654	-0.100	-0.491	-0.169	0.201	-0.251	-0.138	0.073	0.180	0.868
18	0.441	0.763	0.040	0.003	0.034	-0.192	0.009	-0.174	0.040	0.849
19	0.389	0.253	0.205	-0.414	-0.242	0.179	-0.027	-0.381	0.163	0.691
20	0.370	0.562	0.127	0.195	-0.104	-0.159	0.269	-0.431	-0.113	0.813
21	0.293	-0.100	0.552	0.150	-0.145	0.323	0.013	-0.147	-0.083	0.578
22	0.239	0.235	0.096	0.388	0.168	-0.171	-0.482	0.074	0.200	0.607

*To identify variables refer to Table 1.

TABLE 14

Factor Loadings of Variables in the Right to Counsel Cases*

j	a_{j1}	a_{j2}	a_{j3}	a_{j4}	a_{j5}	a_{j6}	a_{j7}	a_{j8}	a_{j9}	h_j^2
1	-0.753	-0.137	-0.084	0.034	-0.027	-0.061	0.011	-0.237	0.046	0.657
2	0.187	-0.306	0.277	0.432	-0.276	-0.027	-0.388	0.096	-0.131	0.645
3	0.244	0.025	0.479	0.533	0.065	-0.177	-0.082	0.099	-0.219	0.674
4	0.140	-0.295	-0.130	0.320	-0.242	0.045	-0.338	-0.148	0.319	0.524
5	0.769	-0.034	-0.101	-0.261	0.030	0.119	-0.126	-0.241	-0.206	0.802
6	0.851	-0.011	0.131	-0.007	-0.194	-0.145	0.269	-0.188	-0.001	0.908
7	0.939	0.107	-0.080	-0.043	0.011	0.035	0.090	0.131	0.009	0.927
8	0.896	0.077	-0.186	-0.069	0.065	0.249	-0.064	0.012	-0.023	0.919
9	-0.549	-0.293	0.193	-0.218	0.289	0.508	0.040	0.205	0.022	0.859
10	0.337	-0.705	-0.064	-0.204	0.082	-0.464	-0.035	0.132	-0.091	0.905
11	0.244	0.229	-0.193	0.496	0.046	0.240	0.340	-0.092	0.274	0.654
12	-0.433	0.595	0.226	-0.175	0.033	-0.044	-0.176	0.294	-0.111	0.756
13	0.114	0.077	0.265	-0.016	-0.027	-0.416	0.391	0.290	0.113	0.513
14	-0.127	-0.456	0.589	-0.124	-0.149	0.094	0.294	-0.227	-0.011	0.756
15	-0.454	-0.278	0.119	0.218	-0.010	-0.258	0.193	-0.077	0.141	0.475
16	0.227	0.297	0.361	0.176	0.650	-0.175	-0.179	-0.190	0.049	0.825
17	0.260	-0.277	0.578	0.009	0.530	0.240	0.061	-0.060	0.049	0.827
18	0.036	0.049	0.550	-0.270	-0.415	0.182	-0.013	-0.217	-0.050	0.634
19	0.231	-0.402	0.262	-0.102	-0.191	0.120	-0.320	0.283	0.302	0.619
20	-0.099	0.661	0.404	-0.152	-0.394	-0.070	-0.065	-0.129	0.053	0.816
21	0.271	0.403	0.219	-0.216	0.146	-0.178	-0.203	0.001	0.369	0.560
22	0.259	-0.159	-0.025	-0.489	-0.026	-0.085	0.098	0.117	0.157	0.387
23	0.255	0.128	0.151	0.303	-0.238	0.303	0.261	0.355	-0.038	0.541

*To identify variables refer to Table 2.

this factor. Of course, this has no bearing on its association with other factors; for example, it has a fairly high loading on factor 3. "Crime subject to capital punishment" (variable 1) has a relatively high negative loading on factor 1; i.e., it is disassociated from factor 1. In other words, the deprivation of the defendant of the services of counsel during *all* main phases of the criminal proceeding is more readily encountered in noncapital cases than in capital cases. (Of course, the absence of counsel during only some of the phases might be sufficient, in combination with other circumstances, for a reversal of the conviction.)

TABLE 15

Factor Loadings of Variables in the Connecticut Workmen's Compensation Cases*

j	a_{j1}	a_{j2}	a_{j3}	a_{j4}	a_{j5}	$h_j{}^2$
1	−0.887	−0.148	0.254	0.160	0.148	0.920
2	−0.369	−0.145	0.122	0.340	−0.358	0.416
3	−0.427	−0.147	−0.140	0.348	−0.207	0.387
4	0.814	0.421	0.024	0.044	−0.055	0.846
5	0.727	0.540	0.105	0.172	−0.007	0.861
6	0.593	0.565	0.168	0.192	−0.011	0.736
7	0.779	0.323	0.028	−0.060	−0.020	0.717
8	0.835	0.343	0.020	0.116	−0.034	0.830
9	0.776	−0.215	0.128	−0.199	−0.180	0.737
10	0.619	−0.301	−0.278	−0.231	0.035	0.606
11	0.692	−0.457	−0.041	−0.270	−0.065	0.767
12	0.173	−0.268	0.522	−0.115	−0.061	0.391
13	0.581	−0.088	0.092	−0.010	0.205	0.396
14	0.176	−0.229	0.659	−0.106	−0.126	0.545
15	−0.656	0.385	0.303	−0.111	−0.032	0.684
16	0.724	−0.501	0.012	0.297	−0.187	0.898
17	0.608	−0.478	−0.056	0.188	0.033	0.638
18	0.194	−0.239	0.249	0.168	0.503	0.438
19	0.454	−0.212	−0.015	0.409	0.187	0.453

*To identify variables refer to Table 3.

The same observation can be made with regard to "no assistance of counsel at any other phase [other than the main phases] of the proceeding" (variable 9) and "detention and trial in a hostile environment or under inflammatory publicity" (variable 15). Both have substantial negative loadings on factor 1. In other words, petitioners invoke the absence of counsel during miscellaneous phases of the proceeding primarily in those cases in which they cannot complain about the absence of counsel during the main phases of the proceeding. This is logically plausible. Furthermore, the factor loadings in question suggest that the detention and the trial of a defendant in a hostile environment or under inflammatory publicity usually is accompanied by the presence of counsel during at least some of the main phases of the proceeding. Indeed, even in *Powell* v. *Alabama* the defendants had a *pro forma* representation by counsel at the arraignment, during the trial, and at the time of sentencing. (The critical point was the absence of counsel between the arraignment and the trial.) It is also interesting to note that the negative loadings on factor 1 suggest a close association between the presence of a crime that is subject to capital punishment, a complaint about the absence of counsel during other than the main phases of the proceeding, and the detention and trial in a hostile environment or under inflammatory publicity. Again, this is plausible.

TABLE 16

Regression Coefficients for the Estimation of Factors in the Involuntary Confession Cases

Variables*	Factors								
	1	2	3	4	5	6	7	8	9
1	0.207	0.123	0.005	0.940	−0.084	0.048	0.608	0.518	0.373
2	0.063	0.415	−0.326	−0.584	−0.240	0.544	−0.017	0.952	−0.431
3	0.006	−0.095	0.478	−0.060	−0.183	0.122	−0.569	−0.235	0.006
4	0.141	−0.295	0.404	−0.595	0.159	−0.481	0.718	0.537	−0.187
5	0.010	0.075	0.656	−0.148	0.027	−0.634	−0.467	0.161	0.052
6	0.090	0.032	0.109	0.240	−0.366	0.033	0.731	0.241	0.735
7	0.433	0.332	0.108	1.343	−0.038	0.061	−0.511	0.952	−1.037
8	−0.064	−0.374	−0.326	0.239	−0.064	−0.788	−0.972	−0.191	0.611
9	0.059	0.284	0.476	0.107	0.371	0.324	0.188	0.769	1.816
10	0.414	−0.301	−0.209	0.112	−0.156	0.203	0.097	−0.431	0.485
11	0.386	−0.462	0.042	0.080	−0.124	0.354	−0.259	−0.249	−0.070
12	0.462	−0.017	0.095	−0.152	1.206	0.246	−0.158	−0.303	−0.349
13	0.183	0.590	−0.030	−0.737	−0.483	0.601	−0.602	0.145	0.128
14	0.306	−0.194	0.307	−0.027	−0.309	0.341	0.101	0.365	−0.257
15	0.420	−0.347	−0.016	−0.011	−0.353	0.138	−0.017	0.075	−0.124
16	−0.259	−0.112	0.189	0.256	0.382	0.847	−0.215	−0.248	0.565
17	0.698	−0.135	−0.981	−0.374	0.564	−0.921	−0.708	0.413	1.351
18	0.238	0.612	0.057	0.036	0.027	−0.294	0.027	−0.356	0.264
19	0.218	0.122	0.235	−0.533	−0.352	0.324	−0.054	−0.769	0.474
20	0.115	0.190	0.052	0.124	−0.118	−0.102	0.309	−0.460	−0.187
21	0.112	−0.050	0.241	0.078	−0.122	0.255	0.014	−0.151	−0.082
22	0.051	0.089	0.062	0.273	0.130	−0.122	−0.473	0.111	0.374
C	2.667	−0.426	0.573	−0.134	0.697	0.345	−0.977	0.384	3.038

*To identify variables refer to Table 1.

From the foregoing example, it can be seen that some factors are "bipolar," that is, they contain high positive as well as high negative factor loadings.[17] This feature may be given the following interpretation. A bipolar factor in a state criminal case would give the petitioner some advantages and some disadvantages in seeking a reversal of his conviction. For example, in a right to counsel case, factor 1 would enable the petitioner to argue that he has been deprived of the services of counsel during all or most main phases of the state criminal proceeding. On the other hand, factor 1 probably would not make it possible for him to argue that he was charged with a crime subject to capital punishment and that he had been detained and tried in a hostile environment or under inflammatory publicity. Moreover, he might not find it feasible to stress the absence of counsel during miscellaneous phases, in view of the fact that such absence would be overshadowed by the absence of counsel during the main phases of the proceeding. Correspondingly, factor 1 in the workmen's compensation cases would enable the

TABLE 17

Regression Coefficients for the Estimation of Factors in the Right to Counsel Cases

Variables*	1	2	3	4	Factors 5	6	7	8	9
1	−0.128	−0.082	−0.115	0.004	0.004	−0.033	0.025	−0.401	0.093
2	0.075	−0.208	0.249	0.509	−0.331	0.078	−0.584	0.153	−0.260
3	0.054	0.001	0.292	0.491	−0.006	−0.093	−0.095	0.205	−0.454
4	0.043	−0.173	−0.044	0.236	−0.188	0.070	−0.401	−0.175	0.541
5	0.220	−0.040	−0.138	−0.524	0.054	0.293	−0.479	−0.951	−0.914
6	0.527	−0.041	0.451	0.008	−0.544	−0.415	1.256	−0.867	0.081
7	0.733	0.327	−0.060	−0.121	0.076	0.079	0.482	1.186	0.241
8	0.677	0.082	−0.483	−0.216	0.164	1.024	−0.642	−0.022	−0.150
9	−0.184	−0.304	0.252	−0.482	0.357	0.937	0.246	0.565	0.021
10	0.151	−0.825	−0.025	−0.515	0.178	−1.088	−0.197	0.487	−0.254
11	0.037	0.045	−0.190	0.558	0.076	0.189	0.498	−0.089	0.618
12	−0.093	0.562	0.311	−0.380	0.069	−0.200	−0.226	0.816	−0.508
13	0.013	0.167	0.285	−0.053	0.047	−0.562	0.804	0.777	0.371
14	−0.046	−0.467	0.750	−0.207	−0.336	0.264	0.635	−0.565	−0.082
15	−0.093	−0.165	0.061	0.277	0.008	−0.261	0.333	−0.106	0.414
16	0.158	0.529	0.582	0.388	1.684	−0.724	−0.658	−0.803	0.289
17	0.161	−0.347	0.986	0.068	0.975	0.481	0.181	−0.199	0.242
18	0.024	−0.038	0.522	−0.370	−0.517	0.260	−0.170	−0.347	−0.159
19	0.137	−0.358	0.375	−0.081	−0.444	−0.186	−0.809	0.594	1.196
20	−0.006	0.597	0.616	−0.475	−0.617	−0.200	−0.270	−0.170	0.212
21	0.064	0.185	0.137	−0.294	0.117	−0.231	−0.284	0.035	0.876
22	0.008	−0.006	−0.001	−0.141	−0.001	−0.027	0.032	0.042	0.122
23	0.045	0.025	0.142	0.321	−0.202	0.218	0.300	0.537	−0.150
C	1.860	−0.074	0.821	−0.675	−0.228	−0.064	0.758	0.552	0.035

*To identify variables refer to Table 2.

claimant to relate his injury to an accident. On the other hand, factor 1 would not make it possible for him to argue that his injury is the result of unhealthy work conditions, or an occupational disease, rather than the result of an accident.

Although most bipolar factors in this study are more advantageous than disadvantageous to the petitioner or to the claimant, a few have the opposite effect. For example, factor 5 in the right to counsel cases shows substantial positive loadings for "deception of the defendant by a distorted and misleading presentation of charges" (variable 16) and "no explicit presentation of charges to the defendant" (variable 17). In that respect, factor 5 gives the petitioner a distinct advantage in seeking a reversal of his conviction. But 12 out of the 23 variables have negative loadings on factor 5. Particularly noteworthy are "coercion or intimidation of the defendant to plead guilty" (variable 18) and "request for additional time for consultation with counsel and for the preparation of a defense denied" (variable 20). Both variables have negative loadings on factor 5. This means that, to the extent

TABLE 18

Regression Coefficients for the Estimation of Factors in the Connecticut Workmen's Compensation Cases

Variables*	Factors				
	1	2	3	4	5
1	−0.495	−0.300	1.367	1.030	0.920
2	−0.174	−0.005	0.140	0.622	−1.219
3	−0.135	−0.006	−0.306	0.567	−0.577
4	0.243	0.419	0.142	0.088	−0.063
5	0.232	0.587	0.338	0.525	0.131
6	0.095	0.329	0.278	0.304	0.012
7	0.145	0.157	0.116	−0.146	0.078
8	0.236	0.295	0.092	0.289	0.083
9	0.160	−0.178	0.414	−0.479	−0.350
10	0.099	−0.152	−0.262	−0.270	0.228
11	0.193	−0.380	0.117	−0.633	0.055
12	0.088	−0.211	1.043	−0.382	−0.141
13	0.084	−0.058	0.097	−0.037	0.350
14	0.110	−0.249	1.739	−0.541	−0.475
15	−0.122	0.234	0.469	−0.213	−0.317
16	0.322	−0.859	0.140	1.296	−0.856
17	0.110	−0.246	−0.055	0.226	0.251
18	0.186	−0.244	0.402	0.208	1.561
19	0.072	−0.094	−0.059	0.402	0.405
C	1.351	−0.774	4.254	0.657	1.037

*To identify variables refer to Table 3.

that factor 5 is prevalent in a case, the defendant (the petitioner before the Supreme Court) usually has been protected during the state criminal proceeding against such procedural infractions as those represented by variables 18 and 20, although he has not been protected against the type of irregularities represented by variables 16 and 17. Considering the net balance of loadings on factor 5, one might suspect that the *total* effect of this factor is a disadvantage rather than an advantage for the petitioner in seeking a reversal of his conviction; and it will be seen later that the final regression analysis does in fact assign a negative weight to factor 5.

Some attention has to be given now to the question whether or not names can be assigned to the factors. It should be noted again that the principal axes that represent the factors are statistical constructs and do not necessarily represent the entities in terms of which the justices think.[18] Nevertheless, if a name for a factor is desired, an attempt can be made to describe the factor in terms of the variables that have high loadings on the factor. Accordingly, factor 1 in the involuntary confession cases could be called "tactic to keep the defendant in isolation, uninformed of the charges against him, and uninformed of his procedural rights, but no denial of consultation

TABLE 19

Factor Estimates in the Involuntary Confession Cases

Cases*	1	2	3	4	5	6	7	8	9
1	1.323	0.583	−0.225	2.902	−0.068	0.220	0.927	1.111	0.254
2	1.011	0.787	0.892	−1.098	−0.572	0.492	−1.593	−1.299	0.842
3	1.043	0.407	0.794	1.515	0.226	−0.376	−1.448	0.278	−0.796
4	−2.047	−0.128	1.816	0.420	−0.654	1.265	−0.229	0.028	−1.009
5	1.283	1.507	−0.039	0.253	−0.314	0.650	−1.498	1.610	−1.105
6	−0.016	−0.721	1.919	−0.695	0.669	−0.721	−0.652	1.110	−0.508
7	−0.813	−1.193	−2.063	0.180	−1.830	−1.359	−0.882	−0.767	−0.786
8	−0.063	−1.003	0.049	0.142	0.580	1.565	−0.548	−0.379	0.302
9	0.918	−0.187	1.264	−1.229	−0.060	−0.468	0.200	−1.018	0.153
10	0.347	−1.112	0.920	−0.856	0.384	−0.397	−0.082	0.567	−0.398
11	0.431	−0.984	0.552	−0.557	0.200	−0.486	1.218	1.044	0.332
12	0.783	−0.182	0.660	−0.396	0.109	−0.882	1.554	0.228	0.409
13	0.361	−0.700	−0.991	0.088	−0.228	0.067	0.665	−1.584	−2.459
14	0.140	−0.332	−1.185	−0.716	0.263	0.885	0.205	1.208	−0.617
15	0.237	0.200	−0.916	0.134	0.598	−0.141	0.471	−1.076	0.066
16	0.228	0.967	0.201	−0.875	0.689	−0.774	0.473	0.953	−0.321
17	−0.179	−1.052	0.266	0.643	−2.281	−1.039	−1.355	0.495	1.858
18	−0.120	0.952	−0.272	0.317	1.112	−1.394	−0.158	−1.188	0.511
19	−1.426	2.191	−1.376	−1.419	−0.457	−0.090	−0.135	1.539	0.091
20	1.212	1.355	−0.469	−1.384	−1.270	1.600	0.939	−0.602	0.527
21	−0.795	−0.367	−0.720	0.240	1.425	0.963	−0.063	−0.584	0.677
22	−0.437	−0.575	−0.915	0.425	1.324	0.725	−0.567	−0.247	1.010
23	−0.019	−0.819	−0.367	0.475	0.893	1.321	−0.452	−0.032	0.670
24	−2.420	0.941	1.680	0.857	−0.824	0.398	1.277	−0.767	−0.320
25	−1.034	1.525	−0.157	0.001	1.510	−1.948	−0.304	−0.048	0.284
26	0.049	−0.127	−0.690	0.633	−1.424	−0.179	2.038	−0.580	0.337

*To identify cases refer to Table 4.

with counsel if the defendant makes such a request." Factor 1 in the right to counsel cases could be described as "absence of counsel during *all* main phases of the state criminal proceeding, which is most likely in a noncapital case, where probably no claim is made that counsel was absent during miscellaneous phases of the proceeding, and where probably no detention and trial in a hostile environment or under inflammatory publicity are involved." Factor 1 in the workmen's compensation cases could be called "a combination of circumstances which relate the alleged injury to an accident, and which probably preclude a claim of an occupational disease." Other factors can be described in similar ways. There are factors, however, which cannot be readily given names, because they do not show any high loadings. Nevertheless, such factors must be included, by virtue of the criteria that are controlling for factoring.[19] In any case, for the purpose of the analysis, *exclusive* reliance is placed on the quantitative statement of the factors.

TABLE 20

Factor Estimates in the Right to Counsel Cases

Cases*	1	2	3	4	5	6	7	8	9
1	−1.264	−1.719	1.083	1.425	−0.940	−1.976	1.018	−1.044	0.414
2	−2.032	1.146	0.232	0.008	−0.457	−0.860	−0.827	0.295	0.674
3	0.828	0.809	0.996	1.216	2.682	0.174	−0.097	−1.355	1.706
4	0.349	0.614	−0.957	0.327	0.100	0.673	1.160	−0.418	0.213
5	0.414	−0.466	−1.140	0.053	0.094	−0.379	0.587	−0.506	0.592
6	0.376	−0.511	−0.950	−0.505	0.018	−0.568	0.090	−0.417	−0.026
7	0.365	1.483	1.224	−0.456	−1.378	0.329	−0.682	0.327	−1.575
8	0.452	1.128	0.463	−1.416	−1.184	0.330	−0.399	−0.902	1.310
9	0.612	−0.408	−0.402	0.161	−0.195	−0.437	0.302	0.768	−0.601
10	−1.255	0.170	1.549	−0.942	−1.682	−0.328	1.042	−2.977	−0.432
11	−1.304	−1.003	−0.202	0.819	−0.018	−1.238	−1.710	0.045	−1.006
12	−1.232	−0.443	−1.349	−0.306	0.618	2.356	−2.010	−1.436	−0.444
13	0.797	−0.821	−0.076	−0.657	−0.647	−0.556	−1.548	0.850	1.938
14	0.505	−0.429	−0.835	−0.510	0.014	−0.535	0.065	−0.016	−0.119
15	0.416	0.021	−0.846	0.568	−0.542	1.193	−1.127	−1.128	−0.496
16	0.505	−0.718	−0.408	0.495	−0.319	−0.583	−0.589	−0.059	−0.741
17	0.505	−0.429	−0.835	−0.510	0.014	−0.535	0.065	−0.016	−0.119
18	0.466	0.233	−0.752	1.072	−0.419	0.821	0.175	−0.439	0.493
19	0.470	−0.262	−0.791	−0.887	0.201	−0.631	0.497	0.201	−0.537
20	0.401	−1.380	1.197	−1.508	1.198	1.050	1.560	0.002	−0.356
21	0.717	−0.994	−0.211	−0.081	−0.761	−0.271	−1.328	0.731	0.817
22	0.503	−0.286	−0.794	−1.450	0.196	−0.738	0.627	0.368	−0.048
23	0.462	−0.256	−0.791	−0.746	0.202	−0.605	0.466	0.159	−0.660
24	0.910	−0.280	1.319	0.710	2.525	−0.864	−0.689	−0.486	−0.843
25	−2.436	−0.614	−0.085	−0.061	1.001	1.083	0.896	0.849	0.884
26	0.487	2.444	1.172	−0.502	1.271	−0.965	−0.870	−0.246	0.009
27	0.580	−0.070	−0.362	−0.550	0.313	−0.929	0.087	0.399	−0.238
28	0.771	−2.124	2.732	−0.261	−0.488	1.796	−0.232	0.926	0.235
29	0.539	0.389	0.209	1.580	−0.520	0.593	0.189	0.771	−1.724
30	−2.253	0.417	−0.088	−0.236	0.705	0.206	0.091	1.205	−0.059
31	−2.253	0.417	−0.088	−0.236	0.705	0.206	0.091	1.205	−0.059
32	0.339	0.897	0.437	1.933	−1.297	0.453	0.589	0.983	1.015
33	0.394	0.639	−0.815	0.648	−0.102	0.891	1.460	0.119	0.063
34	0.544	0.469	−0.275	1.865	−0.301	0.774	0.868	0.355	−0.305
35	0.321	1.939	0.439	−1.060	−0.610	0.071	0.182	0.889	0.025

*To identify cases refer to Table 5.

2. ESTIMATION OF FACTORS IN THE CASES.

On the basis of the obtained factor loadings of the variables, it is now possible to restate the combination of variables in each case in terms of factors. The Shortened Estimation Method has been used in this study for that purpose.[20] The object of the method is to obtain an estimate of each factor in each case. Tables 16, 17, and 18 list the regression coefficients for the estimation of factors. Factor estimates are computed as follows: The observed values of the variables in the case (see note 11 and Tables 7-9) are multiplied by their corresponding regression coefficients (Tables 16-18).

TABLE 21

Factor Estimates in the Connecticut Workmen's Compensation Cases

Cases*	Factors 1	2	3	4	5
1	0.126	−1.392	−0.422	−0.269	−0.504
2	−1.377	−1.194	0.211	2.546	−1.420
3	0.552	−1.183	−0.446	−0.488	0.012
4	−1.719	−0.002	0.459	0.013	−0.067
5	−1.584	0.004	0.765	−0.553	0.511
6	0.061	1.284	−2.498	0.284	1.497
7	0.648	0.480	0.335	1.135	−0.401
8	1.024	−0.110	0.287	0.196	0.232
9	0.526	0.291	−0.360	1.453	0.449
10	−0.602	0.727	−0.606	−1.911	−0.165
11	1.024	−0.110	0.287	0.196	0.232
12	1.024	−0.110	0.287	0.196	0.232
13	0.613	−0.969	−0.426	−0.597	−0.260
14	1.024	−0.110	0.287	0.196	0.232
15	−1.500	−0.075	−1.502	0.602	1.708
16	0.344	−0.469	−0.860	0.478	0.384
17	0.940	−0.052	0.190	0.232	−0.117
18	0.928	−0.439	0.009	−0.109	0.220
19	−1.672	0.214	−0.278	−0.172	0.652
20	−1.428	−0.148	0.803	−0.188	1.265
21	0.094	1.819	0.720	−0.600	−0.113
22	0.483	0.811	−1.025	1.959	0.439
23	−1.390	−0.324	0.237	0.061	1.232
24	0.924	0.043	0.549	0.465	0.004
25	−0.165	2.157	0.377	−1.211	−2.079
26	0.746	−0.229	0.174	0.198	−0.357
27	0.928	−0.439	0.009	−0.109	0.220
28	0.670	0.372	−0.169	0.485	−0.018
29	−1.944	0.243	0.504	−0.140	−2.269
30	1.024	−0.110	0.287	0.196	0.232
31	1.024	−0.110	0.287	0.196	0.232
32	−1.647	−0.097	0.400	0.415	0.339

*To identify cases refer to Table 6.

TABLE 21
(Continued)

Factor Estimates in the Connecticut Workmen's Compensation Cases

Cases*	Factors 1	2	3	4	5
33	−1.352	−0.476	0.240	−0.114	1.078
34	−1.685	−0.095	0.847	0.470	−0.303
35	0.073	−1.897	−0.679	−0.865	−0.009
36	0.105	1.855	0.875	−1.039	−0.168
37	0.470	1.229	0.672	−1.540	0.521
38	−1.512	−0.090	0.706	−0.151	0.916
39	−1.584	0.004	0.765	−0.553	0.511
40	0.913	0.136	0.343	−0.031	−0.019
41	0.537	−0.582	−0.121	−0.763	−0.618
42	0.757	−0.193	0.330	−0.241	−0.413
43	1.024	−0.110	0.287	0.196	0.232
44	0.560	0.694	0.189	1.081	0.276
45	0.697	−1.026	−0.329	−0.634	0.090
46	1.024	−0.110	0.287	0.196	0.232
47	−1.428	−0.148	0.803	−0.188	1.265
48	0.171	−0.635	−0.889	−0.886	−2.150
49	−1.215	−1.202	0.485	1.938	−0.267
50	0.552	−1.183	−0.446	−0.488	0.012
51	−1.584	0.004	0.765	−0.553	0.511
52	0.454	−1.445	−0.471	−0.721	0.152
53	−0.138	2.091	0.364	−0.523	−0.168
54	−0.010	−1.839	−0.776	−0.828	−0.359
55	0.648	0.480	0.335	1.135	−0.401
56	1.024	−0.110	0.287	0.196	0.232
57	0.470	1.229	0.672	−1.540	0.521
58	−1.584	0.004	0.765	−0.553	0.511
59	0.928	−0.439	0.009	−0.109	0.220
60	1.024	−0.110	0.287	0.196	0.232
61	1.024	−0.110	0.287	0.196	0.232
62	0.731	0.422	0.432	1.098	−0.052
63	0.135	−1.682	−0.660	−0.974	−0.281
64	0.146	−1.646	−0.504	−1.412	−0.336
65	1.024	−0.110	0.287	0.196	0.232
66	0.062	−1.588	−0.601	−1.375	−0.686
67	−0.324	2.335	−0.037	−0.732	−1.729
68	0.830	0.194	0.245	0.006	−0.368
69	−1.388	−1.206	0.625	2.559	−1.485
70	0.549	0.763	0.546	0.470	−0.708
71	0.526	0.714	0.804	0.922	−0.718
72	0.648	0.480	0.335	1.135	−0.401
73	−1.548	0.004	0.765	−0.553	0.511
74	0.239	1.552	−0.329	−0.215	1.132
75	−0.264	2.456	−2.476	0.801	0.854
76	−1.387	0.615	−4.822	−0.360	−1.386

Each factor has its own set of regression coefficients, and each coefficient applies to a particular variable. After the observed values of the variables have been multiplied by their corresponding regression coefficients for a particular factor, the products are added, and the applicable value of C is deducted. (The last-mentioned step is necessary where observed instead of standard values for the variables are used[21]). The obtained factor estimates are reported in Tables 19-21.

Since the factor estimates in the cases are based on the factor loadings of the variables, i.e., on measures of association with (or disassociation from) the factors, negative factor estimates are meaningful. A negative factor estimate indicates that the combination of variables in the case is disassociated from the factor in question. (This disassociation does not preclude, of course, a high association with other factors.) For example, if the description of factor 1 in the involuntary confession cases is considered, the negative estimate of factor 1 in *Spano* v. *New York* (case 24) would indicate that the defendant was protected during the state criminal proceeding from being kept in isolation, from being uninformed of the charges against him, and from being uninformed of his procedural rights, but that his request for consultation with counsel was denied. An inspection of Table 7, which shows the presence and absence of variables in the involuntary confession cases, confirms this conclusion.

3. LOCATION OF CASE WEIGHTS

Since the combination of variables in each case has been restated in terms of factors, the analysis can proceed now to finding a numerical value or weight for each combination of factors in each case. The object of weighting is to provide a distinction between combinations of factors which lead to decisions in favor of the petitioner (or claimant in the workmen's compensation cases) and combinations of factors which lead to decisions against the petitioner or claimant. The weights in question have been obtained in this study by using a multiple regression analysis.[22]

An important question has to be raised at this point: What kind of weight would be a proper index for the decision of a case? It must be recognized that the decisions of a multi-judge court, such as the United States Supreme Court and the state appellate courts, do not represent two opposite extremes. They are characterized by various degrees of support (or lack of support) of the contentions of the party seeking review, according to the votes of the justices. In other words, the decisions are represented by a "continuous distribution" rather than by a clearly "dichotomous distribution." For this reason, it is desirable to use the number of votes in favor of the petitioner (or claimant) as the observed value of the decision of the cases.[23] If this number of votes represents a majority of the participating justices (as defined in note 23), it obviously indicates a "pro" decision (in favor of the petitioner or claimant); if it represents only a minority, it indicates a "con" decision (against the petitioner or claimant).

On that basis, the final multiple regression analysis can be given the following meaning. Each case is represented by a "conditional equation." The decision of the case is the "dependent variable" in the conditional equation, and the factor estimates in the case are the "independent variables." The "observed value" of the dependent variable in each case is the number of votes of justices in favor of the petitioner or claimant. The "estimated value" of the dependent variable is obtained as a result of the final multiple regression analysis, and it serves as the case weight. If the correlation between the "observed values" and the "estimated values" can be accepted as significant, it can be concluded that the decision of a case, which is represented by the case weight, is—at a specifiable degree of probability—a function of the combination of factors (the restated combinations of variables). The case weights then can be regarded as approximations to the number of votes in favor of the petitioner or claimant, and, in this manner, they provide the desired distinction between pro and con decisions. The weight of a new case, that is, a case which represents a combination of variables (and a corresponding combination of factors) not previously encountered, can be computed as soon as its variables are identified. (Table 22 provides

TABLE 22

Final Regression Coefficients

Involuntary Confession Cases		Right to Counsel Cases		Connecticut Workmen's Compensation Cases	
Factors	Regression Coefficients	Factors	Regression Coefficients	Factors	Regression Coefficients
0	5.077	0	5.829	0	2.711
1	0.828	1	1.621	1	1.342
2	1.437	2	0.384	2	0.170
3	1.215	3	1.219	3	0.673
4	0.790	4	0.069	4	1.112
5	−0.302	5	−0.636	5	−0.126
6	−0.356	6	−0.372		
7	−0.168	7	0.371		
8	0.264	8	−0.024		
9	0.326	9	0.724		

the information needed for computing the weights of cases, by listing the final regression coefficients for the three groups of cases.)[24] It is in this respect that the quantitative formulation of the legal norms in question exhibits its predictive capacity, namely, in the assignment of case weights which indicate whether a combination of variables not previously encountered can be expected to lead to a decision in favor of the petitioner (or claimant) or to a decision against him.

Tables 23, 24, and 25 present the results of the final multiple regression analysis. In interpreting the estimated value (the case weight) as an index of the nature of the decision (pro or con), the estimated value must be rounded to the closest whole number, in view of the fact that fractions of a vote have no empirical meaning. Accordingly, in the involuntary confession cases and in the right to counsel cases, any numerical value not lower than 4.501 indicates a decision in favor of the petitioner, and a numerical value not higher than 4.500 indicates a decision against the petitioner, provided that all justices participate in the decision (in the sense indicated in note 23). If the full court does not participate in the decision, the separating numerical value is half of the number of participating justices. In the Connecticut workmen's compensation cases, any numerical value not lower than 2.501 indicates a decision in favor of the claimant, and a numerical value not higher than 2.500 indicates a decision against the claimant (the Connecticut Supreme Court of Errors has five justices), with the same qualifications that applies to the United States Supreme Court. It should be noted again

TABLE 23

Weights for the Involuntary Confession Cases

Cases*	Observed Values	Actual Decisions	Estimated Values without Variable 22†	Estimated‡ Decisions without Variable 22†	Estimated Values	Estimated‡ Decisions
1	9	pro	9.020	pro	9.194	pro
2	8	pro	6.718	pro	7.457	pro
3	9	pro	8.765	pro	8.811	pro
4	2	con	5.756	*pro*	5.200	*pro*
5	9	pro	8.382	pro	8.637	pro
6	6	pro	4.963	pro	5.218	pro
7	2	con	1.413	con	1.050	con
8	5	pro	3.417	pro§	3.114	pro§
9	5	pro	6.580	pro	6.065	pro
10	6	pro	4.592	pro	4.268	*con*
11	5	pro	4.552	pro	4.541	pro
12	5	pro	6.500	pro	6.168	pro
13	2	con	3.011	con	1.949	con
14	2	con	2.654	con	2.400	con
15	0	con	4.583	*pro*	4.203	con
16	3	con	3.635	con	3.565	con
17	5	pro	5.108	pro	6.271	pro
18	6	pro	5.622	pro	6.304	pro
19	4	con	5.168	*pro*	4.880	*pro*
20	7	pro	6.296	pro	6.033	pro
21	2	con	2.555	con	2.510	con
22	4	con	2.003	con	2.815	con
23	3	con	2.810	con	3.360	con
24	9	pro	7.081	pro	6.728	pro
25	8	pro	5.869	pro	6.554	pro
26	6	pro	4.929	pro	4.706	pro

*To identify cases refer to Table 4.
†The meaning of these columns will be explained in the concluding section of the study, p. 181.
‡Errors in estimation are italicized.
§These estimates must be interpreted as "pro" because only five justices participated (in the sense indicated in note 23) in the decision.

that the estimated values are approximations to the observed values, and that they are the "best" approximations (in the least-square sense) that can be obtained. Accordingly, negative numerical values should be interpreted as approximations to 0. Actually, negative numerical case values are encountered in very few instances.

An inspection of Tables 23, 24, and 25 shows that not all estimated

TABLE 24

Weights for the Right to Counsel Cases

Cases*	Observed Values	Actual Decisions	Estimated Values	Estimated† Decisions
1	7	pro	6.572	pro
2	0	con	4.043	con
3	9	pro	8.240	pro
4	3	con	5.767	*pro*
5	7	pro	5.674	pro
6	7	pro	5.274	pro
7	8	pro	7.803	pro
8	8	pro	8.914	pro
9	6	pro	6.130	pro
10	8	pro	7.017	pro
11	2	con	2.248	con
12	1	con	0.307	con
13	9	pro	8.094	pro
14	4	con	5.558	*pro*
15	4	con	4.670	*pro*
16	9	pro	5.575	pro
17	4	con	5.558	*pro*
18	5	pro	6.226	pro
19	4	con	5.363	*pro*
20	6	pro	6.472	pro
21	6	pro	7.012	pro
22	9	pro	5.807	pro
23	0	con	5.252	*pro*
24	5	pro	6.713	pro
25	0	con	1.448	con
26	9	pro	8.191	pro
27	9	pro	6.260	pro
28	9	pro	9.278	pro
29	5	pro	6.129	pro
30	4	con	1.651	con
31	3	con	1.651	con
32	9	pro	8.975	pro
33	7	pro	6.081	pro
34	9	pro	6.681	pro
35	9	pro	7.981	pro

*To identify cases refer to Table 5.
†Errors in estimation are italicized.

decisions correspond to the actual decisions. The numerical case values do not indicate correctly the actual decisions in three out of the 26 involuntary confession cases, in six out of the 35 right-to-counsel cases, and in 11 out of the 76 workmen's compensation cases. Nevertheless, the F test shows that the results of the final multiple regression analysis are highly significant in all three sets of cases.[25] This means that considerable confidence can be placed in the obtained results for having identified consistent patterns of

TABLE 25

Weights for the Connecticut Workmen's Compensation Cases

Cases*	Observed Values	Actual Decisions	Estimated Values	Estimated† Decisions
1	0	con	2.123	con
2	5	pro	3.813	pro
3	0	con	2.406	con
4	5	pro	0.735	*con*
5	0	con	0.420	con
6	4	pro	1.457	*con*
7	5	pro	5.200	pro
8	3	pro	4.447	pro
9	0	con	4.783	*pro*
10	0	con	−0.487	con
11	3	pro	4.447	pro
12	5	pro	4.447	pro
13	5	pro	2.451	*con*
14	5	pro	4.447	pro
15	0	con	0.129	con
16	1	con	2.997	*pro*
17	5	pro	4.365	pro
18	5	pro	3.739	pro
19	0	con	0.043	con
20	0	con	0.940	con
21	5	pro	2.976	pro
22	5	pro	4.931	pro
23	0	con	0.862	con
24	5	pro	4.845	pro
25	0	con	2.025	con
26	5	pro	4.054	pro
27	5	pro	3.739	pro
28	5	pro	4.101	pro
29	0	con	0.612	con
30	5	pro	4.447	pro
31	5	pro	4.447	pro
32	5	pro	1.172	*con*
33	0	con	0.714	con
34	0	con	1.563	con

*To identify cases refer to Table 6.
†Errors in estimation are italicized.

TABLE 25
(Continued)

Weights for the Connecticut Workmen's Compensation Cases

Cases*	Observed Values	Actual Decisions	Estimated Values	Estimated† Decisions
35	0	con	1.069	con
36	3	pro	2.621	pro
37	5	pro	2.223	*con*
38	0	con	0.858	con
39	0	con	0.420	con
40	5	pro	4.158	pro
41	5	pro	2.480	*con*
42	5	pro	3.700	pro
43	5	pro	4.447	pro
44	5	pro	4.622	pro
45	5	pro	2.533	pro
46	5	pro	4.447	pro
47	0	con	0.940	con
48	0	con	1.520	con
49	5	pro	3.392	pro
50	1	con	2.406	con
51	0	con	0.420	con
52	0	con	1.936	con
53	0	con	2.565	*pro*
54	0	con	0.986	con
55	4	pro	5.200	pro
56	5	pro	4.447	pro
57	5	pro	2.223	*con*
58	0	con	0.420	con
59	4	pro	3.739	pro
60	5	pro	4.447	pro
61	5	pro	4.447	pro
62	5	pro	5.283	pro
63	0	con	1.114	con
64	0	con	0.759	con
65	3	pro	4.447	pro
66	0	con	0.676	con
67	0	con	2.051	con
68	5	pro	4.075	pro
69	5	pro	4.098	pro
70	5	pro	4.556	pro
71	5	pro	5.195	pro
72	5	pro	5.200	pro
73	0	con	0.420	con
74	0	con	2.692	*pro*
75	0	con	1.891	con
76	0	con	−2.517	con

*To identify cases refer to Table 6.
†Errors in estimation are italicized.

judicial action, because the estimated weights of the decisions are in very close agreement with the observed weights.

2. "Forward" and "Backward" Tests of the Method

Aside from having identified patterns of consistency, would it be possible to predict the chronologically second half of a group of cases from the first half, and vice versa,[26] by means of the proposed analysis? In order

TABLE 26

Weights for the First Half of the Involuntary Confession Cases

Cases*	Observed Values	Actual Decisions	Estimated Values	Estimated Decisions
1	9	pro	8.864	pro
2	8	pro	7.522	pro
3	9	pro	8.750	pro
4	2	con	1.992	con
5	9	pro	9.211	pro
6	6	pro	6.738	pro
7	2	con	2.003	con
8	5	pro	5.308	pro
9	5	pro	5.527	pro
10	6	pro	5.131	pro
11	5	pro	4.671	pro
12	5	pro	5.293	pro
13	2	con	1.991	con

*To identify cases in this and subsequent tables refer to Tables 4-6.

TABLE 27

Weights for the Involuntary Confession Cases Predicted from the First Half

Cases	Observed Values	Actual Decisions	Predicted Values	Predicted* Decisions
14	2	con	5.950	*pro*
15	0	con	6.042	*pro*
16	3	con	4.937	*pro*
17	5	pro	6.659	pro
18	6	pro	5.857	pro
19	4	con	5.281	*pro*
20	7	pro	6.414	pro
21	2	con	3.457	con
22	4	con	6.575	*pro*
23	3	con	6.321	*pro*
24	9	pro	2.146	*con*
25	8	pro	6.046	pro
26	6	pro	5.326	pro

*Errors in estimation and prediction are italicized in this and subsequent tables.

to provide an answer to this question, the involuntary confession cases, the right to counsel cases, and the Connecticut workmen's compensation cases were divided chronologically into two halves, and for each group of cases an attempt was made to predict the second half of cases from the first half, and vice versa. The results are reported in Tables 26 to 39.

Table 38 shows that the estimates for the first half of the involuntary confession cases, which are reported in Table 26, are highly significant. But it also shows that the prediction of the second half of the involuntary con-

TABLE 28

Weights for the Second Half of the Involuntary Confession Cases

Cases	Observed Values	Actual Decisions	Estimated Values	Estimated Decisions
14	2	con	2.327	con
15	0	con	3.846	con
16	3	con	4.058	con
17	5	pro	4.831	pro
18	6	pro	5.839	pro
19	4	con	4.513	*pro*
20	7	pro	6.312	pro
21	2	con	2.281	con
22	4	con	2.065	con
23	3	con	2.015	con
24	9	pro	9.453	pro
25	8	pro	6.385	pro
26	6	pro	5.075	pro

TABLE 29

Weights for the Involuntary Confession Cases Predicted from the Second Half

Cases	Observed Values	Actual Decisions	Predicted Values	Predicted Decisions
1	9	pro	4.733	pro
2	8	pro	7.189	pro
3	9	pro	6.094	pro
4	2	con	6.834	*pro*
5	9	pro	5.198	pro
6	6	pro	5.316	pro
7	2	con	1.489	con
8	5	pro	3.005	pro*
9	5	pro	7.252	pro
10	6	pro	4.931	pro
11	5	pro	5.151	pro
12	5	pro	6.467	pro
13	2	con	3.430	con

*This prediction must be interpreted as "pro" because only five justices participated in the decision (in the sense of note 23).

fession cases from the first half, the results of which appear in Table 27, is not significant. The failure of this prediction can be explained by the fact that the first half of cases provides no information on variable 11.

TABLE 30

Weights for the First Half of the Right to Counsel Cases

Cases	Observed Values	Actual Decisions	Estimated Values	Estimated Decisions
1	7	pro	7.464	pro
2	0	con	−0.433	con
3	9	pro	9.000	pro
4	3	con	3.435	con
5	7	pro	5.691	pro
6	7	pro	6.113	pro
7	8	pro	8.095	pro
8	8	pro	8.890	pro
9	6	pro	5.778	pro
10	8	pro	7.402	pro
11	2	con	2.753	con
12	1	con	0.804	con
13	9	pro	8.196	pro
14	4	con	5.947	*pro*
15	4	con	4.495	con
16	9	pro	7.332	pro
17	4	con	5.947	*pro*
18	5	pro	4.090	*con*

TABLE 31

Weights for the Right to Counsel Cases Predicted from the First Half

Cases	Observed Values	Actual Decisions	Predicted Values	Predicted Decisions
19	4	con	5.189	*pro*
20	6	pro	9.771	pro
21	6	pro	8.253	pro
22	9	pro	3.371	*con*
23	0	con	5.644	*pro*
24	5	pro	8.864	pro
25	0	con	−0.398	con
26	9	pro	9.311	pro
27	9	pro	8.903	pro
28	9	pro	13.406	pro
29	5	pro	5.363	pro
30	4	con	−2.161	con
31	3	con	−2.161	con
32	9	pro	4.255	*con*
33	7	pro	2.855	*con*
34	9	pro	4.892	pro
35	9	pro	6.863	pro

Variable 11 appears in all cases in the first half, i.e., it is a constant in the first half of cases, and consequently no correlation coefficients and no factor loadings are obtained for it. On that basis, the second half of

TABLE 32

Weights for the Second Half of the Right to Counsel Cases

Cases	Observed Values	Actual Decisions	Estimated Values	Estimated Decisions
19	4	con	5.446	*pro*
20	6	pro	6.091	pro
21	6	pro	6.358	pro
22	9	pro	5.424	pro
23	0	con	5.452	*pro*
24	5	pro	4.902	pro
25	0	con	0.890	con
26	9	pro	9.188	pro
27	9	pro	5.443	pro
28	9	pro	8.496	pro
29	5	pro	6.344	pro
30	4	con	3.012	con
31	3	con	3.012	con
32	9	pro	9.267	pro
33	7	pro	6.548	pro
34	9	pro	7.350	pro
35	9	pro	9.777	pro

TABLE 33

Weights for the Right to Counsel Cases Predicted from the Second Half

Cases	Observed Values	Actual Decisions	Predicted Values	Predicted Decisions
1	7	pro	2.459	*con*
2	0	con	4.036	con
3	9	pro	6.335	pro
4	3	con	6.185	*pro*
5	7	pro	4.848	pro
6	7	pro	4.525	pro
7	8	pro	9.792	pro
8	8	pro	7.788	pro
9	6	pro	6.637	pro
10	8	pro	2.086	*con*
11	2	con	1.110	con
12	1	con	2.022	con
13	9	pro	7.268	pro
14	4	con	6.304	*pro*
15	4	con	6.884	*pro*
16	9	pro	4.669	pro
17	4	con	6.304	*pro*
18	5	pro	7.207	pro

cases, in which variable 11 is not a constant, is predicted without attributing any weight to variable 11. A similar problem is encountered in the "backward" test. The second half of the involuntary confession cases yields no information on variables 1, 7, and 9. This is due to the fact that variables 1 and 7 appear in no case in the second half, and that variable 9 appears in all cases in the second half. In other words, these three variables are

TABLE 34

Weights for the First Half of the Connecticut Workmen's Compensation Cases

Cases	Observed Values	Actual Decisions	Estimated Values	Estimated Decisions
1	0	con	1.600	con
2	5	pro	3.619	pro
3	0	con	1.769	con
4	5	pro	0.860	*con*
5	0	con	0.321	con
6	4	pro	2.396	*con*
7	5	pro	4.479	pro
8	3	pro	4.498	pro
9	0	con	3.736	*pro*
10	0	con	0.136	con
11	3	pro	4.498	pro
12	5	pro	4.498	pro
13	5	pro	2.080	*con*
14	5	pro	4.498	pro
15	0	con	1.826	con
16	1	con	1.592	con
17	5	pro	4.510	pro
18	5	pro	3.812	pro
19	0	con	−0.175	con
20	0	con	1.517	con
21	5	pro	4.675	pro
22	5	pro	3.682	pro
23	0	con	1.568	con
24	5	pro	4.648	pro
25	0	con	2.139	con
26	5	pro	3.980	pro
27	5	pro	3.812	pro
28	5	pro	5.686	pro
29	0	con	−0.710	con
30	5	pro	4.498	pro
31	5	pro	4.498	pro
32	5	pro	2.074	*con*
33	0	con	−1.098	con
34	0	con	1.826	con
35	0	con	0.975	con
36	3	pro	3.442	pro
37	5	pro	4.694	pro
38	0	con	1.576	con

constants in the second half of cases. The first half of cases, then, in which these variables are not constants, is predicted without allocating any weight to variables 1, 7, and 9, and so—quite understandably—prediction fails. The results are reported in Table 29, and Table 38 shows that they are not significant. Moreover, the estimates for the second half of cases, which

TABLE 35

Weights for the Connecticut Workmen's Compensation Cases Predicted from the First Half

Cases	Observed Values	Actual Decisions	Predicted Values	Predicted Decisions
39	0	con	0.321	con
40	5	pro	5.949	pro
41	5	pro	2.160	con
42	5	pro	2.747	pro
43	5	pro	4.498	pro
44	5	pro	5.480	pro
45	5	pro	2.061	con
46	5	pro	4.498	pro
47	0	con	1.517	con
48	0	con	1.917	con
49	5	pro	1.845	con
50	1	con	1.769	con
51	0	con	0.321	con
52	0	con	1.723	con
53	0	con	3.179	pro
54	0	con	0.993	con
55	4	pro	4.479	pro
56	5	pro	4.498	pro
57	5	pro	4.694	pro
58	0	con	0.321	con
59	4	pro	3.812	pro
60	5	pro	4.498	pro
61	5	pro	4.498	pro
62	5	pro	4.460	pro
63	0	con	1.286	con
64	0	con	0.053	con
65	3	pro	4.498	pro
66	0	con	0.071	con
67	0	con	1.857	con
68	5	pro	5.968	pro
69	5	pro	2.135	con
70	5	pro	4.697	pro
71	5	pro	4.446	pro
72	5	pro	4.479	pro
73	0	con	0.321	con
74	0	con	4.257	pro
75	0	con	4.155	pro
76	0	con	−1.483	con

appear in Table 28, are not significant (as shown in Table 38), which by itself indicates that prediction would not succeed. Likewise, the second half of the right to counsel cases yields no information on variable 13, and the first half of cases, in which variable 13 is not a constant, thus is predicted without any weight for variable 13. The results of the prediction are given in Table 33, and Table 38 shows that they are not significant.

TABLE 36

Weights for the Second Half of the Connecticut Workmen's Compensation Cases

Cases	Observed Values	Actual Decisions	Estimated Values	Estimated Decisions
39	0	con	−0.519	con
40	5	pro	3.929	pro
41	5	pro	2.151	con
42	5	pro	3.605	pro
43	5	pro	4.709	pro
44	5	pro	4.123	pro
45	5	pro	3.062	pro
46	5	pro	4.709	pro
47	0	con	0.315	con
48	0	con	0.835	con
49	5	pro	4.268	pro
50	1	con	2.750	pro
51	0	con	−0.519	con
52	0	con	2.540	pro
53	0	con	1.767	con
54	0	con	0.970	con
55	4	pro	4.905	pro
56	5	pro	4.709	pro
57	5	pro	2.211	con
58	0	con	−0.519	con
59	4	pro	3.998	pro
60	5	pro	4.709	pro
61	5	pro	4.709	pro
62	5	pro	5.150	pro
63	0	con	1.282	con
64	0	con	0.938	con
65	3	pro	4.709	pro
66	0	con	0.693	con
67	0	con	0.876	con
68	5	pro	3.684	pro
69	5	pro	5.789	pro
70	5	pro	3.781	pro
71	5	pro	5.022	pro
72	5	pro	4.905	pro
73	0	con	−0.519	con
74	0	con	2.287	con
75	0	con	1.847	con
76	0	con	−1.858	con

The failure of this prediction also could have been anticipated on the basis of the estimates for the second half of cases (Table 32), which are not significant, as can be seen from Table 38. The first half of the right to counsel cases contains the necessary information for predicting the second half of cases on all variables. Furthermore, the estimates for the first half,

TABLE 37

Weights for the Connecticut Workmen's Compensation Cases Predicted from the Second Half

Cases	Observed Values	Actual Decisions	Predicted Values	Predicted Decisions
1	0	con	2.179	con
2	5	pro	4.892	pro
3	0	con	2.750	*pro*
4	5	pro	1.064	*con*
5	0	con	−0.519	con
6	4	pro	1.856	*con*
7	5	pro	4.905	pro
8	3	pro	4.709	pro
9	0	con	4.590	*pro*
10	0	con	−1.089	con
11	3	pro	4.709	pro
12	5	pro	4.709	pro
13	5	pro	2.817	pro
14	5	pro	4.709	pro
15	0	con	−0.302	con
16	1	con	3.256	*pro*
17	5	pro	4.464	pro
18	5	pro	3.998	pro
19	0	con	−0.774	con
20	0	con	0.315	con
21	5	pro	2.407	*con*
22	5	pro	4.844	pro
23	0	con	−0.048	con
24	5	pro	4.905	pro
25	0	con	0.927	con
26	5	pro	3.949	pro
27	5	pro	3.998	pro
28	5	pro	3.633	pro
29	0	con	0.111	con
30	5	pro	4.709	pro
31	5	pro	4.709	pro
32	5	pro	1.653	*con*
33	0	con	0.142	con
34	0	con	1.591	con
35	0	con	1.215	con
36	3	pro	2.063	*con*
37	5	pro	2.211	*con*
38	0	con	0.070	con

which appear in Table 30, are significant (see Table 38). Nevertheless, the prediction of the second half of cases from the first half fails. The results of this prediction, which are presented in Table 31, are not significant, as shown in Table 38. The possible conclusion that the Court became inconsistent in the second half of cases cannot be accepted, because the estimates for the total sample are highly significant (see note 25). What

TABLE 38

F Test Results for "Forward" and "Backward" Predictions

Table	SETS OF CASES	Degrees of Freedom m	N-m-1	F	P (Chance Probability of Higher Value of F)	Observed and Estimated or Predicted Values in Significant Agreement
26	First half of involuntary confession cases	8	4	17.754	$P<0.01$	yes
27	Involuntary confession cases predicted from first half	8	4	0.121	$P>0.05$	no
28	Second half of involuntary confession cases	7	5	1.582	$P>0.05$	no
29	Involuntary confession cases predicted from second half	7	5	0.338	$P>0.05$	no
30	First half of right to counsel cases	10	7	4.998	$P<0.05$	yes
31	Right to counsel cases predicted from first half	10	6	0.736	$P>0.05$	no
32	Second half of right to counsel cases	8	8	1.369	$P>0.05$	no
33	Right to counsel cases predicted from second half	8	9	0.694	$P>0.05$	no
34	First half of Conn. workmen's compensation cases	7	30	5.462	$P<0.001$	yes
35	Conn. workmen's compensation cases predicted from first half	7	30	5.131	$P<0.001$	yes
36	Second half of Conn. workmen's compensation cases	6	31	11.237	$P<0.001$	yes
37	Conn. workmen's compensation cases predicted from second half	6	31	7.624	$P<0.001$	yes

might be concluded is that for such a small sample significance at the 0.05 level is not sufficient for predictive purposes and that high significance at the 0.01 level is required.

In the larger sample of the Connecticut workmen's compensation cases, prediction is successful in both directions. Table 34 reports the estimates for the first half of cases, and Table 35 gives the results of the prediction of the second half of cases from the first half. Correspondingly, Table 36 presents the estimates for the second half of cases, and Table 37 presents the weights for the first half of cases as predicted from the second half. Table 38 shows that the results are highly significant in all instances. Furthermore, it can be seen from Table 39 that the estimation and prediction of the Connecticut workmen's compensation cases from the entire sample, from

TABLE 39

Comparison of Estimations and Predictions in the Connecticut Workmen's Compensation Cases

Sets of Cases	Cases in Set	Cases in Set Correctly Estimated or Predicted	Cases in Whole Sample Correctly Estimated	Direction of Test	Chi Square*	P (Chance Probability of Higher Value of Chi Square) (1-tailed)	Estimations and Predictions in Significant Agreement
First half	38	33	31	Forward	19.630	$P<0.001$	yes
Second half predicted from first half	38	31	34	Forward	5.780	$P<0.01$	yes
Second half	38	34	34	Backward	3.454	$P<0.05$	yes
First half predicted from second half	38	29	31	Backward	14.302	$P<0.001$	yes

*See Walker and Lev, *Statistical Inference op. cit. infra* (note 16), pp. 81-108, and in particular pp. 103-106, for an explanation of the use of chi square. In this instance, chi square is used as a correlation measure between the correct and incorrect estimations and predictions of the sets which are compared.

the first half of cases, and from the second half of cases are almost equally successful. The "forward" test yields slightly better estimates for the first half of cases than the entire sample, and its prediction of the second half of cases is slightly less accurate than the estimation obtained from the entire sample. The "backward" test estimates the second half of cases as well as the entire sample, and its prediction of the first half of cases is slightly less accurate than the estimation derived from the entire sample. But these differences are not statistically significant. One can conclude, therefore, that —at least in this area of judicial action—a sample of 38 cases offers considerable stability in the application of the analysis. Moreover, the "backward" test has implications that are particularly noteworthy with regard to the principle of stare decisis. They will be discussed in the concluding section of this study.

Before turning to the purposes and implications of the analysis, some comments about a comparison of the method presented here with other methods seem to be called for. The earlier Kort method[27] used experimentally determined weights for variables and cases. They correctly distinguished pro and con decisions, but they could not be justified—and were not justified—as a unique solution of the problem. In other words, it could not be shown that no other sets of weights would distinguish pro and con decisions as well as the obtained weights. The present method, however, is based on a solution of simultaneous equations; thus, it provides a unique solution by obtaining case weights that are the "best" weights in the least-square sense. Moreover, the earlier Kort method was based on the assumption that the original variables are mutually independent (with the exception of the degrees of the gravity of the crime in the right-to-counsel cases, which are mutually exclusive). The present method does not make this assumption. It determines mutual dependence and independence among the variables by means of the factor analysis, and then proceeds to distinguish the different combinations of variables in terms of the nature of the decision. The Nagel method[28] is superior to the earlier Kort method inasmuch as it is based on correlations between the variables and the decision, but it does not explore the mutual dependence and independence among variables as fully as the factor analysis used in this study. (Of course, the Nagel method has the advantage of simple calculations.) Furthermore, like the earlier Kort method, the Nagel method does not yield unique solutions for the case weights.

3. Purposes and Implications of the Analysis

As already indicated, the proposed quantitative formulation of rules of law which make the decision of cases dependent on unspecified combinations of specified controlling circumstances provides information which the conventional verbal statement of such rules does not reveal. It is the absence of this information in the verbal statement of the right-to-counsel rule that has been deplored,[29] and it is precisely this information that lawyers need for appraising their cases in terms of the rule. To be sure, this information could be provided by a verbal restatement of the rule of law. However, such a verbal restatement would be extremely complex and, from a practical point of view, awkward. It would have to contain all the possible combinations of the circumstances (the permutations of all variables), and it would have to indicate the decision which each combination represents. Moreover, the quantitative formulation of the rule would have to be obtained before the verbal restatement could be prepared. Consequently, the quantitative formulation would be an indispensable step in providing the information, even if a verbal formulation should be preferred.

As far as prediction is concerned, it should be clearly understood that the quantitative formulation of the rule of law under discussion offers a *conditional* and *not an unconditional* prediction of decisions. In other words, a decision is predicted on the assumption that the combination of circumstances which will be accepted by the court is known. To predict the combination of circumstances which actually will be accepted by the court from the submitted briefs and, in the case of an appellate court, from the lower court reports, would be an entirely different task. If such a predictive device can be found, its combination with the method for predicting how the rule will be applied would, of course, permit an *unconditional* prediction of the decisions. If, in the absence of a predictive device for anticipating the combination of circumstances that will be accepted by the court, the utility of the method for predicting how the rule of law will be applied is questioned, the following considerations should be noted, apart from the other purposes discussed here:

1. If an attorney can anticipate which combinations of circumstances will lead to a decision in favor of his client and which combinations will be insufficient for such a decision, he certainly could appraise the prospects of his client, and, secondly, he would be in a position to know which circumstances he should emphasize in his presentation to the court.

2. After the decision of a new case, when the combination of circumstances that has been accepted by the court is known, it can be determined by means of the proposed analysis whether or not the court continues to apply the rule of law consistently. Again, this appraisal requires the precise formulation of the rule of law which has been attained by its quantification.

Independent of prediction, the analysis makes it possible to determine conformance and nonconformance by lower courts to rules of law stated in the indicated flexible form by higher courts. For example, in *Mapp* v. *Ohio*,[30] the United States Supreme Court ruled that the admission of evidence obtained by an unreasonable search and seizure in a state criminal proceeding is a violation of the due process clause of the Fourteenth Amendment. In other words, the same exclusionary rule which has been controlling for federal courts now is also mandatory for state courts. Accordingly, in reviewing a state search and seizure case, a state appellate court will be supposed to make the same evaluation which the United States Supreme Court is presumed to make in deciding a federal search and seizure case. Both will have to determine whether or not the combination of circumstances in the case is of such nature as to amount to an unreasonable search and seizure. After several such cases have been decided, it should be possible to ascertain by means of the proposed quantitative analysis whether or not combinations of circumstances which would be regarded as unreasonable searches and seizures by the United States Supreme Court also are so regarded by state appellate courts.

Furthermore, the analysis that has been introduced here can be used to examine the rationale on which a rule of law with the indicated characteristic is based. For example, consider the involuntary confession cases. Assume that it is not clear whether one or two possible lines of reasoning should be attributed to the Supreme Court in these cases.[31] One line of reasoning would be that an involuntary confession is untrustworthy evidence and that its admission might lead to the conviction of an innocent person.

This line of reasoning could be called the "untrustworthiness" rationale. The other line of reasoning would be that, independent of the untrustworthy nature of the involuntary confession, the admission of such a confession into evidence must be prohibited in order to deter police officials from resorting to tactics that violate fundamental fairness. It would be convenient to call this line of reasoning the "deterrence" rationale. In comparing these two lines of reasoning, variable 22, "no evidence which, apart from the challenged confession, would be sufficient for a conviction," becomes important. For the "deterrence" rationale, this variable would be irrelevant. For even if the confession is shown to be trustworthy by other evidence, it still would be inadmissible because the manner in which it has been obtained is objectionable. For the "untrustworthiness" rationale, however, this variable would be highly relevant. An inspection of Tables 7 and 23 shows that the Court has not been using exclusively the "untrustworthiness" rationale, for it did reverse convictions in cases in which *there was evidence* which, apart from the challenged confession, was sufficient for a conviction.

But has the Court used the "untrustworthiness" rationale *in addition* to the "deterrence" rationale or has it relied *exclusively* on the "deterrence" rationale? In other words, has it given any consideration to the variable "no evidence which, apart from the challenged confession, would be sufficient for a conviction"? In order to obtain an answer to this question, the analysis of the involuntary confession cases was performed twice. The first time, variable 22 was excluded; the second time, it was included. This approach was used with the assumption that if the results of both investigations would offer equally good distinctions between pro and con cases, one could conclude that the Court has used exclusively the "deterrence" rationale. For it would be apparent then that the absence of "evidence which, apart from the confession, would be sufficient for a conviction" had no impact on the decisions. If, on the other hand, the results of the second analysis would offer a better distinction between pro and con cases than the first analysis, one would have to conclude that the Court has used the "untrustworthiness" rationale, in addition to the "deterrence" rationale. The results which were obtained appear in Table 23. In both investigations, the decisions in 23 out of 26 cases were correctly estimated. But with variable 22 the approximation to the actual votes is *highly* significant ($F=3.834$, $P<0.01$), whereas without variable 22 it is merely significant ($F=2.824$, $P<0.05$). It must be concluded, therefore, that the Court has been using the "untrustworthiness" rationale in addition to the "deterrence" rationale, and the Court's expression of an exclusive commitment to the "deterrence" rationale in the *Rogers* case must be accepted as a pronouncement for future use rather than an appraisal of past action.

As far as the implications of the proposed quantitative analysis are concerned, one general and one particular conclusion are suggested by this study. The particular conclusion is that in at least one area of judicial action, namely, in the Connecticut workmen's compensation cases, a pattern of consistency is apparent which exhibits dimensions of regularity beyond the traditional conception of stare decisis. Consistency in terms of stare decisis could explain the success of the "forward" prediction. But it cannot explain the success of the "backward" test, for the consistency which was detected in the earlier decisions by prediction from the later decisions obviously cannot be attributed to a process of basing earlier decisions on later "precedents." It seems, therefore, that, in at least this area of judicial action, consistency must be explained by a pattern of regularity which differs from adherence to precedent. It must be explained by the independent (although convergent) recognition and acceptance of a response pattern to given factual situations by different judges at different times.

The general conclusion is that the model on which the analysis is based represents the decision-making process which judges employ in the specified areas of judicial action. The fact that this model has not been explicitly stated in the applicable court opinions as a controlling pattern of thought cannot be interpreted as evidence that it is not employed. Like many other persons who are engaged in the solution of complicated problems, judges cannot be expected to give a complete analytic account of the complex thought processes through which they reach decisions, not even in systematically developed opinions. Certainly, the explanations which they have given in describing their positions in the specified areas of judicial action do not refute the inference that the proposed model represents their pattern of thought. In the involuntary confession cases and in the right to counsel cases, the majority of Supreme Court justices have repeatedly stated that their decisions depend on the combinations of the applicable circumstances. Essentially, this is the basic structure of the proposed model. The fact that, contrary to the Supreme Court's own summary of its position in the right to counsel cases, this approach has been used by the Court in capital as well as in noncapital cases is noteworthy, but it does not present a serious discrepancy between the Court's own evaluation of its position and the model. Moreover, the fact that the entities to which the justices mentally reduce the circumstances of the cases probably are not identical with the factors to which the variables are reduced by the analysis is not crucial. If the total set of factors accounts for most of the variance of the variables, similar to the way in which the justices restate the controlling circumstances as completely as possible in terms of their conceptual entities, the factors can be regarded as acceptable approximations to the entities in terms of which the justices think. Both can be equally well related to the decisions, for, in terms of factor analysis, the configuration of the variables is not affected by factorial structure.[32] In accordance with the requirements of scientific inquiry, the decisive criterion for accepting the model as an explanation of judicial action in the specified areas is the fact that the model suggests an hypothesis which has been empirically verified with a high degree of probability.

NOTES

1. "In each instance our inquiry must weigh the circumstances of pressure against the power of resistance of the person confessing." *Stein* v. *New York*, 346 U.S. 156,

185 (1953); *Fikes* v. *Alabama,* 352 U.S. 191, 197 (1957); *Thomas* v. *Arizona,* 356 U.S. 390, 393 (1958). Prior to the *Stein* case, the Court had not taken into consideration the different trial procedures used to resolve the questions of fact and judgment on the issue of the voluntariness of the confession. See Bernard D. Meltzer, "Involuntary Confessions: The Allocation of Responsibility between Judge and Jury," *University of Chicago Law Review,* Vol. 21 (Spring, 1954), 318. In the *Stein* case, the Court concerned itself with this point, but the Supreme Court's determination of the voluntariness issue still depends on its evaluation of the "circumstances of pressure" and the "power of resistance of the person confessing."

2. "[The majority of the Court] think that when a crime subject to capital punishment is not involved, each case depends on its own facts. See *Betts* v. *Brady,* 316 U.S. 455, 462. Where the gravity of the crime and other factors—such as the age and the education of the defendant, the conduct of the court or the prosecuting officials, and the complicated nature of the offenses charged and the possible defense thereto—render criminal proceedings without counsel so apt to result in injustice as to be fundamentally unfair, [we hold] that the accused must have legal assistance under the Amendment whether he pleads guilty or elects to stand trial, whether he requests counsel or not. Only a waiver of counsel, understandingly made, justifies trial without counsel." *Uveges* v. *Pennsylvania,* 335 U.S. 437, 440-41 (1948). Although the Court here relates the controlling circumstances only to noncapital cases, it actually has used these circumstances as dominant considerations in capital cases also. Consequently, capital as well as noncapital cases will be included in the analysis.

3. The suggestion of analyzing workmen's compensation cases in terms of the method used in this study was made by Henry H. Foster, New York University Law School.

4. Although the rules of law under discussion are found primarily in case law, they may also appear in statutory form, as a legislative directive to the courts.

5. Glendon Schubert, "The Study of Judicial Decision-Making as an Aspect of Political Behavior," *American Political Science Review,* Vol. 52 (1958), 1017-22.

6. Fred Kort, "Predicting Supreme Court Decisions Mathematically: A Quantitative Analysis of the 'Right to Counsel' Cases," *American Political Science Review,* Vol. 51 (March 1957), 1-12. Stuart S. Nagel, "Using Simple Calculations to Predict Judicial Decisions," *American Behavioral Scientist,* Vol. 4 (December 1960), 24-28.

7. This approach imposes limitations on the predictive capacity of the analysis, which will be discussed later. Moreover, it raises questions in interpreting the votes of justices, a point which also will be discussed later. The alternative, however, would be to attribute to the court considerations it may not have recognized as relevant or significant. In mathematical terms, variables would erroneously be included which the equations representing the cases do not contain. It follows, of course, that only decisions which are accompanied by opinions that discuss the facts and the decision on the merits (or by opinions which give a clear indication how the court would have decided the cases on their merits) can be used. Summary decisions on the merits and jurisdictional decisions, such as Supreme Court denials of certiorari, are therefore excluded from the sets of data appropriate for analysis by the present method.

8. This statement also can be expressed as follows: the general set of circumstances is the universal set of variables; each combination of circumstances is a subset of the universal set; some subsets generate a "pro" decision and other subsets generate a "con" decision.

9. It should be noted that it might not be possible to restate the 20 test scores exclusively in terms of the four main abilities. Assume that 15 of the 20 tests measure exclusively the four indicated abilities, and that the five remaining tests measure the four abilities to some extent, but that, in addition, each of the five remaining tests measures an ability which no other test measures. For each student, then, 15 of the 20 test scores could be restated in terms of the four main ability scores, and five of the test scores could be restated in part in terms of the four main ability scores and in part in terms of the five ability scores that have to be expressed separately. For reasons that are readily apparent, the four main abilities can be referred to as common factors (they are common to several or all tests), and the abilities that must be identified

separately may be called specific factors (each is represented by only one test). Speaking now in general terms, the extent to which a variable (test score in this example) can be accounted for by common factors is known as its common factor variance or its communality; the extent to which it must be expressed in terms of a specific factor is known as its specific variance; the variance which must be attributed to error is called error variance; the combination of the specific variance and the error variance of a variable is called its unique variance or its uniqueness. The sum of the communality and the uniqueness of a variable is defined to equal 1. See L. L. Thurstone, *Multiple-Factor Analysis* (Chicago: University of Chicago Press, 1947), pp. 73-76.

The communality of a variable can be separated from its uniqueness by means of factor analysis. However, its specific variance can be separated from the error variance only if the experiment through which the sample was obtained can be repeated (see Thurstone, *op. cit.*, pp. 84-85). On empirical grounds, this is not possible with court cases. Consequently, it cannot be determined how much specific variance and how much error variance the uniqueness of a variable contains. For this reason, only common factors are used in this study. Accordingly, the term "factors" as used here refers to the *common factors*. It is realized that some accuracy is sacrificed by relying on common factors only. But, if the communality of a variable is sufficiently high, most of its variance is accounted for by the common factors.

10. "Factor loading" is the customary term. More accurately, it should be called the projection of the variable on the factor or the correlation of the variable with the factor. In terms of a geometrical model, each variable can be represented by a vector in *m*-dimensional space; each factor is represented by an axis in that space. The factor loading then is the projection of the vector on the axis, and the projection also is equivalent to the correlation of the variable with the factor. See Thurstone, *op. cit. supra* (Note 9), pp. 87-96, and Harry H. Harman, *Modern Factor Analysis* (Chicago: University of Chicago Press, 1960), pp. 262-64. It is in this sense that the term "factor loading" will be used here.

11. Where a circumstance can have more than one manifestation in a case (a rare situation), multiple values of 1 have to be used, depending on the number of manifestations. These are the "observed values" of the variables, as distinguished from the "standard values."

12. By restating the variables in terms of factors, the final multiple regression analysis has to deal with fewer unknowns than would be the case if it were applied directly to the variables. This difference may be critical so far as it concerns the sufficiency of information for solving the simultaneous equations.

13. Harold Hotelling, "Analysis of a Complex of Statistical Variables into Principal Components," *Journal of Educational Psychology,* Vol. 24 (1933), 417-41, 498-520; "Simplified Calculation of Principal Components," *Psychometrika,* Vol. 1 (March 1936), 27-35. For a complete exposition of this method, with regard to mathematical proof as well as application, see Thurstone, *op. cit. supra* (Note 9), pp. 480-503. The principal axes obtained by this method are orthogonal; i.e., the factors that these axes represent are independent of each other. This is a statistical relationship, and to the extent that factors adequately replicate the thought processes of the justices, the psychological counterparts of the statistical constructs are not necessarily independent. Indeed, the intuitive expectation might be that the psychological factors in sets of cases such as those analyzed here would be intercorrelated. It would be reasonable to argue, therefore, that factors should be obtained that actually correspond to the entities in terms of which the justices actually think. Furthermore, it could be argued that the axes that represent such factors are probably not orthogonal but oblique; i.e., these factors are not independent of each other. For this reason, it might be suggested that the principal axes should be rotated to an oblique position. But the available methods for rotating axes (see Edward F. Gocka, *A Comparison of Some Analytic Methods of Rotation in Factor Analysis* [Seattle: University of Washington Press, 1959], and Harman, *op. cit. supra* [Note 10], pp. 309-34) are based on purely statistical criteria just as much as the location of the principal axes. Consequently, the oblique axes that would be obtained by the established methods of rotation would not necessarily

approximate the entities in terms of which the justices think to a higher degree than the orthogonal axes. For this reason, the principal axes have been retained in this study in their original orthogonal position.

It should be noted again that the factor analysis in this study represents an intermediate, and not a final, stage of inquiry; it is merely a preparatory stage for the multiple regression analysis, which is designed to obtain the case weights. In this context, the most important requirement of factor analysis is to restate the original variables as completely as possible in terms of factors. The Principal Axes Method is particularly suited for this purpose, because it yields the highest possible communalities for the variables in terms of the fewest possible factors (see Thurstone, *op. cit. supra* [Note 9], pp. 503-10).

14. The term "original" correlation matrix is used here in order to distinguish it from the "residual" correlation matrices that are obtained in the process of factoring.

15. Since the correlation matrix is symmetrical, only the half above the major diagonal is presented here. The diagonal cells have been left blank. For some purposes, the proper entry for each cell in the diagonal of a correlation matrix would be 1, because each variable has the highest possible correlation with itself. The correlation matrix then would represent the "complete" correlation matrix. However, if the object of the factor analysis is to extract the common factors only, as in this study, the "reduced" correlation matrix, with estimated communalities in the diagonal, has to be used (see Thurstone, *op. cit. supra* [Note 9], pp. 76-82).

The following procedure has been employed in this study: The highest absolute value in each row of the correlation matrix is used as the first estimate of the communality (see Thurstone, *op. cit.,* pp. 299-300). Factoring proceeds until nearly vanishing entries appear in the diagonal of the residual correlation matrix. (Values smaller than 0.1 have been treated as nearly vanishing in this study.) The communalities that are obtained on this basis are used as the new estimates of communalities in the original correlation matrix, and the factoring process is repeated. The replacement of estimated communalities and the iteration of the factoring process continue until convergence in the communalities is reached. (Differences smaller than 0.1 have been regarded as convergence in this study.)

16. For an explanation of the use and limitations of the phi coefficient, see Helen M. Walker and Joseph Lev, *Statistical Interference* (New York: Henry Holt, 1953), pp. 272-75; J. P. Guilford, *Psychometric Methods,* 2nd ed. (New York: McGraw-Hill, 1954), p. 359; and Edward E. Cureton, "Note on ϕ/ϕ Max.", *Psychometrika,* Vol. 24 (March 1959), 89-91.

17. Generally, it is more convenient to work with factors that have high positive loadings than with factors that have high negative loadings. In order to gain this advantage, it is perfectly legitimate to reverse the sign of *every* loading on a particular factor (see Thurstone, *op. cit. supra* [Note 9], p. 96, especially the example that "minus grouchiness" is equivalent to "plus cheerfulness"). In this study, the sign of every loading on a factor was reversed whenever the sum of negative loadings below —0.5 exceeded the sum of positive loadings above +0.5. The purpose of this sign reversal was to emphasize high positive loadings as distinctive characteristics of the factors. This procedure cannot, however, eliminate the bipolarity of factors, for, obviously, whenever a high negative loading is converted into a high positive loading, a high positive loading on the same factor is changed to a high negative loading.

18. See note 13, *supra.*

19. See note 15, *supra.*

20. This method was first introduced by Walter Lederman in "On a Shortened Method of Estimation of Mental Factors by Regression," *Psychometrika,* Vol. 4 (June 1939), 109-16, and expanded by Harry H. Harman in "On the Rectilinear Prediction of Oblique Factors," *Psychometrika,* Vol. 6 (February 1941), 29-35. For a complete exposition of this method, with regard to mathematical proof as well as application, see Harman, *op. cit. supra* (Note 10), pp. 338-48 (covering the Complete Estimation Method, which must be examined for a proper understanding of the Shortened Estimation Method) and pp. 349-56 (on the Shortened Estimation Method itself).

21. See Harman, *op. cit. supra* (Note 10), p. 346.

22. Numerous references for multiple regression analysis are available. One convenient source is Oscar Kempthorne, *The Design and Analysis of Experiments* (New York: Wiley, 1952), pp. 38-44. The multiple regression analysis which is used at this point of the study will be called "final" multiple regression analysis, in order to distinguish it from the multiple regression analysis which is involved in the estimation of the factors in the cases.

23. The term "number of votes in favor of the petitioner (or claimant)" requires some qualification. Only the votes of justices who accept the facts (circumstances, or variables) as stated in the Opinion of the Court and who support the contentions of the petitioner or claimant on *that* ground can be included (see note 7, *supra*). If a justice justifies his position in the case only on jurisdictional grounds, his vote cannot be included, because his contribution to the decision is *not a part* of the decision *as a function* of the combination of variables (reduced to factors by the analysis). Furthermore, if a justice supports the petitioner or claimant only by accepting *more* facts than the ones stated in the Opinion of the Court, his vote also cannot be included, because no indication is given what his position would be on the facts which are accepted in the Opinion of the Court, i.e., the facts which are controlling for the decision. But, if a justice supports the petitioner or claimant by invoking *fewer* facts than the ones stated in the Opinion of the Court, his vote can be included; for obviously he also would support the petitioner or claimant on the basis of more facts (i.e., circumstances in favor of the petitioner or claimant).

24. The final regression coefficients represent the "weights" of the factors. Most factors have positive weights, because they are advantageous to the petitioner in obtaining a reversal of his conviction or to the claimant in receiving a compensation award; but a few factors, such as factor 5 in the right to counsel cases, have negative final regression coefficients, as previously noted. Accordingly, all variables are presumed to have an effect favorable to the petitioner or claimant, but this is not true of all *factors*, because of negative variable loadings on factors.

To compute the case weights, the factor estimates are multiplied by their corresponding final regression coefficients and the products are added (the first final regression coefficient, designated by 0, is multiplied by 1 in this process). If, instead of a new combination of old variables, a new case contains a *variable* that has not been previously encountered (empirically, a rare situation), a weight cannot be computed on the basis of the information derived from past decisions. But several such cases can be used as additional observations, the entire analysis can be repeated with the new cases, and then the weights of subsequent cases that contain the new variable can be computed.

25. See Quinn McNemar, *Psychological Statistics,* 2nd ed. (New York: Wiley, 1957), pp. 276-80, 389-91, for an explanation of the use of the F test in determining the significance of a multiple regression analysis. The F test measures whether or not the mean square explained by regression is significantly greater than the mean square not explained by regression. Accordingly,

$$F = \Sigma(Y'-\overline{Y})^2/m/\Sigma(Y-Y')^2/(N-m-1),$$

where Y represents the observed values, Y' the estimated values, $\overline{Y}$ the mean of the observed values, m the number of independent variables, and N the number of observations.

| | Degrees of Freedom | | | P (Chance Probability |
Sets of Cases	m	$N-m-1$	F	of Higher Value of F)
Involuntary confession cases	9	16	3.834	$P < 0.01$
Right-to-counsel cases	9	25	3.910	$P < 0.01$
Connecticut workmen's compensation cases	5	70	17.947	$P < 0.001$

Hence we can conclude that observed and estimated values are in significant agreement.

26. The "backward" test for the right to counsel cases was first suggested in July 1957 by Rudolph R. Rhomberg, formerly of the Department of Economics, University of Connecticut, now with the International Monetary Fund.

27. Kort, *op. cit. supra* (note 6).

28. Nagel, *op. cit. supra* (note 6).

29. See *Virginia Law Review,* Vol. 33 (1947), 731; *Southern California Law Review,* Vol. 22 (1949), 259; John Raeburn Green, "The Bill of Rights, the Fourteenth Amendment and the Supreme Court," *Michigan Law Review,* Vol. 46 (1948), 869, 898; and the discussion of these sources in William M. Beaney, *The Right to Counsel in American Courts* (Ann Arbor: University of Michigan Press, 1955), p. 194.

30. 367 U.S. 643 (1961).

31. Until recently, this actually was not clear. See Francis A. Allen, "Due Process and State Criminal Procedure: Another Look," *Northwestern University Law Review,* Vol. 48 (March-April, 1953), 16-35. But in *Rogers v. Richmond,* 365 U.S. 534 (1961), the Court definitely stated that the "deterrence" rationale is controlling.

32. See Thurstone, *op. cit. supra* (note 9), pp. 87-93.

Appendix

The computations involved in the proposed quantitative analysis would be prohibitive without the use of an electronic computer. For this reason, a computer program is included here. It can be used for any set of cases to which one might wish to apply the proposed analysis. The only information required is the appearance of variables in the cases, in the form in which it is presented in Tables 7, 8, and 9. The program is designed to accommodate any number of cases up to 200 and any number of variables up to 40. Should the number of cases or the number of variables exceed the indicated limits, certain simple changes in the DIMENSION statements would have to be made. But careful attention must be given to not exceeding the available storage.

The program is written in FORTRAN language. It has been tested and used for production on the IBM 709 and the IBM 7090. But it can be used on any computer which accepts FORTRAN. This includes not only several IBM computers, e.g., IBM 704, IBM 709, IBM 7090, but also some computers which have been built by other firms. Before using this program on a given computer, the following points must be checked carefully:

1. In what form should the identification card be punched?

2. Can "compilation" and "execution" be accommodated as *one* continuous operation? If not, the FORTRAN deck, which ends with the *last* END statement, has to be compiled first, and then the data deck, which begins with the * DATA statement, has to be processed with the binary deck.

3. What is the available storage? The program presented here uses 21,072 storage locations for data processing only.

4. Which tape is used for input and which tape is used for output? The program which is presented here uses Tape 4 for input and Tape 2 for output. But this is an arrangement which depends on the particular computer being used. Accordingly, the number of the tape which is used for

input (if other than 4) should be substituted in *every* READ INPUT TAPE statement, and the number of the tape which is used for output (if other than 2) should be substituted for 2 in *every* WRITE OUTPUT TAPE statement.

As presented here, the program contains two types of statement. One type consists of statements which contain numbers, various symbols, and *capital letters only. Each* line of these statements must be punched on an 80 column IBM card *exactly* in the form in which it appears here. For example, the line "1140 IF (E (I,J)-0.) 1150, 1150, 1200" states specifically the information which must be punched on the card in the indicated form. If the first character in such a line is an asterisk, it must be punched in column 1 of the card. If the first character in such a line is a number consisting of *one* digit, it must be punched in column 6. If the *first three* characters in such a line are a number consisting of *three digits,* the number should be punched in columns 3, 4, and 5. If the *first four* characters in such a line are a number consisting of four digits, the number should be punched in columns 2, 3, 4, and 5. The *first alphabetical* character in such a line should be punched in column 7, *regardless* of whether it is preceded by an asterisk, by a number, or by blank spaces. All the information in such lines is so arranged that no column after column 72 is used. The computer ignores columns 73-80. The other type of statement contains numbers, various symbols, and *capital and small* letters. These statements are merely *directions* as to what should be punched on the card. For example, the statement "identification card" is a direction to punch such a card; the information to be punched on the card must be determined by the person using the program. If such statements consist of more than one line, each line after the first line in the statement is indented. But the entire statement refers to *one* card *only, unless* an instruction to the contrary is given. *Regardless of the type of statement,* the cards must be arranged *exactly* in the order in which the statements appear in the program.

The program incorporates the mathematical procedures which have been discussed, and for which particular references have been given in footnotes 13, 20, 21, and 24. SUBROUTINE PRINAX covers the process of factoring, based on the Principal Axes method. SUBROUTINE FACEST performs the factor estimation. SUBROUTINE FIMURE covers the final multiple regression analysis. SUBROUTINE PREDIC predicts one half of a group of cases from the other half. SUBROUTINE SIGTES performs the significance test for the final multiple regression analysis and the predicted cases.

The expressions (other than the standard expressions in FORTRAN) used in this program have the following meaning:

E—matrix that indicates appearance of variables in cases
N—number of cases; number of rows in matrix E
M—number of variables; number of columns in matrix E
A, B, C, D—cells in the fourfold tables for computation of phi coefficients
NHALF—index that controls whether or not computer uses SUBROUTINE PREDIC; it is 0
    if the total sample is used and 1 if one half of the sample is predicted from the other
    half

F—in SUBROUTINE PRINAX, sum of two adjacent cells in matrix E; in SUBROUTINE SIGTES, value of F in F test

R—correlation matrix

RA—correlation matrix with absolute values

BIGRA—largest absolute value in a row of correlation matrix

RO—matrix that preserves original correlation matrix for iteration of factoring with new estimates of communalities

CYCLE—index of iteration

COM—communality

COMNEW—new estimate of communality

I—number of factors

SR—sum of a column in correlation matrix

SRA—absolute value of SR

BIGSRA—largest value of SRA

U—trial vector for iterative matrix multiplication

V—product of correlation matrix and trial vector

W—absolute value of V

BIGW—largest value of W

T—new trial vector for iterative matrix multiplication

BLR—product of T (or U) at point of convergence and V

CLR—square root of BLR

FL—factor loading

SFL—sum of factor loadings above 0.5 or below −0.5

S—residual correlation matrix

SA—residual correlation matrix with absolute values

BIGSA—largest absolute value in a row of residual correlation matrix

UFL—uniqueness of variable

P—product of inverse of diagonal matrix with uniqueness of variables in diagonal and common factor matrix

Q—product of transpose of common factor matrix and P

G—matrix of coefficients of unknowns and right-hand side of simultaneous equations

DIVG, FMULG, SIGMA—intermediate values, as defined in program, for solution of simultaneous equations by method of elimination

ALPHA—regression coefficients for factor estimation

EMEAN—column means in matrix E

SDSQ—variance of variables

SD—standard deviation of variables

DC—constant to be deducted from factor estimates, in view of use of observed values of variables

X—factor estimates

Y1—observed values of votes of court for total sample or for the half used as basis of prediction

Y1EST—estimated values corresponding to $Y1$

Y2—observed values of votes of court for predicted half of cases

Y2PRED—predicted values corresponding to $Y2$

SUM—coefficients of unknowns in normal equations in final multiple regression analysis

SUMRHS—right-hand side of normal equations in final multiple regression analysis

BETA—final multiple regression coefficients

Y1MEAN—mean of $Y1$ and, in iteration, mean of $Y2$

SUMNUM—summation in numerator of formula for F

SUMDEN—summation in denominator of formula for F

The program now follows:

Identification card.

```
*      XEQ
*      LIST
       READ INPUT TAPE 4, 100
100 FORMAT (72H
       1                    /72H
       2                              )
       WRITE OUTPUT TAPE 2, 100
       COMMON E, A, RA, RO, P, SUM, B, FL, ALPHA, C, S, G, D, SA, Q,
       1R, SR, V, UFL, EMEAN, SUMRHS, SRA, W, T, SDSQ, DC, U, SD, BETA,
       2COM, COMNEW, X, Y1, Y1EST, Y2, Y2PRED, M, N, I, LV, LW,
       3FMT, FMTA, FMTB, FMTC, FMTD, FMTE
       EQUIVALENCE (A, RA, RO, P, SUM), (B, FL, ALPHA), (C, S, G),
       1(D, SA, Q), (SR, V, UFL, EMEAN, SUMRHS),
       2(SRA, W, T, SDSQ, DC), (U, SD, BETA)
       DIMENSION E(200,40), A(40,40), RA(40,40), RO(40,40), P(40,40),
       1SUM(40,40), B(40,40), FL(40,40), ALPHA(40,40), C(40,40), S(40,40),
       2G(40,40), D(40,40), SA(40,40), Q(40,40), R(40,40),
       3SR(40), V(40), UFL(40), EMEAN(40), SUMRHS(40), SRA(40), W(40),
       4T(40), SDSQ(40), DC(40), U(40), SD(40), BETA(40), COM(40),
       5COMNEW(40), X(200,20), Y1(200), Y1EST(200), Y2(200), Y2PRED(200),
       6FMT(12), FMTA(12), FMTB(12), FMTC(12), FMTD(12), FMTE(12)
       CALL PRINAX
       CALL FACEST
       CALL FIMURE
       READ INPUT TAPE 4, 110, NHALF
110 FORMAT (I3)
       IF(NHALF-1) 130, 120, 120
120 CALL PREDIC
130 CALL SIGTES
       CALL EXIT
       END
*      LIST
       SUBROUTINE PRINAX
       COMMON E, A, RA, RO, P, SUM, B, FL, ALPHA, C, S, G, D, SA, Q,
       1R, SR, V, UFL, EMEAN, SUMRHS, SRA, W, T, SDSQ, DC, U, SD, BETA,
       2COM, COMNEW, X, Y1, Y1EST, Y2, Y2PRED, M, N, I, LV, LW,
       3FMT, FMTA, FMTB, FMTC, FMTD, FMTE
       EQUIVALENCE (A, RA, RO, P, SUM), (B, FL, ALPHA), (C, S, G),
       1(D, SA, Q), (SR, V, UFL, EMEAN, SUMRHS),
       2(SRA, W, T, SDSQ, DC), (U, SD, BETA)
       DIMENSION E(200,40), A(40,40), RA(40,40), RO(40,40), P(40,40),
       1SUM(40,40), B(40,40), FL(40,40), ALPHA(40,40), C(40,40), S(40,40),
       2G(40,40), D(40,40), SA(40,40), Q(40,40), R(40,40),
       3SR(40), V(40), UFL(40), EMEAN(40), SUMRHS(40), SRA(40), W(40),
       4T(40), SDSQ(40), DC(40), U(40), SD(40), BETA(40), COM(40),
       5COMNEW(40), X(200,20), Y1(200), Y1EST(200), Y2(200), Y2PRED(200),
       6FMT(12), FMTA(12), FMTB(12), FMTC(12), FMTD(12), FMTE(12)

       READ INPUT TAPE 4, 1100, M, N
1100 FORMAT (2I3)
       READ INPUT TAPE 4, 1110, (FMT(J), J=1,12)
1110 FORMAT (12A6)
       READ INPUT TAPE 4, FMT, ((E(I,J), I=1,N), J=1,M)
       MB=M-1
       WRITE OUTPUT TAPE 2, 1120
1120 FORMAT (//17H FOUR FOLD TABLES//)
       DO 1225 J=1,MB
       JA=J+1
       WRITE OUTPUT TAPE 2, 1130, J
1130 FORMAT (//10H VARIABLE I3, 25H AND SUBSEQUENT VARIABLES//)
       DO 1220 K=JA,M
       A(J,K)=0.
       B(J,K)=0.
       C(J,K)=0.
       D(J,K)=0.
       DO 1220 I=1,N
```

```
      IF(E(I,J)-E(I,K)) 1140, 1180, 1160
1140  IF(E(I,J)-0.) 1150, 1150, 1200
1150  B(J,K)=B(J,K)+1.
      GO TO 1220
1160  IF(E(I,K)-0.) 1170, 1170, 1200
1170  C(J,K)=C(J,K)+1.
      GO TO 1220
1180  F=E(I,J)+E(I,K)
      IF (F-1.) 1190, 1190, 1200
1190  D(J,K)=D(J,K)+1.
      GO TO 1220
1200  A(J,K)=A(J,K)+1.
1210  FORMAT (4F5.1)
1220  CONTINUE
      WRITE OUTPUT TAPE 2, 1210, (A(J,K), B(J,K), C(J,K), D(J,K),
     1K=JA,M)
1225  CONTINUE
      DO 1230 J=1,MB
      JA=J+1
      DO 1230 K=JA,M
1230  R(J,K)=((A(J,K)*D(J,K))-(B(J,K)*C(J,K)))/
     1SQRTF(((((A(J,K)+B(J,K))*(C(J,K)+D(J,K)))*
     2(A(J,K)+C(J,K)))*(B(J,K)+D(J,K))))
      DO 1240 J=1,MB
      JA=J+1
      DO 1240 K=JA,M
1240  R(K,J)=R(J,K)
      DO 1250 J=1,M
1250  R(J,J)=0.
      DO 1260 J=1,M
      DO 1260 K=1,M
1260  RA(J,K)=ABSF(R(J,K))
      DO 1290 J=1,M
      BIGRA=RA(J,1)
      DO 1290 K=2,M
      IF(BIGRA-RA(J,K)) 1270, 1280, 1280
1270  BIGRA=RA(J,K)
1280  CONTINUE
1290  R(J,J)=BIGRA
      WRITE OUTPUT TAPE 2, 1300
1300  FORMAT (//28H ORIGINAL CORRELATION MATRIX//)
      READ INPUT TAPE 4, 1110, (FMTA(J), J=1,12)
      WRITE OUTPUT TAPE 2, FMTA, ((R(J,K), K=1,M), J=1,M)
      DO 1310 J=1,M
      DO 1310 K=1,M
1310  RO(J,K)=R(J,K)
      DO 1320 K=1,M
1320  COM(K)=0.
      CYCLE=1.
1330  I=0
1340  DO 1350 K=1,M
      SR(K)=0.
      DO 1350 J=1,M
1350  SR(K)=SR(K)+R(J,K)
      DO 1360 K=1,M
1360  SRA(K)=ABSF(SR(K))
      BIGSRA=SRA(1)
      DO 1380 K=2,M
      IF (BIGSRA-SRA(K)) 1370, 1380, 1380
1370  BIGSRA=SRA(K)
1380  CONTINUE
      DO 1390 K=1,M
1390  U(K)=SR(K)/BIGSRA
1400  DO 1410 J=1,M
      V(J)=0.
      DO 1410 K=1,M
1410  V(J)=V(J)+R(J,K)*U(K)
      DO 1420 J=1,M
1420  W(J)=ABSF(V(J))
      BIGW=W(1)
      DO 1440 J=2,M
```

```
      IF (BIGW-W(J)) 1430, 1440, 1440
1430  BIGW=W(J)
1440  CONTINUE
      DO 1450 J=1,M
1450  T(J)=V(J)/BIGW
      DO 1460 J=1,M
      IF (ABSF(U(J)-T(J))-.0004) 1460, 1460, 1470
1460  CONTINUE
      GO TO 1490
1470  DO 1480 K=1,M
1480  U(K)=T(K)
      GO TO 1400
1490  BLR=0.
      DO 1500 J=1,M
1500  BLR=BLR+T(J)*V(J)
      CLR=SQRTF(BLR)
      I=I+1
      DO 1510 J=1,M
1510  FL(I,J)=V(J)/CLR
      SFL=0.
      DO 1530 J=1,M
      IF (ABSF(FL(I,J))-.5) 1530, 1530, 1520
1520  SFL=SFL+FL(I,J)
1530  CONTINUE
      IF (SFL-0.) 1540, 1560, 1560
1540  DO 1550 J=1,M
1550  FL(I,J)=(FL(I,J))*(-1.)
1560  DO 1570 J=1,M
      DO 1570 K=J,M
1570  S(J,K)=R(J,K)-FL(I,J)*FL(I,K)
      DO 1580 J=1,MB
      JA=J+1
      DO 1580 K=JA,M
1580  S(K,J)=S(J,K)
      IF (CYCLE-2.) 1590, 1650, 1650
1590  DO 1600 J=1,M
1600  S(J,J)=0.
      DO 1610 J=1,M
      DO 1610 K=1,M
1610  SA(J,K)=ABSF(S(J,K))
      DO 1640 J=1,M
      BIGSA=SA(J,1)
      DO 1630 K=2,M
      IF (BIGSA-SA(J,K)) 1620, 1630, 1630
1620  BIGSA=SA(J,K)
1630  CONTINUE
1640  S(J,J)=BIGSA
1650  DO 1660 J=1,M
      IF (S(J,J)-.1) 1660, 1670, 1670
1660  CONTINUE
      GO TO 1690
1670  DO 1680 J=1,M
      DO 1680 K=1,M
1680  R(J,K)=S(J,K)
      GO TO 1340
1690  WRITE OUTPUT TAPE 2, 1700
1700  FORMAT (//16H FACTOR LOADINGS//)
      WRITE OUTPUT TAPE 2, FMTA, ((FL(J,K), K=1,M), J=1,I)
      DO 1710 K=1,M
      COMNEW(K)=0.
      DO 1710 J=1,I
1710  COMNEW(K)=COMNEW(K)+(FL(J,K)**2)
      DO 1720 K=1,M
      IF (ABSF(COMNEW(K)-COM(K))-.1) 1720, 1750, 1750
1720  CONTINUE
      DO 1730 K=1,M
1730  COM(K)=COMNEW(K)
      WRITE OUTPUT TAPE 2, 1740
1740  FORMAT (//20H FINAL COMMUNALITIES//)
      WRITE OUTPUT TAPE 2, FMTA, (COM(K), K=1,M)
      GO TO 1800
```

```
1750 DO 1760 K=1,M
1760 COM(K)=COMNEW(K)
     WRITE OUTPUT TAPE 2, 1770
1770 FORMAT (//14H COMMUNALITIES//)
     WRITE OUTPUT TAPE 2, FMTA, (COM(K), K=1,M)
     DO 1780 J=1,M
     DO 1780 K=1,M
1780 R(J,K)=RO(J,K)
     DO 1790 K=1,M
1790 R(K,K)=COM(K)
     CYCLE=CYCLE+1.
     GO TO 1330
1800 RETURN
     END
*    LIST
     SUBROUTINE FACEST
     COMMON E, A, RA, RO, P, SUM, B, FL, ALPHA, C, S, G, D, SA, Q,
    1R, SR, V, UFL, EMEAN, SUMRHS, SRA, W, T, SDSQ, DC, U, SD, BETA,
    2COM, COMNEW, X, Y1, Y1EST, Y2, Y2PRED, M, N, I, LV, LW,
    3FMT, FMTA, FMTB, FMTC, FMTD, FMTE
     EQUIVALENCE (A, RA, RO, P, SUM), (B, FL, ALPHA), (C, S, G),
    1(D, SA, Q), (SR, V, UFL, EMEAN, SUMRHS),
    2(SRA, W, T, SDSQ, DC), (U, SD, BETA)
     DIMENSION E(200,40), A(40,40), RA(40,40), RO(40,40), P(40,40),
    1SUM(40,40), B(40,40), FL(40,40), ALPHA(40,40), C(40,40), S(40,40),
    2G(40,40), D(40,40), SA(40,40), Q(40,40), R(40,40),
    3SR(40), V(40), UFL(40), EMEAN(40), SUMRHS(40), SRA(40), W(40),
    4T(40), SDSQ(40), DC(40), U(40), SD(40), BETA(40), COM(40),
    5COMNEW(40), X(200,20), Y1(200), Y1EST(200), Y2(200), Y2PRED(200),
    6FMT(12), FMTA(12), FMTB(12), FMTC(12), FMTD(12), FMTE(12)
     LV=I+1
     DO 2120 K=1,M
     IF(COM(K)-.99) 2100, 2100, 2110
2100 UFL(K)=1.-COM(K)
     GO TO 2120
2110 UFL(K)=.01
2120 CONTINUE
     DO 2130 K=1,M
     DO 2130 J=1,I
2130 P(J,K)=FL(J,K)/UFL(K)

     DO 2140 L=1,I
     DO 2140 J=1,I
     Q(J,L)=0.
     DO 2140 K=1,M
2140 Q(J,L)=Q(J,L)+FL(J,K)*P(L,K)
     DO 2150 L=1,I
2150 Q(L,L)=Q(L,L)+1.
     DO 2240 K=1,M
     DO 2160 J=1,I
     DO 2160 L=1,I
2160 G(J,L)=Q(J,L)
     DO 2170 J=1,I
2170 G(J,LV)=P(J,K)
     DO 2200 L=1,I
     DIVG=G(L,L)
     DO 2180 J=L,LV
2180 G(L,J)=G(L,J)/DIVG
     IA=L+1
     IF(IA-LV) 2190, 2210, 2210
2190 DO 2200 JA=IA,I
     FMULG=G(JA,L)
     DO 2200 J=L,LV
2200 G(JA,J)=G(JA,J)-G(L,J)*FMULG
2210 ALPHA(K,I)=G(I,LV)
     L=I
2220 SIGMA=0.
     DO 2230 J=L,I
2230 SIGMA=SIGMA+G(L-1,J)*ALPHA(K,J)
     L=L-1
     ALPHA(K,L)=G(L,LV)-SIGMA
```

```
      IF(L-1) 2240, 2240, 2220
2240  CONTINUE
      VN=N
      DO 2250 K=1,M
      EMEAN(K)=0.
      DO 2250 J=1,N
2250  EMEAN(K)=EMEAN(K)+(E(J,K)/VN)
      DO 2260 K=1,M
      SDSQ(K)=0.
      DO 2260 J=1,N
2260  SDSQ(K)=SDSQ(K)+((E(J,K)-EMEAN(K))**2)/VN
      DO 2270 K=1,M
2270  SD(K)=SQRTF(SDSQ(K))
      DO 2280 K=1,M
      DO 2280 L=1,I
2280  ALPHA(K,L)=ALPHA(K,L)/SD(K)
      WRITE OUTPUT TAPE 2, 2290
2290  FORMAT (//42H FACTOR ESTIMATION REGRESSION COEFFICIENTS//)
      WRITE OUTPUT TAPE 2, FMTA, ((ALPHA(K,L), K=1,M), L=1,I)
      DO 2300 L=1,I
      DC(L)=0.
      DO 2300 K=1,M
2300  DC(L)=DC(L)+ALPHA(K,L)*EMEAN(K)
      WRITE OUTPUT TAPE 2, 2310
2310  FORMAT (//42H DEDUCTABLE CONSTANT FOR FACTOR ESTIMATION//)
      WRITE OUTPUT TAPE 2, FMTA, (DC(L), L=1,I)
      DO 2320 J=1,N
      DO 2320 L=2,LV
      X(J,L)=0.
      DO 2320 K=1,M
2320  X(J,L)=X(J,L)+E(J,K)*ALPHA(K,L-1)
      DO 2330 L=2,LV
      DO 2330 J=1,N
2330  X(J,L)=X(J,L)-DC(L-1)
      DO 2340 J=1,N
2340  X(J,1)=1.
      WRITE OUTPUT TAPE 2, 2350
2350  FORMAT (//26H FACTOR ESTIMATES IN CASES//)
      READ INPUT TAPE 4, 2360, (FMTB(J), J=1,12)
2360  FORMAT (12A6)
      WRITE OUTPUT TAPE 2, FMTB, ((X(J,L),J=1,N), L=1,LV)
      RETURN
      END
*     LIST
      SUBROUTINE FIMURE
      COMMON E, A, RA, RO, P, SUM, B, FL, ALPHA, C, S, G, D, SA, Q,
     1R, SR, V, UFL, EMEAN, SUMRHS, SRA, W, T, SDSQ, DC, U, SD, BETA,
     2COM, COMNEW, X, Y1, Y1EST, Y2, Y2PRED, M, N, I, LV, LW,
     3FMT, FMTA, FMTB, FMTC, FMTD, FMTE
      EQUIVALENCE (A, RA, RO, P, SUM), (B, FL, ALPHA), (C, S, G),
     1(D, SA, Q), (SR, V, UFL, EMEAN, SUMRHS),
     2(SRA, W, T, SDSQ, DC), (U, SD, BETA)
      DIMENSION E(200,40), A(40,40), RA(40,40), RO(40,40), P(40,40),
     1SUM(40,40), B(40,40), FL(40,40), ALPHA(40,40), C(40,40), S(40,40),
     2G(40,40), D(40,40), SA(40,40), Q(40,40), R(40,40),
     3SR(40), V(40), UFL(40), EMEAN(40), SUMRHS(40), SRA(40), W(40),
     4T(40), SDSQ(40), DC(40), U(40), SD(40), BETA(40), COM(40),
     5COMNEW(40), X(200,20), Y1(200), Y1EST(200), Y2(200), Y2PRED(200),
     6FMT(12), FMTA(12), FMTB(12), FMTC(12), FMTD(12), FMTE(12)
      READ INPUT TAPE 4, FMTB, (Y1(J), J=1,N)
      LW=LV+1
      DO 3100 K=1,LV
      DO 3100 L=1,LV
      SUM(K,L)=0.
      DO 3100 J=1,N
3100  SUM(K,L)=SUM(K,L)+X(J,K)*X(J,L)
      DO 3110 K=1,LV
      SUMRHS(K)=0.
      DO 3110 J=1,N
3110  SUMRHS(K)=SUMRHS(K)+Y1(J)*X(J,K)
      DO 3120 K=1,LV
```

```
          DO 3120 L=1,LV
 3120 G(K,L)=SUM(K,L)
          DO 3130 K=1,LV
 3130 G(K,LW)=SUMRHS(K)
          DO 3160 J=1,LV
          DIVG=G(J,J)
          DO 3140 L=J,LW
 3140 G(J,L)=G(J,L)/DIVG
          I1=J+1
          IF(I1-LW) 3150, 3170, 3170
 3150 DO 3160 J1=I1,LV
          FMULG=G(J1,J)
          DO 3160 L=J,LW
 3160 G(J1,L)=G(J1,L)-G(J,L)*FMULG
 3170 BETA(LV)=G(LV,LW)
          K=LV
 3180 SIGMA=0.
          DO 3190 L=K,LV
 3190 SIGMA=SIGMA+G(K-1,L)*BETA(L)
          K=K-1
          BETA(K)=G(K,LW)-SIGMA
          IF(K-1) 3200, 3200, 3180
 3200 WRITE OUTPUT TAPE 2, 3210
 3210 FORMAT (//39H FINAL MULTIPLE REGRESSION COEFFICIENTS//)
          READ INPUT TAPE 4, 3220, (FMTC(J), J=1,12)
 3220 FORMAT (12A6)
          WRITE OUTPUT TAPE 2, FMTC, (BETA(K), K=1,LV)
          DO 3230 J=1,N
          Y1EST(J)=0.
          DO 3230 K=1,LV
 3230 Y1EST(J)=Y1EST(J)+X(J,K)*BETA(K)
          WRITE OUTPUT TAPE 2, 3240
 3240 FORMAT (//13H CASE WEIGHTS//)
          WRITE OUTPUT TAPE 2, FMTB, (Y1EST(J), J=1,N)
          RETURN
          END
  *       LIST
          SUBROUTINE PREDIC
          COMMON E, A, RA, RO, P, SUM, B, FL, ALPHA, C, S, G, D, SA, Q,
         1R, SR, V, UFL, EMEAN, SUMRHS, SRA, W, T, SDSQ, DC, U, SD, BETA,
         2COM, COMNEW, X, Y1, Y1EST, Y2, Y2PRED, M, N, I, LV, LW,
         3FMT, FMTA, FMTB, FMTC, FMTD, FMTE
          EQUIVALENCE (A, RA, RO, P, SUM), (B, FL, ALPHA), (C, S, G),
         1(D, SA, Q), (SR, V, UFL, EMEAN, SUMRHS),
         2(SRA, W, T, SDSQ, DC), (U, SD, BETA)
          DIMENSION E(200,40), A(40,40), RA(40,40), RO(40,40), P(40,40),
         1SUM(40,40), B(40,40), FL(40,40), ALPHA(40,40), C(40,40), S(40,40),
         2G(40,40), D(40,40), SA(40,40), Q(40,40), R(40,40),
         3SR(40), V(40), UFL(40), EMEAN(40), SUMRHS(40), SRA(40), W(40),
         4T(40), SDSQ(40), DC(40), U(40), SD(40), BETA(40), COM(40),
         5COMNEW(40), X(200,20), Y1(200), Y1EST(200), Y2(200), Y2PRED(200),
         6FMT(12), FMTA(12), FMTB(12), FMTC(12), FMTD(12), FMTE(12)
          READ INPUT TAPE 4, 4100, N
 4100 FORMAT (I3)
          READ INPUT TAPE 4, 4110, (FMTD(J), J=1,12)
 4110 FORMAT (12A6)
          READ INPUT TAPE 4, FMTD, ((E(J,K), J=1,N), K=1,M)
          DO 4120 J=1,N
          DO 4120 L=2,LV
          X(J,L)=0.
          DO 4120 K=1,M
 4120 X(J,L)=X(J,L)+E(J,K)*ALPHA(K,L-1)
          DO 4130 L=2,LV
          DO 4130 J=1,N
 4130 X(J,L)=X(J,L)-DC(L-1)
          DO 4140 J=1,N
 4140 X(J,1)=1.
          WRITE OUTPUT TAPE 2, 4150
 4150 FORMAT (//36H FACTOR ESTIMATES IN PREDICTED CASES//)
          READ INPUT TAPE 4, 4110, (FMTE(J), J=1,12)
          WRITE OUTPUT TAPE 2, FMTE, ((X(J,L), J=1,N), L=1,LV)
```

```
          DO 4160 J=1,N
          Y2PRED(J)=0.
          DO 4160 K=1,LV
 4160 Y2PRED(J)=Y2PRED(J)+X(J,K)*BETA(K)
          WRITE OUTPUT TAPE 2, 4170
 4170 FORMAT (//23H PREDICTED CASE WEIGHTS//)
          WRITE OUTPUT TAPE 2, FMTE, (Y2PRED(J), J=1,N)
          RETURN
          END
  *       LIST
          SUBROUTINE SIGTES
          COMMON E, A, RA, RO, P, SUM, B, FL, ALPHA, C, S, G, D, SA, Q,
         1R, SR, V, UFL, EMEAN, SUMRHS, SRA, W, T, SDSQ, DC, U, SD, BETA,
         2COM, COMNEW, X, Y1, Y1EST, Y2, Y2PRED, M, N, I, LV, LW,
         3FMT, FMTA, FMTB, FMTC, FMTD, FMTE
          EQUIVALENCE (A, RA, RO, P, SUM), (B, FL, ALPHA), (C, S, G),
         1(D, SA, Q), (SR, V, UFL, EMEAN, SUMRHS),
         2(SRA, W, T, SDSQ, DC), (U, SD, BETA)
          DIMENSION E(200,40), A(40,40), RA(40,40), RO(40,40), P(40,40),
         1SUM(40,40), B(40,40), FL(40,40), ALPHA(40,40), C(40,40), S(40,40),
         2G(40,40), D(40,40), SA(40,40), Q(40,40), R(40,40),
         3SR(40), V(40), UFL(40), EMEAN(40), SUMRHS(40), SRA(40), W(40),
         4T(40), SDSQ(40), DC(40), U(40), SD(40), BETA(40), COM(40),
         5COMNEW(40), X(200,20), Y1(200), Y1EST(200), Y2(200), Y2PRED(200),
         6FMT(12), FMTA(12), FMTB(12), FMTC(12), FMTD(12), FMTE(12)
          READ INPUT TAPE 4, 5100, N, NHALF
 5100 FORMAT (2I3)
          CYCLE=1.
          FI=1
 5110 FN=N
          Y1MEAN=0.
          DO 5120 J=1,N
 5120 Y1MEAN=Y1MEAN+Y1(J)/FN
          SUMNUM=0.
          DO 5130 J=1,N
 5130 SUMNUM=SUMNUM+(Y1EST(J)-Y1MEAN)**2
          SUMDEN=0.
          DO 5140 J=1,N
 5140 SUMDEN=SUMDEN+(Y1(J)-Y1EST(J))**2
          F=(SUMNUM/FI)/(SUMDEN/(FN-FI-1.))
          IF (CYCLE-1.) 5150, 5150, 5210
 5150 WRITE OUTPUT TAPE 2, 5160, F
 5160 FORMAT (//28H F TEST ESTIMATED CASES  F =F7.3//)
          IF (NHALF-1) 5230, 5170, 5170
 5170 CYCLE=CYCLE+1.
          READ INPUT TAPE 4, 5180, N
 5180 FORMAT (I3)
          READ INPUT TAPE 4, FMTE, (Y2(J), J=1,N)
          DO 5190 J=1,N
 5190 Y1(J)=Y2(J)
          DO 5200 J=1,N
 5200 Y1EST(J)=Y2PRED(J)
          GO TO 5110
 5210 WRITE OUTPUT TAPE 2, 5220, F
 5220 FORMAT (//28H F TEST PREDICTED CASES  F =F7.3//)
 5230 RETURN
          END
```

*DATA

Identification card; first character in column 2.

Identification card; first character in column 2.

Number of variables in columns 2 and 3; number of cases in columns 5 and 6, or 4, 5, and 6 if the number of cases exceeds 99.

Format statement for the appearance of variables in the cases, which will be punched on the cards that *follow* this card; on those cards, three columns will be used to indicate the observed value of each variable in each case, going *first* through all the cases for variable 1, then through all the cases for variable 2, *etc.* Consequently, as many as 24 cases can be accommodated on one card. This format statement has to be punched accordingly. For example, if there are 50 cases, the format statement should be punched as follows, starting in column 2: (24F3.1/24F3.1/2F3.1) This means that for *each* variable there are 3 cards; the first card contains the observed values of the variables in the first 24 cases, the second card the observed values in the second 24 cases, and the third card the observed values in the last two cases. For more or fewer cases, the format statement has to be adjusted accordingly.

Appearance of variables in the cases, *punched on as many cards as needed,* in accordance with the preceding format statement, starting in column 1 of each card, 3 columns for each case; i.e., O. for the absence of the variable in the case, 1. for presence, multiple of 1. for several manifestations, whereby a blank space must follow each decimal point.

Format statement for printing the correlation matrix, etc., starting in column 2; e.g., (10F7.3/9F7.3) for 19 variables, (10F7.3/10F7.3/3F7.3) for 23 variables, *etc.,* according to the number of variables.

Format statement for factor estimates, etc., starting in column 2; e.g., (10F7.3/10F7.3 /6F7.3) for 26 cases, (10F7.3/10F7.3/10F7.3/4F7.3) for 34 cases, etc., according to the number of cases.

Observed values of the votes of the court for the total sample, or for the half which is used as the basis of prediction. These observed values must be *punched on as many cards as needed,* in accordance with the preceding format statement, starting in column 1 of each card, 7 columns for each observed value, with the number of votes in the *third* column of each field of 7 columns and the decimal point in the *fourth* column of each field of 7 columns.

(5F9.3/5F9.3/5F9.3/5F9.3) to be punched starting in column 2.

1 in column 3 for prediction of one half of the cases from the other half; otherwise, 0 in column 3.

Number of cases to be predicted in columns 2 and 3 (in columns 1, 2, and 3, if the number exceeds 99), *if* prediction is used.

Format statement for the appearance of variables in the predicted cases (*if* prediction is used), following the pattern of the format statement for the appearance of the variables in the cases on which the prediction is based.

Appearance of variables in the cases to be predicted (*if* prediction is used), in accordance with the preceding format statement.

Format statement for the factor estimates in the predicted cases, etc. (*if* prediction is used), following the pattern of the format statement for the factor estimates of the cases on which the prediction is based.

Number of cases in the total sample, or in the half on which the prediction is based, in columns 2 and 3 (in columns 1, 2, and 3, if the number exceeds 99). 1 in column 6 for prediction of one half of cases from the other half; otherwise, 0 in column 6.

Number of cases to be predicted in columns 2 and 3 (in columns 1, 2, and 3 if the number exceeds 99) *if* prediction is used.

Observed values of the votes of the court in the predicted cases (*if* prediction is used), *punched on as many cards as needed,* following the pattern of the format statement for the observed values of the votes of the court in the half of cases on which the prediction is based.

PART THREE

POLITICAL SOCIOLOGY
AND COURTS

Conscientious Objectors before Norwegian Military Courts

VILHELM AUBERT

HOW DOES A COURT reach a decision in a trial? This question has increasingly emerged as a central one in lego-philosophical discussion, but it does not actually belong in the realm of legal philosophy. It is rather an empirical question which concerns social psychology and sociology. There has always been a question as to what extent legal decisions are logically derived from positive rules, and to what extent they are conditioned by a particular judge's values, personality, and social background. In this question is bound up both the problem of the "rule of law" (*Rechtsicherheit*) and the problem of justice.

The "rule of law" includes, among other things, the principle that it should be possible to predict the legal consequences of citizens' actions. Theoretically, this could occur through stringent laws and their mechanical application by the courts. Any variation would imply that one judge or another had put aside the law, and consequently it would be easy to discern whether the courts had upheld the "rule of law."

The problem of justice involves still another principle: that like cases shall be handled alike. Paradoxically enough, to invoke this principle is to contend that each case shall be treated according to its peculiarities, if we interpret "likeness" to mean something more than that two cases shall be judged exactly alike if they fulfill exactly the same clear and simple conditions which are to be read from the law. There is hardly any doubt that most of people's ideas and beliefs about justice, unclear and ambiguous as they probably are, are based on something more than a mechanical-juridical "likeness." Moreover, even if the cases which are judged to be alike are alike in all their relevant moral aspects, a human being, with his unique values, personality, and social relationships, must make this judgment of what is alike and what is not. Consequently, it has always been recognized

The substance of this chapter was originally published in Norwegian in *Tidsskrift for Rettsvidenskap,* Vol. 69 (1956), 403-23. The data were collected in 1955 under a grant from the Norwegian Research Council.

that the decisions of a judge involve more than a mechanical application of abstract rules to available facts. It has not, however, been easy to develop an alternative theory of how legal decisions are arrived at.

One thing is certain: no valid theories of the decision process can be framed if one is limited exclusively to the reasons that the judge himself states when he gives an opinion. His articulated premises for judgments are of course important, but it would seem a questionable approach to interpret judicial opinions in *psychological* terms in order to yield a cue to the judge's mind and motivation (as for example, Alf Ross does several places in his treatment of these questions).[1] The grounds for sentencing are obviously meant as an officially correct argument for the judgment, not as a scientifically valid introspective analysis. After all, the judge has not been charged with the latter task.

If one cannot determine on what bases a judge's decisions are made by relying solely on his official arguments, how, then, is it possible to investigate decision-making? Naturally, the possibility exists that, in addition to their official opinion, judges might be encouraged to furnish an introspective report analyzing their own decision-making process. But such a procedure is hardly feasible. There is, however, another way of answering this question of why a judge acts as he does, and that is by examining the ways in which the characteristics of the case and those of the decision are statistically correlated. Which factors are actually present in a judgment for conviction or a judgment for acquittal, for example? The best results would be reached if one could chart the cases without having to rely upon the opinions of the courts, which of course cannot be expected to give any exhaustive picture of the facts. But even if this is not possible, a statistical treatment of the elements of the decision's premises can reveal significant correlations—for instance, the relationship between the decision and the traits of the accused, or the accused's milieu—relationships which might not otherwise be recognized. It may in this way be possible to discover some of the judge's secrets without having to go beyond his own premises.

If such an objective, quantitative analysis were to expose relationships with no evident warrant in the legal doctrine, would this not imply a defect in the "rule of law" or in justice? Of course, if all cases came before the same judge, the results would not necessarily deviate from the principle that "like cases shall be treated alike." But most cases (including those which will be treated here) are brought before different judges, and it is likely that the motives which unknowingly influence the decisions will be expressed in different ways by different judges. Therefore, an examination of several judges' patterns of reasoning will often tell one something of the problems of "rule of law" and justice. This assumption underlies the investigation which will be reported here.

1. Legal and Organizational Context

This study deals with military court verdicts in cases involving objectors to military service. The choice of subject is in part due to a special interest

TABLE 1

A Description of the Sample as a Function of Judicial Statements about the Defendants' Personal Beliefs and Intention of Permanently Avoiding Military Service

	Intention to Avoid	
Defendants' Beliefs	*YES (Art. 35 cases)*	*NO (Art. 34 or Art. 77 cases)*
Serious belief found (acquittals)	190	3
No serious beliefs found (convictions)	53	—
	243	3

in the problem of conscientious objectors. In part it is also due to the fact that we here are concerned with a comparatively limited, and therefore manageable, number of cases divided among a total of seven courts. The discretionary character of the statutory provisions offers a good opportunity to study what occurs when the judge's personal values and personality have the greatest possibilities to manifest themselves in the decisions. But on the same account the investigation cannot lay claim to being representative beyond the sphere it covers.

The material embraces those cases which apply the military penal law, Article 35, Section 4:

Anyone who with the express intention of permanently avoiding military service trespasses as stated in Art. 34,[2] or after being in attendance or present for military service, illegally refuses to fulfill in any way his military duty is liable to punishment by prison from three months to two years, but up to three years if this occurs during military duty with craft on mission.

In cases of repetition the penalty is from one to three years.

If the accused appears voluntarily within seven days for purpose of fulfilling his military duty, or within the same period of time indicates his willingness to do so, he is liable to punishment up to two years; under especially extenuating circumstances arrest can be used.

Punishment according to Sections 1, 2, and 3 is not imposed if the accused is liable to conscription (officers or conscripts) and maintains that it is against his serious conviction to do military service of any sort. In cases in the assize courts in which the question of guilt is answered negatively, the jury shall in its opinion state if any jurors have voted for acquittal on the basis of this exemption and if so, how many.

This investigation is based exclusively on those cases in which the court's decision touched on the question whether doing military service is in conflict with the accused's serious beliefs (see Table 1). (This should cover virtually all cases in which strong beliefs have been claimed by the accused. Of course, it is not inconceivable that a few cases might be found where the accused has strong beliefs but has not placed them before the court. However, by definition, such cases cannot be identified.) The investigation is exclusively based on the protocols of the courts.

The delimitation mentioned in the description of the material implies three types of judicial decisions: (1) decisions where the accused is acquitted on the basis of Art. 35, Section 4; (2) decisions where the accused is convicted on the basis of Art. 35, because the conditions in Section 4 are not considered fulfilled; and (3) some decisions in which the accused is convicted and given milder penalties according to Art. 34 or Art. 77. There are only three cases which belong in the last category, in which the court, on the one hand, establishes that strong beliefs are claimed, but that on the other hand, no intention of permanently avoiding military service is present. Otherwise, all cases in which the court decides that such an intention is not present lie outside this investigation. Likewise excluded are those few cases where the court decides that an intention permanently to avoid conscription is present, but where no strong beliefs are mentioned in the evidence.

All sentences were passed by military courts. These courts are presided over by a military judge (generally a district judge or city judge) and also include two lay judges. One of these latter is an officer, the other an ordinary soldier. The proceedings were nearly the same as judicial proceedings in civilian criminal cases. It should be noted, however, that the cases on which this study is based occurred during the period from 1949 to 1954. Although the substantive laws concerning military objectors have not been altered, the manner of handling these cases has since been changed. In 1957, the Norwegian legislature adopted a law which in practice transfers the judicial authority of the military courts to the civilian courts in time of peace.[3]

A sentence of acquittal, according to the military penal code Art. 35, Section 4, entails the right and duty to do civil work in place of military duty. Thus an acquittal brings about the same result as an administrative transfer to civil work granted a petitioner by the Justice Department.[4] In a number of the cases of those investigated the accused applied to the Justice Department but was denied a transfer. In other cases no petition was sent in. When the case concerns transfer to civil work, the military courts thus function both as courts of first instance on the same level as the Justice Department and as courts of appeal in relation to the decisions of the Justice Department. It has been asserted that the rulings of the Justice Department differ from those of the military courts. The Justice Department has considerable discretion in its decision-making, while the military courts are bound by the usual principles of the burden of proof in a criminal action, and therefore will more often find strong beliefs to be of consequence. The comparatively large number of conscientious objectors who have been acquitted in military courts after having applications refused by the Justice Department would indicate that this assertion is correct.

Nevertheless, the majority of civil workers have been transferred as the direct result of favorable decisions by the Justice Department. In the period 1947-1954, a total of 3317 objectors to military service were transferred to civil work by administrative decision, as compared to 193 military court "transfers," in the cases studied in this investigation. The Justice Department's method of deciding cases has therefore played, practically speaking, a greater role than the practice of the military courts. As an authoritative expression of valid rules, however, each judicial decision may be attributed greater weight than each administrative decision.

2. Sampling Procedure and Method of Analysis

The present study has been based on an examination of the records of the five military courts from January 1, 1949, to July 1, 1954. The decisions in all relevant cases were carefully perused and the contents classified according to a code set up on the basis of a pretest. For the most part, the information fell into three main groups: (1) circumstances concerning the decision itself (the sentence, which court, which judge, what period of time, etc.); (2) the external characteristics of the objector (age, occupation, income, previous service, appeal for transfer, previous punishment, etc.); and (3) the specific aspects of the objector's beliefs that were revealed (religious or not, emotional or rational, political or not, etc.). All the information was classified in fairly precise general categories. The greatest problems in this classification arise from the court's description of an objector's convictions. The classification in Nordland was especially difficult because the decisions often are long and contain quite detailed discussions of the objector's views.[5]

An objective classification permits the material to be transferred to punchcards and handled statistically. In this way one can, for example, draw some conclusions concerning the relationship between the characteristics of the accused on the one hand and the properties of the decision on the other. Indeed, it is difficult to see how one could treat a large number of sentences without using, at least in part, some such objective classification. The content analysis technique used in this study provides significant insights into the behavior of the military courts. By the same token, we should note that this method has certain limitations as well. First and foremost, it is very difficult to quantify the more complex patterns in the judge's argumentation. Here we have in mind the fact that we are concerned not only with the question of how the meaning associated with each element varies as a function of the combinational context, but also how these same elements combined in a given case take on different meanings and yield different results from case to case. It may always be necessary, therefore, to supplement statistical analyses with more intuitive considerations of the total *Gestalt* of specific decisions.

The 246 cases included in this investigation are divided among five military court districts: Østlandet (Eastern), 83; Sørlandet (Southern), 26; Vestlandet (Western), 35; Trøndelag (Central), 34; and Nordland (Northern), 68. Up to and including October 30, 1953, the military court for Nordland also handled cases from Troms (Far Northern) which are covered in this investigation. Afterward, a separate military court for Troms was established. For practical reasons it was not possible to go through cases which were handled by this court or cases of the military court in Finnmark (Far Northeastern) in the time allotted for the investigation. There were 14 such cases, four in Troms and ten in Finnmark.

Table 2 summarizes the decisions of the military courts in all of the cases included in the sample. Seventy-eight per cent of the defendants were acquitted; and of the remaining defendants, who were convicted, 77 per cent

TABLE 2

Summary of the Military Courts' Decisions

NUMBER OF CASES

Sentence	No Parole	Parole	Total
> 90 days	8	1	9
90 days	26	15	41
< 90 days	3	0	3
Acquitted	—	—	193
			246

received 90-day prison terms, although over a third of them were paroled. Only 15 per cent of the defendants actually were imprisoned as the result of these decisions.

There are on record only three cases where the decisions of the military courts in the present sample have been appealed to the Supreme Court and where the court has reviewed the previous decision. In one of these cases, the defendant had been found not guilty by the military court (Norsk Rettstidende, 1950, 917 ff.), while in the other two the defendant had been found guilty (R. T. 1954, 523 ff.; R. T. 1955, 1247 ff.). In all three cases the Supreme Court upheld the decision of the lower court. In the years since this study, however, the Supreme Court has reversed some subsequent cases.

3. Geographic Districts

What is it, then, that distinguishes the basis for judgments of acquittal from those of conviction? First and foremost, it was found that the proportion of convictions to acquittals varied from one military court to another. This variation is shown in Table 3.

The probability that an objector will be convicted is greater in Nordland than in other areas. It is also significantly larger in Sørlandet than in Østlandet, Vestlandet, or Trøndelag. Seen statistically, these variations can hardly be

TABLE 3

Geographic Variations in Percentage of Convictions

Military District	Convictions	Acquittals	Percentage of Convictions
Northern (Nordland)	37	31	54
Southern (Sørlandet)	9	17	35
Central (Trøndelag)	2	32	6
Eastern (Østlandet)	4	79	5
Western (Vestlandet)	1	34	3

due to random circumstances. (These would be evened out over time.) On what then do these variations depend? Can they be due to a greater number of lawbreakers, in Nordland and in Sørlandet, of this special type, namely, military objectors who claim to have conscientious objections that in reality they do not have? Or are they a result of the Nordland and Sørlandet military courts' following idiosyncratic juridical practices? If the first explanation is correct, the statistical variation in itself does not provide a valid basis for criticizing the decisions. If the second explanation is correct, however, we come up against a situation that is relevant to the question of justice in this area. These data would then show that like cases are not always treated alike.

In order to answer this most important question it is necessary to view these relationships in connection with some of the other results. Let us then compare the decisions of the individual judges in the military courts of Nordland and Sørlandet, as shown in Table 4.

TABLE 4

Individual Judicial Variations in Percentage of Convictions

Judges	Convictions	Acquittals	Percentage of Convictions
N. (incumbent)	24	8	75
N. (predecessor)	9	16	36
N. (assistant)	4	7	36
S. −A	0	6	0
S. −B	6	7	46
S. −C	3	4	43

Even though the number of cases involved is small, it is evident that the differences between the geographical districts in the proportion of convictions and acquittal sentences are not simply due to different rates of "criminality." These figures offer some evidence for assuming that the judges' personal attitudes can have an effect on their judgments in conscientious objector cases. Another fact lends support to our assumption: the laws according to which the judges must decide such cases are of a pronounced discretionary nature. It is rare to find other laws which leave so much to the judge's opinion with regard to the contents of the transgression.

4. Religious Affiliation and Beliefs

The differences among the military courts in the proportion of acquittals and convictions may be due more to the judges' attitudes than to dissimilarities in the frequency of offenses against this law, as was indicated. But we need further evidence here. In order to explore the question further, we shall look at those factors other than jurisdiction and the judge that are statistically related to whether a sentence is one of conviction or of acquittal. The most important of these factors is probably the religious convictions of the objector (see Table 5), or to be more exact, the judges' evaluation of the objector's religious sincerity (here we have only the records of the court as a guide). For example, if the conscientious objector belongs to a religious sect (usually Jehovah's Witnesses), it is practically certain he will be acquitted.

TABLE 5
Religious Differences and Percentages of Convictions

Claims of Defendants	Convictions	Acquittals	Percentage of Convictions
Nonreligious beliefs	33	16	67
Religious beliefs unknown	14	22	39
Nonsectarian religious beliefs	5	30	14
Sectarian religious beliefs	1	125	1

Whether the objector is religious or not, has, accordingly, an important effect on the outcome of the case. For many readers this discovery will not be surprising. But the clause in the military penal law Art. 35 gives no authority for such discrimination between the objectors who have religious convictions and those whose conscientious objections rest on a different basis. The proposal of a legislative committee in 1955 stated explicitly (p. 15): "Whether the motive for conscientious objections are of a religious, ethical, political, or other character is immaterial." This should be the juridically correct interpretation of the law. In principle, its correctness is hardly at issue. But the information our investigation revealed in the actual decisions points out that the judicial practice followed in Nordland, and to lesser degree in Sørlandet, is definitely at variance with this interpretation.

Since the religious element plays so crucial a role, we shall regard the matter from another angle. We find that the jurisdiction, the judge, and the religious convictions of the objector each are related to the decision in these cases. But what are the intercorrelations among these factors? Are religious objectors more frequently found in the military courts which have a high percentage of acquittals?

Table 6 shows the decisions of the military courts in each region in cases involving religious claims by defendants. The rank correlation between the percentage of religious sectarians and the percentage of acquittals in each area (the last two columns) is $+0.80$, at a significance level of about 0.042. This substantiates the finding that judicial attribution of religious sectarianism to defendants is an important factor in acquittals in all five districts.

It appears that the proportion of those who are classified as nonreligious is far higher in Nordland and Sørlandet (44 per cent) than in the other districts. But again we must consider the possibility that the courts vary in their evaluation of who is religious and who is not. Let us first look at those

TABLE 6

Geographic Variations in Religious Differences and in Percentages of Religious Sectarians and Acquittals

CLAIMS OF DEFENDANTS

Military Districts	Nonreligious Beliefs	Non-sectarian or Unknown	Religious Sectarians	Totals	Percentage of Religious Sectarians	Percentage of Acquittals
Northern (Nordland)	32	17	19	68	28	46
Southern (Sørlandet)	9	7	10	26	38	65
Eastern (Østlandet)	5	32	46	83	55	95
Central (Trøndelag)	2(?)	11(?)	21	34	62	94
Western (Vestlandet)	1(?)	4(?)	30	35	86	97
Totals:	49	71	126	246	51	78

belonging to sects, where the basis for religious beliefs is clear and observable so that the descriptions ought not to be so subject to bias by the particular judge's evaluation. As Table 6 shows, only half as many defendants (31 per cent) are classified as belonging to religious sects in Nordland and Sørlandet as are so classified (64 per cent) in the other three districts. The variations in the sentences among the military courts may, conceivably, depend upon the fact that military court judges consider sect membership to be especially convincing as a sign of sincere religious beliefs, and that members of sects appear less often in Sørlandet and in Nordland than in other places. But does this explain the entire divergence?

If we look at the more ambiguous categories in terms of religious faith, we again find differences among the courts. In Østlandet, 14 per cent of the non-sectarian objectors were considered nonreligious; the comparable statistic for Nordland is 65 per cent, and for Sørlandet 56 per cent. Yet there is no real evidence that there actually are more nonsectarian but religious objectors in Østlandet than in Sørlandet and Nordland. We must in any case allow the possibility that the relationship may, in fact, be the following: When so many objectors before the Southern and Northern courts are characterized as nonreligious, it may be that the courts have found them guilty on other grounds but relied on the argument of lack of religious belief, since it can reasonably be invoked to indicate the absence of sufficiently serious beliefs against doing military service.

5. Group Affiliations

Other dissimilarities were found among the jurisdictions which may conceivably influence the tendency to convict. One is the fact that refusal to do military service is more widespread in certain districts in Nordland and Sørlandet than other places. In this also lies the greater probability of objection to military service originating in the milieu, derived from group norms and social pressures. Does the individual's relation to his milieu affect the outcome of the case? And if so, in what way?

The legislative committee considered this question and concluded (p. 15): "There must exist a serious personal conviction. Membership in an organization which has the abolishment of military service as a part of its program is not in itself sufficient." However, in the courts' practice it appears that the interpretation of the milieu factor varies greatly. On the one hand, membership in a sect makes acquittal practically a certainty. Thus here it turns only upon the acceptance of a group norm. The military courts also have shown clearly at various times that they do not consider it necessary to waste words in discussing the sect member's personal views. In a case in Nordland against a Jehovah's Witness, the judge stated expressly: "As a basis for serious conviction the movement's own authority is enough for its adherents, in any case in most instances." On the other hand, five of seven cases in Nordland and in Sørlandet where association with *Folkereisningen mot Krig*[6] (a pacifist group) was mentioned ended in conviction.

More important, however, is how the military courts for Sørlandet and Nordland handle the objector's relation to his "natural" milieu, the family or community. In seven cases conformity to the milieu's norms was produced as an argument for acquittal; in four others it was considered as reason for conviction. In two cases a lack of conformity to the milieu was interpreted as an argument for acquittal, while in three other cases it was viewed as a reason for conviction. In twelve cases conformity with the milieu was mentioned less specifically, but four of these cases resulted in acquittal and eight in conviction. This variation corresponds well to the general impression one forms by reading the decisions. The objector's relation to the milieu is an element which judges use variously, sometimes one way and sometimes another. It should, however, be noted that in the rare instances when the remaining military court judges (for Østlandet, Vestlandet, and Trøndelag) mention the objector's association with the milieu, they consistently do so as an argument for acquittal.

6. *Other Factors in the Northern and Southern Subsample*

1. OCCUPATION

In the following examination of the dissimilarities between acquittal and conviction sentences we shall limit ourselves to Sørlandet and Nordland, since the number of convictions in the other three military courts is so small. Let us first look at the extrinsic factors of the objector and his situation. Occupation appears to have a definite connection with the outcome of these cases. Table 7 summarizes the relationship between occupation and convictions in the Northern and Southern military court cases.

Of the 42 unskilled workers in the court records, only 14 were acquitted. In all other occupational categories the proportion was considerably more favorable; taken together there were 34 acquittals in 52 cases. There seems to be no clear difference between the different income groups, but information on income is lacking for a good many of the cases. Possibly the difference between unskilled workers and others indicates that the probability for acquit-

TABLE 7

Correlation of Occupational Class with Convictions

Occupation	Convictions	Acquittals	Totals
Unskilled workers	28	14	42
All others	18	34	52
Totals:	46	48	94

$\phi = +0.319$ $\qquad$ $X^2 = 9.494$ $\qquad$ $P < 0.01$

tal is reduced as the accused's socio-economic status decreases. Whether this can be explained by a higher rate of lawbreakers among low-status defendants, whether these objectors have more difficulty in managing an effective defense, or whether some of the judges discriminate according to status, it is not possible to say. That there has occasionally been a slight tendency toward social discrimination is apparent in the following quotation of the incumbent military judge in Nordland. He is referring to an objector who pleaded serious beliefs: "It is not reasonable to believe that, given his supposed lack of ability to let ideas and counter-ideas assert themselves—he has not impressed anyone who has seen him as being more than a simple, ordinary man —he could have developed an independent conscientious objection to taking part in military service of any kind."

2. TYPE OF MILITARY SERVICE

As might be expected, it makes a difference what kind of service the defendant has objected to, as shown in Table 8. The probability for conviction is greater when the case involves initial military service than for call-up exercises for the home guard. This may signify that the judge places a great emphasis on how great the loss is for the army in the different types of service. For it is difficult otherwise to discern any general reason why re-enlistment and home guard conscripts should more frequently hold serious beliefs, and thus be convicted in fewer cases, than those who object to initial military service.

TABLE 8

Types of Military Service and Percentage of Convictions

Type of Military Service	Convictions	Acquittals	Percentage of Convictions
Initial Service	29	19	60
Re-enlistment	11	17	39
Home Guard	4	12	25

$X^2 = 7.2$ $\qquad$ $P < 0.05$ $\qquad$ $df = 2$

3. PREVIOUS ADVERSE ADMINISTRATIVE DECISIONS

Apparently the decision is also influenced by whether the objector has or has not previously applied for transfer to civil work. Over two-thirds of those who sought transfers were convicted, while over two-thirds of those who had not sought transfers were acquitted. However, nearly all of those who had not sought transfer and were acquitted were Jehovah's Witnesses, who do not accept civil work either. Without them, the difference between those who sought transfer and those who did not is insignificant.

The military court in Nordland vacillates in its view towards the lack of application for transfer, as can be shown by several decisions. In one case where the accused maintained he was not acquainted with the application procedure, the court said: "Such an arrangement has existed, however, for so long a time and was at the time in question [Jan.-Feb., 1953] so well known that the court cannot put decisive weight on the defendant's claim." And in another case, it stated: "This opportunity [to seek transfer to civil work] is so well known that the possibility that the accused was not aware of it must be excluded." But then the court reversed its thinking in another case when it declared: "Against this it can be stated that the accused had not sought transfer to civil work until he had been in camp for some time. To this it must be added that it has not been shown that he was aware of this possibility earlier." In this case the court considered it quite reasonable that the objector had not been aware of the application procedure.

4. CRIMINAL RECORD OF DEFENDANT

Whether the objector previously had been punished or not is clearly related to the outcome of the decision, as Table 9 makes clear. The high percentage of convictions in the 28 cases in which this factor was not mentioned at all demonstrates that the connection between the record of the accused and the outcome of the case is not unambiguous. Equally important as the fact of

TABLE 9

Previous Criminal Convictions and Percentage of Present Convictions

Previous Criminal Convictions*	Convictions	Acquittals	Percentage of Convictions
Serious offense	5	1	83
Unknown	17	11	61
Minor	7	6	54
None	17	30	36

$X^2 = 7.678$ $P =$ about 0.06   df $= 3$

*The distinction between "minor" and more "serious" offenses is arbitrary.

a record of previous conviction appears to be whether the judge chooses to emphasize the *absence* of such a record, in opinions supporting judgments of acquittal. One might infer from this that the presence or absence of a criminal record often is used by the judges as a rationale to support judgments arrived at on some other basis.

5. MORAL, EMOTIONAL, AND RATIONAL CRITERIA

Aside from the religious factor it is possible to distingush three other factors in the judge's description of the objector's beliefs: the moral ("conscience," the Fifth Commandment, etc.), the emotional, and the rational (e.g., political). Of course, these three categories are often regarded as inseparable components of an individual's beliefs from a psychological point of view. Here, however, we are not classifying beliefs, but rather the judge's description of them. The elements in these descriptions can, therefore, in many cases be classified in terms of one or more of these three categories.

Table 10 summarizes the courts' consideration of the moral basis of belief. Of the eight cases where the court explicitly maintains that objection to military service has no moral basis, none ended in acquittal. But the outcome is not so very different in the cases where the court states that the objection to military service is based upon the absolute prohibition to kill. On the other

TABLE 10

Moral Basis for Defendants' Claims, and Percentage of Convictions

Moral Basis	Convictions	Acquittals	Percentage of Convictions
None	8	0	100
Absolute prohibition against killing	11	3	79
Unknown	17	27	43
Abstract ideals	7	18	28
$X^2 = 19.40$	$P < 0.001$	df $= 3$	

hand, three-fourths were acquitted where abstract moral elements were mentioned, such as conscience, honor, idealism, pacifism, or just "morality" itself. But also favorable to the defendant was the situation in which moral elements are not mentioned at all; a majority of these cases resulted in acquittals. In particular the cases against Jehovah's Witnesses ended in acquittal even if the moral aspect is not mentioned.

The most surprising finding is the court's evaluation of a conviction based on the Fifth Commandment. Part of the explanation lies in the following argument:

The court considers it obvious that the accused's view that it is wrong to kill cannot have caused any problem in his conscience when appearing as a conscript at Setermoen on April 16, 1951. He was not appearing there to kill anyone but to receive military training. It is of course possible that the accused, at some time in the future, as a result of a number of interrelated reasons, among them military training, could be confronted by a situation in which there is a possibility he would take a person's life. He may test his view when that time comes. In any case, it cannot be acknowledged that such an unknown possibility should be any hindrance to appearing for military service in peacetime.

Another Nordland decision a little later stated:

The defendant relies exclusively on the Commandment against killing. He has not been called up for 40 days of repetition exercises to kill anyone, but rather to practice against the military training he received earlier. His appearance and his service will not bring him into any actual conflict with the Commandment at issue.

When the court mentions emotional factors, the sentence as a rule is conviction. By emotional factors, we refer to the content of such expressions as "feelings," "psychologically based," "aversion," "anxiety," etc., in the decisions. Table 11 summarizes the findings of the courts in those cases in

TABLE 11

Correlation of Emotional Factors and Convictions

Emotional Factors	Convictions	Acquittals	Totals
Present	21	2	23
Absent	25	46	71
Totals:	46	48	94

$$\phi = +0.482 \qquad X^2 = 21.84 \qquad P < 0.001$$

which emotional factors are so mentioned. Of the 23 cases where emotional factors were mentioned, only 9 per cent ended in acquittals, while 65 per cent of the remaining cases, in which the emotional component was not introduced at all, resulted in acquittals. The relationship is obvious. However, there are exceptions, as shown by the following quotation from a Nordland decision where emotional factors were used as an argument for acquittal in the case. The judge says of the objector: "His opinion, which appears to be predominantly based upon emotions, has according to the opinion of the court permeated his whole personality."

As far as the rational elements in objectors' beliefs are concerned, no consistent trend is apparent. There were six cases in which it was asserted that objection to military service was rationally based; four of these ended in acquittal. Of 30 cases in which it was pointed out that the rational basis was inadequate, 14 ended in acquittals. Of the 58 cases where this element was not directly discussed, 30 ended in acquittal. From a statistical point of view, the odds are the same for conviction or acquittal, irrespective of whether rational factors are mentioned or not; and also irrespective of whether, if mentioned, they are deemed by the court to be adequate or inadequate.

Political or opportunistic motives are seldom noted, but when mentioned

they are factors which tend to be associated with convictions. Both this quantitative information and the qualitative impression formed by reading the
decisions indicate a lack of clarity in the two courts' views of the significance
of the rational and intellectual aspects of pacifist convictions. It is easy to
point to examples showing that the military court for Nordland handles this
question differently from one case to the other.

The following is a quotation which may be considered representative of
the Nordland court's attitude toward logical reasoning and intellectual quality
in cases against members of religious sects:

The court finds it therefore substantiated that the accused's view that it is wrong to
perform military service rests on a religious belief not susceptible to rational argument,
and that he may therefore feel this view a compelling belief, even though he is unable
to adduce any reasons for it, and even though his views, in terms of ordinary logic or
its consequences, cannot be considered especially convincing for others.

A second quotation gives the impression of a completely different emphasis,
though not directed to the specifically religious objectors:

In order that the opinions of the accused should have fulfilled the criteria in the law
concerning conscientious objections the accused must to some extent in any case have
taken counter arguments into account.

And in a third case:

The court assumes that there is doubt whether the accused really has such a well
thought-out view of the consequences to which his position on the Commandment against
killing might lead that it can be spoken of as a serious belief. Quite apart from the
shortcomings which obviously exist when it comes to carrying these thoughts to their
logical end, it is difficult to comprehend how the accused actually can have convinced
himself that he is right and society is wrong with regard to this question. It seems
unlikely that the accused can seriously have meant that he is better qualified than society
to undertake an objective evaluation of the meaning of the commandment in question and
its relation to the legality of taking part in the country's defense.

The opposite argumentation is, however, also used by the court in cases
against objectors who are not members of sects:

Any belief exempts from punishment provided it is serious, and must be considered,
according to the person's sense for logical relationships, to imply the consequences which
he infers with regard to military service.

And in another case the court declared:

The decisive point is not how the court views the thoroughness and adequacy of the
reasons, or the legitimacy of the confidence that the accused reposes in his own set of
values. It is not impossible that the accused, on the basis of intellect, knowledge, and
socially supported beliefs, is sincere in his convictions, even if inadequacies are found
when compared with the most objective evaluation which seems possible.

The foregoing examples of the arguments used by the military court judges
in their opinions raise a general question that is taken up by Alf Ross in
his treatment of cultural tradition as a source of law.[7] Ross maintains that
in addition to such sources of law as statutes, precedent, and custom there
exists a source of law which has often been called the "nature of the case."

He chooses to call this source "cultural tradition," evidently because, in this way, he hopes to find a better empirical referent for statements on valid law. His point is that the judge, when he finds himself in an area where law and usage provide insufficient guide lines, or where he must interpret an ambiguous law, must fall back on the collective cultural tradition of society. By knowing this cultural tradition, one should therefore find it possible to make predictions as to how the judge will be ideologically motivated in specific cases.

The fact is that the above-mentioned arguments used by military judges have a certain place in the Norwegian cultural tradition. These are ways of thinking and patterns of argumentation that separately, in one relation or another, are approved and sanctioned by Norwegian culture. This applies, for example, to the argument that to be serious, an individual's belief must to some extent be reasonably reflected upon by introducing counter-arguments for consideration. On the other hand, it also includes the viewpoint that there are matters of faith that are so deep-seated emotionally that questions of reason and deliberation are not relevant. Furthermore, Norwegian culture in certain ways may be said to favor the viewpoint that an individual who stands in opposition to his milieu must be deemed to hold serious beliefs. But this same culture, under certain circumstances, also favors the exact opposite view, namely, that a belief that has grown out of ties to the milieu must be taken especially seriously.

Arguments that appear to be logically incompatible are thus derived from the same cultural heritage. Consequently, the military court decisions and opinions referred to can be culturally justified, but still used in ways which are partly contradictory. It shows how difficult it would be on the basis of Ross's assumption to reach more certain conclusions about a judge's ideas or motivation in a specific case.

Culture is not a logically worked-out system of interrelated norms. It is rather a conglomeration of patterns that can be woven together in special situations, but without that form of inner consistency that could make knowledge of cultural patterns yield predictions on how a person of that cultural background will be motivated in given situations. One must interpret the present data as a sign that knowledge of cultural norms furnishes no adequate basis for prediction of the subtle deliberations that take place in a judge's mind as he makes a decision. In other words, even if we know that military court decisions in cases involving conscientious objectors are full of argumentation patterns deeply rooted in Norwegian culture, this knowledge does not enable us to predict the result of the decision with any greater certainty than if we had disregarded the "cultural tradition" as a source of law.

7. Length of Judicial Descriptions of Defendants' Beliefs

It can, however, be said of the judge's *description* of the objector's beliefs that the shorter it is, the surer one can be that acquittal will result. Tables 12 and 13 summarize the situation. With the exception of the military courts for Nordland and Sørlandet, it is rare (19 of 152 cases) for the judge

TABLE 12

Length of Judicial Descriptions of Defendants' Beliefs and Percentage of Convictions

Lines in Judicial Descriptions	Convictions	Acquittals	Percentage of Convictions
Over 60	9	3	75
41-60	13	7	65
20-40	15	16	48
Under 20	9	22	28
	$X^2 = 10.22$	$P<0.02$	$df = 3$

TABLE 13

Correlation of Military Districts with Length of Judicial Descriptions of Defendants' Beliefs

Military District	Length of judicial descriptions		Total
	Over 40 Lines	40 Lines or Less	
N, S	32	62	94
C, E, W	1	151	152
Totals:	33	213	246
$\phi = +0.496$	$X^2 = 60.516$	$P<0.001$	

to use more than 20 lines to describe the seriousness of the defendants' beliefs, and only in one case were over 40 lines employed. Therefore, it is understandable that the moral, emotional, and rational elements, which so often are mentioned by the military courts in Sørlandet and Nordland, rarely are brought to the fore by the three other courts.[8]

8. Dissenting Judicial Behavior

Nearly all the sentences were unanimous. Only in seven cases were there dissents. In five of these it was one of the lay judges who dissented; four of these cases ended with convictions. In two of the cases of acquittal the professional judge voted against the decision; there were no cases in which professional judges dissented against convictions. Of the seven dissents, five were in Nordland and two in Sørlandet.

9. Conclusions

The foregoing investigation deals with judicial behavior. The method used has been somewhat different from the usual juridical treatment of legal opinions. Through a statistical analysis of the relationships between different factors mentioned in the opinions and the results of the decisions, we have tried to arrive at some new understanding of the judge's motives. Has this investigation led to any findings of more general significance?

It is known that in many fields of law, variations are found in sentencing tendencies among the courts and among the judges, and these variations cannot be fully explained by dissimilarities in the nature of the cases. In this study, our findings strongly suggest that different judges' dissimilar views of a problem can lead to varying court decisions. This conclusion has, of course, long been accepted by most students of the law. Concrete underpinnings may perhaps be of interest anyway. Our investigation has further shown that the courts in these cases have formed a legal practice which, to a certain extent, is uniform, but nevertheless does not seem to have any legal authority. We refer here to the treatment of religious as contrasted to nonreligious objectors. In these cases judges follow an implicit, and to a certain extent uniform, ideological pattern. But it is doubtful if this pattern can be said to have the characteristics of common law. The idea that religious motives are to be given greater weight than nonreligious motives is not explicitly maintained.[9]

The present investigation of the decisions of military courts in cases concerning conscientious objectors can also be seen from another viewpoint, namely, that of a criminological study. It illuminates the relationship between a group of 53 "criminal" objectors to military service and a group of 193 noncriminal objectors. The investigation shows, of course, some clear statistical dissimiliarities between these two groups. One could, for example, say on the basis of these statistical relationships that the probability that an objector to military service will be deemed a lawbreaker is greatest when he is nonreligious but emotional, when he lives in Nordland (especially Velfjord and Bindal), is an unskilled worker, attempts to avoid initial service, has previously been punished, etc. The relative degree of association of such characteristics of defendants with sentences of conviction is shown in Table 14.

Such statistical relationships can be interpreted to provide pertinent information on dissimilarities between criminal and noncriminal objectors to military service. This approach may not have any great criminological interest,

TABLE 14

Correlates of Convictions

Computed from Table	Factor	Correlation
5	Lack of religious beliefs	+0.692
2	Northern and Southern military districts	+0.524
11	Emotional	+0.482
7	Unskilled occupation	+0.319
8	Initial military service	+0.263
9	Previous criminal conviction	+0.246

but it is one possible interpretation of the material. However, another interpretation of these materials does, indeed, have criminological significance. We refer to the use of these same factors to provide data on the dissimilarities among the acting judges. This investigation shows, therefore, something which concerns most lawbreakers: that which usually passes as criminality—the disclosed, usually indicted offenses—is the result of two processes, one which develops on the lawbreakers' side and one which develops on the part of the acting authorities. This principle, which here comes emphatically to view, has, according to my judgment, great and significant consequences in more important areas of criminology.[10]

In terms of methodology this investigation represents an application of the quantitative method of content analysis to the analysis of court decisions. The use of the method creates no special problems until one comes to the more complicated arguments found in the grounds for the decisions. It can, with greatest certainty, be used to analyze the relation between the outcome of cases and different objective properties of the judging authority, of the defendants, etc. The quantitative method is also a practical tool in exploring the variations in the meting out of punishment, and the relation between lay judges and professional judges and dissents in the courts. And it can also be used to analyze the manner of argumentation in the decisions and thereby cast new light on the role played by the judges' value patterns as the basis on which decisions are made.

NOTES

1. *Om Ret og Retfaerdighet* (On Law and Justice), Copenhagen, 1954, p. 47. Cf. p. 55.

2. Article 34 reads as follows: "Anyone who illegally leaves or stays away from that place where he is to fulfill military duty is liable to punishment by fine or arrest. If the guilty is a conscript, he is liable to punishment for such specified illegal absence by arrest or imprisonment for up to three months; should the absence last longer than seven days, by imprisonment for up to two years; but under especially extenuating circumstances by arrest only. In the same manner, anyone contributing to or encouraging absence of another person from that place at which he is to fulfill military service is liable to punishment."

3. An amendment to *Lov om Rettergangsmaaten i militaere Straffesatker,* May 6, 1921, No. 1, Sec. 1, Art. 19.

4. Cf. law of June 17, 1937, concerning civilian workers as among those liable to military service.

5. This part of the material has been read and classified by the author. The rest of the coding was done by appeals court barrister Randi Haaland, law student Arne Bjoern Rtoenhaug, and M.A. candidate Arne Martin Klausen.

6. The Norwegian section of the War Resister's International.

7. *Op. cit. supra* (note 1), pp. 116-20.

8. Of the 53 cases in the total sample that ended with convictions, the deterrence of other potential defenders was mentioned as a reason for punishment in 14 of the opinions, while in two others this reason was mentioned but was set aside as irrelevant.

9. Cf. report from the committee for revision of the law concerning civil workers, p. 15, which explicitly states that this distinction in itself is without legal significance.

10. Cf. Vilhelm Aubert, "White Collar Crime and Social Structure," *The American Journal of Sociology,* Vol. 58 (1952), 263-71.

The Role of the Supreme Court
in the Norwegian Political System

ULF TORGERSEN

IF ONE COMPARES the Supreme Court of Norway with the Supreme Court of the United States, one is struck by both similarities and differences in the political role of these two courts.

The most important similarity is the role that both courts have played in resolving political conflicts in the two countries during the latter part of the Nineteenth Century and well into the 1930's. Although the length of this period differs somewhat for each country, the courts in both countries functioned as a conservative check on reform legislation.[1] Though the particular historical circumstances differ, and despite national dissimilarities and variations, one can discern a similar trend in the political function of these two Supreme Courts: In both political systems the demands for social reforms were to some extent checked by the existence of the institution of judicial review of legislation; in both systems there was a period when this institution was used by an essentially conservative Supreme Court to block social and economic reforms; in both countries the system of judicial review (or the way in which it was used) was criticized by representatives of the left;[2] in both this trend was brought to an end before World War II had begun; and in both this use of judicial review as a conservative measure is almost entirely absent at the present time.[3] This represents in broad outline the essential similarity between the political roles of the two Supreme Courts in their respective political systems.[4]

There have been, of course, important differences between these Courts as well. The most pertinent difference lies in the relative strength of the conservative wave in the two countries. Although the Supreme Courts in both

This chapter is based on an article which appeared in the March 1960 issue of the Norwegian journal *Tidsskrift for samfunnsforsking* under the title "Höyesteretts rolle i norsk politikk." The original article has, however, been extensively revised and enlarged. The data in the article are drawn from the Archives of Norwegian Elite Personnel, established at the Institute for Social Research in Oslo, through a generous grant from the Rockefeller Foundation.

countries played a conservative role in this period, the United States Supreme Court did so much more vigorously, consistently, and for a longer period of time than the Norwegian Court. The diehard adherence of the American Supreme Court to laissez-faire ideology had only a rather pale counterpart in Norway. Moreover, the substantive importance of the cases in which the United States Supreme Court invalidated state and federal legislation was far greater than that of the cases in which the Norwegian Supreme Court followed a similar line.

The United States Supreme Court represented more and more clearly, in the last part of the nineteenth century, a political position decidedly friendly to big business interests and industrial management, together with a clearly skeptical attitude—and at times a hostile one—toward social welfare legislation. In a series of decisions it wrote this attitude, which in legal terms was a change of the original intent of the due process clause, into American constitutional law. During the period between 1890 and 1937 this orientation prevailed; and it was only after a drastic conflict with the Presidency that the United States Supreme Court eventually modified its position.

The situation in Norway was quite different. Not only were the decisions in which the Norwegian Supreme Court invalidated legislation of lesser importance, it is also quite clear that the Norwegian court used its power with much greater care.[5] This orientation seems to have been very generally accepted among Norwegian Supreme Court judges. "It is presumably considered as one of the best features of the Norwegian Supreme Court," declared Supreme Court Judge Edvard Hagerup Bull, in a speech in honor of Chief Justice Löchen "that only reluctantly has it been willing to take stands on the basis of principles. It is always difficult to anticipate how a general rule will work out in all the individual instances."[6]

This statement is not merely the opinion of a single man, or of a minority of legal thinkers; rather it represents the predominant ideology of the Norwegian Supreme Court. This orientation toward the single case at hand had also been voiced earlier by Chief Justice Lambrechts (1886-1900), who often reminded his subordinate judges that they did not sit in order to discuss matters of law, but rather to decide the case at hand.[7] And nearly two-thirds of a century later this ideology of concrete orientation to legal problems and legal conflicts was still being articulated with approbation in Norway.[8]

Just as the Norwegian Supreme Court's trend toward conservative orientation had been more careful, its reversal was less drastic. It did not in any way approximate the dramatic battle between President Roosevelt and the "nine old men." Business interests were not nearly as firmly entrenched in the Norwegian Supreme Court, and they yielded more gradually, more gracefully, and with less open conflict.[9]

What is the reason for the more cautious orientation that has prevailed in the Norwegian Supreme Court? In my opinion, there are two sets of reasons: the first relates to the power position of the court, and the possibilities for using it as an effective weapon against radical legislation; the second relates to the disposition of the judges to pursue such lines of decisions. Both reasons are closely related to the nature of the Norwegian bureaucracy and its relation, in turn, to the rising industrial and mercantile middle classes during the course of the last hundred years.

We will make some inquiries into both these reasons, and their possible interrelations, by first examining the power potential of the Supreme Court, and secondly examining the occupational, social, and political background of the judges. Where it is possible, we shall try to see the data in relation to Schmidhauser's study of the United States Supreme Court.[10] By seeing the Norwegian situation in this perspective, some of its features may stand out with greater clarity.

1. Judicial Review in Norway

The relative weakness of conservatism in the Norwegian Supreme Court is related to differences in the acceptance, within the two societies, of judicial review as a check on legislative activity. While the United States Supreme Court early in its history claimed for itself the right of judicial review of national legislation, this was by no means true in Norway. In the works of those who wrote legal treatises on the Norwegian Constitution, one finds conflicting attitudes toward the question of the right of the Supreme Court to declare legislation unconstitutional. Some of the writers answered in the negative, and considered judicial review of acts of parliament to be a measure so grave that it could only be considered justified if the government and parliament were to inaugurate a virtual policy of suppression. Moreover, these commentators considered the very existence of a power of judicial review to be extremely dubious. They argued that it only should be used in the gravest of events, and that these were not very likely to occur.[11]

Typical in this respect was the position taken by the most influential commentator on Norwegian constitutional law in the Mid-nineteenth Century, the future prime minister, Frederik Stang. Until well into the 1880's his work was *the* authoritative treatise on constitutional law. Frederik Stang's view of the political functions of the courts starts with an analysis of the proper role of the courts. He took the position that it is only in a very special sense that the courts can be said to be a special branch of the government.[12] Stang did concede that for many practical reasons courts ought to be organized separately, and with special stress on their independence and moral fiber. But apparently he was thinking of the qualities generally required of civil servants, circumscribed by such institutional devices as the right to hold one's position until convicted of a crime, a right which he felt had to be safeguarded, and which was required to an even greater extent among judges. For the time this was not an unreasonable approach, because the type of administrative work that occurred in the central and local government was much more strictly an application of laws than it was the policy-making and planning of civil servants today. At any rate it is obvious that this orientation meant that the courts were not conceived of as major guardians of the constitution.

Stang belonged to the dominant bureaucratic elite in Norway, and his position on the question of judicial review must be understood in a strictly political context. In the period before 1884, the cabinet was responsible to the King, not to the parliament. The parliament was still elected on the basis of a rather restricted suffrage, and while it had the right to legislate and tax, it could not intervene in questions pertaining to the executive branch of state. The King had the right to veto legislation, though this veto was only suspensive. The cabinet was appointed by the King, and he invariably selected his cabinet from the dominant social class, and particularly from the academically trained professionals, most of whom held governmental office as ministers, as administrators, or as judges, or served in other posts requiring legal education. This social class held bureaucratic positions without fear of losing them, since they could be removed only if convicted of crime. (For positions at the ministerial level, of course, the King was legally free to appoint and to remove.) This social elite enjoyed security and high income, and they constituted an important proportion of the parliament, too.

The political cleavages in Norway were, on the whole, rather limited, except for occasional periods of dissatisfaction among the farmers and in the lower strata in the cities. On the basis of this peaceful political situation, and with a cabinet removed from direct parliamentary control—thus enabling it to function in part as a conservative second chamber—it is understandable that a spokesman for the civil servant class would feel slight need for judicial review, as a check on "popular majorities."

It was only later, when the parliament began to insist more and more strongly on a change in the institutional structure of the government, and after the introduction of the system of cabinet responsibility became a possibility, that the bureaucratic class started to search for other possible conservative guarantees in the Constitution.

One consequence of this was a revision of the ideas that previously had been current concerning the courts. The new orientation was introduced by a professor of law at the University of Oslo, Torkel Halvorsen Aschehoug, who completely reversed the thesis presented by Stang a generation earlier. Aschehoug not only raised the courts to the position, in theory, of an equal and independent branch of government, he also emphasized the role that the (new) judicial branch had in protecting vested interests of citizens. He went on to reinterpret the Norwegian clause concerning ex post facto laws in such a way that it now bore a close resemblance to the change in function attributed to the due process clause of the American constitution by the United States Supreme Court.[13] And in reinterpreting Clause 97 (prohibiting ex post facto laws) in the Norwegian constitution of 1814, Aschehoug did very much the same theoretical job as was being performed by his American contemporary Thomas M. Cooley in his theory about due process of law. In both cases an old clause dealing with forms was given a new substantive content. Aschehoug thus presented a Norwegian Supreme Court of real power and vigor; and it is significant that he explicitly built his new conception of the role of the Norwegian judiciary after the American model.

There was a corresponding change in the behavior of the Norwegian Supreme Court. After 1890 a series of decisions came in conflict with parliamentary legislation (see Table 1), and gradually the principle was established that the courts had a right to decline to apply unconstitutional legislation.[14] But even as late as 1918 it was possible for the Chief Justice of the Supreme Court to declare that he considered judicial review to be highly doubtful, in a case decided in favor of the state.[15] This testifies to the relative weakness of judicial review in Norway, as compared to the American situation. There

TABLE 1

Private Rights Cases Involving Clause 97 Decided by the Norwegian Supreme Court

Cases	1814-79	1880-99	1900-19	1940-59	1920-39
Total private rights cases	0	17	30	44	15
Decided in favor of private rights	0	2	9	6	1

it was established almost a century earlier, and has not been seriously challenged on legal grounds (at least, by Supreme Court justices themselves) since the end of the American Civil War.

The political structure, too, helped to emphasize this conflict. Since the idea of judicial review occurred in connection with the introduction of parliamentarism, the former can be seen as an attempt to stem the tide of the liberal forces which had captured the state apparatus. But the same situation that had brought the possibility of a more active, conservative court also curbed its power. The scope of the Court's resistance to the policies of the government and the parliament is limited. Consequently, judicial review by the Supreme Court tended to be rather modest in scope, even in the period of conservatism, before new appointments brought into the Supreme Court persons more sympathetic with the major popular movements (or else neutral civil servants with no intention of speaking out against the state).

2. Occupational Bases for Judicial Recruitment

It is clear that the possibility of using the Norwegian Supreme Court as a check on reform legislation was limited, simply because the Court had limited opportunity for pursuing a policy of its own in opposition to the other branches of the government. The United States Supreme Court, placed in a very strategic position as arbiter of problems that might arise in a federal system and from the separation of powers implicit in the Presidential system of government, by that token had a great deal more potential power. Appointments to the Supreme Court of the United States are therefore more important than appointments to the Supreme Court in Norway. Perhaps for that reason persons appointed to the American Court, as Schmidhauser's data indicate, have tended to be persons with substantial political experience, while this seems to have been much less the case in Norway.[16] Indeed, appointment to the Supreme Court in Norway has tended to be relatively nonpolitical and to represent the peak of an administrative or court career.

If we look at the Norwegian Supreme Court judges appointed in the

periods 1814–1884, 1885–1920, and 1921–1959, we find that a rather limited proportion of them have at one time or another been members of the
parliament. For the first period, 16 out of 43 (37 per cent) had been members of parliament, for the second period 7 of 24 (29 per cent), and in
the third period only 4 of 47 (9 per cent). We shall comment later on the
declining proportion of the judges who have been members of the parliament. At present we are just concerned with emphasizing that the proportion
is rather small in all three periods. Indeed, it is even smaller than the data
above indicate, because they include not only the positions in the parliament
held before appointment to the Supreme Court, but *afterward* as well. If we
limit ourselves to the proportion of parliamentary positions held *before* appointment to the Supreme Court, it is even smaller: in the first period, 9 of
43; in the second period, 6 of 24; and in the third period, 4 of 47. This
relatively low proportion (17 per cent) for all three periods suggests that the
political element has been rather limited, and that appointees to the court
overwhelmingly have been recruited from among the bureaucracy, although
the extent to which this was the case has varied somewhat from time to time.

This finding is supported by the data presented in Table 2 which shows
the positions the judges held just before they were appointed to the bench.
Three-fourths of the Supreme Court appointees come from the bureaucracy.

TABLE 2

Occupation at Time of Appointment to the Norwegian Supreme Court

Types of Occupations	1814-1884	1885-1920	1921-1959	Totals
Lower court judge	19	16	25	60
Private attorney	4	3	10	17
Civil servant (central government)	4	2	9	15
Civil servant (local government)	7	2	1	10
Cabinet member	2	1	2	5
Law professor	5	0	0	5
No information	2	0	0	2
Totals:	43	24	47	114

Over half of them have been judges, and another 22 per cent come from
either central or local governmental civil service. Private attorneys represent
a small proportion (15 per cent), increasing, however, from less than 10 per
cent in the first period to slightly over 20 per cent in the last period. The
number of persons appointed straight from the cabinet is only 5 for the
whole period (4 per cent). The five professors in the first period is the result
of the somewhat disorganized situation immediately following 1814, when
the lack of personnel was great and the university was not as attractive for
many people as it later became. If we compare these findings with Schmid-

hauser's data from the United States Supreme Court it is clear that the proportion of lawyers who were primarily attorneys before appointment to the Supreme Court is about the same in the United States as in Norway.[17] However, it appears that there is a difference in the extent to which the judges of the two courts have had experience as private attorneys. (The data for Norway are presented in Table 3.) That element is much stronger in the United States than in Norway.

TABLE 3

Norwegian Supreme Court Judges' Pre-Judicial Occupational Experience

Occupation	1814-1884	1885-1920	1921-1939	1945-1959	Total
Lower court judge	29	18	18	14	79
Central administration	24	11	9	15	59
Private attorney	16	15	12	10	53
Local administration	14	7	4	4	29
Number of Judges:*	43	24	26	21	114

*These are not totals since many judges had several different occupations before their appointment.

The high proportion of lower court judges appointed to the Norwegian Supreme Court—over twice as high as in the United States—makes it advisable to comment upon the differences between the career opportunities of judicial office in Norway and in the United States. In Norway, for instance, it is quite proper to count judges among the bureaucracy, although such a statement would not be very accurate in the United States with its system of predominately elective judgeships (at least in the state courts) and its theory of separation of powers.

All judicial offices in Norway have been appointive posts exclusively, for the last 150 years. It is the government that decides the question of the appointment of a judge, and the appointment does not need to be confirmed by any other authority, as in the United States, where the Senate has to consent to Presidential nominations of all federal judges. It is true that the appointment of judges is subject to public criticism and comments by the Parliamentary Control Committee, which audits this and many other aspects of governmental administration and suggests remedial measures for the future. But the government's legal power to make judicial appointments without parliamentary advice and consent is far more than a mere formality. As is also true of all federal judges in the United States, Norwegian judges have tenure and cannot be removed by the government.

Norwegian judges are drawn from among law graduates trained at the University of Oslo, formerly the Royal University of Fredrik. There are also some more detailed qualifications for the higher courts, for which a certain level of academic achievement is required, but the crucial point is that the degree in law is the only formal requirement. There is nothing to correspond to the French *corps des magistrats*. French judges must have passed a certain training in order to be qualified, whereupon they become members of a closed body of government professionals with a high professional solidarity in which they remain for the rest of their lives. This system, based on a rather strict application of the doctrine of the *séparation des pouvoirs,* does not exist in Norway.

The same training thus qualifies a person for a position in the administration, in the courts, and in the courtrooms; and one may move back and forth among these various legal activities.[18] To be sure, lawyers must have passed their law exam with *laudabilis* (the best mark in the graduation examinations) in order to become higher judges or lawyers with the right to plead before the Supreme Court, but there are no insurmountable barriers separating the various legal activities. The extent to which such interchange happens and has happened is an empirical matter closely related to the political role of the individual judge, and will be discussed later. The judges themselves tend to believe that this mobility is to some extent distinctively a Norwegian practice. A recent report concerning the International Congress of Judges (Rome, 1958) fully underscores this:

What struck a Norwegian participant was the extent to which almost all countries— outside of the English-speaking nations and some of the Scandinavian countries—are protagonists of a system based on special education and even special exams for young lawyers who want to become judges, and in which the personal qualities and practical experience from other fields of legal activities are given a rather subordinate importance. In a short statement in the afternoon I found it appropriate to sketch our Norwegian system, and to stress our concern with finding the right type of man, not with the education of specialists.[19]

The main reason for the establishment of this system is cultural. Its small size has almost forced Norway to adopt this system of training the incumbents of rather diversified activities in essentially the same way. There was a period of severe shortage of teachers in law at the University and also a great shortage of Norwegian legal textbooks when Norway broke away from Denmark. There simply were not teachers who could take the responsibility for an examination system based on more cameralistic disciplines. These factors, however, are only minor parts of a broader picture. Norway at that time also was suffering from a lack of academic manpower (as was true of the Central European States after World War I and is true of the African nations today) and the small size of the country aggravated this situation. It was impossible to have a system with different types of training; such a system just could not work. What was needed was a system in which people could move around according to needs. This is the origin of the one-education—many-activities system that exists today.

This system, once introduced, seems to have had certain consequences. The common education has led to a certain amount of solidarity and understanding among people from highly varied walks of legal life, and the interchange of personnel between the various organizations in which the legally trained man works has tied the professional subcultures together. More specifically, the judges, who to a considerable extent have been recruited from the administration, tend to feel loyalty to the state administration, and are somewhat reluctant to act against the government when faced with the problem of determining the legality of some measure.

But within this general framework, with its concomitant high level of loyalty of the judges toward the government, some changes have been going on which have brought about important modifications in the relation of the judges to the state bureaucracy. These changes were inherent in the growth of the legal profession, and in its internal structural differentiation.

Table 4 presents data showing the growth of the legal profession and its various parts. It is characterized by rather different rates of growth for the

TABLE 4

Absolute and Relative Development of Major Legal Occupations in Norway (selected years)*

	1815		1844		1864		1885		1905		1930		1950	
Occupation	%	No.	%	No.	%	No.	%	No.	%	No.	%	No.	%	No.
Judge	30	96	21	94	15	116	13	138	11	157	8	163	6	178
Local admin-istration	34	106	37	174	31	177	18	202	14	214	10	203	12	330
Central adminis-tration	9	27	18	82	30	226	29	315	22	321	18	346	25	694
Private attorney	28	87	25	117	24	230	41	449	53	784	63	1232	57	1624
Total:	101	316	101	467	100	739	101	1104	100	1476	99	1944	100	2828

*The data in this table do not include all law graduates for these years, since we are interested here only in particular professional groups and their relative development. Among the groups omitted are, e.g., lawyers employed in private business firms as executives, and lawyers who own their own business firm.

different parts of the profession. While the number of judges has almost doubled, increasing from 96 in 1815 to 178 in 1950, the proportion of judges was only one-fifth as great at the end of this century and a half as it was at the beginning. Similarly, the number of lawyers employed in local administration has tripled in absolute terms, while declining sharply on a relative basis. The central administration on the other hand has increased over 25-fold (in absolute terms) and also has tripled in proportionate size. It is not quite appropriate to use the figures from 1815 as a base for the description of the growth, however, because in 1815 Norway was compelled —because of its separation from Denmark, under which it had had no central administration at all—to start from scratch and build a central administration. But even if we use later figures as the basis, it appears that the central administration has, by any standard, increased much more rapidly than that part of the legal profession employed as judges or in local administration. A similar expansion is found in the group of private attorneys, whose numbers increased almost 20-fold and whose relative size doubled, and presently includes over half of all law graduates in the occupations discussed here.

It is thus clear that, as is true of professional employment, judicial office and local government service have become increasingly *less* important sources of legal employment, while employment by central government and in private practice have become increasingly *more* important. One may say that the three most important roles in the legal profession are these: the judge, the administrator, and the private attorney. In 1815 and for some time afterward, these three types of legal activity were much closer to each other than they later came to be. The practice of law was not unrestricted, so the attorney was appointed, and was much more closely bound to the courts than in later times. The type of administrative activity required of attorneys corresponded more closely to the activities of the judge than it did later on when a certain amount of initiative and policy-making, as well as loyalty to the political leaders, was added to the administrator's role. The bureaucrats were administering the law in their jobs very much as were the judges in their positions. And again, we see that the small number of the attorneys —and particularly those who were entitled to plead before the Supreme Court—enabled them to have a reasonable expectation of becoming judges themselves.[20]

This situation was fundamentally altered later on, however. The change in the direction of more dynamic administrative policy-making and, with the introduction of parliamentarism, the demand for loyalty not only to one's own independent judgment of the matters at hand, but also to the political line drawn up by the cabinet ministers, changed the character of the administrative bureaucracy. At the same time, the attorney became a free professional; and he gradually came to be associated more than previously with his clients, and particularly with business interests, as this offered gradually increasing monetary rewards. These attorneys were able to earn such a high income that it entailed considerable financial sacrifice for them to become judges, and in any event, only the best of the lawyers could hope to become judges.

To what extent can we discern any traces of this internal differentiation in the recruitment to the Supreme Court? Have there been any changes in the background of the judges that can be linked to this trend?

If we again look at Table 2, it appears that there are some few changes from period to period. It appears that the private attorneys named to the Court become somewhat more numerous, that the central administrative element is more dominant, and that local administration experience is greatly reduced. The increase of those with central administration background is rather what one should expect, but not so with the attorneys. How can this be explained?

One clue can be found when we look somewhat more closely at the attorneys. It is clear that these attorneys represent a politically and socially deviant element within the legal profession. Three of the 10 attorneys were socialists; three of them were known to be left-wing liberals; and a majority of them belonged to old civil-servant families. They could, with one exception, be said not to be of the "corporation lawyer" type. Thus the facts actually reinforce—in spite of the seemingly inconsistent increase in the number of private attorneys appointed to the Supreme Court—the previously stated character of the Supreme Court. To the extent that the Supreme Court has included judges drawn from the ranks of private attorneys, these have tended to be persons with a radical orientation who are loyal to the state and have few ties to the business elements in society.

If we look again at Table 3 we get a somewhat broader picture of the Supreme Court justices' occupational backgrounds. It is clear from that table that the proportion of justices who, before being appointed to the Supreme Court, had been (at some time or other) practicing attorneys has not changed very much in the course of the past 150 years. The proportion who have had experience in local administration has dropped, while the proportion of justices with experience as civil servants in the central administration played a smaller role in the first three periods than in the fourth. The proportion of judges with experience from lower courts is, for all periods, roughly two-thirds of the total.

The same trends are supported by the data given on judges in Norway in Table 5. In this regard it is important to realize the prestige associated

TABLE 5

Some Attributes of Norwegian Judges

Attribute	PERCENTAGES BY EXAMINATION YEARS						
	1810-29	1830-49	1850-69	1870-89	1890-1909	1910-29	1930-39
Reached peak of career as judge	75	73	80	75	79	*	*
Experience as private attorney	63	47	66	63	51	43	28
Experience in central administration	40	61	45	31	29	46	51
Number of judges:	75	142	139	208	242	190	74

*Information not available.

with *any* judicial office in Norway. If a person has at some time become a judge, he has tended to stay in that position unless appointed to a higher court. Table 5 shows that throughout the past century and a half, about four out of five persons who became judges reached the peak of their careers as judges. The remaining fifth have belonged to a variety of categories, including high administrators and a few members of the cabinet. The data for other occupational experience relate predominantly, therefore, to *pre-judicial* experience. Thus relatively fewer judges have had experience as private attorneys in the most recent period; while experience in central administration has tended to fluctuate reciprocally to private attorney experience, with a corresponding *increase* for central administrative experience in the most recent period.

What is it that has brought about these changes in the recruitment pattern? Several factors seem to have been at work at the same time. Partly, as already mentioned, the pecuniary inducement of the bench for attorneys who are really good—so good that they are possible candidates for judicial positions—is rather small. That is, the income possible for outstanding success in private business is much higher than the salary of a judge. This situation is satisfactory to the government, too, because a high percentage of judges with previous attachments to business circles might handicap the government in many lawsuits, since it might increase the chances that the state would lose in expropriation cases, tax cases, and the like. Finally, one must consider the specific needs of one special section of the central administration, the Ministry of Justice, especially its Law Division. The Ministry now plays an important role as a basis for recruitment to the bench. The function of the Law Division is to assist the different ministries in the drafting of statutes, and to give the government expert legal advice in such matters as treaties, general administrative law, constitutional law, and problems arising in connection with the administration of law in the various legal areas. It is important for this branch of the central administration to attract highly qualified young law graduates; and since the division itself does not furnish a sufficient number of high positions to ensure advancement for the ambitious graduates who seek employment there, it is highly advantageous for the division to be able to send many of those who have been employed there into judicial positions.

3. Social Background of Supreme Court Judges

We have already noted that the judge has been a person who has enjoyed high prestige in Norwegian society. Throughout the Nineteenth Century, Supreme Court judges belonged to the second highest rank in the official state precedence, and the Chief Justice belonged to the very first rank. Although lower court judges did not enjoy quite that exalted a position, nevertheless they were accorded great respect. Such status differentials have been somewhat reduced in the course of the development toward greater social equality, but the judge is still a highly respected member of society. He is also a highly respected member of the legal profession and only the very best lawyers can become judges. As will be seen from Table 6, the proportion of the judges who have the *laudabilis* is consistently higher than for any other branch of the legal profession. Graduation with honor is simply a condition *sine qua non* for Supreme Court judges.

As is the case with most high prestige occupations, judges come from families in the higher social strata. Though there have been some changes in this, it remains true that the judge is more likely to come from an upper middle class background, and in about half the cases (since 1814) from families where the father was trained in a profession requiring academic preparation.[21] From a statistical point of view, it is apparent from Table 7 that there are no great differences between the samples of fathers and of

TABLE 6

Proportion of Honor Graduates of Law School, among Major Legal Occupations, at Age 40

	HONOR GRADUATES, BY EXAMINATION YEARS											
	1810-29		*1830-49*		*1850-69*		*1870-89*		*1890-1909*		*1910-29*	
Occupation	*%*	*No.*	*%*	*No.*	*%*	*No.*	*%*	*No.*	*%*	*No.*	*%*	*No.*
Judge	84	25	78	45	79	18	86	34	90	34	89	42
Local admin-ministration	72	43	70	130	66	65	47	149	58	181	48	178
Private attorney	79	81	66	154	67	189	57	371	56	646	56	592
Central admin-istration	65	25	49	151	64	154	50	230	57	290	58	246

fathers-in-law for the period as a whole. Supreme Court judges and their wives, in other words, have come from the *same* social class. Sixty per cent of both judges and their spouses have come from families associated with either the higher civil service or independent businesses; while only 13 per cent have come from families identified with farming, fishing, or the lower civil service. There have been *some* changes in the family connections of the Supreme Court judges, such as the somewhat decreasing proportion of the sons of higher public employees, but they represent mainly shifts among the upper social strata. No son of an industrial worker so far has been appointed to the Supreme Court; those assigned to the category "other occupations, occupation unknown" belong, to the extent that we know the

TABLE 7

Occupations of Fathers (F) and Fathers-in-Law (FIL) of Supreme Court Justices

	1814-1884		1885-1920		1921-1959		Totals	
Occupation	*F*	*FIL*	*F*	*FIL*	*F*	*FIL*	*F*	*FIL*
Higher civil service	21	14	13	6	13	18	47	38
Independent business	11	12	3	7	12	9	26	28
Lower civil servant	3	3	1	2	6	2	10	7
Higher private employee	1	4	1	0	4	2	6	6
Farmer, fisherman	3	0	3	2	2	2	8	4
Independent professional	1	2	0	4	4	1	5	7
Other occupations, and occupation unknown	3	5	3	2	6	6	12	13
Total:	43	40	24	23	47	40	114	103

Judges who did not marry:	3	1	7	11

title of the occupation, to some sub-category of middle-class occupations.

In general, one can say that recruitment and marriage data indicate upper middle-class affiliations. This picture is not very different from the one that Schmidhauser gives of the American Supreme Court justice:

The typical Supreme Court justice has invariably been white, generally Protestant with a penchant for a high social status denomination, usually of ethnic stock originating in the British Isles, and born in comfortable circumstances in an urban or small town environment. In the earlier history of the court, he very likely was born in the aristocratic gentry class, while later he tended to come from the professionalized upper middle classes.[22]

This indicates that both courts were recruited from the better-off groups in society. There are also some differences: The gentry class did not exist in Norway, and Norwegian Supreme Court judges seem to have been to some extent less frequently recruited from among business and independent professionals' sons and more often from the civil servant class. This reflects the difference in the upper strata in the two societies. The decline of the civil servant element in Norway as a recruitment basis for the Supreme Court is thus matched by a decline, in the same respect, of the gentry in the United States.

His high status and social origins suggest that, politically, the judge would be inclined toward a sympathetic attitude toward the "establishment." He will be familiar with the opinions and ideas of the higher social strata, and he will associate mainly with people from these classes. This must, however, be considered only a tentative first approximation to the political orientation of judges. One must be careful in drawing too quick conclusions from the facts of origin and status. And even if one should be able to characterize the political outlook of the judges as "conservative," it would be highly desirable to specify the character of this conservatism. Rather than to accept these inferences as conclusive, we ought also to examine the special characteristics of the political position of the judge, and particularly with reference to other high status groups in Norwegian society.

4. Political Background and Participation of Judges and Lawyers

Differentiation similar to that already noted within the legal profession has also occurred in politics, resulting in changing patterns of recruitment to political positions as well as in changing values and orientations. The political regime of the Nineteenth Century, extending from 1814 to 1884, gave the university-trained civil servants a very strong position in Norwegian politics. The cabinet members were invariably selected from among this class; and they also played a very important role in the parliament, as well as in locally elected bodies. This had important implications for the dominant conception of the norms to which a politician should conform, and particularly in relation to his activity and his duties. Indeed, the conception of the ideal politician did not differ significantly from that of the ideal judge:

they both were supposed to act on the basis of "universalistic" criteria, to represent the whole (not parts) of society; and, to that end, to be "independent" and to have "character," in order to be able to withstand temptations to act otherwise.[23]

Gradually, however, and to the detriment of this conception, two other ideas about what the politician should be like gained increasing popularity. One was the "realistic" idea of the politician as a representative of interests, loyal to "his" people and groups, in close contact with them, sensitive to their wishes, loyal to their demands and not just to abstract conceptions of the public good.

The other ideal type was that of the politician as a crusader for a cause, a leader with a gospel, a prophet fighting to overcome evil. Such a politician should not be a careful and conscientious man, weighing the pros and cons, but rather should be a man who had made his mind up about the relevant questions, and now had set out to reform the world, either by demanding that new values should be introduced and old ones discarded, or else by restoring the temple to its ancient truths.[24]

It is easy to see how either of these new ideal types ran counter to the old "judge-like" ideal of what a politician should be like. A politician who represented interests was incompatible with a politician who was uncommitted and independent; and a crusader-politician was utterly incompatible with the idea of value-neutrality and matter-of-fact orientation. The two new ideals were also, of course, mutually inconsistent with each other; but at present we are concerned with the fact that both of these new conceptions of political man gained increasing popularity, and as a consequence they changed completely the political climate in Norway.

The introduction of the parliamentary system of government was one of the tokens of this change. The demand that the members of the cabinet should be responsible to the parliament and resign if they did not have the support of the parliament meant that one of the more important institutional safeguards of the old conception of politics had disappeared.

Similarly, the new conceptions came to permeate the whole orientation to the qualities that were to be demanded of persons who were elected to public office. As a consequence, the "fit" demanded between the qualities of a judge and of a politician grew smaller and smaller; and thus it became more and more difficult for judges to participate in politics.

This change in political ethics was based on the rise of broad social movements, and on the increasing political participation by the lower social classes. The idea that politics is an objective question, which must be decided by neutral and well-educated men, is almost invariably more prevalent in conservative and upper-class social groups than among other classes of the population; and it is probably correct to regard this change in political norms as having been directed *against* the high level of political influence enjoyed by Norwegian civil servants generally, and by the judges.

The dramatic events that indicated a change in these questions took place around 1884, but the intensity of conflict must not be interpreted to indicate that *all* the important changes took place at that time. Rather one can talk about a gradual erosion of the political power of the civil servants, and an intensification of the resistance to this process at a time when the process had already gone very far but was not yet quite finished. The exit of the judges from important political positions was a continuous process that started considerably before 1884 and lasted for quite some time afterward, too.

This exit from elective positions is seen very clearly if one looks at the Supreme Court judges. In the first period (1814-1884), they played a rather important part in such positions: out of a total of 27 elections, there were only three (in 1850, 1865, and 1882), or 11 per cent in which no Supreme Court judge was elected as either representative or vice-representative to the parliament. During the period from 1884 to 1920 there were 12 elections, and in seven, or 57 per cent of these, no judge from the Supreme Court was elected. From 1920 to 1940 there were seven elections, and in six of these (86 per cent) no Supreme Court judge was elected; in the six parliamentary elections since the end of World War II, none has been elected. In view of the fact that both the parliament and the Supreme Court have been substantially enlarged in size during the period since 1814, the significance of the exclusion of Supreme Court judges from parliament seems rather clear.

A similar tendency appears if we look at the appointment of Supreme Court judges to the cabinet. Such appointments were not uncommon before 1884, and they were not considered to pose any problem. In subsequent years, however, these appointments were made less frequently: Ferdinand Roll in 1891, Einar Löchen in 1900, Bull in 1907, Scheel in 1912, and Paal Berg in 1924. Berg was the last Supreme Court justice to become a member of the cabinet *after* his appointment to the court. Generally, one might say that with the redefinition of the role of the politician, and particularly with the change in the principles of recruitment of cabinet members, the sequence in which political and Supreme Court positions normally are held has been reversed. It used to be common to be a judge first, and then to be elected to the parliament or appointed to the cabinet afterward; but during the last four decades the reverse has been true.

The appointment of a politician to the bench of the Supreme Court may, of course, serve several functions. It may be just another way of paying political debts. But it may also be a way in which to influence the character of the decisions of that court. The withdrawal of the court from political affairs did not mean that it was not one of the cabinet's interests to see that the "right" people were appointed. This probably has been most evident in the choice of the Chief Justice.

After the Radicals' victory in 1884, when the Left forced the King to call for his cabinet's resignation and appoint a new one that enjoyed the confidence of the parliament, the question arose of who should be appointed as Chief Justice to succeed I. S. Thomle (who had resigned in 1886). Chr. Hansteen was the only applicant for the position, and it appeared that, technically, the cabinet had no choice. Hansteen, however, was known to be a die-hard Conservative and a staunch enemy of the parliamentary system of government. The government, therefore, informed the Supreme Court that it could not accept Hansteen, as they wanted somebody less intransigent as Chief Justice; additional applications were requested. Faced with this peremptory demand, the Court yielded, and a younger judge named Lambrechts applied for the position and got it. Lambrechts, like all of the ten incumbent judges of the Supreme Court (with one possible exception) was also a Conservative, but he was deemed to be considerably more flexible than Hansteen.

The issue arose again when Lambrechts died in 1900. Instead of appointing one of the older judges as Chief Justice the Liberal government chose the Minister of Justice, Einar Löchen. This created a storm of protest among the Conservatives and vitriolic comments in the press, tempered only by the consideration that somebody even "worse" (i.e., somebody even more leftist) had been discussed as an alternative. There was less discussion when Löchen resigned in 1908 to be replaced by a judge, Kristoffer Karenus Thinn. The government that appointed him was Liberal, and it was no secret that Thinn held very much the same political and social ideas. Some, indeed, considered him to be to the left of the government; and although he had never entangled himself in party politics, he was known to be friendly to labor. His brilliant judicial career made him eminently qualified for the post, and so his appointment met with wide approval.

Thinn served until 1920, when he resigned because of the age limit and the Conservative Minister of Justice H. C. J. Scheel was appointed by the incumbent Conservative government. In 1929 the position was once more vacant, and the Liberal government appointed a Liberal, Paal Berg, who had served in a Liberal government. When he resigned in 1946, the Labor government appointed Laborite Emil Stang. Stang was followed in 1952 by Sverre Grette, who was politically neutral and strictly a civil servant, with a central administrative background. He died in 1958, and the present Chief Justice, Terje Wold, former Secretary of State and member of the parliament, took over. One might say consequently that the exit of Supreme Court judges from national politics has not meant that the government is not interested in maintaining some vague sort of control by letting the "right people" get important positions on the court.

The exit of the Supreme Court from politics was not restricted to national politics. The judges at one time had played a quite important part in local politics in Oslo. From 1837 (when local self-government was introduced) until 1884, there was only one election in which the city council was without representation from the Supreme Court. In the 21 elections from 1884 to 1940, however, the court was represented in only ten, or less than half; and in the period since World War II there have been no Supreme Court judges on the Oslo city council.

It is quite clear that this gradual elimination of judges from politics is not limited to members of the Supreme Court. The combined total of judge representatives and vice-representatives in the parliament has been decreasing steadily since 1814: in 1815 there were 24 judges, 19 in 1841, 13 in 1865, 10 in 1880, and 3 in 1900. Since 1900 (with the exception of 1913, when there were nine judges elected) the number has ranged between two and six. During this same period the size of the parliament has increased considerably, so it is clear that the relative role which the judges play in the parliament has been rather drastically limited. (See Table 8.)

So far we have described the exit of the judges in general and the Supreme Court judges in particular as a result of the democratization of political life, and as a brief generalization this is true. But running parallel to this broad trend, and closely connected with it, is another trend that also deserves some concern. One of the basic reasons for Norway's growing democratization was the development toward urbanization and industrialization. This develop-ment in itself had very important effects on the structure of the upper strata of Norwegian society, and thus for the political leadership of the Conserva-tive Party. Alongside the previously powerful civil servant elite, the new captains of industry and trade became increasingly more powerful. The old Conservative Party, which had been formed to restore the political system to the pre-parliamentary political order, was gradually transformed into a party in which the older, bureaucratic element gradually lost their positions, while business elements and their closest connections within the legal profession,

TABLE 8

The Representation of Judges and Attorneys in the Norwegian Parliament

Period*	Total Number of Representatives	Number of Judges	Number of Attorneys	Percentage of Judges	Percentage of Attorneys
1815-20	242	68	10	28	4
1823-29	235	60	15	26	6
1832-38	289	56	22	19	8
1841-47	307	46	19	15	6
1850-56	324	27	35	8	11
1859-65	339	39	33	12	10
1868-73	333	34	26	10	8
1876-82	339	25	43	7	13
1885-91	341	20	49	6	14
1894-1900	342	15	27	4	8
1903-09	363	16	25	4	7
1912-18	372	18	36	5	10
1921-27	450	10	31	2	7
1930-36	450	10	29	2	6
1945-57	600	18	35	3	6

*Each period includes several successive parliaments.

the private attorneys, took over the helm.[25] At first, however, when the growing bourgeoisie was still weak, and the political position of the civil servants still firm, the alliance between the two social classes remained strong. But by the end of the nineteenth century, when the political power of the civil servants had disappeared and the bourgeoisie was in the ascendancy, the need for a close relationship between the old and new classes in the Conservative Party was considerably reduced. From the point of view of the business element, the benefits that were to be gained from such a relationship largely had disappeared. The civil servants were now more often appointed from among politically leftist groups, but even the older type of conservative civil servants felt the strains between the new bourgeoisie and its values, and their own orientations.

Lawyers, as a class, held their own much better, as Table 8 indicates. The number of private attorneys in parliament was in the beginning rather small, and did not reach as many as ten until 1848. After that, there was usually a considerable number in parliament. Since 1884 there have always been more private attorneys than judges in the parliament. Of course these trends are in sharp contrast to the practice in America where it is common in many legislative assemblies for attorneys to be the largest single group; while incumbent state or federal judges rarely serve as legislators because of conflict-of-interest prohibitions.

Table 9 shows the same trend: the increasing importance of the private

TABLE 9

Occupational Experience of Lawyers Who Served in the Cabinet and Parliament (by examination periods)

Occupation	PERCENTAGE IN THE YEARS:						
	1810-29	1830-49	1850-69	1870-89	1890-1909	1910-29	1930-49*
Private attorney	45%	49%	64%	71%	72%	66%	80%
Local administration	71	67	51	43	27	38	24
Central administration	40	48	43	38	21	44	28
Judicial	50	40	45	37	19	21	4
Total number of lawyers:	58	118	67	87	85	61	25

*Data may not be complete for this column since it is possible that persons in this period may still become members of parliament or cabinet members.

attorney in politics, and the decreasing importance of the judge. A great proportion of those in the legal profession who have become cabinet politicians have had varied occupational experience within the different branches of the legal profession. The relatively stable importance of a central administrative background is evident, as is the decreasing importance of local administrative experience. The data for the very last period are subject to revision, because of the possibility that lawyers in this category may yet become members of parliament or cabinet members.

Table 10 shows that the growth in the size of the legal profession has outstripped the growth in the size of the parliament; and that consequently the proportion of lawyers (in all major experience categories) in parliament has steadily declined. Indeed, during the past 40 years (represented by the two most recent examination periods) there has been no important difference

TABLE 10

Representation in Parliament of Major Categories of Legal Experience
(by examination periods)

Legal Experience	1810-29 % of Total		1830-49 % of Total		1850-69 % of Total		1870-89 % of Total		1890-1909 % of Total		1910-29 % of Total	
Judge	40	68	29	147	20	127	16	178	6	224	4	173
Local administration	27	147	21	358	15	215	13	266	7	296	5	304
Private attorney	22	111	15	230	13	313	10	557	6	945	3	779
Central administration	23	91	15	337	8	275	8	337	3	416	5	411
Law graduate	21	259	13	775	7	695	6	1044	4	1620	2	1575

in the *proportion* of different types of lawyers; there have, however, been differences in the number of representatives from these different occupational groups. Obviously, the most numerous group, private attorneys, has provided the most representatives, while the least numerous group, judges, has provided the fewest. For the period 1910-29, for example, there were 25 private attorneys and only six judges, although the proportion of judges (4 per cent) was slightly higher than that of private attorneys (3 per cent). And the lawyers, to a large extent because of the expansion of the profession, have become more and more important figures within the Conservative Party, and outside it as well.

Paralleling the growing democratization, which played a considerable part in stripping the judges of their political offices, another trend thus was present: the changes in the nature of the upper class and in the composition and character of the legal profession. The political position of the judge not only was threatened from below; it also was threatened from another group within the legal profession, the private attorneys, a group that grew increasingly different from the judges. This cleavage within the legal profession, a cleavage which occurred simultaneously with the pressures of the new popular movements, must have weakened the dispositions of the judges to support conservative business-oriented policies. While in the United States both the bar and the bench moved equally in the direction of pro-business positions in the last years of the nineteenth century, the cleavage that occurred within its legal profession served to soften this trend in Norway.

5. Conclusions

We have now described some of the causes that made Aschehoug's orientation to the courts fail as a policy. The most important reason was probably
the strategic situation in which the court was placed; unlike the United States
Supreme Court, it was not one of three separate branches of a government
in which the legislative branch was often in conflict with the executive.
Neither could the Norwegian court base its power on the strategic position
that the federal constitution accords the United States Supreme Court. Quite
the contrary, after the introduction of parliamentarism, the Norwegian
Supreme Court was faced with a united front of the cabinet and parliament.
Paradoxically, one might say that the idea of the court as a censoring device
was not invented until its power to fulfill this function had been eliminated.
When the court could have played this role, the requisite theoretical justification was lacking; and when the conservatives began to formulate such a
theory, the parliamentary form of government had made its implementation
all but impossible. These are important and strong reasons why the attempt
to copy the Cooley doctrine in Norway turned out to be a pale shadow of
the potent conservative force that the Supreme Court became in the United
States.

But alongside these influences, which derive from the very structure of the
government, other related factors have been at work. And the loyalty of the
judges toward the government has been one of the most important of these
factors. The conservatism of civil servants is not the same as the conservatism of business and industry. It is inevitable that those who have been
trained in the public bureaucracy (and quite a few of them specifically in
the drafting of laws and statutes, as we have pointed out) should retain a
substantial part of their loyalty to the administration and its political leaders
after they reach the bench. Thus they will look with sympathy upon the
government and its legislative program, and they will be extremely reluctant
to propose, without the most compelling reasons, that an enacted measure is
unconstitutional. As we showed in our analysis of the changes in recruitment
patterns, this orientation has probably been intensified by the change in the
major components of judicial experience away from the private legal practice and in the direction of the central civil service. However, the basic
orientation must have been present more or less throughout the entire period.

In addition, however, this framework has been modified by other broad
processes that have affected the position of the courts and the judges in
political life in Norway. The democratization of politics and the structural
differentiation of the legal profession—two transformations going on in
Norwegian society throughout the period that we have described—can be
seen as the essence of the changes just described. Although separable for
purposes of analysis, it is of course true that these two transformations have
been closely interrelated and have reinforced each other.

The process of democratization represents the advance of lower social
groups to political influence. This ascendancy of less privileged classes

meant a thoroughgoing change in political ethics, and it made inevitable the decline of the political role of the judge. The judges protested, to be sure, against this broad wave of popular movements, because they felt ties of loyalty to the established industrial and mercantile groups. This loyalty, however, was always softened by a loyalty to the state; and the latter tended to become stronger as the judges were recruited to a decreasing extent from among private attorneys. At the same time, the change in the conservative party leadership meant an increased amount of influence for the private attorneys and a decreased amount of influence for judges. Or, to put it another way, the new group of private attorneys were gradually pulled closer to private enterprise. The gradually closer recruitment relationship between the state and the bench and the accompanying loosening of the ties between attorneys and government resulted, politically, in a decrease in the political role of the judge, who was likely to have been a civil servant and to have been recruited from nonbusiness-oriented graduates of the University of Oslo law school. The Conservative Party was transformed into a more business-oriented party, and it was the rise of the new class of businessmen that was the precondition for the great increase in the number of lawyers; often the attorneys were businessmen themselves. Thus the social and political decline of the judges and civil servants generally was not just the result of broad democratization, but also the product of changes within the upper ranks in society. The judges were no longer representative of the business classes, because businessmen were in fact representing themselves.

In broader perspective the fate of judicial review testifies to the egalitarian character of Norwegian society and political life. The reason why the attempt to use it was not really carried very far can be attributed to the inherent political vulnerability of the older elites. The attempt was made because the independent power of the cabinet had been broken—an event which also is indicative of the weakness of the bureaucracy and its allies among the upper classes. From this point of view the weakness of the court can be seen as another sign of the weakness of the established elites, and of the absence of ascriptive orientations that limited the entrance to the upper classes or made them resist the pressures from below. Instead, the Norwegian upper classes have been characterized by permeability and flexibility, and our interpretation of the changing role of the Norwegian Supreme Court rests upon this fundamental characteristic of Norwegian political society.

NOTES

1. A thoroughgoing analysis of the initial phase of conservative judicial review in the United States is presented in Arnold M. Paul, *Conservative Crisis and the Rule of Law: Attitudes of Bar and Bench, 1887-1895* (Ithaca, N.Y.: Cornell University Press, 1960). For a more general description, see Alfred H. Kelly and Winfred A. Harbison, *The American Constitution: Its Origin and Development* (New York: Norton, 1948), particularly chaps. 19 and 20; this book also contains a good bibliography on the subject. See also Henry J. Abraham, "Machtkampf: The Supreme Court of the United States in the Political Process," *Parliamentary Affairs*, Vol. 13 (1960), 424-41, where some information about the frequency of invalidation of federal statutes is presented. For a

description of the cases in which state laws have been declared null and void, see Felix Frankfurter, *Mr. Justice Holmes and the Supreme Court* (Cambridge: Harvard University Press, 1939). For the parallel development in Norway, see Ulf Torgersen, *De generelle synspunkter pa grunnlovens § 97: En historisk undersökelse av juridisk argumentasjon* (1955) [Magister thesis; typescript; Oslo University Library, Manuscript Division.] See also Finn Sollie, *Courts and Constitutions: A Comparative Study of Judicial Review in Norway and the United States* (Johns Hopkins University, unpublished Ph.D. dissertation, 1957).

2. For a Norwegian criticism of judicial review in constitutional matters, see Mikael H. Lie, *Domstolene og Grunnloven* (Kristiania, 1923). Also published as *Stortingsdokument nr. 13, 1923.*

3. This tendency to look for support against the threats of democratic and left-wing legislation was by no means confined to the United States and Norway. There were similar tendencies and sentiments in Great Britain. Writing in 1888, Bryce reported that the existence of judicial review in the United States had made people who previously had been skeptical of the egalitarian traits in that country look at the United States with envy: "They lament that England should have no Supreme Court." James Bryce, *The American Commonwealth,* abridged ed. (New York: Capricorn Books, Putnam, 1959), p. 62.

4. I want to emphasize that in this article I am not concerned with the function of the Norwegian Supreme Court in cases of impeachment. According to the Norwegian Constitution, this system functions in a way which demands the participation of the regular members of the Supreme Court *in* the jury, together with the members of one of the two chambers in the Norwegian Storting (the parliament). This institution played some part in the political life of the country up to 1884, when the cabinet was condemned for having advised the King to veto constitutional amendments aiming at a more parliamentary form of government. Although the judges all voted for the acquittal of the cabinet, it was found guilty by a majority of the jury. Since then, however, impeachment has only been used in one instance, because other types of control have taken the place of this device, which had some importance only in a system where the members of the cabinet were *not* responsible to the national assembly.

5. One author of a treatise on constitutional law in Norway expresses the idea in these terms: ". . . the Norwegian judges are much more reluctant than their American colleagues when it comes to using their own opinions about right and justice as against the view accepted by the national assembly." Johs. B. Andenaes, *Statsforfatningen i Norge* (Oslo: Johan Grundt Tanum, 1948), p. 237.

6. *Norsk Retstidende* (1908), p. 881. Also quoted in G. Hallager: *Norges Höiesteret 1815-1915. Andet bind, 1864-1915* (Kristiania, 1916), p. 225.

7. Hallager, *op. cit. supra* (Note 6), p. 151.

8. In an obituary of a Supreme Court judge, a colleague of his stated: "As judge he avoided, if possible, according to a long-standing custom in the Supreme Court, taking a stand on theoretical or more general questions. He limited his reasoning to the case at hand." *Medlemsblad for den norske dommerforening* (March, 1960). This should, however, not be taken to imply support of any "Freirechtslehre." The particularistic orientation of that school of legal thought has never had any real support among Norwegian lawyers.

9. One consequence of this more careful attitude has been that there have been no "famous dissenting opinions"; similarly there has been a relative absence of clear divisions between conservative and liberal "blocs" in the court.

10. John C. Schmidhauser, "The Justices of the Supreme Court: A Collective Portrait," *Midwest Journal of Political Science,* Vol. 3 (1959), 1-57.

11. For a more detailed description of this group of writers, see Ulf Torgersen, *op. cit., supra* (Note 1) pp. 10-21.

12. Frederik Stang, *Systematisk Fremstilling af Kongeriget Norges constitutionelle eller grundlovbestemte Ret* (Christiania, 1833), and unpublished lectures from 1830, Oslo University Library, Manuscript Division.

13. T. H. Aschehoug, *Norges nuvaerende Statsforfatning,* Vol. III (Christiania, 1885).

14. This is not the place for discussing the question of when a Supreme Court decision that clearly established judicial review of legislation first occurred. Aschehoug, who was eager to find precedents, found clues in a decision in 1844. Most other authors on the subject tend to place the date of acceptance of this institution by the Supreme Court quite a bit later, generally from about 1890. See Frede Castberg, *Norges Statsforfatning,* 2nd ed. (Oslo, Aschehoug, 1947), Vol. II, p. 221. Similarly Andenaes, *op. cit. supra* (Note 5), p. 223.

15. *Norsk Retstidende* (1918), p. 426.

16. Schmidhauser, *op. cit. supra* (Note 10), p. 37.

17. Schmidhauser, *op. cit. supra* (Note 10), p. 33.

18. This system was modified in one way only: by the introduction of an examination which did not base the legal training on Latin and which was called the "Norwegian Law Degree." Because it did not require extensive knowledge of Latin, it was considered to be inferior to the "Latin Law Degree," and it was introduced largely because of the temporary shortage of legally trained personnel after 1814. In 1826 a declaration stated that the "Norwegian" candidates could not become judges except in cases of temporary vacancies, and in 1846, when the shortage of manpower had abated—by then there was, in fact, a surplus—they could not serve as judges even temporarily, according to an official declaration. Finally, the examination itself was abolished.

19. Axel Heiberg, "Den 1. Internasjonale dommerkongress i Rom 11-13. oktober," *Medlemsblad for norsk dommerforening* (1959), p. 23.

20. This is in part seen from Table 4. The Supreme Court lawyers were, to begin with, not quite as numerous as the Supreme Court judges; but their numbers have grown very rapidly, and at a proportionately faster rate than lawyers as a whole.

21. Vilhelm Aubert, with co-authors Ulf Torgersen and Karl Tangen, "Norske jurister fra 1814 til den annen verdenskrig" (Institute for Social Research, Oslo, 1960; mimeographed), p. 93.

22. Schmidhauser, *op. cit. supra* (Note 10), p. 45.

23. Jens Arup Seip, *Et regime foran undergangen* (Oslo, 1945), p. 97.

24. The relevance of these changes in the definition of political types, for political participation of university professors, has been described in my article: "Universitetet og politikken," *Tidsskrift for samfunnsforskning,* Vol. 2 (March, 1960) 17-36. For a discussion of comparable political types and theories in American political society, see Glendon Schubert, *The Public Interest* (Glencoe: The Free Press, 1961), *passim,* and with particular reference to judges, see pp. 74-78, 123-35, and 186-97.

25. The transformation of the Norwegian conservative party from a party dominated by civil servants to a party in which business interests prevailed is a phenomenon that has been noticed by many writers but analyzed by few. Some suggestions are contained in Johan Vogt, *Tanker om politikk* (Oslo, Aschehoug, 1947), pp. 178-91. A penetrating analysis on this development in the city of Trondheim is presented in Rolv Danielsen, *Trondhjem bys historie. Det nye bysamfunn. 1880-1914* (Trondheim kommune, 1958), particularly chap. 10.

The Role of the Judiciary
in American State Politics

HERBERT JACOB and KENNETH VINES

POLITICAL SCIENTISTS have usually slighted the political relevance of the courts in favor of legalistic and institutional analysis, conceiving of the courts in terms of jurisprudential theory and formal organization. The proposition that courts are an integral part of the political system has rarely been suggested. In consequence, the legal and institutional traits of the courts have been examined carefully, but their political functions, the role of court participants, and the relationship of courts to the political and social structure have received little attention. Moreover, courts in general have rarely been examined; the few existing studies which concern the political character of courts focus on the national Supreme Court, its members, and their activities.

While often embroiled in political controversy, the state courts have been virtually neglected. The condition of research on the state judiciary may be summed up by the fact that the eclectic V. O. Key in his book on state politics does not mention either judges or courts.[1] Not even the forward-looking SSRC report on state politics formulated by the Committee on Political Behavior considers the state judiciary in making its suggestions for research in state politics.[2] The void left by the omission of courts from the state political system is nowhere better illustrated than in the failure by students of state and local government to consider them politically. Charles Adrian, one of the most politically oriented of the state and local government authors, barely mentions the political functions of state courts.[3]

Most of our information concerning the operation of state courts comes from the writing and research of scholars in the field of public administration.[4] The structure and organization of state courts, their personnel problems, judicial administration, and the legal process have been considered, and it is from this body of material that scholars have drawn their conceptions of the place of courts in local politics. Some ten years ago, to illustrate, when the *Journal of Politics* published a symposium on the Southern political scene, "The Southern State Judiciary" was written by a specialist in public administration from the viewpoint of organization, staffing, and judicial administration; the political functions of the courts were not considered.[5] Were it not for such studies the contributions of political scientists to the study of local courts would be extremely slight. But as it is, a vacuum, created by the lack of concern with the political functions of the courts by students of the state political system, exists in both theory and research.

When we observe the judiciary in action, we quickly become aware of how acutely "political" it may be. Not only judges, but sheriffs, prosecutors, and coroners are usually elected officials. In Louisiana, where judges have been indicted for income tax evasion and listed on the board of directors of oil and gas companies, we may infer that their ceremonial insulation from the public has not prevented their getting in on the "big barbecue" that is by now customary in Louisiana politics. Moreover, the cases brought before the courts frequently have immediate and sharp political consequences. In Mississippi the courts are used to hinder Negro activities through breach of the peace convictions. In Louisiana they serve as the arena for clashes between New Orleans and up-state factions of the Democratic Party. In all the states, they frequently decide disputes over election laws and thus help one party or faction defeat another.

Within the last two or three years a few scholars, largely under the influence of Glendon Schubert's tutelage, have begun to pay attention to the state courts.[6] Their efforts have, however, been limited in both scope and technique. Most frequently they have used the bloc analysis of dissenting opinions of state supreme courts modeled on the examination of the national Supreme Court by Pritchett and Schubert.[7] The most important results of such bloc analysis have been negative. The rate of dissent is only a small fraction of that of the U. S. Supreme Court and in no case exceeds more than 20 per cent of the total number of cases. The possibilities for bloc analysis are thus severely limited, and the conclusions that can be drawn from such analysis concerning the political role of the state courts are distinctly meager.[8]

A second limitation of the recent studies of state courts is their conception of judicial politics solely in terms of supreme court judges, a bias in judicial scholars that Jerome Frank has called "the upper court myth."[9] This bias has led to the neglect of the judicial process in its entirety. On the state level the functions of the prosecutor, the jury, and the entire output of the lower courts have not yet been included in the study of the judiciary. One suspects that those scholars who take the supreme courts as their definition of judicial politics simply echo the myopia of students of the national judiciary where the functions of the Attorney General's Office, the role of the United States' Attorneys and the flow of claims through lower federal courts have been neglected for refined quantitative analysis of the Supreme Court.[10]

In the light of our political history it is puzzling that state courts have been so seldom considered as policy-makers by observers of local politics. During the Jacksonian era struggles ranged all over the United States in the movement to elect state judges rather than keep them appointive as during the Federalist period. The Jacksonians' motivation was to thrust courts and their judges into the political arena within reach of the popular interests unleashed by the Jacksonian movement. In most states they succeeded in having judges elected, though in winning the battle they perhaps lost the war. The long terms of office, the frequent nonpartisan character of judicial elections, and especially the lack of publicity given the records and roles of judges have again removed them from attention in the political process and from the political perceptions of the electorate. The mysterious realm of the law has effectively insulated the judge from both voter and scholar of politics alike. Whereas we know that public information and perception of legislative and executive politics is slight, the ceremonies and mysteries of the judiciary have so hidden the state courts from public view that the question of their role as policy-maker has seldom even been raised.

These considerations, then, lead us to ask: What is the role of the judiciary in a state's political system? How may it profitably be studied?

I

Systematic analysis can locate the distinctive political functions of the courts and consider the relationship of the judiciary to other institutions of state government. By considering the courts in state politics as a whole, we can more accurately define their political functions through comparison and contrast with other institutions of state government.

A useful division of functions in a political system is between the making of claims upon government and the processing and granting of such claims. Political parties and pressure groups, for example, make claims upon the state while the executive, the legislature, and the courts decide upon these claims.[11] Thus the three branches of government share the prerogative of making decisions. To some extent the practices and safeguards inspired by the principle of separation of powers divide the areas in which different institutions can grant claims, although in practice there is a great deal of overlapping, i.e., the same claim may be considered by any or all of the institutions of government.

Courts, then, are one of the agencies of government which meet demands, settle disputes, and resolve arguments in the political system. Some problems find their way into the courts but others do not. For what reasons do claims come before a court rather than some other agency of government? The first and best understood is the formal framework within which the courts must act. The state constitution, statutes governing the operation and functions of the courts, and the conceptual requirements of the common law all set limits upon the kind of cases which can come before the courts. Constitutional provisions and statutes, for example, require some claims to come before the courts and specifically exclude others, leaving many which may or may not come before the courts. The common law provides that only those interests which are part of an adversary action, a conflict between opposing parties, may be brought before the courts.

A simple example will illustrate the importance of such formal boundaries.

A group may approach the legislature and demand special treatment because it has political power or would promote the welfare of the state; such claims, at least in that form, could not be entertained by the courts. The group would have to put its claim in such a fashion (e.g., generate a controversy involving legal rights) as to come within the formal boundaries marking the court's jurisdiction.[12] But it is easy to overestimate the restrictive effects of the courts' formal boundaries. Friendly disputes can usually be easily arranged among interests desiring access to the courts. The flexibility of equity remedies elasticizes the boundaries of the courts. Often a taxpayer may obtain standing before a court if there is expenditure of public monies and ask for an injunction or other remedy.

Indeed, the business of the courts has increased in modern times in response to the growing complexity of the political system just as has the business of other branches of government. The ever-changing nature of the common law as well as the eclectic character of state constitutions seem to have made the courts adaptable to modern political situations. Getting access to the courts is, thus, not necessarily more difficult than to any other agency of government, given an understanding of the nature of the formal boundaries. Some claims may be easier to process through the courts; others are more difficult.

A second determinant of the character of the courts' business is related to values institutionalized by the courts. In a certain sense the courts may be said to embody a lag in political culture because of their built-in conservatism. This conservatism is a function of legal education which emphasizes attachment to precedent, to the interests of the past, and to stability of legal procedures. Furthermore, the judiciary is considerably less involved in the changing political mood and movements of the time. While the legislature and the executive are forging ahead in new directions, the courts may provide a place for those interested in resisting political change. Minorities may find refuge in the courts from majority-dominated legislatures and governors. Vested interests representing property rights or the claims of institutions can find surcease in the courts from hostile attacks.

On a different level, but again involving social change, any shift in the equilibrium of the political system may create business for the court. The role of the federal courts in civil rights has created additional business for the state courts since interests resistant to Negro rights and civil rights in general turn to the state courts both to mitigate and to offset the effects of federal court decisions.[13] Even in the face of a specific Supreme Court decision, there is much discretion left to the decision-making authority of state courts. The final outcome is often determined by the state courts.[14]

Another limitation that may deter interests from coming before the courts lies in the kinds of remedies the courts can grant. Courts cannot institute an integrated program of action; they cannot dip into the public treasury for appropriations. While they can direct an action, they can neither administer nor supervise its execution; indeed, they depend on the acquiescence of other governmental institutions to effectuate their decisions.

Once more caution is necessary in interpreting the effect of these restrictions. Courts can and do initiate far-reaching social changes; they may effect the distribution of wealth through decisions on various property rights. Though they may not directly supervise a policy, they can influence its execution through the application of sanctions they control.

Finally, the perceptions of the interested claimant are important in determining the business of the court, for there are a number of institutions to which an interested claimant may turn. We have already suggested that vested interests and minority groups habitually perceive the courts as more hospitable than other agencies.[15] In addition, groups that find themselves defeated at the polls and hence out of favor with the legislature and executive may turn to the courts. When the Longs were in power in Louisiana, the oil, gas and sulfur interests were prone to perceive the courts as a more favorable haven for processing claims until the courts fell under the Longs' domination.

For some groups the courts offer the only arena in which claims may be effectively presented. On the national level such interests as the Communists, the N.A.A.C.P., or Jehovah's Witnesses perceive the courts as the only feasible point of access to government.[16] We may expect to find that groups in a similar position in a local social structure perceive the state courts similarly. On occasion the courts may offer the quickest or the most direct way to settle a claim. Although much can be said about overloaded dockets and slow, costly litigation, the courts can act quickly if they choose, particularly when those involved have encountered the delaying and obstructive tactics possible in the legislature and the cautious instincts of a careful executive.

II

A description of the courts as one of the arenas in which conflicts are resolved does not adequately show their political character. To further understand the role of the courts in the political system, it is necessary to consider the flow of judicial action and to show at which points the judicial process impinges on other parts of the political system.

Let us first take criminal cases. The kind of cases that enter the courts and their disposition are markedly determined by the character of the local political structure. They depend on the actions of the prosecuting attorney, an elected official with enormous discretionary powers[17] that often allow him to become the key figure in a local political machine. A criminal case begins with the commission of an allegedly illegal act and the apprehension of the suspected perpetrator by the police. After booking the individual, the police turn the suspect over to the prosecuting attorney's office for investigation. It is then up to the discretion of the prosecutor to determine what law, if any, has been violated. His direct action results either in the release of the suspect or in his indictment.[18] If the suspect is to be indicted, the prosecutor enjoys great freedom in determining the character of the charge. Let us say the suspect apparently caused some disorder. The prosecutor may charge him with inciting a riot, breaching the peace, or simply loitering.

Which charge the prosecutor selects often depends on the political circumstances surrounding the case. "Throwing the book" at a defendant may win support from the press; leniency may strengthen political alliances.[19]

Even when indicted, the suspect often does not stand trial. The prosecutor, always alert for additional support, may find it to his advantage to dismiss the charges before trial or simply not to prosecute them by entering a plea of *nolle prosequi*. The crime surveys of the 1920's indicated that between one-fifth and one-half of all indictments were disposed of in this fashion; a cursory review of New Orleans court records indicates a similar performance there today.[20] Even when the indictment is pressed, it often leads to conviction on a lesser charge. Contrary to popular stereotype, most convictions are not the result of trial by jury; rather they are the result of guilty pleas, usually to reduced charges. Once more it is entirely within the discretion of a prosecutor whether he offers or accepts a lesser charge in return for a guilty plea.[21] As most prosecutors run for re-election on their record of convictions,[22] they are anxious to pad it and avoid the expense and work of a jury trial by inducing defendants to plead guilty. The crime surveys of a generation ago indicated that this was a widespread practice; there is nothing to indicate its abandonment today.

Once a defendant has been found guilty, his sentence depends on the discretion of the judge and the recommendations of the prosecuting attorney. In most states, the law allows the judge considerable latitude in sentencing prisoners. While the general public is rarely informed of his actions in particular cases, the defendants and their families are acutely aware of them. A light sentence, bench parole, or suspended sentence can be justified in the press as justice tempered by mercy; in many instances, it can be turned to real political advantage. Studies of judicial sentencing behavior indicate that the discretionary powers of judges may indeed be used for political purposes, for much evidence exists that sentences for similar crimes vary considerably.[23] As judges, like prosecutors, must seek office by election in most states, it seems likely that electoral considerations are a factor in the sentencing process.

Thus, elected officials sensitive to the political process charge, prosecute, convict, and sentence criminal defendants. This means that such decisions are made in response to cues from the political structure; thereby the political system provides channels by which local claims and local interests can influence judicial outcomes.[24] In this way, the judiciary helps create the conditions necessary for the re-election of court officials or for their frequent promotion to higher offices in the state or nation.[25] In short, criminal prosecutions provide opportunities for the political system to affect judicial decisions and for the judicial process to provide favors which nourish political organizations.

While criminal proceedings appear to be closely linked with a community's political machinery, civil proceedings appear to reflect its interest group structure. Clashes between interest groups often find their way to the courts. Conflicts between labor and management, between consumers and public utilities, between a dock board and park board over land usage are typically found among the cases on a civil docket; their outcome has important political consequences for the community. Moreover, certain groups may sometimes influence court procedure in their favor. In Manhattan, for instance, commercial cases are heard without delay while personal injury suits usually must wait several years.[26] It would be a good guess that such a bias toward the commercial community reflects the general primacy of business interests in the political perceptions of judicial politicians in the world's commercial capital. Finally, some interest groups use civil litigation to obtain out-of-court settlements. Insurance companies and finance firms, for instance, may threaten to go to court to win settlements.

One of the interests with special influence in judicial proceedings is the bar. The availability and quality of counsel available to each side often foreshadows the outcome of judicial proceedings. It is no accident, for instance, that many civil rights cases involving Negroes in the South have to be handled by Northern lawyers, for the number of Negro lawyers in the South is quite limited and most white lawyers refuse such cases. Likewise, when legal counsel is expensive, some litigants simply abandon their case.[27] Thus, the bar acts as a gatekeeper to the courts; it determines which groups shall have access to judicial proceedings. Moreover, by providing superior legal services to some, it enhances their chance for success.

The bar also plays an important role in acting as a conduit by which novel political ideas can be conveyed to the courts in legal terminology so that judicial decisions can be based upon them. During the last century, protection of private property won judicial recognition as a result of the bar's advocacy of the substantive interpretation of the due process clause.[28] In this century, the N.A.A.C.P.'s Legal Defense Committee has played a similarly successful role in changing the constitutional guarantees available to Negroes.

Finally, the bar plays a crucially important role in the training and selection of judges.[29] Almost without fail, judges come from the ranks of the bar, and in an increasing number of states the bar helps select judges either through a "nonpartisan" selection plan or by rating candidates for judicial office and seeking to influence the outcome of the election.[30] The bar has thus assumed the role of guardian of the judiciary. When one adds this to its other roles as gatekeeper of the courts and legalizer of popular notions, the bar's political importance for the judiciary becomes clear.

III

The links we have so far described between the political system and judicial process are those stemming from the making of judicial decisions. Decisions, however, are not the only outputs of the judicial process. Other aspects of the judicial system provide the political structure with important sources of strength. One might indeed hypothesize that judicial patronage provides an important resource that allows political machines to flourish in this age of the welfare state and civil service. A generation ago political machines survived through their ability to provide favors for the poor and

jobs for the needy. The rise of government welfare programs and the acceptance of civil service reform has shifted the dispensation of largesse from
political machines to nonpartisan bureaucrats. The judicial system, however,
constitutes a major exception. Political friendships may minimize the legal
consequences of a misdeed as we have already seen. Likewise, jobs are
available at all levels. Judgeships (paying as much as $45,000 annually)
are prizes for which some lawyers will work many years. Moreover, judicial
appointments to receiverships of bankrupt corporations and to appraisers of
estates may provide a handsome side income to lawyers associated with the
winning party. For nonlawyers who help a machine, hundreds of clerical
positions remain outside the civil service system in the judiciary. Finally,
court officials may direct business to favored bail-bond firms and thus
assure their political allies of a profitable business. In short, the judiciary
provides many of the resources that make the organization of factions or
machines possible.[31]

The political system affects the judiciary in still another way, for the
decisions of other political institutions determine to a large degree the conditions under which judges must work. Indeed, the structure of the courts
is mostly the result of legislative edicts. The most important consequence
has been that in most states the legislatures have failed to create a judicial
hierarchy, leaving trial courts almost entirely autonomous. While appellate
courts may upset lower-court rulings, they often have no other control over
the trial courts. In most states, each court draws up its own budget request
and determines its own work schedule. Lower courts are almost completely
free from centralized personnel controls. If a judge happens to be elected in
a jurisdiction with little work, he can take life easy while his colleague
in a neighboring county finds himself swamped by an overloaded docket.[32]
This almost complete absence of administrative machinery in the judiciary
is probably a reflection of the parochial attitude of many state legislators.
They perceive themselves as ambassadors from a country rather than as
representatives of a state; they come to the capital to protect the local
political structure from outside interference.[33] In most states, they have
succeeded in defending the autonomous and anarchic structure of the
judiciary.

Finally, no discussion of the role of the judiciary in the political system
is complete without a consideration of the ways in which judicial decisions
affect outcomes in other spheres of the political process. Some decisions affect
the formal conditions under which other political institutions operate, e.g.,
decisions regarding how officials in other agencies are to be elected. Other
decisions affect the resources that other participants in the political system
may commit to political activity—for instance, court decisions affecting political contributions by labor unions. Still others settle disputes with such
finality that they are not brought to other political arenas for redress; most
private litigation falls in this category. Finally, some judicial settlements
so frustrate the loser that he transfers his dispute to the legislative or executive arena in the hope of obtaining a more favorable outcome. In short,

just as election returns or legislative outcomes shift the balance of the political system, so judicial decisions affect the system's equilibrium.

IV

We have argued in this paper that the jurisdiction of the courts depends not so much on its legal definition as on the functions of the local political structure and upon the perceptions of potential litigants. We have also suggested that the judicial process is intimately affected by the remainder of the political system and in turn judicial actions have repercussions on other political institutions. Consequently, if we are to understand the operations of the political system, it is necessary to increase our knowledge of the judicial process.

Studies of judicial organization and administration have prepared the way by providing a foundation, and the studies of the Supreme Court using quantitative methods have provided an elegant example how the study of the judiciary may be operationalized with precision and imagination. But such studies, we have suggested, do not go far enough. They do not provide us with the requisite information concerning the operation of the courts in the state political system.

We may gain some valuable suggestions as to how to proceed from studies undertaken a generation ago. The Crime Commission Reports suggest that attention to court records on the local level can produce a wealth of data on the operation of the judicial process. Raymond Moley's *Politics and Criminal Prosecution* and Hugh Fuller's *Criminal Justice in Virginia* show the effectiveness of analysis utilizing court statistics in producing clues on the functioning of the judicial system. Although such studies lacked the conceptual and analytical treatment available to political scientists today, they indicate the value of observing judicial politics as a whole.

The basic weakness of previous studies has been their inadequate conceptualization of the judicial system—the fact that their basic questions were posed in institutional or reformative terms. A more adequate explanation necessitates the use of operational inquiries whenever possible, for operational procedures focus on the activities and functions of the different parts of the judicial system and allow more careful analysis of it.

Present-day political science provides a rich variety of tools and theoretical concepts adequate for the study of the judicial system. The following are some of the approaches which can be used.

1. The study of the state judiciary should be comparative. The comparative method has proved itself in the study of state legislatures and electoral systems. It can prove equally valid in promoting generalization of function and descriptive variety and in avoiding parochialism. Comparative analysis of state judicial systems might focus especially on seeking differences between states which have centralized in their supreme court control over the local courts (e.g., New Jersey) and those who retain autonomous local courts. The consequences of party politics may be observed by contrasting judicial

politics in those states which have a two-party system and those where one party dominates, those where all judicial officers are elected on a partisan ballot and those where some are elected on a nonpartisan ballot. Finally, such comparative analysis could contrast judicial systems where court personnel are appointed and those where they are elected.

2. Sampling and coding procedures should be utilized in studying the judicial process. Because the output of the local court system is tremendous, sampling presents a means by which cases can be selected from among a large number and still be representative within limits of statistical confidence. By using a standardized coding form, the sample cases can be systematically checked for items which will show the nature and extent of the business of the courts.

3. Interviews with participants in the judicial process as well as systematic observation of the courts should supplement the statistical analysis. These techniques might be used to determine the perceptions and attitudes of claimants before the court as well as of court officials themselves. Systematic observation may reveal the roles peculiar to court participants and their distinctive functions in the judicial process.

4. The use of content analysis might be explored more fully in analyzing judicial opinions and trial transcripts. The traditional analysis of Supreme Court decisions already examines the content of decisions using intuitive categories. A more rigorous content analysis may reveal clues concerning the functioning of the courts. When applied to trial transcripts, content analysis may reveal the differing appeals which trial lawyers make to juries and judges in various sorts of cases.

Applying these techniques, among others, we would suggest that the following questions be asked.

1. What is the role behavior of judges? Observation indicates that judges differ in the way they handle claims and perceive their function in quite as distinctive a fashion as do legislators.

2. What is the role behavior of prosecuting attorneys and other court officials?

3. What is the recruitment process by which judges and other judicial officials win office? What role do political parties play? What is the function of the bar? What effect does a community's social structure have on the recruitment of judicial officers?

4. By what process do judicial officials learn their proper role and undergo socialization for participation in the judicial system?

5. How do interest groups decide upon and gain access to the state courts? What are the perceptions of interest groups concerning the judiciary and its officials?

6. What is the role of judicial patronage? What part do the jobs, rewards, and favors dispensed in the courts play in the functioning of the local political process?

7. What is the style and rationale of judicial opinions? What role do federal court decisions, decisions from other state courts, social science

evidence, law reviews, and submitted briefs play in the perceptions and cognitions of judges as revealed in their decisions?

8. What is the political relationship of the judiciary to other agencies of state government? What cues do judicial officials furnish to legislators and executives, and what cues do they pick up from them?

We suggest such investigations of the judicial process, for we believe that without them our understanding of state politics must remain incomplete. We now rely on an impressionistic realization that courts play an essential role in American state politics; only systematic study can supplant that with the hard facts that will lead to a real understanding of the political system. What is needed is that the state judiciary be examined with the same care as other political institutions.

NOTES

1. V. O. Key, Jr., *American State Politics: An Introduction* (New York: Knopf, 1956).

2. Social Science Research Council, Committee on Political Behavior, "Research in State Politics" (December 1954, mimeographed).

3. Charles Adrian, *State and Local Governments: A Study in the Political Process,* (New York: McGraw-Hill, 1960).

4. See any of the standard texts on state and local government. On the Southern judiciary, see Lee S. Greene, "The Southern State Judiciary," *Journal of Politics,* Vol. 10 (1948), 441-64. For a carefully done study, see especially Forrest Talbott, *Intergovernmental Relations and the Courts* (Minneapolis: University of Minnesota Press, 1950).

5. Greene, *op. cit. supra* (Note 4).

6. Glendon Schubert studies the Michigan Supreme Court in *Quantitative Analysis of Judicial Behavior* (New York: The Free Press of Glencoe, 1959), pp. 129-43. See also Stuart S. Nagel: "Testing Relations between Judicial Characteristics and Judicial Decision-Making," *Western Political Quarterly,* Vol. 15 (1962), 425-37, and "Unequal Party Representation on the State Supreme Courts," *Journal of the American Judicature Society,* Vol. 45 (1961), 62-65.

7. C. Herman Pritchett, *The Roosevelt Court* (New York: Macmillan, 1948); Schubert, *op. cit. supra* (Note 6).

8. Edward Ferguson, III, "Some Comments on the Applicability of Bloc Analysis to State Appellate Courts" (paper prepared for delivery at Midwest Conference of Political Scientists, May 1961, mimeographed); for a rather more optimistic use of bloc analysis see Schubert, *op. cit. supra* (Note 6).

9. Jerome Frank, *Courts on Trial* (Princeton: Princeton University Press, 1949).

10. Jack W. Peltason, *Federal Courts in the Political Process* (New York: Random House, 1955) attempts to correct this view to some extent.

11. For a more extended treatment of the possibilities of systematic analysis, see David Easton, "An Approach to the Analysis of Political Systems," *World Politics,* Vol. 9 (1957), 383-400, and Gabriel Almond, "Introduction," in Almond and James S. Coleman (eds.), *The Politics of the Developing Areas* (Princeton: Princeton University Press, 1960), pp. 3-64.

12. Lewis Mayers, *The American Legal System* (New York: Harper, 1955), pp. 209-38.

13. See the discussion of *Williams* v. *Georgia* and *Florida ex rel Hawkins* v. *Board of Control,* in Walter F. Murphy and C. Hermann Pritchett, *Courts, Judges, and Politics* (New York: Random House, 1961), pp. 602-18.

14. "Evasions of Supreme Court Mandates in Cases Remanded to State Courts since 1941," *Harvard Law Review,* Vol. 67 (1954), 1251-59.

15. Clement Vose, *Caucasians Only* (Berkeley and Los Angeles: University of California Press, 1959), pp. 50-73.

16. Glendon Schubert, *Constitutional Politics* (New York: Holt, Rinehart and Winston, 1960), p. 78.

17. "Prosecutor's Discretion," *University of Pennsylvania Law Review,* Vol. 103 (1955), 1057-81.

18. The prosecutor plays the controlling role even when the indictment is by grand jury action, for he is its official advisor.

19. For an elaboration of this point, see Raymond Moley, *Politics and Criminal Prosecution* (New York: Minton, Balch, 1929), pp. 27-94.

20. Dismissals other than by jury acquittal were as follows: New York City (1925), 19.8 per cent; Chicago (1926), 45.4 per cent; New Orleans (1961), 52.1 per cent. New York and Chicago data are from *ibid.,* p. 41; New Orleans data are tabulated from New Orleans *Times-Picayune* for September, 1961.

21. Moley, *op. cit. supra* (Note 19), pp. 166-92; Hugh N. Fuller, *Criminal Justice in Virginia* (University of Virginia Institute for Research in the Social Sciences, Monograph No. 10, 1931), pp. 151-55.

22. Observation indicates that prosecutors usually compute their record as follows: (guilty pleas + convictions)/jury acquittals.

23. Albert Somit, Joseph Tanenhaus, and Walter Wilkie, "Aspects of Judicial Sentencing Behavior," *University of Pittsburgh Law Review,* Vol. 21 (1960), 613-20; Fuller, *op. cit. supra* (Note 21), pp. 102-17, 151.

24. For some interesting examples, see V. O. Key, Jr., *Southern Politics in State and Nation* (New York: Knopf, 1950), pp. 21-22 and 53-54.

25. The importance of law-enforcement positions in the career ladders of state politicians is described by Joseph A. Schlesinger, *How They Became Governor* (East Lansing, Michigan: Governmental Research Bureau, 1957), pp. 74-96.

26. Hans Zeisel, Harry Kelven, Jr., and Bernard Buchholz, *Delay in the Court* (Boston: Little, Brown, 1959), pp. 201-05.

27. Emery A. Brownell, "Availability of Low Cost Legal Services," *Annals of the American Academy of Political and Social Science,* Vol. 287 (1953), 121-23.

28. Benjamin R. Twiss, *Lawyers and the Constitution* (Princeton: Princeton University Press, 1942).

29. See, for instance, John R. Schmidhauser, "Justices of the Supreme Court: A Collective Portrait," *Midwest Journal of Political Science,* Vol. 3 (1959), 1-57, as well as Schmidhauser's *The Supreme Court: Its Politics, Personalities, and Procedures* (New York: Holt, Rinehart and Winston, 1960), pp. 6-27.

30. Raymond Moley, *Our Criminal Courts* (New York: Minton, Balch, 1930), pp. 227-57.

31. An excellent discussion of this aspect of a judicial system is Wallace Sayre and Herbert Kaufman, *Governing New York City* (New York: Russell Sage Foundation, 1960), pp. 522-54; see also Moley, *Our Criminal Courts, op. cit. supra* (Note 30), pp. 48-56, and M. T. Bloom, "Your Unknown Heirs," *Harper's Magazine* (August, 1961), pp. 29-33.

32. Arthur T. Vanderbilt, *The Challenge of Law Reform* (Princeton: Princeton University Press, 1955); Maxine B. Virtue, "Improving the Structure of Courts," *Annals of the American Academy of Political and Social Science,* Vol. 287 (1953), 141-46; and Willard G. Woelper, "Work of the Modern Administrator of Courts," *loc. cit.,* 147-53.

33. A similar point is made by William J. Keefe, "Comparative Study of the Role of Political Parties in State Legislatures," in H. Eulau, S. J. Eldersveld, and M. Janowitz (eds.), *Political Behavior: A Reader in Theory and Research* (New York: The Free Press of Glencoe, 1956), p. 313.

Bibliography

General

Cohen, Felix S., "Field Theory and Judicial Logic," *Yale Law Journal*, Vol. 59 (1950), 238-72.

Cohen, Felix S., "Transcendental Nonsense and the Functional Approach," *Columbia Law Review*, Vol. 35 (1935), 809-49.

Cohen, Julius, "Factors of Resistance to the Resources of the Behavioral Sciences," *Journal of Legal Education*, Vol. 12 (1959), 67-70.

Douglas, William O., "The Supreme Court and its Case Load," *Cornell Law Quarterly*, Vol. 45 (1960), 401-14.

Fagen, Richard R., "Some Contributions of Mathematical Reasoning to the Study of Politics," *American Political Science Review*, Vol. 55 (1961), 898-99.

Haines, Charles G., "General Observations on the Effects of Personal, Political and Economic Influences in the Decisions of Judges," *Illinois Law Review*, Vol. 17 (1922), 96-116.

Kort, Fred, "A Review of: Glendon Schubert, *Quantitative Analysis of Judicial Behavior*," *Modern Uses of Logic in Law*, Vol. 60D (December, 1960), 143-46.

Loevinger, Lee, "Jurimetrics, The Next Step Forward," *Minnesota Law Review*, Vol. 33 (1949), 455-93.

Nagel, Stuart S., "Testing Relations between Judicial Characteristics and Judicial Decision-Making," *Western Political Quarterly*, Vol. 15 (1962), 425-37.

Schubert, Glendon, *Constitutional Politics: The Political Behavior of Supreme Court Justices and the Constitutional Policies that They Make* (New York: Holt, Rinehart and Winston, 1960), pp. 7-171.

Schubert, Glendon, *Quantitative Analysis of Judicial Behavior* (Glencoe: The Free Press, 1959).

Schubert, Glendon, "The Study of Judicial Decision-Making As an Aspect of Political Behavior," *American Political Science Review*, Vol. 52 (1958), 1007-25.

Tanenhaus, Joseph, "The Uses and Limitations of Social Science Methods in Analyzing Judicial Behavior" (American Political Science Association Annual Meeting, September 1956, mimeographed), pp. 1-22.

Ulmer, S. Sidney, "Researching the Judicial Process: Some Comments on a Quantitative Approach" (Midwest Conference of Political Scientists, May 1961, mimeographed), pp. 1-26.

Part One: Social Psychology and Judges

Allport, Floyd H., *et al.*, "The Effects of Segregation and the Consequences of Desegregation: A Social Science Statement," *Minnesota Law Review*, Vol. 37 (1953), 427-39.

Anonymous, "Mr. Justice Reed: Swing Man or Not?" *Stanford Law Review*, Vol. 1 (1949), 714-29.

Bernard, Jessie, "Dimensions and Axes of Supreme Court Decisions: A Study in the Sociology of Conflict," *Social Forces*, Vol. 34 (1955), 19-27.

Bevan, William, Robert S. Albert, Pierre R. Loiseaux, Peter N. Mayfield, and George Wright, "Jury Behavior as a Function of the Prestige of the Foreman and the Nature of His Leadership," *Journal of Public Law*, Vol. 7 (1958), 419-49.

Broeder, Dale W., "The University of Chicago Jury Project," *Nebraska Law Review*, Vol. 38 (1959), 744-60.

Cahn, Edmond, "Jurisprudence [A Dangerous Myth in the School Segregation Cases]," *New York University Law Review*, Vol. 30 (1955), 150-69.

Cahn, Edmond, "Jurisprudence [The Lawyer, the Social Psychologist, and the Truth]," *New York University Law Review*, Vol. 31 (1956), 182-95.

Clark, Kenneth B., "The Desegregation Cases: Criticism of the Social Scientist's Role," *Villanova Law Review*, Vol. 5 (1959-60), 224-40.

Curran, William J., "Behavioral Science Research in Judicial Administration: A Lawyer's Reply," *Boston University Law Review*, Vol. 39 (1959), pp. 164-71.

Danelski, David J., "Assignment of the Court's Opinion by the Chief Justice" (Midwest Conference of Political Scientists, May 1960, mimeographed), pp. 1-57.

Danelski, David J., "The Influence of the Chief Justice in the Decision Process of the Supreme Court" (American Political Science Association Annual Meeting, September 1960, mimeographed), pp. 1-24.

Editorial, "Psychoanalysis of Judges," *Law Notes*, Vol. 29 (1925), 122-23.

Ferguson, Edward, III, "Some Comments on the Applicability of Bloc Analysis to State Appellate Courts" (Midwest Conference of Political Scientists, May 1961, mimeographed), pp. 1-10.

Frank, Jerome, "Are Judges Human?" *University of Pennsylvania Law Review*, Vol. 80 (1931), 17-53, 233-67.

Frank, Jerome, *Law and the Modern Mind* (New York: Coward-McCann, 1930).

Garfinkel, Herbert, "Social Science Evidence and the School Segregation Cases," *Journal of Politics*, Vol. 21 (1959), 37-59.

Gaudet, Frederick J., "Differences between Judges in the Granting of Sentences of Probation," *Temple Law Quarterly*, Vol. 19 (1946), pp. 471-84.

Gaudet, Frederick J., "Individual Differences in the Sentencing Tendencies of Judges," *Archives of Psychology*, Vol. 32, No. 230 (1938).

Gaudet, Frederick J., George S. Harris, Charles W. St. John, "Individual Differences in Penitentiary Sentences Given by Different Judges," *Journal of Applied Psychology*, Vol. 18 (1934), 675-80.

Gaudet, Frederick J., George S. Harris, Charles W. St. John, "Individual Differences in the Sentencing Tendencies of Judges," *Journal of Criminal Law, Criminology, and Police Science*, Vol. 23 (1933), 811-18.

Green, Edward, *Judicial Attitudes in Sentencing: A Study of the Factors underlying the Sentencing Practice of the Criminal Court of Philadelphia*, Cambridge Studies in Criminology, No. 15 (London: Macmillan, 1961).

Haggard, Ernest A., and Soia Mentschikoff, "Responsible Decision-Making and Decision-Consensus: An Experimental Analysis of a Case in Commercial Arbitration," in Haggard and Mentschikoff (eds.), *Rule of Law in Commercial Groups: How Decisions Are Made* (forthcoming).

Herzog, Alfred W., "A Psychoanalyst of Judges," *Medico-Legal Journal*, Vol. 34, No. 7 (1917), 10-12.

Hutcheson, Joseph B., "The Judgment Intuitive: The Function of the Hunch in Judicial Decisions," *Cornell Law Quarterly*, Vol. 14 (1929), 274-88.

Knowles, William H., "Mediation and the Psychology of Small Groups," *Labor Law Journal*, Vol. 9 (1958), 780-84.

Kubie, Lawrence S., "Research in Judicial Administration: A Psychiatrist's View," *Boston University Law Review*, Vol. 39 (1959), 157-63.

Lasswell, Harold, "Impact of Psychiatry upon Jurisprudence," *Ohio State Law Journal*, Vol. 21 (1960), 17-27.

Lasswell, Harold, *Power and Personality* (New York: Norton, 1948), pp. 64-88.

Lasswell, Harold, "Self-Analysis and Judicial Thinking," *International Journal of Ethics,* Vol. 40 (1930), 342-62.

Lazar, Joseph, "Human Sciences and Legal Institutional Development: Role and Reference Group Concepts Related to the Development of the National Labor Relations Board," *Notre Dame Lawyer,* Vol. 31 (1956), 414-50.

Loeb, Louis S., "Judicial Groups and Judicial Values: A Study of the Value Relationships between Voting Groups on Selected U.S. Courts of Appeal and State Supreme Courts and the United States Supreme Court, 1957-60" (American University, Ph.D. dissertation), listed in *American Political Science Review,* Vol. 55 (1961), 693.

Maslow, Will, "How Social Scientists Can Shape Legal Processes," *Villanova Law Review,* Vol. 5 (1959-60), 241-46.

Meloney, James P., "An Exploration of the Application of the Theory of Games to the Supreme Court Decision-Making Process" (Michigan State University Bureau of Social and Political Research, February 1958, mimeographed), pp. 1-30.

Mott, Rodney L., "Measurement of Judicial Personnel," *New York University Law Quarterly,* Vol. 23 (1948), 262-77.

Mott, Rodney L., Spencer D. Albright, and Helen R. Semmerling, "Judicial Personnel," *Annals of the American Academy of Political and Social Science,* Vol. 167 (1933), 143-55.

Nagel, Stuart S., "Ethnic Affiliations and Judicial Propensities," *Journal of Politics,* Vol. 24 (1962), 92-110.

Nagel, Stuart S., "Judicial Attitudes and Those of Legislators and Administrators" (American Political Science Association Annual Meeting, September 1962, mimeographed), pp. 1-20.

Nagel, Stuart S., "Judicial Backgrounds and Criminal Cases," *Journal of Criminal Law, Criminology, and Police Science,* Vol. 53 (1962), 333-39.

Nagel, Stuart S., "Judicial Characteristics and Judicial Decision-Making" (Northwestern University, Ph.D. dissertation in political science, 1961).

Note, "Content Analysis—A New Evidentiary Technique," *University of Chicago Law Review,* Vol. 15 (1948), 910-25.

Pritchett, C. Herman, *Civil Liberties and the Vinson Court* (Chicago: University of Chicago, 1954), pp. 177-85.

Pritchett, C. Herman, *The Roosevelt Court: A Study in Judicial Politics and Values, 1937-1947* (New York: Macmillan, 1948).

Redmount, Robert S., "Pantoscopic View of Law and Psychology," *Journal of Legal Education,* Vol. 10 (1958), 436-51.

Redmount, Robert S., "Psychological Discontinuities in the Litigation Process," *Duke Law Journal* (1959), 571-87.

Redmount, Robert S., "Psychological Tests for Selecting Jurors," *Kansas Law Review,* Vol. 5 (1957), 391-403.

Redmount, Robert S., "Psychological Views in Jurisprudential Theories," *University of Pennsylvania Law Review,* Vol. 107 (1959), 472-513.

Roper, Elmo, "A Study of Voter Awareness of Judicial Candidates in Elections" (Institute of Judicial Administration, November 1954, mimeographed), pp. 1-23.

Salisbury, Robert, "The United States Court of Appeals for the Seventh Circuit, 1940-1950: A Study of Judicial Relationships" (University of Illinois, Ph.D. dissertation in political science, University Microfilms No. 13,558; 1958).

Schmidhauser, John R., "Judicial Behavior and the Sectional Crisis of 1837-1860," *Journal of Politics,* Vol. 23 (1961), 615-40.

Schmidhauser, John R., *"Stare Decisis,* Dissent, and the Background of the Justices of the Supreme Court of the United States," *University of Toronto Law Journal,* Vol. 14 (1962), 194-212.

Schmidhauser, John R., and David Gold, "Scaling Supreme Court Decisions in Relation to Social Background," *Political Research: Organization and Design,* Vol. 1, No. 5 (May 1958), 6-7.

Schroeder, Theodore, "The Psychologic Study of Judicial Opinions," *California Law*

Review, Vol. 6 (1918), 89-113.

Schubert, Glendon, "The 1960-61 Term of the Supreme Court: A Psychological Analysis," *American Political Science Review*, Vol. 56 (1962), 90-107.

Schubert, Glendon, "Policy without Law: An Extension of the Certiorari Game," *Stanford Law Review*, Vol. 14 (1962), 284-327.

Schubert, Glendon, "Psychometric Analysis of Judicial Behavior: The 1961 Term of the Supreme Court," *Law and Contemporary Problems*, Vol. 28, No. 1 (Winter, 1963).

Schubert, Glendon, "A Psychometric Model of the Supreme Court," *American Behavioral Scientist*, Vol. 5, No. 3 (November 1961), 14-18.

Schubert, Glendon, "Psychometric Research in Judicial Behavior," *Modern Uses of Logic in Law*, Vol. 2, No. 3 (March 1962), 9-18.

Schubert, Glendon, "A Solution to the Indeterminate Factorial Resolution of Thurstone and Degan's Study of the Supreme Court," *Behavioral Science*, Vol. 7, No. 4 (October 1962), 448-458.

Silving, Helen, "Psychoanalysis and the Criminal Law," *Journal of Criminal Law, Criminology and Police Science*, Vol. 51 (1960), 19-33.

Snyder, Eloise C., "A Quantitative Analysis of Supreme Court Opinions from 1921-1953: A Study of the Responses of an Institution Engaged in Resolving Social Conflict" (Pennsylvania State University, Ph.D. dissertation in sociology, 1956).

Snyder, Eloise C., "The Supreme Court as a Small Group," *Social Forces*, Vol. 36 (1958), 232-38.

Snyder, Eloise C., "Uncertainty and the Supreme Court's Decisions," *American Journal of Sociology*, Vol. 65 (1959), 241-45.

Somit, Albert, Joseph Tanenhaus, and Walter Wilke, "Aspects of Judicial Sentencing Behavior," *University of Pittsburgh Law Review*, Vol. 21 (1960), 613-19.

Spaeth, Harold J., "An Analysis of Judicial Attitudes in the Labor Relations Decisions of the Warren Court" (Midwest Conference of Political Scientists, April 1962, mimeographed), pp. 1-25.

Spaeth, Harold J., "An Approach to the Study of Attitudinal Differences as an Aspect of Judicial Behavior," *Midwest Journal of Political Science*, Vol. 5 (1961), 165-80.

Spaeth, Harold J., "Judicial Power as a Variable Motivating Supreme Court Behavior," *Midwest Journal of Political Science*, Vol. 6 (1962), 54-82.

Spaeth, Harold J., "Measuring Ideational Identity by Pairing Justices," *Political Research: Organization and Design*, Vol. 3, No. 9 (May 1960), 22-23.

Subcommittee to Investigate the Administration of the Internal Security Act and Other Internal Security Laws, Committee on the Judiciary, United States Senate, "Recording of Jury Deliberations," *Hearings* of October 12-13, 1955 (84th Congress, 1st Session), and *Report* of March 20, 1956 (84th Congress, 2nd Session).

Tanenhaus, Joseph, "Social Science in Civil Rights Litigation," in Milton Konvitz and Clinton Rossiter (eds.), *Aspects of Liberty* (Ithaca: Cornell University Press, 1958), pp. 91-114.

Tanenhaus, Joseph, "Supreme Court Attitudes toward Federal Administrative Agencies," *Journal of Politics*, Vol. 22 (1960), 502-24.

Tanenhaus, Joseph, "Supreme Court Attitudes toward Federal Administrative Agencies, 1947-1956—An Application of Social Science Methods to the Study of the Judicial Process," *Vanderbilt Law Review*, Vol. 14 (1961), 473-502.

Thurstone, Louis L., and J. W. Degan, "A Factorial Study of the Supreme Court," (University of Chicago, Psychometric Laboratory *Report No. 64* (March 1951), pp. 1-7, reprinted in National Academy of Sciences, *Proceedings* (1951), pp. 628-35, and also summarized in Benjamin Fruchter, *Introduction to Factor Analysis* (New York: Van Nostrand, 1954), pp. 176-79.

Trosper, Emory T., "A Scalogram Analysis of the Right to Counsel Decisions of the Supreme Court, 1940-1957" (Michigan State University Bureau of Social and Political Research, mimeo. paper, pp. 1-26, February 1958).

Ulmer, S. Sidney, "The Analysis of Behavior Patterns on the United States Supreme Court," *Journal of Politics*, Vol. 22 (1960), pp. 629-53.

Ulmer, S. Sidney, "Homeostatic Tendencies in the United States Supreme Court," in

Ulmer (ed.), *Introductory Readings in Political Behavior* (Chicago: Rand, McNally, 1961), pp. 167-88.

Ulmer, S. Sidney, "Judicial Review as Political Behavior: A Temporary Check on Congress," *Administrative Science Quarterly*, Vol. 4 (1960), 426-45.

Ulmer, S. Sidney, "Label Thinking and the Supreme Court: A Methodological Note," *Political Research: Organization and Design*, Vol. 2, No. 1 (September 1958), 25-26.

Ulmer, S. Sidney, "A Note on Assignment Procedure in the Michigan Supreme Court" (1962, mimeographed), pp. 1-16.

Ulmer, S. Sidney, "A Note on Attitudinal Consistency in the United States Supreme Court," *Indian Journal of Political Science*, Vol. 22 (1961), 195-204.

Ulmer, S. Sidney, "Polar Classification of Supreme Court Justices," *South Carolina Law Quarterly*, Vol. 12 (1960), 407-17.

Ulmer, S. Sidney, "The Political Party Variable in the Michigan Supreme Court," *Journal of Public Law*, Vol. 11 (1962, in press).

Ulmer, S. Sidney, "Scaling Judicial Cases: A Methodological Note," *American Behavioral Scientist*, Vol. 4, No. 8 (April 1961), 31-34.

Ulmer, S. Sidney, "Supreme Court Behavior and Civil Rights," *Western Political Quarterly*, Vol. 13 (1960), 288-311.

Winick, Charles, "The Psychology of Juries," chap. 5 in Hans Toch (ed.), *Legal and Criminal Psychology* (New York: Holt, Rinehart, and Winston, 1961), pp. 96-120.

Winick, Charles, Israel Gerver, and Abraham Blumber, "The Psychology of Judges," chap. 6 in Hans Toch (ed.), *Legal and Criminal Psychology* (New York: Holt, Rinehart, and Winston, 1961), 121-45.

Wresinski, James E., "Voting Behavior in Non-Unanimous Decisions of the Warren Court, 1953-1957" (Michigan State University Bureau of Social and Political Research, February 1958, mimeographed), pp. 1-30.

ZoBell, Karl M., "Division of Opinion in the Supreme Court: A History of Judicial Disintegration," *Cornell Law Quarterly*, Vol. 44 (1959), 186-214.

Part Two: Statistical Prediction and Decisions

Allen, Layman E., Robin B. S. Brooks, and Patricia James, "Storage and Retrieval of Legal Information: Possibilities of Automation," *Modern Uses of Logic in Law*, Vol. 60J (June 1960), 68-84.

Bartholomew, Paul C., "Supreme Court and Modern Objectivity," *New York State Bar Journal*, Vol. 33 (1961), 157-64.

Boole, George, *An Investigation of the Laws of Thought* (New York: Dover Publishing Co., reprint of 1854 edition), pp. 376-98: chap. 21, "Probability of Judgments."

Burgett, William A., "Discretionary Review and Summary Decisions of the Warren Court, 1953-1957" (Michigan State University Bureau of Social and Political Research, February 1958, mimeographed), pp. 1-42.

Dickerson, Reed, "Electronic Law Searching," *Modern Uses of Logic in Law*, Vol. 60S (September 1960), 97-98.

Fiordalisi, Vincent, "Progress and Problems in Application of Electronic Data Processing Systems to Legal Research," *Modern Uses of Logic in Law*, Vol. 60D (December 1960), 174-79.

Fisher, Franklin M., "The Mathematical Analysis of Supreme Court Decisions: The Use and Abuse of Quantitative Methods," *American Political Science Review*, Vol. 52 (1958), 321-38.

Fisher, Franklin M., "On the Existence and Linearity of Perfect Predictors in 'Content Analysis,'" *Modern Uses of Logic in Law*, Vol. 60M (March 1960), 1-9.

Horn, Robert A., "A Quantitative Study of Judicial Review," *Political Research: Organization and Design*, Vol. 1, No. 1 (September 1957), 27-30.

Kort, Fred, "Predicting Supreme Court Decisions Mathematically: A Quantitative

Analysis of the Right to Counsel Cases," *American Political Science Review,* Vol. 51 (1957), 1-12.

Kort, Fred, "The Quantitative Content Analysis of Judicial Opinions," *Political Research: Organization and Design,* Vol. 3, No. 7 (March 1960), 11-14.

Kort, Fred, "Ramifications of the Denial of Certiorari in the 'Right to Counsel' Cases for Quantitative Analysis" (University of Chicago Law School, October 1958, mimeographed memo), pp. 1-7.

Kort, Fred, "Reply to Fisher's Mathematical Analysis of Supreme Court Decisions," *American Political Science Review,* Vol. 52 (1958), 339-48.

Lasswell, Harold, "Current Studies in the Decision Process: Automation versus Creativity," *Western Political Quarterly,* Vol. 8 (1955), 398-99.

Levin, A. Leo, and Edward A. Woolley, *Dispatch and Delay: A Field Study of Judicial Administration in Pennsylvania* (Philadelphia: University of Pennsylvania, The Law School, Institute of Legal Research, Studies in Law and Administration, 1961).

Loevinger, Lee, "Jurimetrics," *Modern Uses of Logic in Law,* Vol. 59S (September 1959), 15-16.

Melton, Jessica S., and Robert C. Bensing, "Searching Legal Literature Electronically: Results of a Test Program," *Minnesota Law Review,* Vol. 45 (1960), 229-48.

Mott, Rodney L., "Judicial Influences," *American Political Science Review,* Vol. 30 (1936), 295-315.

Nagel, Stuart S., "Using Simple Calculations to Predict Judicial Decisions," *American Behavioral Scientist,* Vol. 4, No. 4 (December 1960), 24-28; reprinted in *The Practical Lawyer,* Vol. 7 (1961), 68-74.

Nagel, Stuart S., "Weighting Variables in Judicial Prediction," *Modern Uses of Logic in Law,* Vol. 60S (September 1960), 93-96.

Riker, William H., and Ronald Schaps, "Disharmony in Federal Government," *Behavioral Science,* Vol. 2 (1957), 283-84.

Rosensweig, Simon, "The Opinions of Judge Edgerton—A Study in the Judicial Process," *Cornell Law Quarterly,* Vol. 37 (1952), 164-66.

Ulmer, S. Sidney, "Supreme Court Behavior in Racial Exclusion Cases: 1935-1960," *American Political Science Review,* Vol. 56 (1962), 325-30.

Zeisel, Hans, Harry Kelven, Jr., and Bernard Buchholz, *Delay in the Court* (Boston: Little, Brown, 1959).

Part Three: Political Sociology and Courts

Arnes, Richard, and Harold Lasswell, *In Defense of Public Order* (New York: Columbia University, 1961).

Aubert, Vilhelm, Ulf Torgersen, and Karl Tangen, "Norske jurister fra 1814 til den annen verdenskrig" (Oslo: Institute for Social Research, 1960, mimeographed), pp. 1-168.

Ayoub, Victor, "Review: The Judicial Process in Two African Tribes," in Morris Janowitz (ed.), *Community Political Systems* (Glencoe: The Free Press, 1961), pp. 237-50.

Bashful, Emmett W., *The Florida Supreme Court: A Study in Judicial Selection* (Florida State University, Bureau of Governmental Research and Service, 1958).

Berns, Walter, "*Buck* v. *Bell:* Due Process of Law?" *Western Political Quarterly,* Vol. 6 (1953), 762-75.

Beutel, Frederick K., "Elementary Semantics: Criticisms of Radical and Experimental Jurisprudence," *Journal of Legal Education,* Vol. 13 (1960), 67-75.

Beutel, Frederick K., "Outline of Nature and Methods of Experimental Jurisprudence," *Columbia Law Review,* Vol. 51 (1951), 415-38.

Beutel, Frederick K., *Some Potentialities of Experimental Jurisprudence as a New Branch of Social Science* (Lincoln: University of Nebraska, 1957).

Bohannan, Paul, *Justice and Judgment Among the Tiv* (London: Oxford University, 1957).

Bulock, Henry A., "Significance of the Racial Factor in the Length of Prison Sentences,"

Journal of Criminal Law, Criminology, and Police Science, Vol. 52 (1961), 411-17.

Cavers, David F., "Science, Research, and Law: Beutel's Experimental Jurisprudence," *Journal of Legal Education*, Vol. 10 (1957), 162-88.

Cohen, Julius, Reginald A. H. Robson, and Alan Bates, *Parental Authority* (New Brunswick: Rutgers University, 1958).

Cowan, Thomas A., "Law, Morality, and Scientific Method," *Nebraska Law Review*, Vol. 38 (1959), 1039-47.

Dahl, Robert A., "Decision-Making in a Democracy: The Role of the Supreme Court as a National Policy-Maker," *Journal of Public Law*, Vol. 6 (1957), 279-95.

Dozeman, Alvin, "A Study of Selected Aspects of Behavior of the Judges of the United States Court of Appeals for the Tenth Circuit" (Michigan State University, Master's thesis in political science, 1960).

Ewers, Thomas A., "A Study of the Background of the Successful and Unsuccessful Candidates for the Iowa Supreme Court" (State University of Iowa, Master's thesis in political science, 1959).

Ewing, Cortez A. M., *The Judges of the Supreme Court, 1789-1937* (Minneapolis: University of Minnesota, 1938).

Gluckman, Max, *The Judicial Process among the Barotse of Northern Rhodesia* (Glencoe: The Free Press, 1955).

Gluckman, "Comment: The Role of the Barotse King in the Judicial Process," *Stanford Law Review*, Vol. 14 (1961), 110-19.

Hakman, Nathan, "Business Influence in the Judicial Process," *Western Business Review*, Vol. 1 (1957), 124-30.

Herndon, James F., "The Relationship between Partisanship and the Decisions of State Supreme Courts," (University of Michigan, Ph.D. dissertation in political science), listed in *American Political Science Review*, Vol. 53 (1959), 900.

Herndon, James F., "The Role of the Judiciary in State Political Systems: Some Explorations" (Midwest Conference of Political Scientists, April 1962), mimeographed, pp. 1-19.

Higgins, Timothy G., "The Justices of the Wisconsin Supreme Court," *Wisconsin Law Review*, Vol. 1949 (1949), 738-60.

Hoebel, E. Adamson, *The Law of Primitive Man* (Cambridge: Harvard University, 1954).

Hoebel, E. Adamson, "Three Studies in African Law," *Stanford Law Review*, Vol. 13 (1961), 418-42.

Hoebel, E. Adamson, and Karl N. Llewellyn, *The Cheyenne Way: Conflict and Case Law in Primitive Jurisprudence* (Norman: University of Oklahoma, 1941).

Hoopes, Todd, "Experiment in Measurement of Judicial Qualifications in the Supreme Court of Ohio," *University of Cincinnati Law Review*, Vol. 18 (1949), 417-66.

Illinois Association for Criminal Justice, *The Illinois Crime Survey* (Chicago: Illinois Association for Criminal Justice, in cooperation with the Chicago Crime Commission, 1929).

James, Rita M., "Status and Competence of Jurors," *American Journal of Sociology*, Vol. 64 (1959), 563-70.

Keefe, William J., "Judges and Politics: The Pennsylvania Plan of Judge Selection," *University of Pittsburgh Law Review*, Vol. 20 (1959), 621-31.

Krastin, Karl, "Group Interest and the Law," *Journal of Legal Education*, Vol. 13 (1960), 59-66.

Krislov, Samuel, "Constituency versus Constitutionalism: The Desegregation Issue and Tensions and Aspirations of Southern Attorneys General," *Midwest Journal of Political Science*, Vol. 3 (1959), 75-92.

March, James G., "Sociological Jurisprudence Revisited, A Review (More or Less) of Max Gluckman [*The Judicial Process Among the Barotse of Northern Rhodesia*]," *Stanford Law Review*, Vol. 8 (1956), 499-534.

Maslow, Will, "The Legal Defense of Religious Liberty—The Strategy and Tactics of the American Jewish Congress" (American Political Science Association Annual Meeting, September 1961, mimeographed), pp. 1-21.

Mavrinac, Albert A., "From *Lochner* to *Brown* v. *Topeka:* The Court and Conflicting Concepts of the Political Process," *American Political Science Review,* Vol. 52 (1958), 641-64.

McHargue, Daniel S., "Sectional Representation on the Supreme Court," *Marquette Law Review,* Vol. 35 (1951), 13-28.

Nagel, Stuart S., "Culture Patterns and Judicial Systems," *Vanderbilt Law Review,* Vol. 16 (1962), in press.

Nagel, Stuart S., "Political Parties and Judicial Review in American History," *Journal of Public Law,* Vol. 11 (1962), in press.

Nagel, Stuart S., "Political Party Affiliation and Judges' Decisions," *American Political Science Review,* Vol. 55 (1961), 843-50.

Nagel, Stuart S., "Sociometric Relations among American Courts," *Southwestern Social Science Quarterly,* Vol. 43 (1962), 136-42.

Nagel, Stuart S., "Unequal Party Representation on the State Supreme Courts," *Journal of the American Judicature Society,* Vol. 40 (1961), 62-65.

Newland, Chester A., "Legal Periodicals and the United States Supreme Court," *Midwest Journal of Political Science,* Vol. 3 (1959), 58-74.

Oikawa, S., "Application of Beutel's Experimental Jurisprudence to Japanese Sociology of Law," *Nebraska Law Review,* Vol. 39 (1960), 629-47.

Patric, Gordon, "The Impact of a Court Decision: Aftermath of the McCollum Case," *Journal of Public Law,* Vol. 6 (1957), 455-63.

Peltason, Jack W., *Federal Courts in the Political Process* (New York: Random House, 1955).

Peltason, Jack W., *Fifty-eight Lonely Men* (New York: Harcourt, Brace and World, 1961).

Peltason, Jack W., "A Political Science of Public Law," *Southwestern Social Science Quarterly,* Vol. 34 (1953), 51-56.

Riesman, David, "Toward an Anthropological Science of Law and the Legal Profession," *American Journal of Sociology,* Vol. 57 (1951), 121-35.

Rose, Arnold M., and Arthur E. Prell, "Does the Punishment Fit the Crime? A Study in Social Valuation," *American Journal of Sociology,* Vol. 61 (1955), 247-59.

Sayre, Wallace, and Herbert Kaufman, *Governing New York City* (New York: Russell Sage Foundation, 1960), pp. 522-54.

Schmidhauser, John R., "The Justices of the Supreme Court: A Collective Portrait," *Midwest Journal of Political Science,* Vol. 3 (1959), 1-57.

Schmidhauser, John R., *The Supreme Court: Its Politics, Personalities, and Procedures* (New York: Holt, Rinehart and Winston, 1960).

Schubert, Glendon, "A Review of: Frederick K. Beutel, *Some Potentialities of Experimental Jurisprudence as a New Branch of Social Science,*" *Administrative Science Quarterly,* Vol. 2 (1957), 264-68.

Sirotkin, Phillip, "The Supreme Court and the Legislative Process: Two Case Studies in Policy Formation" (University of Chicago, Ph.D. dissertation in political science, University of Chicago microfilm thesis No. 1361, 1951).

Sonnenfield, Peter H., "Participation of *Amici Curiae* by Filing Briefs and Presenting Oral Argument in Decisions of the Supreme Court, 1949-1957" (Michigan State University Bureau of Social and Political Research, February 1958, mimeographed), pp. 1-26.

Sorauf, Frank J., "*Zorach* v. *Clauson:* The Impact of a Supreme Court Decision," *American Political Science Review,* Vol. 53 (1959), 777-91.

Strodtbeck, Fred L., Rita M. James, and Charles Hawkings, "Social Status in Jury Deliberations," *American Sociological Review,* Vol. 22 (1957), 713-19.

Torgerson, Ulf, "Hoyesteretts rolle i norsk politikk," *Tidsskrift for Samfunnsforskning,* Vol. 1 (1960), 94-104.

Ulmer, S. Sidney, "Congressional Predictions of Judicial Behavior," *Political Research: Organization and Design,* Vol. 3, No. 7 (March 1960), 15-17.

Ulmer, S. Sidney, "An Empirical Analysis of Selected Aspects of Lawmaking of the United States Supreme Court," *Journal of Public Law,* Vol. 8 (1959), 414-36.

Ulmer, S. Sidney, "Public Office in the Social Background of Supreme Court Justices," *American Journal of Economics and Sociology*, Vol. 21 (1962), 57-68.

Vose, Clement E., *Caucasians Only: The Supreme Court, the NAACP, and the Restrictive Covenant Cases* (Berkeley and Los Angeles: University of California Press, 1959).

Vose, Clement E., "The Judiciary and the Local Power Structure: An Interest Group Approach" (American Political Science Association Annual Meeting, September 1960, mimeographed).

Vose, Clement E., "Litigation as a Form of Pressure Group Activity," *Annals of the American Academy of Political and Social Science,* Vol. 319 (1958), 20-31.

Williams, Robin M., Jr., Burton R. Fisher, and Irving N. Jarvis, "Educational Desegregation as a Context for Basic Social Science Research," *American Sociological Review,* Vol. 21 (1956), 577-83.

Woodward, Julian, "A Scientific Attempt to Provide Evidence for a Decision on Change of Venue," *American Sociological Review,* Vol. 17 (1952), 447-52.

Case Index

Subject Index

Abraham, Henry J., 242n1
Administrative Office of the United States Courts, 113
Adorno, Theodore W., 44n11
Adrian, Charles R., 245, 255n3
Allen, Francis A., 187n31
Almond, Gabriel, 255n11
American Law Institute, 114
American Soldier, The, 3
Amicus curiae, 5
Andenaes, Johs. B., 243n5, 244n14
Approaches to judicial decision-making: behavioral, 2-7; game theory, 6-7, 117; psychological, 3-4, 7-8, 29-53; small group, 4-5, 7, 13-27; sociological, 6-8; *see also* Content analysis of judicial opinions; Cue theory; Cumulative scaling; Judicial leadership
Aschehoug, Torkel Halvorsen, 224, 241, 244n14
Ash, Maurice A., 27n5
Attorney General of the United States, 246
Aubert, Vilhelm, 3, 6-8, 201, 219n1, 244n21

Bales, Robert F., 27n1, n7, n8
Beaney, William M., 187n29
Beard, Charles A., 8n2
Berelson, Bernard R., 45n11
Berg, Paal, 236-237
Beveridge, Albert, 6
Black, Eugene F., 17-19, 21-22, 24-26, 27n4
Black, Hugo, 59-61, 63-67, 69-71, 74, 81-89, 92-98, 100, 102n26
Bloc analysis, *see* Approaches to judicial decision-making, small group
Bloom, M. T., 256n31
Blumberg, Abraham, 9n19
Borgatta, Edgar F., 27n1
Brandeis, Louis D., 6
Brennan, William J., 59-61, 63-67, 69-71, 74, 77n25, 80-87, 89, 92-98, 100, 102n22
Brownell, Emery A., 256n27
Bryce, James, 243n3
Buchholz, Bernard, 256n26
Bull, Edvard Hagerup, 222, 236
Burchinal, Lee G., 46n19
Burton, Harold H., 59-61, 63-66, 71, 77n26, 80-89, 92-100, 102n22, 131n27

Carr, Leland W., 17-19, 22-25, 27n4

Cartwright, Dorwin C., 9n15, 27n1
Castberg, Frede, 244n14
Centers, Richard, 45n11, 46n27
Certiorari, discretionary exercise of: game theory applied to study of, 117; Gibbs' theory of, 117; hypotheses about, 116-117; lack of theory on, 117; and rule, 19, 113-116; *see also* Cue theory
Certiorari, writ of: applications for, 112-113; "blacklists" of applications, 112-113, 118; *in forma pauperis,* 112-113; origin and history, 111
Chessman, Caryl, 36
Chief Justice, 16, 27, 225, 232, 236-237
Circuit Court of Appeals Act of 1891, 111
Clark, Tom C., 59-60, 63-72, 74-75, 77n27, n30, 80-87, 89, 92-98, 100
Coleman, James S., 255n11
Connecticut workmen's compensation cases: appearance of variables in, 147-148; "backwards" test of, 173-178; content variables in, 139; discussion of, 157, 159-160; factor estimates in, 161-162; factor loadings of variables in, 155; final regression coefficients for, 164; listed, 143-144; original correlation matrix for, 152; predictions of decisions in, 167-168, 178; regression coefficients for estimation of factors in, 158; *see also* Content analysis of judicial opinions
Conscientious objectors, *see* Courts-martial cases (Norwegian)
Conservatism, 55; and civil liberties, 32-33; defined, 29-31; economic, 83-84, 98-100; of judges, 31-34, 38-40, 43, 83-84, 98-100; in Norway, 221-225, 234-242
Content analysis of judicial opinions, 8; compared with other methods, 254; in Connecticut workmen's compensation cases, 136, 141, 147-169; in conscientious objector cases, 202-219; in courts-martial cases (American), 62-63, 66-72; criteria for sample selection of cases, 135; and factor analysis, 135-169; FORTRAN computer program for, 187-197; identification of relevant variables for, 136-140; in involuntary confession cases, 135, 140, 142-169; and the precise formulation of rules of law, 133-134, 179-181; predictive capacity of, 169-179; in right-to-counsel cases,